ALSO BY PHILIP F. GURA

Jonathan Edwards: America's Evangelical
(2005)

C. F. Martin and His Guitars, 1796–1873
(2003)

*Buried from the World: Inside the Massachusetts
State Prison, 1829–1831*
(2001)

America's Instrument: The Banjo in the Nineteenth Century
(with James F. Bollman, 1999)

The Crossroads of American History and Literature
(1996)

*A Glimpse of Sion's Glory: Puritan Radicalism in
New England, 1620–1660*
(1984)

Critical Essays on American Transcendentalism
(with Joel Myerson, 1982)

*The Wisdom of Words: Language, Theology, and Literature
in the New England Renaissance*
(1981)

American Transcendentalism

American Transcendentalism

A HISTORY

Philip F. Gura

 HILL AND WANG

A DIVISION OF FARRAR, STRAUS AND GIROUX

NEW YORK

Hill and Wang
A division of Farrar, Straus and Giroux
18 West 18th Street, New York 10011

Copyright © 2007 by Philip F. Gura
Distributed in Canada by Douglas & McIntyre Ltd.
Printed in the United States of America
Published in 2007 by Hill and Wang
First paperback edition, 2008

The Library of Congress has cataloged the hardcover edition as follows:
Gura, Philip F., 1950–
    American transcendentalism : a history / Philip F. Gura.— 1st ed.
        p. cm.
    Includes bibliographical references (p.   ) and index.
    ISBN-13: 978-0-8090-3477-2 (hardcover : alk. paper)
    ISBN-10: 0-8090-3477-8 (hardcover : alk. paper)
    1. Transcendentalism (New England)   I. Title.

B905 .G87 2007
141'.30973—dc22

                                                            2007015344

Paperback ISBN-13: 978-0-8090-1644-0
Paperback ISBN-10: 0-8090-1644-3

Designed by Jonathan D. Lippincott

www.fsgbooks.com

5   7   9   10   8   6   4

The figure on the front cover is derived from that on the title page of
William B. Greene's Transcendentalism *(1849) and combines symbols from*
various religious traditions. The central figure depicts the Zoroastrian "Farohar,"
its outstretched hand signifying the human soul striving for union with God; the
encircling ring symbolizes eternity. The snake represents mankind's struggle
with evil, and the three intersecting circles represent the Christian Trinity.

For
Bob Richardson, always a guide on these trails

They called themselves "the club of the like-minded"; I suppose because no two . . . thought alike.

—James Freeman Clarke

No single term can describe them. Nothing can be more unjust to them, or more likely to mislead the public, than to lump them all together, and predicate the same things of them all.

—Orestes Brownson

Thus, by mere attraction of affinity, grew together the brotherhood of the "like-minded," as they were pleasantly nicknamed by outsiders, and by themselves, on the ground that no two were of the same opinion.

—William Henry Channing

The new Boston school of philosophy [hold] no very precise doctrines, and [are] without any one band of union . . . They comprise an independency of opinion. They unite to differ.

—"J"

[Transcendentalism] is the practical philosophy of belief and conduct. Every man is a transcendentalist; and all true faith, the motives of all past action, are transcendental.

—J. A. Saxton

CONTENTS

CONTENTS

PREFACE

Most educated Americans identify Transcendentalism as a nineteenth-century intellectual movement that spawned Ralph Waldo Emerson, Henry David Thoreau, and Margaret Fuller. They recall such iconic gestures of individual conscience as Emerson's studied insult of the Harvard faculty in his "Divinity School Address," Thoreau's sojourn at Walden Pond and the great book that resulted, and the pioneering feminist Fuller's declaration, "I accept the universe!" The more sophisticated know as well that the Transcendentalists comprised one of the nation's first coherent intellectual groups: movers and shakers in the forefront of educational reform; proselytizers for the rights of women, laborers, prisoners, and the indigent and infirm; and agitators for the abolition of slavery.

For a twenty-year period between 1830 and 1850 they met in one another's homes, attended one another's lectures and sermons, and read and reviewed one another's writings. Along with the "expatriate" generation of the 1920s and the Beat generation of the 1950s, they remain one of the nation's most compelling and influential intellectual coteries, and as well are the source of many ideas that have come to define what is "American." Writing in *The Dial*, the Transcendentalists' house organ, the journalist J. A. Saxton summed it up well. The very existence of the United States is "transcendental," he observed, for "its right to be a nation was broadly and unequivocally legitimated upon the instinctive truth of the principle of the equality and brotherhood of universal man."[1]

We cannot overestimate the excitement the Transcendentalists' ideas generated and the commitment they engendered. Orestes Brownson, the group's member most identified with the cause of the laborer, put it best late in his life when he recalled how, forty years earlier, he and his friends had threatened to turn the world upside down. Addressing a new cadre of reformers, he reminded them that the Transcendentalists had been first at the barricades. "What have any of you to teach me who participated in the Boston intellectual movement from 1830 to 1844?" he asked. "We Bostonians," he proudly proclaimed, "were a generation ahead of you."[2] The Unitarian minister and erstwhile Transcendentalist Cyrus Bartol concurred, viewing his contemporaries as the present-day guarantors of America's millennial promise. Transcendentalism was nothing less than "a new vessel, a better Mayflower for the Truth's escape from her foes."[3]

Emerson described the almost palpable excitement at the Transcendentalist flowering and its promise of a new world. "No one," he wrote in 1840, "can converse much with the different classes of society in New England, without remarking the progress of a revolution," even as "the spirit of the time is felt by every individual with some difference." To one person, the zeitgeist comes "in the shape of special reforms in the state; to another, in modifications to the various callings of men, and the customs of business; to a third, opening a new scope for literature and art; to a fourth, in philosophical insight; to a fifth, in the vast solitude of prayer." It is, he concluded, "in every form a protest against usage, and a search for principles."[4] His young friend James Freeman Clarke agreed. "I find social life in a precious state of fermentation," he observed to a correspondent that same year. "New ideas are flying, high and low," and "every man," as Emerson recently had remarked, "carries a revolution in his waistcoat pocket."[5]

To many people, however, the Transcendentalists were unsettling, and as often ridiculed or reviled as respected. On his famous trip to the United States at the height of the Transcendentalist ferment, for example, the English novelist Charles Dickens observed that when he inquired of some of his American friends what Transcendentalism signified, he was given to understand that "whatever was unintelligible would be certainly transcendental."[6] The Scottish

writer and reformer Thomas Carlyle, following a visit from the Transcendentalist George Ripley, who had resigned his ministry to start
a socialist community at Brook Farm, a few miles from Boston, was
equally acerbic: Carlyle termed his recent New England guest "a
Socinian [that is, Unitarian] minister, who has left the pulpit to reform the world by cultivating onions."[7] Even fellow travelers could
not resist such humorous characterizations. In her old age, Annie
Russell Marble, who had lived at Ripley's Brook Farm community,
quipped that the Transcendentalists, for all their goodwill, were "a
race who dove into the infinite, soared into the illimitable, and
never paid cash."[8] The historian Henry Adams, no stranger to New
England's ways, concluded that they were "unutterably funny."[9]

These gibes masked a profound uneasiness with the Transcendentalists' challenge to contemporary beliefs and mores, based as it
was in radical European philosophical and social thought that puzzled and frightened many Americans. The staunch Unitarian Francis
Bowen put it baldly. The "new philosophy" of the emergent Transcendentalist group, he wrote, is "abstruse in dogma, fantastic in its
dress, and foreign in its origin." It comes from Germany, he continued, "and is one of the first fruits of a diseased admiration of every
thing from that source," amounting in many individuals to nothing
less than "sheer midsummer madness."[10] Nor did it help that the
Transcendentalists often expressed their thoughts in what seemed
to many an arcane and affected vocabulary and diction, making
their style as frequent a target as their substance (or supposed lack
thereof). "Their favorite method of composition," one skeptic
complained, "seems to be transposition, a conciseness approaching
to obscurity."[11] A wit in the *Boston Post*, commenting on the Transcendentalist Bronson Alcott's dreamy "Orphic Sayings," observed
that their content "resembled a train of 15 railroad cars with one
passenger."[12] Another critic, voicing a similar objection to the Transcendentalists' seemingly willful tendency to obfuscation, noted that
their philosophy seemed more a "manner than a creed."[13] Simply
put, the Transcendentalists' message was more ridiculed than understood or appreciated.

And yet the group was undeniably seminal to American cultural
and intellectual history. In the nation's centennial year, Transcendentalism's first historian, O. B. Frothingham, summed it up well.

The movement, "though local in activity, limited in scope, brief in duration, engaging but a comparatively small number of individuals," left "a broad and deep trace on ideas and institutions." It "affected thinkers, swayed politicians, guided moralists, inspired philanthropists, created reformers."[14] By reexamining the Transcendentalists' intellectual genealogy and the development of their philosophical and cultural agenda, I return this eclectic group of New England thinkers to the transatlantic stage whose boards they so eagerly trod and examine their attempts to reform American society along more democratic lines. From their emergence in the early 1830s—the first American to use the word "Transcendentalist" in print did so in 1833—at least through the early 1850s, they cultivated a vibrant openness to social and cultural ideals that directly challenged the materialism and insularity that were already hallmarks of American culture.[15]

The Transcendentalists were split, however, over how best to effect such reformation. One group, which Emerson epitomized, championed introspection and self-reliance—what one precursor to the movement termed "self-culture"—as keys to the spiritual life, an ethic that fitted conveniently with the antebellum economic expansion known as the Market Revolution.[16] Another group, centered on Ripley and Brownson, stressed the brotherhood of man and outer-directed behavior for the common good, an ethic inherited from the civic republicanism of the post-Revolutionary generation as well as from contemporary European socialism. Friction between those who emphasized hyper-individualism—what one participant called "egotheism"—and those who championed men's and women's irreducible equality marked Transcendentalism from the time of its initial coalescence as an identifiable movement.

For a while, however, the movement held together, and what began as parochial religious controversy over the relative values of reason versus emotion in the spiritual life spawned a vital culture of reform. But as the sectional crisis of the 1850s challenged Americans to confront the immense fact of chattel slavery, hitherto prominent dimensions of such reform—the rights of women, labor, and the indigent, for example—were lost in the maelstrom, viewed as less significant than the horrors of the Southern plantation. Unfortunately, it was decades before such issues again came front and center, for in the post–Civil War era, the uneasy balance between the parties of self and of society tipped in the direction of the former, whose philosophy supported individual rights and market capitalism—or what is now called democratic liberalism—rather than humanitarian socialism. Emerson's demanding philosophy of self-reliance, an artifact of the early 1840s, became simplified and was adopted as a chief article of national belief. More and more, American Transcendentalism became identified through his vision of the imperial self, a process only accelerated after his death in 1882.

Transcendentalism thus was another in a long line of attempts to redirect the still incomplete American experiment, in this case by anchoring it in the sanctity of each individual's heart. The Transcendentalists' unique position in, as well as their final contributions to, the cultural life of the new nation resided in their attempts to reenergize and redirect what they increasingly regarded as the country's misguided and faltering democratic experiment. This book records the story of how these early-nineteenth-century Americans awakened to the possibility of a fully egalitarian brotherhood, encouraged it, and then, under the pressure of insular politics, finally lost their battle to maintain its relevance to the meaning of America. It answers the question of how a movement whose roots were so catholic and universal eventuated in a discourse that promoted an American exceptionalism based on self-interest.

Philip F. Gura
Antiquarian Hall
Worcester, Massachusetts
2007

American Transcendentalism

INTRODUCTION:

LOCATING THE "LIKE-MINDED"

n 1869, Louisa May Alcott, under the cognomen Tribulation Periwinkle, submitted to the *Springfield* (Massachusetts) *Republican* a tongue-in-cheek letter with the "Latest News from Concord," Massachusetts. The town had long been associated with such residents as Ralph Waldo Emerson; her father, Bronson Alcott; and other representatives of the Transcendentalist movement that had flourished in New England thirty years before. "No gossip concerning this immortal town seems to be considered too trivial for the public," she observed, and thus she thought it her duty to add "the last rumor afloat."

Her humorous report was filled with jokes and puns today accessible mainly to scholars but in her time in common circulation. A new hotel was about to be established, she reported, called the Sphinx's Head, where "pilgrims to this modern Mecca" would be entertained in the most hospitable and appropriate style. "Walden water, aesthetic tea, and 'wine that never grew in the belly of the grape'" would be on tap for the refreshment of thirsty guests. "Wild apples by the bushel, orphic acorns by the peck, and Hawthorne's pumpkins, in the shape of pies," could be had "at philosophic prices." The accommodations themselves were special, for the inn would be furnished "with Alcott's rustic furniture, the beds made of Thoreau's pine boughs, and the sacred fires fed from the Emersonian woodpile." Moreover, the thoughtful proprietors would provide telescopes for those who wished "to watch the soarings of the Oversoul, when visible." The innkeeper would supply, gratis, samples of "Autumn Tints, Mosses from the Manse, Rhodora, and herbs from the Garden," as well as "photographs of the faces divine which have conferred immortality upon one of the dullest little towns in Massachusetts."

Most important to those eager to catch a glimpse of the community's famous residents (who by this time included Alcott herself), the hotel also would provide a daily bulletin to announce "the most favorable hours for beholding the various lions" who still roamed Concord's landscape. It would look something like this:

> Emerson will walk at 4 p.m.
> Alcott will converse from 8 a.m. till 11 p.m.
> Channing may be seen with the naked eye at sunset.
> The new Hermit will grind his meal at noon, precisely.
> The ladies of Concord will not be exhibited on Sundays.

The need for such an establishment, Periwinkle concluded, had been long and deeply felt, especially because each spring brought "with the robins, a flock of reporters" who, like the inquisitive birds, "roost upon Concordian fences, chirp on Concordian doorsteps, and hop over Concordian fields and hills, scratching vigorously, as if hoping to unearth a new specimen from what is popularly believed to be the hot-bed of genius."[1]

Obviously, by 1869 Transcendentalism was part of the nation's popular mythology. But as much as Concord and its environs had become shorthand for this important and well-known group of thinkers, writers, and social activists, precisely who they were, beyond those whom Alcott specifically named, has always been a vexed question. There was no central creed that signaled membership in the Transcendentalist coterie nor any roll that certifiably recorded participants. Definition and boundaries are further vexed by the fact that, as with the word "Puritan" in seventeenth-century England, at first the movement's detractors most commonly used "Transcendentalism" as an epithet. Not until the 1840s were some advocates of what was known as the "New Thought" comfortable describing their beliefs with the label Transcendentalist.

One of Ralph Waldo Emerson's earliest biographers, James Elliot Cabot, went to the heart of the matter. He observed that the movement's supporters comprised an ever-shifting and open-ended group. The Transcendental Club (so named, he claimed, by "the public" and not by its participants) comprised "the occasional meetings of a changing body of liberal thinkers, agreeing in nothing but their liberality," a statement he qualified by quoting his friend the Reverend James Freeman Clarke, a Unitarian clergyman and one of the group's original members. Clarke had wittily noted that "they called themselves 'the club of the like-minded,'" primarily because "no two . . . thought alike."[2] Frederic Henry Hedge, another Unitarian minister and a herald of the group's interests in German philosophy, agreed. "There was no club in any strict sense," he wrote, "only occasional meetings of like-minded men and women."[3]

Soon enough the catchphrase entered the public domain. The Unitarian minister and Transcendentalist William Henry Channing observed that "the brotherhood of the 'Like-Minded'" was a "nickname" used by outsiders as well as his friends in the group, "on the ground that no two were of the same opinion."[4] This characterization of the group as amorphous was common even outside Boston, where the Transcendentalists were centered. In New York City, for example, one wit, writing in the fledgling literary journal *Arcturus* in 1841, observed that those in "the new Boston school of philosophy" held "no very precise doctrines," did not have "any one bond of union," and "unite to differ."[5] Transcendentalists agreed. "No single term can describe them," said erstwhile member Orestes Brownson, and "nothing can be more unjust to them, or more likely to mislead the public than to lump them all together, and predicate the same things of them all."[6] Liberality was the group's hallmark, another noted. Among them "the only guest not tolerated was intolerance."[7]

Such statements are maddeningly vague but were common among these "like-minded." Some contemporaries, however, thought that they knew how to characterize them. First, most Transcendentalists were indeed New Englanders, with ties to Harvard College and the Boston area. Second, at some point in their lives, almost to a person, they had been associated with Unitarianism and thus were considered "liberal Christians" whose reading of scripture made them reject Calvinism's harsh and, to them, unreasonable tenets. Finally, although a loosely knit group of thinkers and activists, they had a distinct philosophical bent toward German Idealism rather than British Empiricism, that is, toward the revolution wrought by Immanuel Kant, Johann Gottlieb Fichte, and others who championed the inherent powers of the human mind, against the philosophy of John Locke and his followers, who believed that external circumstances primarily formed man's consciousness. Noah Porter, a conservative Trinitarian minister at the Andover Theological Seminary, early on acknowledged this profile. The Transcendentalists, he opined, were alike in "their intellectual and moral predispositions, their favorite philosophical and literary sympathies," and they possessed a "strong family likeness of their modes of thought and expression."[8] The conservative Unitarian Francis Bowen was not as polite. He had no sympathy, he wrote, "with that ill-regulated admiration, which seeks to transplant German roots to an English soil,—to cultivate a hot-bed, where plants shall be forced to lose their native character." Indeed, the only result he had seen thus far was an "insufferable arrogance" among young people so inclined.[9]

Writing pseudonymously, the Transcendentalist Theodore Parker humorously parodied such caricatures and in so doing provided an index to the fears the group engendered in the general populace. In *The Christian Register* he offered a fictional account of a Boston layman who encountered the word "Transcendentalism" in the daily press and wondered what it meant. "I thought of *Trans*-sylvanian, and *Trans*-substantiation," the fellow explained, "but found no light." Neither could he find the novel term in any standard dictionary. Then he turned to a pamphlet recently published by some conservative clergy at Princeton who had weighed in on New England's recent religious turmoil, from which he learned the truth. "*Trans*-cendentalism," he said, is "a very naughty thing." Indeed, what he read so upset him that he subsequently had a frightening dream in which all the Transcendentalists "and countless others" were thrown together "in the greatest confusion, without regard to age, opinion or character." The outcome was frightening.

Alas for churches in New England! We be all dead men, for the Transcendentalists have come! They say there is no Christ; no God; no soul; only "an absolute nothing," and Hegel is the Holy Ghost. Our churches will be pulled down; there will be no Sabbath; our wives will wear the breeches, and the Transcendentalists will ride over us rough shod.[10]

Who precisely were these shadowy figures associated with all things German? A large number were Unitarian clergymen—Cyrus Bartol, Charles Timothy Brooks, Orestes Brownson, William Henry Channing, James Freeman Clarke, Christopher Cranch, John Sullivan Dwight, Ralph Waldo Emerson, Convers Francis, William Henry Furness, William B. Greene, Frederic Henry Hedge, Sylvester Judd, Samuel Osgood, Theodore Parker, George Ripley, Samuel Robbins, Caleb Stetson, and Thomas T. Stone the most prominent. Some remained in the ministry as Unitarians; others redefined the nature of the churches they led—Clarke and Parker, the most notable examples; while still others left the church altogether. Brownson became an editor and social reformer, for example; Dwight became the nation's foremost music critic; Cranch a poet and painter; and Emerson a lecturer and writer.

There also were many in the cohort—among them, prominent women—who found the path to Transcendentalism in other ways, often through association with one or more of the above-named individuals. Such was the case with Elizabeth Palmer Peabody, who served as amanuensis to the great Unitarian clergyman William Ellery Channing before joining the educational reformer Bronson Alcott as a teacher in his primary school, which was based on Transcendentalist principles. George Ripley's wife, Sophia, was at his side when he decided to begin a socialist commune; she oversaw its well-regarded school. Margaret Fuller's closest teenage friend was James Freeman Clarke, with whom she studied German and prepared herself for a career as a writer and women's rights advocate. In turn, she influenced such younger women as Caroline Healey Dall, Caroline and Ellen Sturgis, and Anna Ward, all of whom gravitated in the Transcendentalist orbit. Still other fellow travelers were

Emerson's protégés, Henry David Thoreau, the most famous, and younger aspiring writers such as Jones Very, Charles King Newcomb, and Charles Stearns Wheeler also taking inspiration from him. The poet William Ellery Channing, nephew of the Unitarian clergyman of the same name, owed much to his association with Thoreau.

Finally, there were important second-generation representatives who carried the Transcendentalist standard into the Gilded Age. Octavius Brooks Frothingham, Unitarian minister and the movement's first historian, was among these, as were fellow clergy David Wasson, John Weiss, Samuel Johnson, Samuel Longfellow (younger brother of Henry Wadsworth Longfellow), and Moncure Conway. Thomas Wentworth Higginson began his career as a clergyman but achieved most fame as editor of *The Atlantic Monthly* and of Emily Dickinson's poetry. Franklin Sanborn, abolitionist, social reformer, and biographer of many individuals in the movement, rounds out these important late-nineteenth-century representatives.

Before 1830, however, there was no cohesive or identifiable movement, simply "like-minded" people who for different reasons were critical of contemporary religious and philosophical thought and had discovered in a novel body of European ideas a way to address this dissatisfaction. In these years Transcendentalism is best considered as a way of perceiving the world, centered on individual consciousness rather than on external fact. This hallmark persisted for five decades, even as adherents quarreled among themselves as to the implication of such an epistemology. Evident among a remarkably varied group of thinkers, more than anything else this emphasis on the primacy of self-consciousness defined American Transcendentalism.

Beginning in the 1830s, there were points of convergence or intersection when certain thinkers recognized common interests and concerns, times that Herman Melville, speaking of his chance encounter with Nathaniel Hawthorne's works that changed his life, memorably termed "shock[s] of recognition." Such moments of heightened self-awareness—when adherents, supporters, and critics alike came to use the term "Transcendentalism" in full confidence that it had an identifiable, if not fully agreed on, meaning—are crucial to the group's history. The year 1836 in particular saw the appearance of several books and pamphlets that exemplified the religious and philosophical interests of the group but also considerably confused the public as to the term's precise meaning. By the early 1840s, however, participants and observers began to publish detailed analyses that now provide convenient benchmarks for understanding how the general public perceived Transcendentalism. In particular, in 1842 the movement's identity came into sharp focus.

This year was important in the lives of several key Transcendentalists. Tragedy struck both the Emerson and Thoreau families, with the losses of the Emerson's five-year-old son, Waldo, to scarlet fever, an event that marked a decisive shift in this thinker's philosophy, and of Thoreau's older brother John, who succumbed to painful death from lockjaw. That same year, Theodore Parker published *A Discourse of Matters Pertaining to Religion*, his magnum opus of comparative religion, and Orestes Brownson his *Mediatorial Life of Jesus*, a pamphlet that marked an important turning point in his journey from Transcendentalism to Roman Catholicism.

Adding to the heightened self-consciousness such events engendered, two years earlier the first issue of *The Dial*, a quarterly periodical first edited by Margaret Fuller and devoted to the intellectual and social interests of the group, had appeared, and by 1842 its reputation as the chief organ of the New Thought was well established. At around the same time, on West Street in Boston, Elizabeth Peabody opened a foreign-language bookstore and lending library, making available a remarkable range of journals and books from France, Germany, and England. In 1841 George Ripley had resigned his pulpit at Boston's Purchase Street Church to found the Brook Farm Institute of Agriculture and Education, the period's most famous utopian experiment; and Horace Greeley assumed editorship of the daily *New-York Tribune*, in which he touted his reformist agenda (and any who supported it, particularly the Transcendentalists).

By 1842, then, Transcendentalism was squarely in the public eye, and Americans wanted to know more about it. Serendipitously, three important assessments of it, one by an insider, the other two by more objective observers, appeared. In December 1841 Emerson himself, never wholly comfortable with the Transcendentalist label but now more frequently acknowledged as one of the movement's chief representatives, delivered a lecture in Boston on "The Transcendentalist" in a series called "Signs of the Times." The following month he published the piece in *The Dial*, then under his editorship. Charles Mayo Ellis, a Massachusetts attorney active in the antislavery movement, anonymously provided a book-length account in his *Essay on Transcendentalism*. Finally, James Murdock, who had recently been a professor at the Andover Theological Seminary, brought forward a third assessment in his *Sketches of Modern Philosophy*, a lengthy analysis of the rise of German Idealism that concludes in a discussion of its American incarnations. What did these three say of the radical philosophical and religious principles that most identified Transcendentalist thought and united such varied individuals?

Ellis is the most helpful because he is analytic. Having in mind the public's great discomfort with Transcendentalism, vague and threatening as it seemed, he tried to calm such fears. Simply put, he said, Transcendentalism maintains "that man has ideas, that come not through the five senses, or the powers of reasoning; but are either the result of direct revelation from God, his immediate inspiration, or his immanent presence in the spiritual world."[11]

How could this be objectionable or dangerous? The problem lay in the implications of such belief. When Ellis discussed God's "immanent presence in the spiritual world" a few pages later, for example, he made a critical distinction:

> This, then, is the doctrine of Transcendentalism, the substantive, independent existence of the soul of man, the reality of conscience, the religious sense, the inner light, of man's religious affections, his knowledge of right and truth, his sense of duty . . . his love for beauty and holiness, his religious aspirations—with this it starts as something not dependent on education, custom, command, or anything beyond man himself.[12]

Innately present in each individual, in other words, is a spiritual principle that, of itself, without any external stimuli, allows one to distinguish between right and wrong, good and bad, God and Satan, and it supersedes any outward laws or injunctions. Transcendentalism, he continued, is thus predicated "on the reality of the spiritual or religious element in man; his inborn capacity to perceive truth and right, so that moral and religious truths can be proved to him with the same degree of certainty that attends all material demonstrations."[13] The highest law comes from the promptings of the spirit, a potentially anarchic belief held in check, Transcendentalists believed, by the universality of the religious sentiment.

Ellis contrasted this conception of spirituality to that predicated on the opposing worldview. The other, the "old" way of thinking about man's acquisition of knowledge, he writes, is one in which he "derives all ideas from sensations, [and which] leads to atheism, to a religion which is but self-interest—an ethical code which makes right synonymous with indulgence of appetite, justice one with expediency and reduces our love of what is good, beautiful, true and divine, to habit, association, or interest."[14] The "old," in other words, is based in the empirical philosophy of John Locke—who believed that knowledge derived from sensory experience—and his disciples in the Scottish Common Sense school—Dugald Stewart, Thomas Reid, and Thomas Brown—who adumbrated his ideas. Whatever else Transcendentalists represented, in other words, they revolted against this empiricism and the putative self-interest on which it was based.

Throughout his small book, Ellis eschewed denominational backbiting as he argued for this universal religious sentiment. Ellis sought, in other words, to move the discussion from debates over doctrine to consideration of the philosophy of religion. Rightly understood, he explained, Transcendentalism was not concerned with "the divine origin of the Sabbath or church," nor with "the authenticity or authority of the old or new testament, their infallible or plenary inspiration," questions that for years had fueled heated debates between Unitarians and their more conservative Trinitarian brethren. Addressing the Unitarians' conservative wing, he explained that Transcendentalism did not have anything to do with "the trinity or unity, the humanity or divinity of the Saviour." Such questions, he explained, were for "critics, historians, divines, [and] theologians," while this new faith pertained to one's personal relation to the spirit. Writing in *The Dial* the year before, the minor Transcendentalist J. A. Saxton put it more bluntly: "All men mostly, perhaps, unconsciously, believe and act upon [this spiritual principle]." Transcendentalism is thus "the practical philosophy of belief and conduct," and "every man is a transcendentalist."[15]

In contrast, James Murdock, until 1829 a professor of sacred rhetoric and ecclesiastical history at Andover, who retired to New Haven to pursue scholarship in church history, devoted the last three chapters of his study of German Idealism to an elucidation of how Americans had appropriated and extended the European "speculative" tradition. Essentially a genealogy of Idealist philosophy from Kant through Fichte, Friedrich Wilhelm Joseph von Schelling, Friedrich Heinrich Jacobi, and Georg Wilhelm Friedrich Hegel, the book is remarkable for how thoroughly and lucidly it introduces so potentially abstruse a topic.

Murdock devoted his first chapter to Samuel Taylor Coleridge's redaction of Kant in *Aids to Reflection*, and thus Coleridge's influence, in the 1820s, on James Marsh, a Trinitarian Congregationalist who was president of the University of Vermont. Marsh's explanation of the distinction, in his lengthy "Preliminary Essay" to Coleridge's work, between "Reason"—that is, intuition or conscience—and "Understanding"—the rational, logical faculty—did much to bring German philosophy to public attention. Similarly, in his final chapter, Murdock discussed Frederick Rauch, the late president of Marshall College in Pennsylvania, whose *Psychology, or A View of the Human Soul* (1840) similarly popularized Hegel's ideas. Most germane, however, is Murdock's chapter sandwiched in between—"American Transcendentalism"—in which he explored several recent publications by members of that group, including a lengthy essay in *The Dial* in which Harvard Divinity College graduate William Dexter Wilson traced America's interest in German philosophy to earlier turmoil within the Unitarian ranks.

As Murdock noted (citing Ripley, Brownson, and Emerson), some Unitarians, "laboring to improve their system of theology," eventually "cast their eyes on foreign countries." There they found a different philosophy—the "speculative"—that suggested an entirely new version of Christianity and invested it "with more spiritual character, with more power to move the soul, to call forth warm emotions, and to produce communion with God" than any contemporary faith. In Murdock's view, when several such disaffected Unitarians noted their mutual interest in this novel way of philosophically grounding their belief, American Transcendentalism was born.[16]

He cited as this group's main inspiration the French philosopher Victor Cousin, not Coleridge, Thomas Carlyle, or any of the Germans directly, thus challenging what many subsequently identified as the most important route for the transmission of these ideas.[17] Through Cousin's synthesis of Idealism with the Scottish Common Sense philosophy of Thomas Reid and Thomas Brown, Murdock explained, Americans learned that "*Spontaneous Reason* acquaints us with the true and essential nature of things."[18] This principle makes "all the doctrines of natural religion the objects" of man's direct, intuitive knowledge. Thus, to know the realm of the spirit, men do not need any explanation or confirmation from teachers or books. Rather, they have only to listen to "the teachings of [their] own souls, the light that shines within [them]."[19]

Murdock's emphases are significant. As much as Idealist philosophy was central to the movement's coalescence, Transcendentalism began as a religious demonstration.[20] No American Transcendentalists were "philosophers by profession," Murdock noted, and nearly all of them were clergymen "of the Unitarian school." As a result, their "habit of thought, their feelings, and their aims" were "manifestly theological."[21] Only later, as they discovered the social implications of their acknowledgment of "spontaneous reason" did they realize that they were prophets of a wholly new secular as well as spiritual order.

Ellis's and Murdock's assessments resonated among other contemporaries as well as with early historians of the movement. In 1876, O. B. Frothingham, for example, noted that although Transcendentalism was usually spoken of as a philosophy, it was more justly regarded "a gospel." Running through it all, he continued, was a belief in "the living God in the Soul, faith in immediate inspiration, in boundless possibility, and in an unimaginable good."[22] Similarly, Ezra Stiles Gannett, a prominent Unitarian minister with friends among the more radical in his denomination, observed that Transcendentalism "implied a universal law of access and communion." It affirmed "inspiration fresh as well as old; Revelation constant; Miracle but the human spirit's pinnacle of action; God the living God, not a deity then and there" but rather "indwelling here and now in every presence."[23] George Ripley concurred. Many years later, recalling the excitement of the antebellum period, he observed that Transcendentalism was but "the assertion of the high powers, dignity, and integrity of the soul; its absolute independence and right to interpret the meaning of life, untrammeled by tradition and conventions."[24] Simply put, it was another American Revolution, spiritual in nature and remarkably varied in its practical implications.

Emerson's assessment is more complicated because it is revelatory of his attempt to control the meaning of an increasingly unruly movement as those associated with it broke into different parties, depending on how they understood those implications. Six years earlier he had provided one of the New Thought's first manifestos in his book *Nature*, but its difficult prose did not provide the explanation the public sought. Reviewing it for *The Christian Examiner*, Francis Bowen found the author's ideas and his manner of expression abstruse and offered advice to those who found the book's ideas of interest: "If the partisans of the New School," he wrote, "still insist upon it, let them manufacture a treatise on the rudiments of Transcendentalism, [so] that tyros may begin with the alphabet of the science, and toil slowly but surely up its cloud-capt heights."[25] Late in 1841 and early the next year, Emerson, solidifying his career as a lecturer, attempted just that when he delivered eight "Lectures on the Times" at the Masonic Temple in Boston and devoted his fourth offering to "The Transcendentalist."

Those looking for a clear and concise rendering of the term, however, were disappointed, for Emerson couched his presentation in the same abstractions that already marked his thought. He was maddeningly vague, declaring that the *"new views* here in New England"—he had in mind Orestes Brownson's *New Views of Christianity, Society, and the Church*, issued the same year and by the same publisher as his *Nature*—were not new, "but the very oldest of thoughts cast into the mould of these new times." "What is popularly called Transcendentalism among us," he observed, is simply "Idealism as it appears in 1842."[26]

He opposed Idealists to "Materialists," the other party that always vied for mankind's allegiance. The latter, he explained, base their philosophy on "experience," the former "on consciousness." Emerson also noted that Materialists reason "from the data of the senses," while the Idealists insist that the senses "are not final," because they cannot explain things themselves. "The materialist," he continued, "insists on facts, on history, on the force of circumstances, and the animal wants of man," while the Idealist focuses on "the power of Thought and on Will, on inspiration, on miracle, on individual culture." For him, "mind is the only reality."[27]

Emerson spun out the implications of the Idealist's point of view. He "believes in miracle, in the perpetual openness of the human mind to the new influx of light and power." He also believed "in inspiration, and in ecstasy," even as such things were experienced differently by different individuals, with different results. Thus, despite the public's fantasy of a conspiracy of American acolytes of all things German, Emerson opined that there was "no such thing as a Transcendental *party*" and "no pure Transcendentalist." Rather, all around him Emerson saw "prophets and heralds" of a resurgent Idealism, eager to return it to public attention. Transcendentalism, he continued, was simply "the Saturnalia or excess of Faith," indicative of a religion "proper to man in his integrity."[28]

Nor did Emerson provide a roster of those whom he thought were bona fide examples. Indeed, he mentioned none among his contemporaries who by then would have been considered Transcendentalists. Rather, he spoke in generalities about their comportment. Dismissing the notion that they comprised an intimidating battalion ready to storm the conservative ramparts, he described Transcendentalists as few, and "lonely" in their habits, conversation, and writing. They tended to shun "general society" and "shut themselves in their chamber in the house, to live in the country rather than in town, and to find their tasks and amusements in solitude." This, however, was puzzling obfuscation, for many of Emerson's cohort, including some of his close friends, at that very moment were assiduously laboring around Boston to remedy the plight of the poor and others disadvantaged by circumstance—prisoners, say, and the developmentally challenged. Emerson chose to ignore these individuals and instead associate Transcendentalism with those who championed an individualistic ethos like his own. He observed approvingly, for example, that the Transcendentalists chose self-imposed isolation "both from temperament and from principle," as if mere rejection of the crass materialism of their contemporaries guaranteed moral integrity.[29]

He did, however, correctly note the Transcendentalists' strident cultural criticism, for much of the public's discomfort with them arose from their demands for personal regeneration. "That, indeed, constitutes a new feature in their portrait," Emerson explained, "that they are the most exacting and extortionate critics." Contemporary Idealists were greatly disappointed in their fellow men and women for their obliviousness to or denial of the banality of their lives, given as they were to selfishness and monetary gain. Disgusted by the "vulgarity and frivolity" of the majority of their compatriots, Emerson observed, Idealists chose separation rather than keeping such "bad company."[30]

Emerson's omissions and mischaracterization are accounted for by a simple fact: his friends' commitment and labors did not square with his own notion of the regenerate life. It was too easy, he believed, to become absorbed in larger causes and to think that such participation validated one's moral rectitude, when in fact such outward activities might mask a continuing moral callousness. Thinking of church sewing circles where collections were taken for the poor, religious tract societies whose members solicited contributions to bring God's word to the underprivileged, and other such "benevolent" organizations, Emerson explained caustically that each such cause becomes too speedily "a little shop, where the article, let it have been at first never so subtle and ethereal, is now made up into portable and convenient cakes, and retailed in small amounts to suit purchasers."[31] The better route was to purify one's own soul and live with full integrity, becoming a model, rather than a nagging goad, to others.

Emerson understood that to effect social transformation in this more individualistic way took time and that, until the Idealists' criticism of contemporary life was more widely shared, they would be known, too, by their seeming extravagance. There still will be "cant and pretension" as well as "subtilty [*sic*] and moonshine," he said wryly. Further, another drawback, the Idealist pioneers whom he described were not yet "proficients" but only "novices" in their philosophical quests and thus only haltingly pointed the road that all people would walk "when the soul has greater health and powers." Yet, he insisted, these "novices" had to be seen as sincere harbingers. "Amidst the downward tendency and proneness of things," Emerson asked his audience rhetorically, "when every voice is raised for a new road or another statue, or a subscription of stock, for an improvement in dress, or in dentistry, for a new house or a larger business, for a political party, or the division of an estate—will you not tolerate one or two solitary voices in the land, speaking for thoughts and principles not marketable and perishable?"[32]

Emerson's lecture did little to satisfy the public demand for clarification of the "new views," but it highlighted an emergent struggle within the group over Transcendentalism's social implications, one that only intensified through the decade. By 1842 Transcendentalists presumed certain theological and philosophical ideas and had begun to act on the social implications of them. To these individuals, political freedom did not necessarily produce "liberality of mind, nor freedom in church institutions." "These brave souls," Margaret Fuller wrote in 1840, thus tried "to quicken the soul, that they may work from within outwards" and thus help their fellow men and women find more meaning in their lives, pulled as they were into the currents of the nation's rising economic tide. "Disgusted with the vulgarity of a commercial aristocracy," she wrote, "they become radicals; disgusted with the materialistic working of 'rational' religion, they become mystics." Simply put, she concluded, "they quarrel with all that is, because it is not spiritual enough."[33] At virtually the same time, two conservative clergymen, themselves popularizing German philosophy, also decried the nation's tawdry pursuit of gain. "Here and there," they wrote, "an individual may be found who is wary of this ceaseless stir, of this insane eagerness after the perishable and the transient." His ears "are pained by the incessant clamor of buyers and sellers," they continued, and he longs "for repose, for calm meditation, for a secure retreat from his jostling and inquisitive contemporaries." Such men, however, they concluded, were still few and far between.[34] To swell their ranks became the Transcendentalists' goal.

In another letter from the same period, Fuller praised Emerson's recent lectures in Providence, Rhode Island, on "The Present Age" and "Human Life," in terms that make clear how important she regarded his, and her cohort's, work. With the flames of religious revival licking at New England's churches as evangelical clergy promised salvation only to those who had an experiential awareness of saving grace, Fuller applauded Emerson's very different, ecumenical work. "You really have got up a revival there," she said, "though [the townspeople] do not know it." Because of Emerson's insistence on the universality of the religious sentiment, she continued, daily they grew "more vehement in their determination to become acquainted with God."[35]

A notion of such universal divine inspiration—grace as the birthright of all—was the bedrock of the Transcendentalist movement. As one late-nineteenth-century historian put it, "the fundamental ideas which make the basis of the religious life,—the idea of God, of duty, of immortality,—the Transcendentalists asserted, are given outright in the nature and constitution of man, and do not have to be learned from any book or confirmed by any miracle."[36] But the practical implications of this heady premise, the spiritual equivalent of the democratic ideal that all men (and women) are created equal, was problematic, and particularly so in a nation that did little for the rights of women or labor, and that still protected slavery.

The Transcendentalists' belief in a democracy of the spirit, Frothingham wrote, thus opened the door to speculation "which carried unlooked-for heresies in its bosom." To them, "all things" had to be "new." Toward that end they called "for immediate application of ideas to life," so that in this brave new world a thinker "was called on to justify himself on the spot by building an engine, and setting something in motion." For this group, Frothingham concluded, the test of a truth was its "availability," its potentially transformative power.[37] How the Transcendentalists found their "truths," subsequently built their various "engines," and adjusted them to the evolving meaning of America occupies the remainder of these pages.

1

SEARCHING THE SCRIPTURES

n the late summer of 1812, Harvard students and professors, local clergy, scholars, bibliophiles, and curious onlookers gathered in Boston "at the Mansion-House of the late Rev. Mr. Buckminster" for the sale of the minister's library, one of the largest in New England. Although he was only thirty-eight when he died, for the previous eighteen years Joseph Stevens Buckminster had presided over Boston's prestigious Brattle Street Church. A civic, intellectual, and religious leader, he was widely regarded as one of New England's most influential ministers, a bold and moving pulpit orator as well as a scholar of the first rank; his premature death was much lamented.[1] Over two days the auctioneers Whitwell & Bond sold more than eleven hundred volumes from his collection, some titles individually, others in lots grouped by topic, many published in London or on the Continent. Given the recent embargo of European goods attendant on the War of 1812, these volumes were particularly enticing. The auctioneers requested payment in "Cash, Boston-money," and the quality of the library guaranteed good prices: during the two days the sale brought close to six thousand dollars.[2]

The bidding was spirited, at no point more so than when the Reverend Moses Stuart, professor of sacred literature at the recently founded Andover Theological Seminary north of Boston, went head-to-head over one set of books with eighteen-year-old Edward Everett, a recent Harvard graduate with clerical aspirations who two years later would be installed over Buckminster's Brattle Street Church.[3] Making this competition seemingly incongruous were the very different religious affiliations of the two bidders. The thirty-two-year-old Stuart, a Yale graduate, was charged at Andover with defending the strictest form of Calvinist theology, based in the works of Jonathan Edwards and his followers Samuel Hopkins and Joseph Bellamy. Everett, on the other hand, had been raised among Boston's liberal Christians, in Buckminster's church, where parishioners were suspicious of overtly emotional religion and were tutored in a rational view of the Bible that revealed a unitary rather than triune God. What in Buckminster's library could have attracted the interest of two such different men?

It was a four-volume work in German, J. G. Eichhorn's *Introduction to the Old Testament*, published between 1780 and 1783, the first comprehensive modern treatment of the Old Testament's books. Years later Stuart still remembered, "with lively and pleasant emotion," how Everett and he had jousted for it. Stuart had gone to the auction thinking Eichhorn's work "unknown to our literary community." Moreover, the set was not even beautifully made or bound—"moderate octavo on coarse hemp paper," he recalled. Thus, he was surprised at Everett's aggressive bidding, up to the extraordinary price of six dollars per volume. But the young man stopped when Stuart subsequently bid a quarter more per book. Stuart had to have it, he explained, and he believed it worth the price. The acquisition of that book, he recalled in 1841, spread its influence over his whole life.[4]

Other attendees were similarly enthralled by the offerings and surprised at the prices fetched, particularly for European theology. The Salem minister William Bentley, for example, was chagrined to be outbid on another of Eichhorn's works, an edition of his multivolume *Universal Library of Biblical Literature* (1787–1801). Why were the works of this scholar, a faculty member at the universities in Jena and Göttingen, so prized? Why were so many of the other volumes in the Buckminster sale similarly in German and devoted to scriptural criticism? What was the fascination of such abstruse works, in a language few New Englanders read? And why among bidders at the sale did bitter interdenominational rivalries seem forgotten? As a result of their meeting at the Buckminster auction, for example,

Stuart tutored his new friend about other German works and even encouraged Everett to undertake the translation of some. Why was it that during this period, as the Unitarian clergyman Ezra Stiles Gannett recalled, "he who could buy nothing else bought a [J. J.] Griesbach," that is, the work of another German biblical scholar?[5] The answers lie in the crucible in which New England Transcendentalism was formed, a widely prevalent interest in scriptural language and its meaning.

The intellectual genealogy of Transcendentalism began in early-nineteenth-century New England among clergymen caught up in unresolved theological battles initiated more than half a century earlier, specifically between "New Light" supporters of the widespread religious revivals known as the Great Awakening and their "Old Light" opponents. The pro-revivalists, epitomized by the great theologian Jonathan Edwards, stressed the necessity of an emotional conversion experience, a change of heart that realigned one's priorities from selfishness to selflessness. The anti-revivalists, led by Boston clergyman Charles Chauncy, argued for the primacy of reason in religion and found the New Lights' emphasis on an emotional religious experience—a "New Birth"—an insult to human intelligence. To Chauncy and his supporters, religion was a matter of the head and not of the heart.[6]

Over the remainder of the eighteenth century, the Old Lights continued to stress reason in religion, a point of view that eventually led some of them—Buckminster, for example—to become what first were termed "liberal Christians" and then, early in the next century, "Unitarians." That is, they rejected the notion that the Bible described a Trinitarian deity—Father, Son, and Holy Spirit—and argued instead for a unitary God. In this reading, Jesus Christ, rather than being a part of the Godhead, was simply the supreme model for humanity, God's gift to show that to which all good Christians should aspire.[7]

Before 1820, those who traveled the full distance to Unitarianism remained few and were vociferously opposed by significant numbers of Trinitarians who controlled the majority of New England's—indeed, of America's—pulpits. The warring camps jousted with scholarly—primarily historical and philological—weapons on the fields of scriptural exegesis.[8] These clergy fought over language, over what precisely the Bible said with regard to the personality of the deity. They sought to know whether scripture was the direct, unmediated word of God or merely the words of men who interpreted the divine Logos in their own languages and through their own cultural predispositions. To spar in this arena required knowledge of the language and culture of the Bible, information at that time best provided by contemporary German scholars. Thus, Eichhorn, Griesbach, and others had become significant for New England intellectuals.

Until the second decade of the nineteenth century, most participants in these battles over scriptural interpretation began from similar premises about the relation of language to meaning, derived from John Locke's famous discussion of the subject in Book III of his *Essay Concerning Human Understanding* (1689). Specifically, they seized upon his declaration of the arbitrariness of language. To Locke, words were merely external stimuli, and the "truth" of language consisted in its utility. The source of meaning, Locke wrote, was simply "rational usage derived from sensory perception." Words were contrivances designed for human convenience. If they came to be used by men as the "*signs* of their *ideas*," it was not through any "natural connection, that there is between particular articulate sounds and certain ideas," but only through "a voluntary imposition, whereby such a word is made arbitrarily the mark of an idea." The world's languages thus had no underlying unity, and words in their primary or immediate signification stood only for ideas "in the mind of him that uses them." Concomitantly, if men employed terms for which they had not experienced sensory analogues, they did not truly know the meaning of what they said. Words could not be universal symbols, for each man to whom the word-idea was expressed had to learn the truth of the idea empirically.[9]

Language was thus an artificial construct that rested upon a contract voluntarily entered, or, more precisely, upon a contextual arrangement. As with laws in the political state, neither vocabulary nor syntax had inherent rationale but were created to serve particular needs—in this case, human communication. Words were not gifts from God that stood as ciphers to reality, but only noises with no direct correspondence to what they named. Words had "meanings" that were narrowly cultural, and acts of human communication were only approximations of experience, not magical invocations of it. Language thus had to be interpreted by the intellectual tools that men, as rational creatures, possessed.

The stakes in these debates were high when one applied such ideas to the language of the Bible. Was the word of God merely contextual, for example, or did it possess transcendent significance? According to Locke's logic, if the Bible was the word of God, it was in a vocabulary set down *by men* in a *particular* place and at a *particular* time, and so had been affected by the vagaries of human circumstance. In this light, scripture did not consist of divinely inspired words but rather of a vocabulary that was the result of the time and chance above which no human being, Trinitarian or Unitarian, could rise.

Settling the matter of what precisely the Bible said—and what it meant for subsequent generations of Christians—became the work of scriptural exegetes like Eichhorn, Griesbach, and a host of other European and American scholars who pioneered the "Higher Criticism" of the Bible, a term that Eichhorn coined.[10] Higher Critics enlisted the rational, critical tools of modern inquiry to discover the deeper truths of Christianity. In general terms, they focused on historical documents and tried to establish their authorship, date, and place of composition, as opposed to the Lower Critics, who worked primarily on the language and grammar of biblical texts. In particular, Higher Critics challenged the idea that Moses was the author of the first five books of the Old Testament, positing several different sources for the book of Genesis alone, and they urged the study of the Bible as a literary artifact rather than as divinely inspired text. To them, it was a book like any other, to be interpreted through immersion in the cultures and languages of its various authors. In the late eighteenth and early nineteenth centuries, advanced scholars in this discipline transformed the debates about biblical and, by implication, figurative language.

American scholars' interest in the Higher Criticism also coincided with their discovery of Germany's rich religious and artistic culture.

At first they got their information secondhand, particularly from the widely circulated *Germany* (1810), by Anne-Louise-Germaine Necker, the baroness of Staël-Holstein (better known as Madame de Staël), which was available in French and, after 1813, in English translation. In addition to providing a road map to the "manners," literature, and arts of the nation, de Staël devoted many pages to a discussion of the country's philosophical and religious thinkers, particularly Kant, and demonstrated the richly symbiotic relationship between their thought and national culture. Here American readers encountered for the first time a lengthy discussion of philosophical Idealism. For those who chafed under the rationalism and materialism to which Locke's empiricism led, an introduction to German Idealism and its ethical implications was both liberating and exhilarating.

De Staël also touted the superiority of the German educational system; and with the conclusion of the War of 1812 and the reopening of safe travel to Europe, Americans began to visit the Continent and to study at German universities. Among the most prominent of these pioneers were George Ticknor, Edward Everett, George Bancroft, and Frederic Henry Hedge, all of whom eventually carved out positions of intellectual leadership in New England and led efforts to disseminate German language and thought.

By the time Ticknor was nineteen, and a Dartmouth graduate, for example, he had read in de Staël of the great university at Göttingen and was determined to sample its educational resources. He knew little German, however, and turned to his friend Edward Everett for guidance. Everett provided him with a German-French dictionary, with which he began his tutorial. Eventually, in 1815 he, Everett, and two others sailed for Europe and made their way to Germany's cultural centers. At Göttingen, Ticknor took classes with, among others, Eichhorn himself, whom he found "lively, gay, full of vigour, though not young, and interested in everything." The young Bostonian luxuriated in this intellectual hothouse.

During his European sojourn Ticknor met other prominent intellectuals, including at Weimar the writer Johann Wolfgang von Goethe, and in Paris the philosophers A. W. von Schlegel and Alexander von Humboldt. He continued his introductions in London, where he greeted the American author Washington Irving and the English writers William Hazlitt, William Godwin, and Charles Lamb, among others. Upon his return to the United States in 1819 Ticknor assumed the position of Smith Professor of French and Spanish Languages and Literature at Harvard, which had been held for him while he studied abroad. Although he was not responsible for teaching the German language per se, his experience abroad made him attentive to students' needs, and in 1825 he convinced Harvard to hire Karl Follen (1796–1840), a German expatriate whom he had met in Switzerland, to teach the language.

Upon his arrival at Göttingen, Ticknor's traveling companion Everett, similarly promised a chair (in Greek) at Harvard upon his return, took private classes with Eichhorn in Hebrew and Arabic and engaged him as well for a tutorial in German literature. In addition, Everett pursued advanced studies in Greek to fulfill his obligation to Harvard, and in 1817 he received a doctorate in philosophy, the first such awarded an American from a German university. After his and Ticknor's audience with Goethe in 1816, Everett prepared an essay on him, published in 1817 in the *North American Review*, the first important notice of this writer to appear in the United States.[11] The following winter Everett continued his travels. In Paris he met the German naturalist and explorer Wilhelm von Humboldt, the philosopher Benjamin Constant, and de Staël herself. He returned to the United States the same year as Ticknor to assume his duties at Harvard. From that position he influenced countless students, many of whom sought him out to learn more of German language and thought. Years later Emerson testified to this professor's large influence, observing that "the genius of Everett" was "almost comparable to that of Pericles in Athens," as even "the rudest undergraduate found a new morning open to him" in Everett's lecture hall.[12]

In the summer of 1818 eighteen-year-old George Bancroft, later a prominent Democratic politician and one of the country's most distinguished historians, followed in Ticknor's and Everett's footsteps for study at Göttingen, with Frederic Henry Hedge, the twelve-year-old son of Harvard professor of logic Levi Hedge (with whom Bancroft had boarded), in tow. Everett had convinced Harvard's president Kirkland to provide Bancroft a stipend to study philology and biblical criticism, and shortly after his arrival in Göttingen he enrolled in two of Eichhorn's courses, in the New Testament and Syriac. In a letter written in 1819 to Harvard's own biblical exegete, Andrews Norton, Bancroft provided a good description of how he spent his day at the great German university. "5 a.m., Hebrew and Syriac," he reported;

7–8, [Arnold Hermann Ludwig] Heeren in Ethnography; 8–9, Church history by the elder [Gottleib Jakob] Planck; 9–10, Exegesis of the New Testament by old Eichhorn; 10–11, Exegesis of the Old Testament by old Eichhorn; 11–12, Syriac by old Eichhorn; 12–1 p.m., Dinner and Walk; 1–2 Library; 2–4, Latin or French; 4–5, Philological Encyclopedia by [Ludolph] Dissen; 5–7, Greek; 7–8, Syriac; 8–9, Tea and Walk; 9–11, Repetition of the old lectures and preparation for the new.[13]

It was a rigorous schedule, but Bancroft made remarkable scholarly progress and received his doctorate from the university in 1820.

In the interim he also visited Berlin, where for five months he took courses from that university's distinguished faculty. He attended lectures under the renowned philosopher G.W.F. Hegel and as well enrolled in the theologian Friedrich Schleiermacher's offering on the philosophy of education, a memorable experience that prompted him to report to Kirkland that Schleiermacher brought to his subject "a mind sharpened by philosophical meditation and enriched with the learning of all ages and countries." Although much in Bancroft's education prepared him for a career as a biblical scholar, early on he decided against it, believing it destructive of true spirituality. As a case in point, he noted that exegetes like Eichhorn seemed little interested in religion per se. In their courses, Bancroft complained, "the bible is treated with very little respect, and the narratives are laughed at as an old wife's tale, fit to be believed in the nursery."[14] After his return to the United States in 1823, Bancroft took Kirkland's advice to start a secondary school on the model of the German "gymnasium." At his Round Hill

School in Northampton, Massachusetts, he put into practice many of the progressive educational ideas to which he had been exposed abroad, particularly in Schleiermacher's course.

While Bancroft studied at Göttingen, he installed his young traveling companion Frederic Hedge in a gymnasium in the city and later at one in Ilfeld. The precocious teenager flourished in the German educational system and immersed himself in German language and philosophy. Upon his return to the United States five years later Hedge was placed in Harvard's junior class and eventually graduated from its infant Divinity School. By the early 1830s he was hands down the Unitarian most at home in German language and culture. He later told Caroline Dall that when he published his essay on Samuel Taylor Coleridge, another exponent of German thought, in *The Christian Examiner* in 1833, no one else in the United States had ever studied German metaphysics "*in the original.*" She saw no reason to doubt his claim.[15]

Others, too, made the pilgrimage to Germany. By 1824, for example, Emerson's older brother William, influenced by fellow Bostonians Everett and Ticknor, also had found his way to Göttingen. He wrote Waldo to "learn German as fast as you can" and urged a visit. "Read Eichhorn's critical, but not his historical works," he added, signaling his own exposure to biblical criticism.[16] He repeated the advice to his college classmate John Fessenden and added, "My mind seems to have undergone a revolution" through "the books and lectures of Eichhorn."[17]

Such enthusiastic reports to New England of German culture and scholarship prompted a great interest in the German language. Before long Harvard began to cast about for native instructors and found them among recent émigrés who not only provided basic instruction in the language but also firsthand knowledge of some of Germany's most prominent biblical scholars and philosophers. The most important of these teachers was Karl Follen, well known for his German nationalist sentiments.[18] He had been a leader in the influential student movement that arose after the defeat of Napoleon in 1815 and resisted the subsequent formation of the German Confederation. This group, which began at the University of Jena but then spread to other campuses, had as its goal the creation of a German state based in democratic and constitutional principles, including freedom of expression. For years Follen taught law at Jena, another great center of learning, but he went into exile following his implication in the assassination of the reactionary playwright August von Kotzebue, who supported the Confederation and ridiculed the insurgent student movement.

Follen and his friend Karl Beck (1798–1866), the stepson of the renowned biblical scholar Wilhelm de Wette, had visited the family of Karl Sand, Kotzebue's assassin, shortly before the murder and thus were, erroneously, linked to the plot, as was de Wette himself.[19] Although the prominent literary historian Wolfgang Menzel testified that Follen had nothing to do with Kotzebue's death, Follen thought it prudent to emigrate to Paris, where he met the philosophers Benjamin Constant and Victor Cousin; and then to Basel, where, following his own interrogation by the German authorities, de Wette also had gone, resigning his post at the University of Berlin. There Follen and de Wette edited a literary magazine that promoted German patriotism, and they numbered among their friends and supporters none other than J. F. Fries, another eminent Idealist philosopher, as well as other German nationalists. Continually hounded by Prussian authorities because of the Sand affair, however, Follen and Beck began to consider leaving Europe altogether.

In 1824 they crossed the Atlantic to Philadelphia. Ticknor thereupon recommended Follen for a position at Harvard as instructor in German, the school's first. A few years later he offered courses in ethics to the divinity students, among whom were George Ripley and James Freeman Clarke, both destined to be great students of German thought. In 1830 Follen became Harvard's first professor of German, a position he held until 1835, when the administration did not renew his contract, purportedly because of his increasingly strident antislavery views.[20] Having previously studied for the Unitarian ministry, he turned to the pulpit and was soon installed over a new church in East Lexington, Massachusetts, which he served until his untimely death in 1840 in a steamboat accident.

Follen's comrade Beck had an equally illustrious career. From Philadelphia he found his way to George Bancroft's Round Hill School in western Massachusetts, where he taught Latin and gymnastics. Then, in 1832, he too was called to Harvard, as professor of Latin, a position he held until late in his life. These two émigré scholars, personally acquainted with de Wette, one of the greatest living biblical exegetes, as well as with Cousin, Constant, and Fries, introduced a generation of Harvard students to German language and culture.

Follen threw himself into this work. Lacking German textbooks, he prepared a reader at his own expense. "Dr. Follen was the best of teachers," Unitarian clergyman Andrew Preston Peabody recalled. "Under him we learned the grammar of the language, in great part *in situ.*" He worked through "forms and constructions" as the students met them in their reading lessons, explaining them "with a clearness and emphasis that made it hard to forget."[21] Keeping tabs on the young man whom he had recommended for the position, George Ticknor concurred. Follen "is a fine fellow," he wrote to a friend in 1826, "an excellent scholar, and teaches German admirably . . . [He] will do good among us."[22] Writing after Follen's death, Elizabeth Peabody paid him the highest compliment. "I never knew any foreigner," she said, "who seemed to be so easily and widely understood by Americans." "In fact," she continued, Follen "was less of a German than a Christian cosmopolite."[23]

By the end of the 1830s the study of German was all the rage. From his bastion at Andover, Moses Stuart observed that "our youth are every day resorting to Germany for education; and our colleges are filling up with Professors, who have been educated there." The German language, he continued, is "becoming an object of classical study in our public seminaries of learning, and in a multitude of ways, through the medium of translations as well as by the knowledge of the German language," its literature was transforming what constituted serious scholarship in a variety of fields.[24] Divinity students and clergymen—Unitarian or Trinitarian—exposed to the language never were the same.

Joseph Buckminster was one of these, and he had assembled his library in great measure to help him examine the scriptural canon in terms of its history and language, a project well under way in Europe. Given his position as a leading Unitarian, he sought to decide to his satisfaction the degree of consistency among New Testament accounts of the life of Christ, a task in which he was particularly encouraged by the works of the German biblical scholar Johann David Michaelis, the Anglican bishop and scholar Robert Lowth, and Griesbach.

Michaelis taught at the Universities of Halle and Göttingen and specialized in the changes in the Hebrew language over time; his philological works were much studied. Lowth, in his *Lectures on the Sacred Poetry of the Hebrews* (1753) and commentary on Isaiah (1778), presented the Old Testament as a complex literary creation penned by various groups of religious people and thus not easily reducible to one clear story or doctrine. He argued as well that the Bible was a complex mixture of history and myth that had to be disentangled before one arrived at the core of Christian doctrine. His insights led Buckminster to observe that "to understand the unconnected writings of any person, written in a remote period, and in a foreign language," one had to consider "the character of the writer, the opinions that prevailed in his time, his object in writing, and every circumstance peculiar to his situation." Then one might be "sure of having reached the whole of his meaning."[25]

Like many other Unitarians, Buckminster was frustrated by the metaphysical hairsplitting that preoccupied New England clergy, and he believed that enlightened attention to the history and language of the Bible might end such divisive and fruitless bickering. Griesbach was the biblical exegete whose work most immediately encouraged him. Griesbach's two-volume edition of the Greek Testament and its elaborate critical apparatus encouraged Buckminster in his attempts to ascertain the veracity of the New Testament books. He was so taken with Griesbach's scholarship that he even convinced Harvard to subsidize, for those who sought easier access to his criticism, a reprint of an abbreviated manual on the New Testament that this scholar had prepared. In print and from his pulpit Buckminster touted Griesbach's conclusions, arguing that one should not regard the Bible as God's word but only as its vehicle and, as such, a text one had to interpret through sophisticated philological and historical scholarship.

By 1811 Buckminster's proselytizing for the Higher Criticism eventuated in his appointment at Harvard as the first Dexter Lecturer in Biblical Criticism, an indication of the institution's growing commitment to the new European scholarship. Buckminster posthaste wrote European booksellers to acquire other key scholarly works that he needed, and he also began to learn the German language so that he could read them in the original.

Following his untimely death, his torch passed to Andrews Norton, who had read theology with both him and the equally well regarded Unitarian Henry Ware, whose appointment to the Hollis Chair of Divinity at Harvard in 1805 had ignited a firestorm of criticism from conservative Trinitarians who viewed his elevation as Harvard's capitulation to liberal Christianity.[26] In 1813 Norton succeeded William Ellery Channing as Dexter Lecturer, a position Channing had held for only a year and which in 1819 (after much lobbying on Norton's part) became the Dexter Professorship. Norton, now proficient enough in German to read Eichhorn's *Introduction to the New Testament* in the original, began his lifelong project of proving the "genuineness" of the Gospels. With his seminal *Statement of Reasons for Not Believing the Doctrines of the Trinitarians* (1819), the locus classicus of the Unitarians' understanding of scripture, Norton initiated a long-running battle with none other than Stuart, who, from his influential position at the Andover Theological Seminary—which was founded in the wake of Ware's appointment to the Hollis Chair to provide a comparable seminary for Trinitarians—resorted to the same Higher Critics to defend a very different notion of scriptural language and meaning.

Andrews Norton was a small man with a "delicate physical organization," one friend recalled, and had a "light and rather pallid complexion." Feeble-voiced—he did not have "sufficient compass to fill a large house"—he was at his best in his study and was an assiduous scholar.[27] His colleague James Walker, professor of moral philosophy, recalled that Norton never troubled himself "to comprehend the ignorance or errors of other people," including his students. This led to a rather limited pedagogy, for "he saw things so clearly himself, and stated them so clearly, that if a pupil failed to be convinced, he soon gave him up."[28] The Transcendentalist Orestes Brownson, who despised all that Norton stood for, was more pointed. "It is said," he wrote in a review of one of Norton's works, "that he usually sits in his room with the shutters drawn, which has the double effect of keeping the light out and the darkness in." "This may be a calumny," he continued archly, but his writings "afford no satisfactory refutation of it."[29] George Ripley, who also had put in time sparring with Norton, was more measured and yet verified the accuracy of both reports. Late in his life he observed that "the predominant qualities of [Norton's] mind were clearness of perception, rigidity of judgment, accuracy of expression, and a chaste imagination."[30]

Stuart directly attacked William Ellery Channing's sermon *Unitarian Christianity* (1819), the most famous manifesto of liberal Christianity, and the bullheaded young Norton quickly jumped to its defense with his *Statement of Reasons*. Moses Stuart was then probably the best-read scholar in biblical criticism in New England, his immersion in German scholarship so profound that at one point the Andover trustees, who every five years required each professor's sworn allegiance to a formal creed, feared for his orthodoxy. They realized, however, that if their faculty were to defend the Trinitarian reading of the Bible position against that of liberal Christians, they had to adopt similar methods of textual scholarship, so Stuart escaped with just a censure.[31]

The heated exchange between Stuart and Norton turned on the ultimate authority of biblical language. For Stuart the chief question was, what did the writers mean to convey in the biblical passages? His position, dictated by unwavering commitment to scriptural revelation, was that when the textual scholar had examined the Bible with the same philological, grammatical, and literary tools that he brought to any other ancient book—that is, when he had discerned the word's *meaning*—the text, as the divinely ordained word of God, was authoritative. "It is orthodoxy in the highest sense of the word," Stuart declared, and "everything which differs from it, which modifies it, which fritters it away, is *heterodoxy*, is heresy." The biblical exegete's only query should be, what thought did this or that passage convey? When this was answered philologically, a Christian was compelled "to believe what is thought, or else to reject the claim of divine authority." One conducted scriptural studies by one's philology, independent of one's philosophy. But after such investigation, what he discerned was binding, because the Bible was inspired.[32]

Stuart depended for his analysis on a group of mid-eighteenth-century Higher Critics subsequently known as the Neologians, specifically Michaelis (1717–91), J. A. Ernesti (1707–81), and, most important, J. S. Semler (1725–91). These scholars and their disciples, many of whom were conservative, evangelical Pietists who took pains not to allow their beliefs to dictate the results of their biblical research, had undertaken a radical reevaluation of Christian revelation and dogma on philological and grammatical grounds. Their highly rationalist view of the exegete's task provides a textbook example of how the Age of Reason affected the study of the Bible, and their influence lingered well into the nineteenth century. Stuart was attracted to them because of their continuing respect for Trinitarian orthodoxy, attendant on their Pietism, for they still believed in Christ's miracles as a demonstration of his divinity.[33] Despite its novelty, their research supported a conservative understanding of scripture such as Stuart had sworn to maintain at Andover.

Channing, however, took the same propositions in a different direction. He was influenced by the important distinction, popularized by Semler, that the Bible, rather than being *literally* the word of God, instead only *contained* it, a semantic distinction that opened the gates to linguistic and historical research that eventually undermined orthodox readings of scripture. Channing contended, following Semler, that before any text could be considered authoritative, it had to agree with the general spirit of the Bible, part of the universal truth Christ and his disciples revealed in the New Testament. The question Channing posed addressed not only what the original writer meant to convey, but whether his text was valid for all ages or merely referred to local, temporal situations, a distinction an informed interpreter could make. Channing also maintained that in many places the Bible dealt with issues about which men had received ideas from sources other than scripture itself, that is, from the writer's culture. The biblical exegete thus had to restrain and modify scriptural language by known truths furnished by observation and experience, in a textbook application of the Common Sense philosophy.

Trinitarians like Stuart rejected this idea because it placed final authority in man's reason rather than in revelation. No one could modify a scriptural proposition to make it agree with man's flawed judgment, a result of his fallen state. To Stuart, the significance of God's word never changed over time, and assertion to the contrary only displayed man's innate depravity. Because he sought to establish the theological authority of scripture *within* the tradition of orthodox Calvinism, Stuart used German scholarship to reinforce beliefs he already held. In a crucial admission, he vowed that he and his fellow Trinitarians never would undertake to "describe affirmatively the distinctions of the Godhead," because such terms as "proceeding from the Godhead" and "the Logos made Flesh" were merely "a language of approximation," feeble attempts to describe the indescribable. While language expressed enough of the truth of such matters to "excite our highest interest and command our best obedience," words were only suggestive.[34]

Although installed as Buckminster's successor as Dexter Lecturer, Channing was not a profound textual scholar, and he never replied directly to Stuart's attack on his sermon. Channing was much more important in his homiletic role and was widely regarded as America's foremost Unitarian—Emerson even termed him, affectionately, "our Bishop"—who served as a model of the liberal Christian piety.[35] The redoubtable Andrews Norton, however, needed little prompting to reply to Stuart, and in his inaugural discourse as Dexter Professor he clarified the role of the biblical scholar. In studying the Bible, he said, the responsible exegete had to acquaint himself "with all that collection of facts and rules, by the application of which the original text of the sacred writings is recovered as far as possible." In addition, he had to master the languages in which they were written and thus be, "in the most comprehensive sense of the word, a philologist." By studying the character of scriptural language, he continued, the philologist discovers "its intrinsic ambiguity and imperfection," for "words taken alone" (that is, without exegesis) were "often inadequate to convey any one definite meaning." Further, that meaning itself might be "loose and unsettled," and thus could be fixed only by the exegete's attention to "extrinsic considerations."[36]

In defending Channing, Norton elaborated these ideas and invoked Locke's principles of language to argue that biblical words, like any others, were only "human instruments for the expression of human ideas." Words expressed nothing but an idea or an aggregate of ideas that men associated with certain sounds or letters. Language represented what "the human understanding is capable of conceiving." Thus, all that had ever been recorded (in scripture or elsewhere) could be understood rationally by intelligent men, for so far as words have meaning, Norton magisterially declared, "they are intelligible." He was humble enough to admit that some truths finally were incomprehensible, but these could not be expressed explicitly through verbal signs. He did not speculate on hypothetical matters: his research led him to grapple only with "the historical circumstances surrounding scriptural language, its peculiarities of idiom, and the prepossessions of writer and audience."[37] He did not condescend to consider how divine wisdom was transmitted to earthly creatures, especially when it contradicted common sense, and he had no time for or interest in language's "intrinsic ambiguity."

Intuition, then, the flights of imagination during an inspired state, had nothing to do with understanding scriptural truth. Cultural differences and lack of linguistic sophistication accounted for most misrepresentations of biblical language and misunderstanding of Christian doctrine (like those, for example, between Unitarians and Trinitarians) because "figures and turns of expression familiar in one language are strange in another." Correct interpretation of passages that seemed to "bear a Trinitarian sense" but in fact, on closer study, supported a Unitarian reading, could be achieved only by considering the writer's character, his "habits of thinking and feeling," his "common state of expression," his "settled opinions and beliefs," the "general state of things during the time in which he lived," and the "particular local and temporary circumstances present to his mind while writing."[38] A writer's specific words, Saint Paul's or Tertullian's, were the result of social and historical context.

This seminal debate over the import of Higher Criticism on American Christianity involved figures from two distinct and opposed denominational camps, each drawing different conclusions from similar historical and linguistic exploration of the Bible. The influence of the Higher Criticism, however, also was felt within individual denominations, with equally divisive effects. The Unitarian clergyman Orville Dewey recalled, for example, how after attending Williams College, a bastion of orthodoxy, he entered Andover with the thought of using the new biblical criticism to buttress orthodoxy. "But the more I studied it," he wrote, "the more I doubted." Ironically, Stuart himself was the problem. In his "crucible," Dewey continued, "many a solid text evaporated and left no residue of proof." Dewey eventually found his way to Unitarianism and ministered to its largest New York congregation.[39]

James Marsh was another orthodox scholar challenged by the Higher Criticism. Born in Hartford, Vermont, in 1794, he was raised in a staunchly orthodox household. When in 1817 he decided to pursue a career in the ministry, his family assumed that he would attend Andover. He was not happy with that institution's academic regimen, however, and late in 1820, as Channing's sermon on Unitarian Christianity was making such a stir, he thought that the stimulation of Cambridge might cure his intellectual unrest. Two months there convinced him of the Unitarians' moral and spiritual failings, and he soon reentered Andover, where Stuart won him over to the new exegetical studies. By February of 1821 Marsh reported that under Stuart's guidance he felt as though he had "conquered" the German language. He plunged into biblical exegesis head-on by undertaking a critical reevaluation of both testaments.[40]

In 1824 Marsh was ordained to the Congregational ministry in Hanover, New Hampshire, where he served for two years, until the University of Vermont in Burlington, seeking new intellectual leadership, offered him its presidency. Throughout his association with that institution—in 1833 he stepped down to become professor of moral and intellectual philosophy—the influence of the new German thought on his writings was everywhere apparent. He believed that because of the Higher Criticism, Christians needed a new way to describe and discuss religious experience; that is, they had to rethink the power of language to capture and make accessible Christianity's essence—the same problem that preoccupied Stuart and Norton.

Marsh's interest in this subject was evident as early as 1829 in a review of his mentor's *Commentary on the Epistle to the Hebrews*, in which Stuart sought to reconcile belief in an intuitive faith—one based in the heart rather than the head—with Trinitarian Calvinist dogma. Arguing that the fragmented state of New England's churches resulted from misconceptions of the vocabulary deployed by differing factions, Marsh moved inexorably toward Stuart's position, that language was best understood as figurative rather than literal. The concept of "redemption," for example, was comprehensible only when one realized that rational analysis of scriptural language yielded only that which could be comprehended by one's logical faculties. To have a true sense of what the ancients meant by "redemption," one had to consider the term *imaginatively* or *intuitively*, coming to know, as Marsh put it, "the inward and subjective nature of it." Unfortunately, most scholars neglected to do so. "Situated as we are in society," Marsh wrote, "we unavoidably learn words before we can have much insight into the meaning of them." Men acquired the habit "of using them without any definite and precise meaning."[41]

The apostle's description of the doctrine of redemption once had been vital, but it no longer made sense in analytic or rational terms. "For those who have the whole of the New Testament in their heads," Marsh wrote, "and read it aright, and feel its powers, the language of the Apostles ought to mean more, than these metaphorical representations, literally interpreted, could express." Head and heart thus had to be reconciled; and anyone, Unitarian or Trinitarian, who set out to explain the doctrines of faith through logical analysis alone evinced a failure of imagination.

Where did Marsh get such ideas? In good measure through his receptive reading of Johann Gottfried von Herder's *On the Spirit of Hebrew Poetry* (1782), whose first American edition he translated and shepherded through his brother-in-law's press in Burlington the same year that he resigned his university presidency. Herder had long been of interest to American biblical scholars. As far back as 1812, for example, Stuart had tried to persuade his young friend Everett to translate Herder's works and was willing to lend his own copies for that purpose. Everett made some progress but never published the result, and it was left to Stuart's younger student

Marsh to complete the task.[42] In 1826 he published several install-
ments of his translation in the *Biblical Repertory*, and seven years
later he made the entire work widely available.[43]

Herder was a progenitor of the "mythical" school in biblical
criticism. He argued that the Bible's stories, like Greek or Roman
mythology, were not factual but true only *poetically*, whetting mankind's appetite for higher things by appeals to the imagination. The
historical appurtenances of a biblical story were thus incidental to
its main instructional and inspirational purposes, which the reader
could grasp if he treated the text as he would any other example of
complex literature. Further, Herder believed that such inspirational
texts derived from a people's culture, their "spirit," a notion of literature that saw religious belief as formative of a people's nationhood, an idea that resonated in Europe, caught as it was in the
throes of nationalist aspirations. Inspired poetry thus was the fount
of both national identity and spiritual inspiration.

When young George Ripley reviewed Herder's eighteen-volume
collected works in *The Christian Examiner* in 1835, he provided
readers with a detailed intellectual pedigree of the German scholar.
Herder, Ripley wrote, derived from Semler, Ernesti, and Michaelis,
who had sought to make theology "a science resting on its own
merits." But their descendant was unique in having recognized that
scripture had to be read as sacred poetry—"Oriental writings" that
belonged "to the infancy of the world." If any doubted the importance of this observation, Ripley continued, in Herder's voluminous writings one "found the germ of most of the important
thoughts, which have since produced such a mighty revolution in
the prevalent conceptions of religion."[44] Ripley's comment proved
prescient, for Marsh's role in the transfer of European culture to the
United States was not restricted to the Higher Criticism. With the
introduction of Herder, however, to a wider audience through his
translation of *On the Spirit of Hebrew Poetry*, anyone interested in
the topic could entertain a wholly new way of understanding the
language and meaning of scripture.

One such person was Elizabeth Palmer Peabody (1804–94), a Salem, Massachusetts, native then working as an assistant in Bronson

Alcott's Temple School in Boston. Peabody had strong Unitarian credentials and in 1834 was well enough known among Boston's intelligentsia for *The Christian Examiner*, the Unitarian publication of record, to ask her to evaluate Marsh's edition of Herder's *On the Spirit of Hebrew Poetry*. She admired Herder's work enough to use it as a text for discussion in a series of "conversations" she held for women in Boston, and she welcomed the opportunity to weigh in on the work's significance.[45]

Given her Unitarian upbringing, Peabody began her review predictably. She stressed that the words of the Old Testament were the product of men "limited in their power of taking in what was so freely poured upon them by their partaking in the spirit and character of the age in which they lived." But she quickly recognized that the uniqueness of Old Testament texts resided in their poetry, what she described as the "expression of abstract and spiritual truths by sensible objects, by the forms, colors, sounds, changes, [and] combinations of external nature." This poetic language, she wrote, existed because the human mind "in its original principles," and natural creation "in its simplicity," were but different images of the same creator, who had linked them "for the reciprocal development of their mutual treasures."[46]

Primitive languages thus were "naturally poetic." But as society "ramified" and people communicated more by imitation and custom than spontaneously, "a thousand arbitrary and accidental associations connected themselves with words" and deadened the impressions they naturally made. Language moved to a level of analytical or technical expression in which words were no longer pictures of the natural world but merely social conventions, as Locke had argued. This language she termed "prose," which, although it provided a more precise expression of the differences among things, sacrificed, Peabody noted, the "force, impressiveness, and exciting power" of poetry. While the most poetic expression existed only in the earliest stages of the human civilization, it remained as a part of all subsequent language through metaphor. Herder had recognized this when he investigated the primitive poetical radicals of the Hebrew language, pointing out that the true genius of the Hebrew tongue was displayed in its "formation and derivation of words from the original roots, and of those original roots from external and internal nature."[47]

Peabody coupled this with what she knew of Greek mythology, for she discerned congruence between the allegorical truths in the poetry and mythology of both the Greek and Hebrew cultures. She regarded primitive man as an original poet who named everything around him through the interaction of his instinctual speech and his environment. Originally, there was a reason why such a word meant such a thing, a position radically opposed to Locke's notion of the arbitrariness of language. Peabody welcomed Herder's suggestion that if one went back far enough in the study of a language, he not only located a tongue's original roots but also could ascertain how these roots themselves were derived from nature. This suggested universality to the oldest forms of languages, which, if properly understood, revealed a universal grammar. In addition to providing a key to the more economic assimilation of the various modern languages, such insight, she believed, demonstrated the common origin of thought in nature.

Her reading of Herder led her to search for an *ur*-language, the parts of which were intimately connected to the exterior world—what we might term a "language of nature" that others like Emerson soon enough elaborated with even more sophistication. Peabody's interest in this subject eventually led her as well to sponsor and publish the work of language theorists who similarly argued a universal origin to speech. In the hands of readers like Peabody and an ever-expanding group of sympathetic readers, the Higher Criticism thus had the potential to alter radically their understanding of language and symbol.

The young Waldo Emerson's struggle with the tenets of his Unitarian faith offers a final example of the potential for the Higher Criticism to challenge long-established tenets in organized religion as well as of its liberating effect on notions of representation. In the early 1830s, shortly after his wife's death from tuberculosis, Emerson, a minister to Boston's Second Church, gave a series of lectures to his congregation's young people that display his growing allegiance to the Higher Criticism and indicate his increasing disenchantment with the Unitarian fellowship. Like Elizabeth Peabody, he believed that the Higher Critics had erred in trying to resolve hermeneutical questions through reason or logic alone. "My friends," he addressed his youthful parishioners in 1831, "if we leave the letter and explore the spirit of the apostles & their master, we shall find that there is an evidence that will come from the heart to the head, an echo of every sentiment taught by Jesus, that will make the evidence to us as strong as that of the Primitive Church."[48] This is precisely what Peabody had discovered through her comparison of Herder's work on Hebrew poetry with her knowledge of classical mythology.

Emerson came to similar conclusions. For example, he based his sermon "The Lord's Supper"—delivered after he had decided that he could no longer in good conscience administer the sacrament of Holy Eucharist—on the same exegetical principles as those of the Unitarians whose judgment in matters of doctrine he had begun to question. His rejection of the sacrament came from rational examination of the scriptural evidence for administering it. After reviewing the relevant scriptural evidence, he concluded that "Jesus did not intend to establish an institution for perpetual observance when he ate the Passover with his disciples." The ritual of the Supper was based in local, Hebraic custom, and Christ's followers (particularly Saint Paul) had erred in their assumption that he wished his disciples to maintain the institution permanently after his death. Moreover, Emerson reminded his contemporaries that on such doctrinal matters they should seek a judgment more in accordance with the spirit of Christianity than had been "the practice of the early ages [that is, the early church fathers]."[49] Sifting through historical and textual evidence, he turned the Unitarians' exegetical principles against them and claimed that the commonly accepted practice of Communion was not in line with the deeper, more intuitive truth of the Christian religion.

Over the next few years, particularly in his book *Nature* (1836) and his address to the graduating students of Harvard's Divinity School in 1838, his reasoning on scriptural language evolved more radically, ending in his decisive break with Unitarianism. In particular, Emerson believed that the literal, contextual meaning of scriptural language was not as important as its more symbolic function, a view ironically congruent with that of the archconservative Stuart. Speaking of Christ's parables, Emerson noted that over time, "the idioms of His language and the figures of His rhetoric" had "usurped" the place of his truth, resulting in churches being built on Christ's "tropes" rather than on his principles. Mankind was left to derive Christ's principles intuitively and subjectively, and not merely through study of the historical context of scriptural language. Emerson thus looked not for more biblical scholars but for "the new Teacher" who would "follow so far those shining laws" of nature that he could see the world as "the mirror of the soul."[50] Truth was not such because the Evangelists had so recorded it, but because they had witnessed it and spoken it in words that were themselves the expression of the laws of God and nature.

Scriptural exegesis lost none of its interest or force over the next two decades. Beginning in 1837, for example, Andrews Norton published the first of what became a three-volume magnum opus on the subject, *Evidences of the Genuineness of the Gospels*, and younger ministers like Ripley and William Henry Furness offered their own refinements of the scholarship. Thus, among those who soon enough were termed Transcendentalists, there was interest in a philosophy of language that took distinctive shape from debates that the Higher Criticism initiated. As these debates became more strident, and as their participants expanded their reading to other European thinkers whose work had fertilized influential biblical scholars, what began as an attempt to discredit erroneous interpretations of scriptural language opened the doors to a novel theory of literary symbolism that placed individual consciousness front and center.

Some theologians began to view human communication as more than man's arbitrary imposition of meaning on sound. Having advanced the idea that scripture was a kind of primitive poetry of the soul, some biblical scholars advanced the concomitant notion that this poetry had been draped most effectively in the imagery of nature. Natural eloquence, they believed, stemmed from the poetic language nature provided men. If one also agreed that verbal signs originally stemmed from man's observation of the natural world, one might posit a "natural" language analogous to the spiritual truths for which men for so long had sought adequate expression. But to arrive at such an understanding of the relations among the individual, nature, and God, dissatisfied Unitarians had to substitute for Common Sense epistemology another that took different account of man's subjectivity. This was expedited by their discovery of philosophical and spiritual Idealism that flowed from the same European founts from which they had taken such deep draughts of the Higher Criticism.

2

REINVIGORATING A FAITH

eginning in 1838 and continuing for the next four years, every few months George Ripley (1802–80), minister at Boston's Purchase Street Church, delivered to the publishing house of Hilliard, Gray, and Company another hefty manuscript for his series *Specimens of Foreign Standard Literature*. Especially interested in making available titles in philosophy, theology, and history, he had conceived the project late in 1836 and proposed to issue each year two or three volumes of about 350 pages each, and to find "true scholars, studious men" among his contemporaries who would translate these works of "truly classical reputation" and append "original notes and dissertations" to guide readers. He needed five hundred subscribers to make the project feasible, and he promised an honorarium of two hundred dollars to each contributor when a thousand copies of each volume were sold, "& in that proportion on every copy, after the first 600."

He offered his friend and potential contributor Convers Francis the following sampler of authors and works he had in mind:

> [Benjamin] Constant on Religion, [Théodore] Jouffroy's Survey of Ethical Systems, Philosophical Miscellanies from [Victor] Cousin, [Theodore Simon] Jouffroy & [Benjamin] Constant, [W.M.L.] De Wette's Lectures on Religion, Selections from [F. H.] Jacobi, [Wolfgang von] Goethe's Autobiography, Selections from [Johann Gottfried von] Herder,

Life of [Jean Paul] Richter & Selections, [Friedrich] Schleiermacher's Discourse on Religion, Miscellanies from [Johann
Gottlieb] Fichte, [G. E.] Lessing's Life & Selections, [Wolf-
gang] Menzel's History of German Literature, Extracts from
Goethe's Correspondence, Historical Notes on German Philosophy.[1]

Ripley successfully assigned many of those titles, with such prominent individuals as the feminist Margaret Fuller and the Unitarian
clergymen James Freeman Clarke, John Sullivan Dwight, and William
Henry Channing (nephew of the Unitarian leader) proffering important translations and introductions. By the time the series ended,
in 1842, when Ripley, having resigned his ministry, was immersed
in a new project, fourteen volumes of translations from French and
German authors had appeared.[2]

Ripley did not restrict his solicitations to Unitarians. It was more
important for editors to have full command of the language of the
authors whom they were to translate and to be sympathetic to the
general tenor of their works than for them to toe some doctrinal
line. As he expressed it to the onetime Congregationalist minister
and now professor of moral and intellectual history at the University of Vermont, James Marsh, the important thing was "to give
some idea of all parts of that enchanted circle in which the German
mind has been revolving for the last seventy or eighty years."[3] Still
believing that Unitarians and Trinitarians might end their divisive
bickering over doctrinal matters and unite in their labors to revivify
Christianity, Ripley sought to ensure that the authors whom he ear-
marked for translation shared one characteristic: they all were part
of that "enchanted circle," that is, contributors to the great philosophical shift from eighteenth-century rationalism to nineteenth-
century subjectivity, typified in such German writers as Goethe but
also in contributors to the new philosophical and theological currents that defined the Romantic age.

At stake for New Englanders like Ripley was the reconciliation
of experimental inquiry, spawned in the seventeenth century and
now fully matured, with their belief that vital religion demanded assent to the heart, to create, in other words, a scientific theology that

included—indeed, welcomed—the emotions. This explains Kant's absence from Ripley's desiderata, testament to his understanding that, as central as this philosopher had been to eighteenth-century philosophical inquiry, a new generation of thinkers had found his rationalism inadequate to their philosophical and theological concerns. Ripley's prospectus thus comprised writers whose work spoke directly to those in search of a revivified, emotional faith.

How did Ripley establish his list of authors, and what were their contributions to the ongoing and increasingly heated debates within New England churches about the true grounds of religious belief? To suggest that Kant's challenge to Lockean epistemology, an eigteenth-century debate, was at the root of some Unitarians' rebellion against the faith of their fathers not only greatly oversimplifies their knowledge of European thought but also gives short shrift to several thinkers whose ideas were formative to this crucial moment in theology and philosophy, in America as well as Europe. Unitarians like Ripley sought a new way to look at the world. It was provided by those who championed man's self-consciousness and, especially, the idea that subjectivity allowed one to reconstitute a vital, heartfelt religion.

James Marsh was one of the earliest and most important purveyors of this New Thought to New England intellectuals. In his attempts to bridge the divide between rational religion, championed by the Unitarians, and an affective faith with its emphasis on personal spiritual experience, advocated by Trinitarians who led the so-called Second Great Awakening of these years, Marsh embraced a new understanding of religious experience, one similar, ironically, to that discovered virtually simultaneously by some of the younger, more radical Unitarians. This explains Marsh's continuing attraction to Ripley, who later also solicited him for contributions to *The Dial*, the Transcendentalist periodical, with the plea that Ripley's party of "heretics and radicals" nevertheless had "large sympathies with ideal conservatives in church and state" such as Marsh.[4]

Marsh's interest in such reconciliation was visible in his first published effort, a review in the prestigious *North American Review* in 1821, a few months before he completed his clerical training at Andover. Assessing a recent book by the Italian scholar Ludovico Gattinara di Breme (1780–1820) defending modern Romantic literature against its detractors, Marsh displayed his familiarity with biblical scholars such as Herder and Eichhorn. Echoing the arguments of Herder, for example, Marsh observed that in the earliest days of the church, religious faith had been based on an imaginative understanding of the natural world.[5] With the Enlightenment's emphasis on science and reason, however, and particularly after the seminal work of Locke in epistemology and Isaac Newton in physics, such poetic use of nature was subordinated to scientific understanding. Marsh believed, however, that for Christianity to remain significant, imagination still had to inform religious sensibility. Because ancient peoples had based their faith in a subjective, affective response to their environment, they "had not learned to write their poetry," Marsh declared, but "had lived it."[6] In contrast, modern writers worked in a world marked by skepticism debilitating to faith. He lamented that, to his contemporaries, it seemed a virtue "to exclude the influence of feeling, and [to] reduce the operations of the whole soul to the measured movements of a machine under the control of our will," a posture that discouraged deep religious faith. Modern man mistrusted emotion, but without it, his faith was not vital.[7]

Marsh's review so impressed readers that some believed that Edward Everett himself had authored it. For his part, Everett, then editor of the *North American Review*, told his friend George Ticknor, who knew of Marsh's intellectual interests and had recommended him for the assignment, that the piece could only have been written by someone with firsthand knowledge of Europe, high praise for a young man who had traveled only as far as Virginia.[8] Marsh's maiden effort was a striking indication of his capability, and thus it was surprising that he waited eight years before again venturing into print, with his review of his mentor Stuart's *Commentary on the Epistle to the Hebrews*. He had spent the intervening years deeply engaged in scriptural exegesis, and this essay located the center of his intellectual agenda, an attempt to reconcile intuitive faith with orthodox, Trinitarian dogma.

Acutely aware of how controversies in scriptural exegesis arose from misunderstandings of language, Marsh predicted that New England's fragmented churches would be united only when Christians considered scriptural language *poetically*, a view akin to that of his mentor, Stuart. Christian doctrine was comprehensible only when one realized that rational analysis of scriptural language could not encompass or describe it. For a true sense of what the ancients meant by a concept like the Trinity, one had to consider the word imaginatively, intuitively, or poetically, coming to know, as Marsh said, its "inward and subjective nature."[9] Thus, while the terms used by the apostles to describe Christ once had been meaningful, now, because of the nineteenth century's slavish adherence to empirical fact, relevant passages had lost their evocative power. Some theological concepts could not be rationally understood, but if approached imaginatively, filled as they were with beauty and grandeur, they might still inspire faith. Through appreciation of such heightened language, the believer could reconcile head and heart.

For the previous year this subject had been much on Marsh's mind, for he was preparing a lengthy introduction to Samuel Taylor Coleridge's *Aids to Reflection*, whose first American edition his brother-in-law, Chauncey Goodrich, published in Burlington, Vermont, in 1829. Marsh applauded Coleridge's attempt to reinvigorate the Church of England, for he viewed the task as congruent with his own efforts to reconcile quarreling factions in American Congregationalism. Marsh's contemporaries demanded a broader and more imaginative understanding of faith, akin to Herder's appreciation of the Hebrew poetry in the Bible, which Marsh thought could be provided through careful study of writers (including Coleridge, but Kant's German successors as well) who emphasized the subjective nature of religious experience. As Marsh read more deeply in the philosophy of religion, he became convinced that a group of German Idealist philosophers provided answers to many of the thorny interpretive questions that the Higher Criticism raised.

Marsh welcomed Coleridge's writings because they helped break the stranglehold of "popular metaphysicians of the day" who continued to champion Lockean empiricism. He objected to a philosophy that tended inevitably to undermine man's belief in the reality of anything spiritual and then "coldly and ambiguously" referred him for the support of his faith to the authority of Revelation. Here he alluded to the Unitarians' illogical opinion of Christ's miracles, which, even as rationalists, they defended, against their own logic, as confirmation of Christ's mission. In contrast, Coleridge argued "the reality of something spiritual in man" and the futility of all modes of philosophizing "in which this was not recognized, or which were incompatible with it."[10]

Marsh's success in spreading Coleridgean thought rested on his reprints of *Aids to Reflection* and *The Friend* in 1831, the former with a lengthy "Preliminary Essay" that became required reading for young Unitarians, even though its author had studied at Andover. Herein Marsh focused on the debilitating split between reason and faith that had preoccupied him for a decade. The central problem, he claimed, lay in the Unitarians' insistence that faith unsupported by reason was mere superstition, while the equally stubborn orthodox maintained that reason alone could never ignite the emotion necessary to vital faith. Redacting contemporary German Idealist philosophers, Coleridge suggested that the painful fragmentation of man's sensibility was based on an inherent division within the mind itself.

In the nineteenth century, Marsh explained, the "natural" or rational mode of knowing had become estranged from the "spiritual" or intuitive, of which one became aware only through persistent examination of one's inner life, a self-consciousness that the empiricists, for whom objective reality was supreme, discouraged. As Marsh put it,

> So long as we hold the doctrines of Locke and the Scottish metaphysicians respecting power, cause and effect, motives, and the freedom of the will, we not only make and defend no essential distinctions between that which is *natural* and that which is *spiritual*, but we cannot even find rational grounds for the feeling of moral obligation, and the distinction between regret and remorse.[11]

Coleridge's importance lay in his emphasis on just this epistemological distinction, which he termed that between Reason and Understanding. As Marsh put it, it was unfortunate that in most contemporary thinkers these two had not merely been "blended and confounded" but "obscured and hidden from our observation in the inferior power."[12] If one grasped the distinction, however, one understood man's religious impulse in a wholly new way.[13] Contemporary religious disputes originated in imprecise terminology, as people talked at cross-purposes without understanding one another. There was a "necessity of associating the study of words with the study of morals and religion," a lesson not lost on those enmeshed in the Higher Criticism.[14]

By the 1830s Marsh's edition of Coleridge was hard to keep in stock in bookstores at Andover and Cambridge, and it initiated debates about the nature of religious experience that, when combined with some New Englanders' firsthand experience with German Idealist thought, reshaped American intellectual history. Karl Follen, the German émigré who taught the language at Harvard, said as much when he wrote Marsh that his edition of Coleridge, with its "excellent prefatory aids," has "done and will do much to introduce and naturalize a better philosophy in this country." It will as well, he continued, make men perceive that "there is still more in the depths of their minds that is worth exploring, and which cannot be cheap and handy in the works of Scotch [*sic*] and English dealers in philosophy," an allusion to the Common Sense philosophers who trolled in Locke's wake.[15] James Freeman Clarke, who came across Marsh's edition of *Aids to Reflection* shortly after it appeared, was equally effusive. Something in him had revolted at all attempts "to explain soul out of sense," he wrote, "deducing mind from matter." He had almost foregone the study of metaphysics, until Coleridge showed him "from Kant that though knowledge begins *with* experience it does not come *from* experience." Whereupon he discovered that he was "a born Transcendentalist."[16]

Marsh later disavowed any connection with such young Turks, even as they praised him for liberating them from an outmoded philosophy. In 1841, for example, he wrote University of Vermont alumnus Henry Jarvis Raymond that he viewed "the whole of Boston Transcendentalism" as a "rather superficial affair." "They have many of the prettinesses of the German writers," he continued caustically, "but without their manly logic and strong systematizing tendency," an assessment with which many contemporaries agreed.[17] Despite Marsh's disclaimers, however, his Coleridge had done its work. By introducing receptive readers to the concept of "Reason," an internal principle not subject to empirical proof, he accounted for a universal religious sentiment, a mysterious source of intuition that informed all belief. It was a lesson that budding Transcendentalists never forgot.

A letter to Marsh in 1832 from his friend Follen revealed the depth of Marsh's interest in the German thinkers who had inspired Coleridge. Follen expressed his pleasure at having heard that Marsh had announced a book "on the basis of Fries."[18] Jakob Friedrich Fries (1773–1843) addressed inconsistencies in Kant's system of knowledge by putting it on more solid psychological ground. Marsh died before finishing the work, but by then Fries's system was widely known in New England intellectual circles, mainly through the translation and publication of several works by his chief student, the philosopher and theologian Wilhelm de Wette.[19] No fewer than four volumes of the fourteen published in Ripley's *Specimens*, for example, were by de Wette, including the two-volume novel *Theodore; or, the Skeptic's Conversion*. Patently autobiographical, *Theodore* illustrates de Wette's endorsement of Fries's revision of Kant, particularly his grounding of faith in a psychological "feeling" that locates the infinite here and now, in the world.

J. D. Morell—an Englishman whose *Historical and Critical View of the Speculative Philosophy of Europe in the Nineteenth Century* (1841) offers a cogent contemporary account of the development of German Idealism—clarifies the attraction of Fries for Marsh and other Americans. He groups this philosopher in his section on "Mysticism in Germany" and places him in a direct line of descent from Friedrich Henry Jacobi (1743–1819), who insisted that human understanding can bring mankind only so far toward the first principles of knowledge and never to the point of knowing absolute truth.[20] Hence, a philosophy based on understanding alone leads to skepticism and, potentially, fatalism. To validate Kant's Idealism, Jacobi posited another fundamental principle, which he termed "faith" or "intuition." As Morell put it, "Just as sensation gives us immediate knowledge of the world, so there is an inward sense—a rational intuition—a spiritual faculty—by which we have a direct and immediate revelation of supersensual things" such as God, providence, freedom, and immortality.[21]

Fries identified intuition as the inward "faith-principle" to which all other thoughts and notions were subordinate. While sensory experience can be fallible, he argued, intuition always provides insight into the true nature of things. Man learns of the absolute not solely through objective knowledge but as well through spiritual intimation.[22] Thus, Fries sought to restore the respect for intuitive feeling that Kant had rejected, for only through it could people know the relationship between this finite world and eternal realities, spirit mirrored in matter. Intuition, in other words, allows us to move from knowledge to faith. With his insistence on the centrality and vitality of the eternal spiritual principle, Fries went far toward overturning Kant's skeptical view of theology. His notion of a "philosophical anthropology," that is, a philosophy of ultimate knowledge dependent on man's subjective awareness, promised a new understanding of religious belief.

At the end of his discussion of Fries, Morell observed that the German philosopher's opinions had gained their greatest fame through their application to religion, particularly in "the celebrated theologian De Wette."[23] Indeed, de Wette credited Fries with rescuing him from the philosophical confusion into which he had fallen after his almost simultaneous introduction to Kant's and Friedrich Wilhelm von Schelling's ideas when he was at university.[24]

De Wette chronicled his experiences at Jena in *Theodore*, published two decades after he had studied there but still revelatory of his intellectual development. Taking courses from Johann Jakob Griesbach and Heinrich Paulus in biblical criticism, for example, young Theodore was disheartened by disagreements over the accuracy and legitimacy of the Gospels and, in particular, the final import of Christ's miracles, confusion that cleared somewhat after his introduction to Kant's works. Thereupon a whole new world opened, for the thought of the "independence of reason," a cornerstone of Kant's system, powerfully seized his mind. Theodore now understood Christ as nothing more than "the Kantian wise man, who taught, in figurative language and emblems suited to his age," what now, after Kant, could be expressed "in clear and pure thoughts."[25]

But the impersonality of this philosophy, as well as Kant's lack of interest in the aesthetic, troubled de Wette, as did Kant's deterministic conception of God. After hearing Schelling lecture, de Wette was impressed by this philosopher's emphasis on the aesthetic element in philosophy and specifically his presentation of nature in light of a transcendent "Absolute." Empirical science takes one only so far into knowledge. Because the aesthetic sense provides subjective ways of comprehending this Absolute, it is essential in man's attempts to know himself and the universe.

De Wette, however, was disappointed that for all his brilliance, Schelling was unable to ground an ethics of personal responsibility through the aesthetic. But de Wette was fortunate enough to meet one more master. When he moved to the University of Heidelberg in 1807 to teach theology, he encountered Fries, his new colleague. As de Wette later wrote to James Freeman Clarke, Fries taught him to "reconcile understanding and faith in the principle of religious feeling."[26] Fries also made him aware of "the dependency and limitation of human knowledge," de Wette explained, allowing him to find a place for emotion in Kant's logic.[27] Fries's concept of intuition fired de Wette's imagination, and he finally overcame his skepticism of the Gospels' authenticity as he realized that spiritual truth could not be verified through historical criticism, but only through intuition.

New Englanders had learned of de Wette as early as 1819, in Moses Stuart's *Letters to the Rev. Wm. E. Channing*, but his main influence was not felt until a decade later.[28] Through various conduits, including Marsh's works and Ripley's series, by the early 1830s Friesian philosophy, as embraced by de Wette and disseminated in *Theodore* as well as other of his works, was central to New Englanders' understanding of philosophical Idealism. In particular, Fries's distinction between knowledge and faith, and his insistence that the infinite can be grasped only by faith, were central to emergent Transcendentalism. His significance was fully apparent in Ripley's testimony to Marsh in 1838, for example, when Ripley reported his "great respect for Fries as a philosophical writer," an indication of firsthand acquaintance with his thought. "I think," Ripley continued, "that he has done much by his recognition of the class of truths which are independent of demonstration, and founded on immediate deduction from our inward nature, to redeem the system of Kant."[29]

In this same letter, Ripley confessed, though, that despite his respect for Fries, he finally found the German's epistemology "too subjective," which is a telling comment. With Fries, Ripley explained, "I am standing on I know not what," for the German philosopher never rose "above the sphere of self." He "gives me the building," Ripley continued, "beautiful in its symmetrical proportions, shown [sic] upon by the clearest light of day." But while some Transcendentalists found Fries's views of the self liberating and empowering, Ripley needed a deeper foundation. For this he turned to Victor Cousin (1792–1867), who, he claimed, "leaves Fries in the rear."[30] Not surprisingly, when Ripley began his series of *Specimens of Foreign Standard Literature*, the first two volumes (which he edited) contained generous selections from this French thinker.[31]

Ripley's sponsorship of Cousin provides another important clue to why and how, in the late 1820s and early 1830s, Idealist thought found its way across the Atlantic. Born in Paris in 1792, Cousin studied at the Sorbonne, where his precocity made him a sensation. Inspired by Pierre Laromiguière's lectures on Locke's works, he made philosophy his career. Another French scholar, Pierre-Paul Royer-Collard, also greatly influenced him through his argument that experiential sensations are dependent on internal principles not accounted for by logic. Finally, Maine de Biran, through his lectures on the will and his emphasis on the power of individual consciousness in epistemology, greatly shaped Cousin's thought. All three of these philosophers were linked in their desire to counter the skepticism and fatalism to which the inquiries of Locke and his successors, including, in France, Étienne Bonnot de Condillac, had led. Cousin eagerly followed the paths they cleared.

His early career culminated in work on religion that most inspired New England Unitarians like Ripley. A major part of Cousin's project was a reintegration of religion into contemporary philosophical debate on a scientific basis; hence, his continuing interest in the empiricist school as well as in that based on self-consciousness. Discerning in such opposed philosophical ideas certain congruence, Cousin worked out his own contribution to contemporary philosophy, a compelling "Eclecticism" that urged mankind to survey all relevant philosophical systems to cull and order their most important principles into one overarching system. Because competing philosophical schools were not so much wrong as partial, and none fully honest regarding the complexity of human consciousness, the Eclectic philosopher scientifically integrated truth from each.

When William Henry Channing, Unitarian minister and soon-to-be Transcendentalist, published in Ripley's series a translation of some of the work of Cousin's understudy, Théodore Jouffroy (1796–1842), he succinctly summarized the principles of this "French school" of philosophy. First, Channing explained, Eclectics declared that "PSYCHOLOGY IS THE BASIS OF PHILOSOPHY," with profound and objective reflection on the powers of the mind being the foundation of any serious philosophical inquiry. Second, "THE HIGHEST PROBLEMS OF ONTOLOGY MAY BE SOLVED BY INDUCTIONS FROM THE FACTS WHICH PSYCHOLOGY ASCERTAINS." When man examines the powers of the mind, in other words, he gains knowledge of the "Infinite Being." Whereas Germany's post-Kantians began with the absolute and descended to man, Channing continued, the French reversed the inquiry. Finally, as the linchpin of the Eclectic system, Jouffroy and others believed that "PSYCHOLOGY AND THE HISTORY OF PHILOSOPHY RECIPROCALLY EXPLAIN EACH OTHER."[32]

By the early 1830s generous selections from Cousin's works that provided the foundation of his Eclecticism were available in English translations that circulated widely, prompting Ripley to venture to say that there was no living philosopher who had "a greater number of readers in this country."[33] When he published his own selections from Cousin's works, he explained that their appeal lay in the Frenchman's clarity, in contrast to the often seemingly willful obscurantism of the German philosophers. He also credited Cousin for his ability to translate "the most sublime contemplations of the philosopher" into "the language of the market," a gift particularly appropriate to American readers. "Our national taste," Ripley admitted, "may certainly be said to repudiate all mystery and concealment." Thus, his countrymen were apt to slight or disregard "truths of unutterable consequence both to society and individuals, on account of the unusual, it may be, the repulsive phraseology in which they are conveyed."[34] Cousin's redaction of German Idealism and its recombination with salient features of the works of other thinkers rendered him the conduit for popular reception of the most significant European thought and helped popularize a "scientific grounding of a spiritual religion."[35]

His disciple, Jouffroy, also drew the attention of young Unitarians. In 1837, for example, Brownson reviewed his *Course of Natural Law* in *The Christian Examiner*, and shortly thereafter William Henry Channing translated for the same journal his "Skepticism of the Present Age," part of the larger work Brownson had treated.[36] More important was Channing's two-volume translation of Jouffroy's major work of moral philosophy, *Introduction to Ethics*, for Ripley's *Specimens of Foreign Standard Literature.* Jouffroy was a student of Thomas Reid, the Scottish philosopher whose works he had translated and brought to the attention of French intellectuals, and in this work he popularized Reid's notion of a "common sense" that binds humanity and provides its moral foundation. Jouffroy's contributions thus lie more in moral philosophy than in metaphysics, but his name always was linked to Cousin's.

In 1842, when James Murdock evaluated the rise of German philosophy in America and its effect on the Transcendentalists, he was explicit about the significance of the Eclectics. "None of the Transcendentalists of this country are Philosophers by profession," he wrote, and they had not produced any work "professionally on the subject, not even an elementary treatise." Instead, as far as he could judge, American Idealists had "merely taken up the philosophy of Victor Cousin, and, after comparing it according to their opportunity with that of the more recent German schools," modified "a little some of its dicta, and applied them freely to scientific and practical theology." He pointed to Henning Gotfried Linberg's translation of Cousin's *Introduction to the History of Philosophy*

(1832) as "the great store house" from which most Americans "derived their peculiar philosophical opinions, their modes of reasoning, and their forms of thought and expression."[37]

Just as Coleridge's works served a turn and were superseded by the Transcendentalists' firsthand experience with German thought, Cousin and the Eclectics' influence also waned as New Englanders enlarged their knowledge at other European "store houses." "I am told that in the city Cousin & Jouffroy & and the opinion of this & that Doctor showed large," Emerson wrote in his journal. "But as soon as we got ten miles out of town, in the bushes we whistled at such matters, cared little for Societies, systèmes, or bookstores." There, he continued, "God & the world return again to mind, sole problem," to be solved by direct experience, not by reading "whole Encyclopedias." Emerson now found "nothing of worth in the accomplished Cousin & the mild Jouffroy," only "the most unexceptionable cleanness, precision, & good sense,—never a slip, never an ignorance, but unluckily, never an inspiration."[38] By then the Eclectics had done their most important work, and the New Englanders looked for inspiration in new places.

One place they found it was in the writings of Emanuel Swedenborg (1688–1772). "There is one man of genius," Emerson wrote in 1837, "who has done much for this philosophy of life, whose literary value has never been rightly estimated." "I mean Swedenborg," he continued, "the most imaginative of men, yet writing with the precision of a mathematician."[39] Emerson's effusive praise was not idiosyncratic, for Swedenborg, founder of the Church of the New Jerusalem, constructed the final wing of the edifice in which disaffected young Unitarians were making themselves comfortable.

Swedenborg studied at Uppsala, Sweden, but also was educated in England, where the young scholar absorbed Locke's philosophy and studied natural science. This first phase of his career eventuated in an administrative position in Sweden's Board of Mines, and he wrote widely on metallurgy, mathematics, and even anatomy. All this changed when Swedenborg was fifty-seven, however, for that year while in London he had a religious experience that reoriented his life. As he described it, after he finished a meal, "a kind of mist" spread before his eyes, and he saw the floor of his room "covered with hideous reptiles, such as serpents, toads and the like." When the mist dissipated, Swedenborg discerned "a man sitting in a corner of the chamber who said to him, 'Eat not so much!'" This was not a dyspeptic dream, however, for the next night the vision reappeared, with a more serious message. "I am God, the Lord," he told Swedenborg, "the Creator and Redeemer of the world," who had chosen the Swede "to unfold to men the spiritual sense of the Holy Scriptures," lessons which he himself would dictate to the astonished Swedenborg.[40]

He took the assignment seriously. For the next five years he professed to have frequent intercourse with the world of spirits, from which he produced scores of theological works that form the cornerstone of the Church of the New Jerusalem. Central among its tenets is what he termed the doctrine of series and degrees, links in the chain from the natural world to the spiritual. The natural series, for example, comprises the mineral, plant, and animal kingdoms, each of which can be traced to its first series or source, from whose simplicity and primacy stems the world's complexity and yet harmony. These series culminate in God, supernal yet announced in the created, physical universe.

Even more important to young Unitarians than Swedenborg's conception of the final unity of the worlds of matter and spirit was his depiction of the natural world as the very emanation of God. The New Jerusalem would come, Swedenborg believed, when humanity used his "key" to the correspondence between the worlds of matter and spirit, and thus discovered the truth of God's word. A seer who sought to bring mankind a true understanding of Christianity, Swedenborg bequeathed to emergent Transcendentalism an insistence that the "correspondential" relationship of nature to spirit is available in and through language, itself an analogue to nature.

Late in his life, when Emerson assessed New England's intellectual life fifty years earlier, he described Swedenborg as a man of "prodigious" mind who had exerted "a singular power over an important intellectual class" in New England.[41] The British Sweden-borgian and biographer of the religion's founder, James John Garth Wilkinson, perhaps best explained Swedenborg's appeal. The doctrine of "Universal Correspondency," Wilkinson wrote, claims "that bodies are the generation and expression of the souls, and that the frame of the natural world works, moves and rests obediently to the living spiritual world." Now, he continued, "this plainly makes all things into signs as well as powers." The "events of nature and the world become divine, angelic, or demonic messages," he concluded, "and the smallest things, as well as the greatest, are omens, instructions, warnings, or hopes."[42]

In the 1820s Swedenborg's thought found its way to New England primarily through early American disciples. First among these was Sampson Reed (1800–1880).[43] A clergyman's son, Reed was introduced to Swedenborgianism as a student at Harvard College (class of 1818), where he also met Emerson. Although Reed subsequently entered the fledgling Divinity School in Cambridge, after taking his M.A. in 1821, he became a wholesale druggist, all the while contributing to Swedenborgian publications, including the *New Jerusalem Magazine*, which he helped found in 1827. His "Oration on Genius," delivered at his commencement, greatly impressed Emerson, who had received his A.B. the same day. The piece had a long afterlife. Reed eventually published this work in Elizabeth Peabody's journal, *Aesthetic Papers*, in 1849.

More significant was his *Observations on the Growth of the Mind* (1826), which Emerson deemed "in my poor judgment the best thing since Plato of Plato's kind, for novelty & wealth of truth."[44] The pamphlet's message was congruent with what readers encountered in Marsh's redaction of Coleridge as well as in their primary readings in Fries and de Wette. Rather than regarding the mind (as empiricists did) as a vacant receptacle to be filled by sensory experience, Reed described it as a "delicate germ, whose husk is the body," put into the world so that "the light and heat of heaven may fall upon it with a gentle radiance, and call forth its energies." The mind must grow, Reed maintained, not from "external accretion," but from "an internal principle."[45] Further, he believed (following Swedenborg) that the growth of the mind was closely linked to a proper perception and interpretation of the natural world. At Creation, God impressed the fabric of nature with a set of correlatives or symbols, which man, after discovering his mind's creative power, could read with ever-increasing clarity. Before this occurred, however, the poetic imagination had to be refined into a "chaste and sober view of unveiled nature" and to find "a resting place in every created object." When man reached this state of meditative attention in which he discerned the relation of the natural object to his mind as well as to its creator, he discovered, in Reed's felicitous phrase, a language "not of words but of things."[46]

A language not of words but of things, a suggestion that utterly contradicts the Unitarians' belief that language consists of conventions based on contrivance and convenience. Reed proclaimed a set of universal symbols that, when made apparent, allowed a more profound comprehension of the Creator than was possible through logically contrived dogma. To Reed, the genius of the age would be he or she who recognized that everything, "whether animal or vegetable," is "full of the expression of that for which it was designed," as a symbol of the infinite. "The very stones cry out," Reed exclaimed, "and we do well to listen to them."[47]

Reed injected into New England's increasingly heated theological atmosphere the heady suggestion that if humanity was to regain its proper relationship to nature and, by extension, the Creator, people had to stop bickering over grammar and syntax and pay more attention to the visible, universal proofs of God. Synthesizing religion and science with poetry, Reed, following Swedenborg, proclaimed "the marriage of the rational with the imaginative powers," which others like Coleridge, Fries, and de Wette also had done, in their own ways.[48]

Reed's pamphlet excited the same young Unitarians who gravitated around Marsh's edition of Coleridge and the English translations of Cousin's works, and they quickly purchased Swedenborg's books when they were republished in the United States. As early as 1838, however, Reed took pains in the third edition of his *Observations* to disavow any connection to the emergent Transcendentalist wing of liberal Christianity. "*Transcendentalism*," he observed, "is the parasite of *sensualism*; and when it shall have done its work, it will be found to be itself a worm, and the offspring of a worm."[49] Two years later, in the *New Jerusalem Magazine*, the Swedenborgian Theophilus Parsons made the divorce more explicit. "The New Church teaches," he explained, "that to be wise, man should look *from* himself." But Transcendentalism "teaches him to look always *to* himself." Whereas the New Church declares "the renunciation of self-love as the beginning of all true wisdom," the Transcendentalist believes "the pride of self-intelligence is itself the beginning and end of all wisdom." "Its whole religion," he concluded, "is self-worship."[50] By this time, many others had begun to associate Transcendentalism with just such excessive egotism, even if this did not characterize all associated with the movement.

Despite Swedenborgians' disavowals of any connection between themselves and Transcendentalists, through the late 1830s Swedenborg's remained a name to conjure with among New England's Unitarians. In 1839, for example, Emerson observed that it was pleasant "to hear of any fine person that he or she is a reader of Swedenborg," for the Swede's influence on the age, he continued, was "an uncomputed force—his Genius still unmeasured."[51] Through the 1840s, however, his influence waned. Meeting Sampson Reed in town one day, for example, Emerson "commended" Swedenborg as "a grand poet." Reed thought that Emerson had missed the point and wished that, if he "admired the poetry," he "should feel it as a fact."[52] A few years later, in his lecture on "Swedenborg; or, The Mystic," later published in *Representative Men* (1850), Emerson concluded that finally Swedenborg's system was too severe and restrictive, the "vice" of this thinker's mind "its theological determinism." This mystic fastened "each natural object to a theological notion," Emerson observed, but forgot that "the slippery Proteus is not so easily caught." In nature, individual symbols played "innumerable" parts, and hence mankind inhabited a symbolic, not an allegorical, universe.[53]

Given the fissure between the New Church and Transcendentalism, George Willis Cooke, an astute historian of the movement, accurately accounted for Swedenborg's influence. He observed that few Transcendentalists were drawn "in any large degree" to the religious element in Swedenborg's teachings. Rather, the Swede influenced them through "the vast suggestiveness of his ideas, and especially by means of his doctrine of the correspondences between the material world and that of spiritual realities."[54] In this light, Emerson's lifelong interest in Swedenborg's doctrine of correspondence makes perfect sense, as does the fact that Linberg, whose translation of Cousin's work was the earliest on the American strand, counted himself a member of the Church of the New Jerusalem.

In the late 1820s and early 1830s, notices of Swedenborg and of other theologians and philosophers were frequently met with in the pages of *The Christian Examiner*, which liberal Christians had founded in 1813 (as *The Christian Disciple*). Prior to the establishment of the American Unitarian Association, in 1825, this journal held together the varied clerical membership of the emergent denomination through its publication of original essays and lengthy reviews of European and American publications. Between 1831 and 1839, under the editorship of James Walker (1794–1874) and his assistant, F.W.P. Greenwood (1797–1843), the journal was particularly receptive to European philosophy, theology, and scriptural exegesis, and it served as the major conduit through which American Unitarians learned of such important Idealist thinkers as Coleridge, de Wette, Jouffroy, and others.

During these years Walker continued as pastor to the Unitarian congregation in Charlestown, Massachusetts. He, too, had contributed to the ferment within Unitarian ranks. In his lecture *The Philosophy of Man's Spiritual Nature in Regard to the Foundation of Faith* (1834), for example, he emphasized how true religious experience derived from internal, intuitive principles; the American Unitarian Association frequently reprinted the piece through the 1830s. After 1839, when he became Alford Professor of Natural Religion, Moral Philosophy, and Civil Polity at Harvard, Walker moderated his theological radicalism but through his classes still exerted much influence in American philosophical circles. On his watch, *The Christian Examiner* provided a highly visible forum for younger clergy increasingly uncomfortable behind the Unitarian standard.

In the process he turned the journal into an index of those in the vanguard of the Transcendentalist movement.

Here, for example, the Unitarian clergymen George Ripley, Orestes Brownson, and Frederic Henry Hedge, soon leaders of the insurgent group, introduced their cohort to the excitement and promise of Idealist philosophy. Asked late in his life what role he had played in the emergence of Transcendentalism, for example, Hedge pointed to his essay on Coleridge in the March 1833 issue of *The Christian Examiner.* He claimed that it was "the *first word* which any American had uttered in respectful recognition of the claims of Transcendentalism," by which he meant the thought of Kant and his followers.[55]

A short, balding man of prodigious intellect, Hedge had been one of the first New Englanders to master the German language and that country's Idealist philosophers. Among the cognoscenti he was known as Germanicus Hedge and a "fountain of knowledge in the way of German."[56] His stubbornness was legendary. His friend Cyrus Bartol, for example, recalled that when someone told Hedge that "the facts were against him," he replied, "So much the worse for the facts."[57] Although he attended meetings of the Transcendental Club, like his friend Theodore Parker, another giant in German studies, he never relinquished his belief in the centrality and efficacy of the Christian church.

Hedge's essay on Coleridge alerted his cohort to the force of German thought, but his influence did not stop there. Within the year he followed this effort with one on Swedenborg's *True Christian Religion*, recently reprinted in Boston, and thus built on the foundation Reed had laid for an appreciation of the theory of correspondence developed by this "constructive mystic."[58] Anticipating Emerson's argument against Swedenborg a decade later, however, Hedge lamented that Swedenborg's vision was being presented as gospel truth. "When the wine of mysticism is poured into sacred vessels and drunken as the inspiration of God," he warned, worship is degraded "into a heathenish mystery."[59]

At the same time, George Ripley, another young Unitarian clergyman, was introducing *The Christian Examiner*'s readership to other European thinkers who decisively influenced the course of

New England Transcendentalism. In the May 1835 issue he reviewed Marsh's translation of Herder's *Spirit of Hebrew Poetry*, published two years earlier, and six months later he treated readers to a rigorous assessment of the same author's eighteen-volume *Complete Works, on Religion and Theology* (1827–30). In his first essay, Ripley argued that Herder's work contained "the germ of most of the important thoughts which have since produced such a mighty revolution in the prevalent conceptions of religion."[60] He further explored this proposition in his second essay.

Ripley most appreciated two of Herder's ideas. First, religion had to be understood apart from theology, for it was "a matter of the inward nature, the higher consciousness of man." Theology, on the other hand, was a set of propositions "for and against which we may dispute" and should never be confounded with religion, verified as it was not by logic but by internal spiritual principles.[61] Second, Herder insisted that men should not "rest the divine authority of Christianity upon the evidence of miracles," for Christ had never claimed that they should be the criterion of his truth nor compared to the value of his "moral endowments." A miracle might direct attention to doctrine but could never prove its truth, which came only through a "conviction of the understanding."[62]

Within a few months the young minister gave more evidence of his mastery of German philosophy and theology (as well as of an astonishing productivity), offering an introduction to and translation of Friedrich Lücke's "Recollections" (1834) of the great German Romantic theologian Friedrich Schleiermacher (1768–1834), whose countrymen, Ripley remarked, placed him "at the head of all theologians of the present day." In his work, Ripley observed, Schleiermacher reconciled the conflicting claims of religion and science by clarifying the essential character of the former. He believed that it is "neither knowledge nor action, but a sense of our dependence on God, and of our need for redemption from sin," not an intellectual proposition, but a *feeling*.[63] This accorded with what Ripley had gleaned from other Idealist philosophers and, through Schleiermacher's moving formulation, became a rallying point as the Transcendentalist group separated from their conservative brethren.

Schleiermacher had been raised in a Moravian pietistic family, and after graduation from the University of Halle he preached locally for several years. He returned to his alma mater in 1802 as professor of theology and four years later assumed a similar position at Berlin. Early in his career he published one of his most influential books, *On Religion: Speeches to Its Cultured Despisers* (1799), in which he argued that religion is a deep emotion arising (as Morell put it) "from the absorption of the man—the individual man—in the infinite."[64] His indebtedness to Schelling and Jacobi was evident, but the force and originality of Schleiermacher's own defense of such propositions marked him as a new lion in German—and, soon enough, American—theological circles. By the spring of 1836 Orestes Brownson, who now read German fluently, had access to a manuscript translation of *On Religion*, very likely Ripley's own.[65] And in his preface to his translation of de Wette's *Theodore*, Clarke asked rhetorically, "Where, in England or America, can minds be found like that of Schleiermacher, to investigate the first principles of the religious life?"[66]

Through the mid-1830s *The Christian Examiner* published other briefs of philosophical Idealism. Brownson, for example, popularized the French Eclectics with essays on recent translations from both Cousin's and Jouffroy's works. New England's intelligentsia also were introduced to Cousin in the pages of the venerable *North American Review* as early as 1829, when Alexander Hill Everett noticed his *History of Philosophy in the Eighteenth Century*, but Brownson's essay spoke more directly to Cousin's applicability to New England's peculiar religious situation. In another issue of *The Christian Examiner*, Brownson assessed Benjamin Constant's *Religion Considered in Its Origins, Forms, and Development* (1824–31), a pioneering work that grounded Schleiermacher's insight about the universality of the religious principle in wide consideration of many of the world's religions.[67]

Noticeably absent, however, from the pages of *The Christian Examiner*—indeed, from any early discussion of philosophical Idealism—was the young Unitarian Ralph Waldo Emerson, even though these European thinkers, in different ways, contributed to what became his cardinal tenet, the supremacy of individual consciousness. Soon enough Emerson joined the incipient revolution, if on his own terms. But in 1836 the growing insurgency's leadership lay in different hands, among individuals more deeply affected by firsthand exposure to European thought who recognized that the Idealists' emphasis on consciousness could lead not only to egotism but also to a profound sense of universal brotherhood. When Transcendentalism burst on the scene, its adherents aligned themselves on one side or the other of this intellectual and moral fault line that defined the movement's ethical dimensions.

3

TRANSCENDENTALISM EMERGENT

n September 12, 1836, thirteen hundred alumni, eighty invited guests, and two hundred undergraduates sat down under a pagoda-like pavilion in Harvard Yard to celebrate the university's bicentennial. Earlier that day the institution's chief marshal had called forward the alumni sequentially by year of graduation, with an eighty-six-year-old member of the class of 1774 leading the procession to Cambridge's Unitarian Church. There the assembly heard the first rendition of Samuel Gilman's song "Fair Harvard," and a two-hour historical address from university President Josiah Quincy. The attendees then filed back into the yard for toasts, libations, and dinner, a celebration that lasted until 8:00 p.m., after which they dispersed, their way lit with lamps in the dormitory windows "arranged in patterns and mottoes." All agreed that it had been a celebration befitting the august occasion, the two hundredth anniversary of the nation's oldest institution of higher learning.[1]

That day marked another meeting, of less immediate significance. At some point during the festivities four alumni repaired to Willard's Hotel in Cambridge to discuss plans for regular meetings of a new discussion club. Frederic Henry Hedge, frequent contributor to *The Christian Examiner* who the year before had left Cambridge to minister to a church in Bangor, Maine, had called the group together. Since June he had corresponded with Ralph Waldo Emerson about what Emerson termed "the project of the symposium."[2] George Ripley and George Putnam, Unitarian ministers in Boston and Roxbury, respectively, joined them. As Hedge later recalled, the four met to "confer together on the state of current opinion in theology and philosophy," which they found very unsatisfactory. In particular, they criticized the empiricist philosophical foundation on which Unitarianism was based. James Marsh's edition of Coleridge's *Aids to Reflection*, as well as some of the essays of the Scot Thomas Carlyle, had moved them to new considerations, and they sensed "a promise of a new era in intellectual life."[3]

The initial discussion went well, and the foursome adjourned until September nineteenth, when a much larger group met at Ripley's home in Boston. Among the number, in addition to Hedge, Emerson, and Ripley, were Amos Bronson Alcott, an educational reformer; Robert Bartlett, a recent Harvard graduate; Cyrus Bartol, another Unitarian minister; Orestes A. Brownson, a social reformer embarking on a new ministry for Boston's laboring classes; the Reverend James Freeman Clarke, visiting from Louisville, Kentucky, where he edited a liberal Christian journal, *The Western Messenger*, and preached to a Unitarian congregation; Convers Francis, minister to Watertown and a prominent Unitarian; Theodore Parker, a recent graduate of the Divinity School; and Charles Stearns Wheeler, a Harvard undergraduate and Emerson protégé. Over the next four years the club, with an ever-shifting membership, but with Emerson, Ripley, and Hedge as anchors, met nearly thirty times, maintaining a focus on significant religious and philosophical issues and occasionally broaching topics of wider social concern, from "Is Mysticism an element in Christianity?" to "the doctrine of Reform."[4]

The meetings had only one cardinal rule, "that no man should be admitted whose presence excluded [discussion of] any one topic."[5] People of less radical sympathies, as long as they were open-minded, were welcome. The great Unitarian preacher William Ellery Channing occasionally attended, as well as James Walker, editor of *The Christian Examiner*.[6] Late in his life Emerson fondly recalled the intellectual give-and-take at these gatherings. One unsympathetic and disgruntled participant, for example, declared that, "it seemed to him like going to heaven in a swing." Another reported that at one knotty point in a discussion a visiting Englishman interrupted one of Alcott's monologues because a lady near him wished "to inquire whether omnipotence abnegates attribute."[7]

By 1840, however, with many competing activities and organizations centering different participants in the Transcendentalist movement, the gathering, sometimes called Hedge's Club in his honor when he returned to Boston for visits, came to a close. In attendance at the last recorded meeting, on September 20 of that year, were the clergyman and reformer (and nephew of the Unitarian leader William Ellery Channing) William Henry Channing; Margaret Fuller, the most remarkable woman in the group; Elizabeth Peabody, who had been William Ellery Channing's amanuensis and recently had opened a foreign-language lending library and bookstore in Boston; and Hedge, Ripley, and Parker. In keeping with the club's focus, that night they debated "the organization of a new church." They could not know it, occupied as they were with so many other plans—they soon would start their own journal, for example—but in retrospect this meeting was as momentous as the first. As one historian of the movement has written, it signaled the end of the Transcendentalist movement as "a unified entity." The proliferation of so many different views of what constituted reform, he observed, prevented their meeting "any longer on common ground."[8]

The remark is just, but of more immediate concern is the group's coalescence in 1836, for they then had quite specific views of what constituted "Reform," specifically as it flowed from their reading in contemporary European philosophy and social theory. That was, indeed, the year of wonders for the movement, as the novel ideas then beginning to circulate began to move American liberal religion in wholly new directions.[9] What motivated Ripley, Hedge, and their cohort to initiate these meetings, and how did their conversations (and other, less formal ones) eventuate not only in challenges to the religious status quo but also in a spectrum of reform activities?

Among the younger Unitarians who attended the Transcendental Club's meetings, none was more remarkable than Orestes Brownson (1803–76). Born with a twin sister, Daphne, in Stockbridge, Vermont, to a poor farming family, Brownson knew years of privation. His father died when the twins were two, leaving his wife with five small children and no means of income. She eventually sent them to live with friends and relatives, and placed six-year-old Orestes with a family in Royalton, fifteen miles away. He did not return to his mother and siblings until 1817, when they moved to Ballston Spa, New York.

While he was in Royalton the boy's interest in religion intensified, particularly after a revival in a nearby church in which conservative evangelical principles reigned. At Ballston Spa, the relatively new creed of Universalism was all the rage; and for a short time he joined his mother, aunt, and other family members at this denomination's services. As Brownson relates in his autobiography, however, he remained religiously unsettled, unable to shake his nagging skepticism about most religious doctrine.

In 1822 a Presbyterian minister comforted him in his spiritual distress. Brownson soon joined this man's church as a full member, having testified to a conversion experience and been baptized. But this spiritual respite proved as brief as his others. Bristling at Calvinism's seemingly unreasonable demands, he returned to the Universalists, admiring their belief in the inherent dignity of each individual and the promise of eventual salvation to all believers. After more geographical and intellectual wandering—he traveled throughout western New York and even as far west as Detroit—Brownson prepared for the Universalist ministry. In June 1826 he was ordained over his first congregation, in Jaffrey, New Hampshire.

The next year, however, he returned to Ballston Spa to marry Sally Healy, and he commenced a series of moves through eastern and central New York, as far west as the Finger Lakes region, ministering to different Universalist groups and working on a number of religious periodicals. In his contributions he expressed what would become lifelong concerns, particularly a distrust of established religion and sympathy for the plight of the lower classes.

Some of these essays drew the attention of prominent freethinkers, including Frances (Fanny) Wright and Robert Dale Owen, leaders of the radical Working Men's Party. When Wright lectured in Utica, New York, she accepted Brownson's invitation to speak in nearby Auburn, where he was living. Her free-thought views met much opposition, however, and soured Brownson's relationship with his parishioners. He spent much time explaining how he could be allied with such a supposed infidel and still maintain his faith. By 1830 his situation had become untenable, and he left his ministry just before the General Convention of Universalists in New England excommunicated him.

During the next two years Brownson edited the *Genesee Republican*, a paper devoted to working-class issues in which he touted such radical proposals as free universal education, strict laws against monopolies, and the abolition of imprisonment for debt. In 1830 he discovered William Ellery Channing's sermons as well as the writings of the French Christian socialist Claude-Henri de Saint-Simon. Fertilized by Channing's emphasis on the inherent goodness of man and Saint-Simon's belief that a true Christian has to work for social justice and harmony among all classes, Brownson took what he saw as the next logical step, to Unitarianism. By the summer of 1832 he had a small liberal congregation in Walpole, New Hampshire, and within two years moved to another, in Canton, Massachusetts, closer to Boston. He continued to read in French thought, particularly Benjamin Constant's writings on religion and Victor Cousin's on philosophy, and he began as well to explore German Idealism, to which he was introduced through the writings of Karl Follen.[10]

Brownson's move to Canton brought him in contact with many other young Unitarians. These clergymen, aware of his powerful articles about the working classes and his advocacy of rational free inquiry, viewed him as an important ally in their attempts to extend their faith to the urban masses. Brownson might offer, through Unitarianism, a Christian alternative to such freethinkers as Abner Kneeland, whose skepticism had led to his total disparagement of religion and several public trials for blasphemy.

Foremost among these younger Unitarians was George Ripley,

who recognized in Brownson a powerful voice in the same register. In 1837 Ripley wrote George Bancroft, a prominent member of the Democratic Party, that with such men as Brownson he "hoped to see the time, when religion, philosophy & politics will be united in a Holy Trinity, for the redemption & blessedness of our social institutions."[11] Through Ripley's efforts, Brownson soon was presented with just such an opportunity—to replace Joseph Tuckerman as minister at large to Boston's poor. Chafing under a low salary and the needs of an ever-growing family, and lobbied heavily by Unitarian friends in the city, Brownson accepted. In the summer of 1836, the year of Harvard's bicentennial and the Transcendental Club's first meeting, he moved his family to Chelsea, near the center of the Unitarian universe. "I am trying to democratize religion and philosophy," he wrote Bancroft.[12] Now he walked shoulder to shoulder with other liberal Christians who derived from Romantic philosophy and religion the impetus to reinvigorate their faith and work toward a realization of more democratic ideals.

In these years Brownson was not easy to miss. He was imposing, over six feet tall and broad-shouldered, his black hair brushed straight back without a part. He had hazel-brown eyes, a long upper lip, and hands in proportion to his large frame. Particularly distinctive was a swallowtail coat, worn "at all hours of the day, even in his study." A powerful speaker, to some he was abrasive; to others, uncouth; and to some, who feared his social radicalism, downright intimidating. His regimen was Spartan: he frequently worked until three in the morning, ate little (but drank strong coffee all day long), and at a time when temperance was in the air, already had sworn total abstinence. His only noted vice, besides being cantankerous, was chewing tobacco.[13]

His intellect was just as striking. Although he had never attended college, making him unusual among his fellow Unitarian ministers, he read Latin, French, and German and had a seemingly boundless appetite for works on religion and philosophy. He also wrote prodigiously. When he did not have enough copy for an issue of his *Boston Quarterly Review*, he dashed off articles and reviews (even of his own works), frequently filling an entire issue and thus lending an ironic justness to the journal's subsequent name,

Brownson's Quarterly Review.[14] His collected works, far from complete, comprise twenty volumes. His friend Isaac Hecker put it baldly: Brownson, he recalled, "was routine in nothing."[15]

He had one other distinguishing characteristic. As the conservative Trinitarian clergyman Noah Porter wrote, Brownson was "manifestly and avowedly in a state of continual transition,—in a certain condition of perpetually *becoming*, but of never *being*."[16] But although he may have been, by his own account, "mercurial" in intellectual matters, he never wavered in his vocation. His was one long attempt to realize a social harmony he had never been fortunate enough to know, and particularly to provide the laboring classes with the education and ministry they needed to better their lot. This devotion to bringing the kingdom of God to earth is what convinced Ripley and his friends that the Canton minister, born and raised on society's margins and yet versed in the same Continental philosophy that captivated them, should succeed Tuckerman as minister at large to Boston's poor.[17]

In Ripley, Brownson found a soul mate. Later in life, long after he had broken with the Transcendentalists, he testified to his friend's influence. "In the formation of my mind," Brownson wrote, "in systematizing my ideas, and in general development and culture, I owe more to him than to any other man among Protestants." Brownson concluded, "I loved him as I loved no other man."[18] In 1836 these two were the de facto field generals of the emergent Transcendentalist movement, popularizing Idealist thought through their seminal publications and applying it to pressing social needs. Despite Frederic Hedge's introduction of European philosophy to readers of *The Christian Examiner*, for example, in Bangor, he was too distant to exercise any concerted influence on his peers. Convers Francis, despite his presence at the Transcendentalist Club's early meetings, was only a fellow traveler in Transcendentalist circles.[19] His good friend, Theodore Parker, eventually a lion among the group, was still at divinity school. Waldo Emerson, another promising foot soldier, had few publications to his credit and none with the intellectual heft of Ripley's or Brownson's essays in *The Christian Examiner*.

Accepting his new position, Brownson lost little time in making himself heard. What he said, both in journals and from the pulpit, derived primarily from the French thinkers whom he had read since his days in New Hampshire. Taking his cue from Benjamin Constant, for example, he argued that man "is determined to [religion] by an interior sentiment," a "fundamental law of his being, a law invariable, eternal, indestructible." He also believed that the world's religious institutions were in dialectical evolution, and as each faith failed to satisfy man's continuing hunger for spiritual truth, another superseded it and moved him closer to that goal. Protestantism's break with Catholicism was one such event, and Unitarianism's revolt from Calvinism another. The current ferment within Unitarian ranks was the most recent example of each age's subsequent rediscovery of the internal, eternal wellspring of religious belief.[20] Brownson also recognized a "distinction between head and heart, the mind and the soul, the understanding and the affections," and thus was convinced of the justness of Constant's belief in a universal religious "sentiment."[21] Locating this in the "heart" or soul opened a way for dissident Unitarians to revivify what they viewed as an emotionally bankrupt faith.

Prior to moving to Chelsea, Brownson had given a series of free lectures on Christianity in the Swedenborgian Chapel in Boston, approvingly reported by the *Boston Daily Advertiser*. Before long he became a sought-after intellectual property in the city. In May 1836 he began to preach at Lyceum Hall on Hanover Street, and soon thereafter he garnered enough support to organize a Society for the Promotion of Christian Union and Progress, his chief congregation for the next three years. This meeting averaged no fewer than five hundred attendees, and after only a few weeks it had to move to a much larger hall, the city's Masonic Temple. Word of Brownson's success, based on his heartfelt response to his parishioners' needs, spread through the city. Soon enough he was ready to offer the general public the principles on which he had founded his "church of the future."

Brownson's *New Views of Christianity, Society, and the Church* appeared late in the autumn of 1836.[22] In it he was most indebted to Constant, particularly to his great *Of Religion*. Brownson's main argument was that his contemporaries misunderstood the true meaning of Christ. What was that? Nothing less than the reconciliation of the two great social systems on which the world had developed: one based in "Spiritualism" and represented by the Eastern world and Asia; the other on "Materialism," which had ruled Greece and Rome. The former, Brownson (again redacting Constant) explained, regarded purity or holiness as a matter of the Spirit alone and Matter as essentially impure. The latter rejected the claims of the Spirit and "count[ed] the body everything, earth all, heaven nothing." These two terms had to be harmonized, and Christ had shown mankind how to do this. This was "the true idea of Christianity." This, Brownson insisted, is the "atonement," the at-one-ment with God.[23]

He also discussed Protestantism's revolt against the Catholic Church after that church had bastardized Christ's message, and Protestantism's subsequent failure, when it had superseded Catholicism, to embrace the world of the spirit. Now Christians raised a universal cry against "the frigid utilitarianism of the last century," its "money-getting" and "desire for worldly wealth and renown." Men were leaving "the Outward for the Inward, and craving something more fervent, living and soul-kindling."[24] Brownson's church of the future would reconcile Spirit and Matter. "We must go forward," he urged, "but we can take not a step forward, but on the condition of uniting these two hitherto hostile principles." "PROGRESS is our law and our first step is UNION." And what of Christ's Second Coming? It would be realized "when the idea which he represents, that is, the idea of atonement, shall be fully realized."[25]

Brownson ranged through world history to illustrate how different religions had emphasized one or the other side of this great duality, Matter and Spirit, pointing out that all faiths had some good in them, originating as they did in man's inherent spirituality. He invoked Cousin's Eclecticism, which synthesized these opposing elements. Other philosophers—Hegel, Fries, and Jacobi, he noted—had anticipated or contributed to this Eclectic method, but Cousin had "perfected" it. He had demonstrated that "Humanity, Nature and God have precisely the same laws, that what we find in Nature and Humanity we may also find in God."[26] All that was needed was a church to embody and act on this philosophy.

Brownson saw glimmerings of hope in Germany's churches, especially in the movement commenced by Herder. He had the most faith, however, in Schleiermacher, "a man remarkable for warmth of feeling, and coolness of thought, a preacher and a philosopher, a theologian and a man of science, a student and a man of business." Brownson also believed that the atonement of which Schleiermacher spoke would be realized first in the United States, where more than in any other country "the man of thought" was united "with the man of action." The time was not distant, Brownson prophesied, "when our whole population will be philosophers, and all our philosophers will be practical men." He sought to align his church along the same great principles that Christ, the "God-Man," symbolized. "UNION" and "PROGRESS" thus was the only authentic creed of the New Church.[27]

Brownson's small book was both paean to and a blueprint for a universal harmony it was his task to help initiate. Everywhere he saw signs of men's eagerness for such a new social order. "There is a universal language already in use," he wrote. "Men are beginning to understand one another, and their mutual understanding will beget mutual sympathy, and mutual sympathy will bind them together and to God."[28] In his Boston ministry he sought to expedite the arrival of this church of the future.

Troubled by the book's social radicalism yet respectful of its author, James Walker, editor of *The Christian Examiner*, apologized in the March 1837 issue for not allotting it more space. He explained that he thought it would not find wide readership because of its "novel application throughout of a few terms, such as *spiritualism*, *materialism*, and *atonement*, which have the effect to give the whole a strange and foreign air," code for Brownson's indebtedness to French and German thought. Walker never doubted Brownson's sincerity but was disappointed that his odd locutions probably would make him lose public sympathy.[29] This did not bother Boston's minister at large, however, who adhered to Saint-Simon's maxim, "Eden is before us, not behind us."[30] For the next several years Brownson preached a gospel of union and progress in ever stronger terms and never flinched from exposing the hollowness he found at the core of American democracy. Constant,

Cousin, and other European thinkers had shown him the dignity of each human being. He would not let his colleagues forget it.

During this period Ripley's interests ran parallel to Brownson's. He touted Cousin's Eclecticism, becoming the Frenchman's foremost American exponent. He also was increasingly committed to social reform, particularly as Boston's poor began to encroach on the neighborhood surrounding his Purchase Street Church. Like Brownson, he, too, welcomed the Higher Critics' scholarship on the New Testament. But more than his friend, he emphasized Schleiermacher's contribution to nineteenth-century theology—specifically, his insistence on the primacy of feeling to the spiritual life. Concomitantly, Ripley grew increasingly concerned with the Unitarians' emphasis on Christ's miracles as proof of Christianity's truth. In several publications at mid-decade Ripley broached these topics in ways that preoccupied Transcendentalists into the early 1840s.

Ripley was born in 1802 in Greenfield, on the Connecticut River in north-central Massachusetts, the second youngest of ten children. Compared with Brownson's, his religious pilgrimage was straightforward. Although his family had been orthodox Christians, during his adolescence his father, a merchant who had moved from Boston, adopted Unitarianism. When his son was ready to enter college, the elder Ripley encouraged him to apply to Harvard rather than to more conservative Yale, the choice of many Connecticut Valley residents. In 1819, to prepare for his entrance examinations, Ripley moved in with relatives near Boston and was tutored by the Reverend Ezra Ripley of Concord, a patriarch among Unitarian ministers. The young Ripley also got reacquainted with his cousin, Ralph Waldo Emerson, then a sophomore at Harvard. Ripley entered the college that fall.[31]

Upon graduation in 1823, not yet fully won over to Unitarianism, he briefly considered attending Andover Theological Seminary, but his father convinced him to stay in Cambridge to study divinity. Ripley's notebooks for the years 1824 through 1827 display much soul-searching about whether to abandon orthodoxy for the new liberal Christianity, and in particular how Unitarians might remedy their seeming inability to invest their faith with heartfelt piety. What sealed his commitment to Unitarianism, however, were the ministry and writings of William Ellery Channing, who epitomized the faith that the young man sought. Meeting Channing, Ripley knew that he wanted to become a Unitarian minister. Accordingly, in September 1826, with the imprimatur of both Channing and Andrews Norton (who had taken a particular interest in him), Ripley laid the cornerstone of a new Unitarian church on the corner of Purchase Street at Pearl Street, near Griffin Wharf in Boston, an occasion at which Henry Ware, Jr., Professor of Pulpit Eloquence and Pastoral Care at Harvard Divinity School, officiated. Later that fall, John Kirkland, Harvard's president, preached the young man's ordination sermon, another sign of Cambridge's high hopes for the young man's ministry.

During these years Ripley was clean-shaven, his brown hair "curled in close, crisp ringlets," and his pale face set off by gold-rimmed spectacles. Although appearing sober, formal, punctilious, and almost ascetic, he actually had "a fund of humor in which his friends delighted" and an intellect every bit as voracious as that of his new friend Brownson.[32] Assuming the pulpit in the small stone Purchase Street Church, over a congregation composed primarily of the "middling" sort, Ripley preached in earnest Unitarianism's central message, a belief in a universal, internal religious principle that validated faith and united all men and women.

Ripley's studies and writings made him America's foremost proponent of Eclecticism, but he also lived by Schleiermacher's theology. Ripley had come to this point after extensive reading not only in the Common Sense philosophers and Kant but as well in Jonathan Edwards, America's foremost eighteenth-century theologian, whose sense of grace as an internal, transformative principle accorded with Ripley's belief in the centrality of intuition or feeling to the spiritual life. As late as 1838, Ripley had praised Edwards for his belief that the human mind, under certain conditions, had "the power of perceiving and judging spiritual truth." Despite Edwards's Calvinist vision, Ripley added, his advocacy of the faculty of the spiritual intuition formed "an invaluable contribution to a sound religious philosophy," a tantalizing suggestion that Transcendentalism was descended from the religion of the heart that the New Lights of the Great Awakening had championed.[33] Schleiermacher postulated a religious element in all mankind from birth, prompting Ripley, as he translated Friedrich Lücke's "Recollections of Schleiermacher" and introduced it to *The Christian Examiner*'s readers, to praise Schleiermacher as someone who sought to reconcile religion and science. His theological principles, Ripley proclaimed, had announced nothing less than "a new era" in religious history.[34]

What precisely did Schleiermacher offer? To Ripley, it was religion "in its primitive elements."[35] For Schleiermacher, religion did not consist in knowledge or action but in feeling, in religious emotion. Grace was one's perception of the divinity of the quotidian through this religious "feeling," an insight that was utterly transformative, making one's entire life an experience of the holy. Schleiermacher's relocation of religion in the heart of each believer powerfully expressed the philosophy of Romantic individualism that swept the Continent. Enshrining as it did the individual consciousness, this belief also was congruent with America's democratic experiment, making Schleiermacher, as Ripley put it, the chief "exponent" of his age.

Ripley's endorsement of Schleiermacher's theology informed his *Discourses on the Philosophy of Religion, Addressed to Doubters Who Wish to Believe* (1836), a book that joined Brownson's *New Views* as a direct challenge to Unitarian orthodoxy and whose title was indebted to Schleiermacher's *On Religion: Speeches to Its Cultured Despisers*. Comprising six discourses that Ripley had preached two years earlier, his book was aimed specifically at those with "a lurking suspicion" that there was something "unsound in the fabric of their faith."[36] Acknowledging his indebtedness to Idealism in general and Schleiermacher in particular, Ripley proposed that every truly religious man was "conscious of an inward nature, which is the source of more important and comprehensive ideas, than any which the external senses suggest." God revealed himself to man through "Reason," the faculty of perceiving "primitive, spiritual truth." Reason, Ripley continued, was "the ultimate standard." "Existing in different degrees, in different men, it is found in some degree in all."[37]

In his fifth discourse, the only one previously published, Ripley addressed the common error of confounding Christianity with the entire contents of the Bible, a topic that related to questions of scriptural exegesis. "How are we to ascertain the real doctrine of Christ?" Ripley asked. Quite simply, by the "rational interpretation of the language of the sacred writers."[38] In other words, if scriptural language, properly translated, suggested something contrary to reason, it was not part of Christ's message.

Here Ripley stepped into the unresolved debate initiated by Channing and Stuart that continued to roil the Unitarian denomination, now challenged by those within its ranks. In an essay in *The Christian Examiner* later the same year, he so infuriated conservative Unitarians (including his mentor Norton) that the Purchase Street minister soon found himself lumped with other young members of the denomination polluted by "German" ideas.

Ripley's occasion was his review of the English Unitarian James Martineau's *Rationale of Religious Inquiry* (1836), a volume that, to Ripley, epitomized responsible scriptural interpretation. Ripley welcomed Martineau's call for fundamental reform in English theology so that "controversy can cease to resemble a contest in the dark."[39] Of particular interest was Martineau's chapter on "Rationalism," in which he raised the question of how to treat scriptural evidence not in accord with reason. Martineau's position was unequivocal. No apparent inspiration can establish anything contrary to reason, for reason is "the ultimate appeal, the supreme tribunal to the test of which even Scripture must be brought."[40] This identified the American Unitarians' logical inconsistency, dependent as they were on belief in Christ's miracles as the seal of their faith.

Ripley offered his own view of what lay behind Martineau's book. How could Unitarians, who professed to base their faith in reason, claim that Christ performed miracles? "As far as we can judge at this distance of time," Ripley wrote, "it was the truth which Jesus Christ announced rather than the wonderful works that he wrought, that called forth the faith of his disciples." Christ's miracles, in other words, were ancillary to his message. Now committed to Idealist philosophy, Ripley deemed it an error "to rest a system of spiritual truth, addressed to the soul, upon the evidence of miracles addressed to the senses."[41] He had learned from Schleiermacher and others that religion was an ineffable, inward feeling of dependence on God and not something validated by sensory experience. He simply set aside as irrelevant the thornier question of whether Christ actually performed the miracles attributed to him. Theology commenced with the study of human consciousness as Cousin and others were examining it, not with debates over such irreconcilable matters as whether Christ turned water into wine or walked on water.[42]

One wonders whether James Walker, editor of *The Christian Examiner*, realized how Ripley's review would offend conservative Unitarians. He did not have to wait long to find out, however, for Norton responded sharply, outraged that the journal of which he was coeditor (Walker had not run Ripley's essay by him) had published such a wrongheaded and insulting piece, by one of his own students. Norton thereupon severed his association with *The Christian Examiner* and turned to *The Christian Register* to explain his resignation and register dissent from Ripley's position. But that journal's editor, not eager for a dogfight, demurred for "personal considerations" and forced Norton to the extraordinary step of publishing his rejoinder in a newspaper, the *Boston Daily Advertiser*. The November 5, 1836, issue carried his letter, in which he made it clear that no callow student, no matter how promising, was going to controvert what his mentor had taught him about Christ's miracles.[43]

Ripley, however, was not cowed. The *Advertiser* published his reply four days later. After thanking Norton for seriously considering his views, he observed that if Norton found heresies in his essay, he also found some in Norton's comments upon it. Ripley reiterated his view that "the evidence of miracles depends on a previous belief in Christianity, rather than the evidence of Christianity on a previous belief in miracles," not his own theological novelty, but a position that had "the sanction of devout and thinking minds of every age of the Church." Further, he resented Norton's condemnation of his ideas without offering any counterproof, save his

Harvard credentials. "I had thought that we lived at too late a day for this," Ripley noted, and "breathed the air of freedom too long, to substitute an appeal to popular prejudice in the place of reason and argument."[44] So much for Norton, the vaunted champion of rationality!

The controversy between Norton and Ripley sat there for two years, until another Unitarian's view of miracles reignited Norton's wrath. In the interim, emergent Transcendentalism had permeated other reform activities—childhood education among them. Although it may seem a long step from the complexities of post-Kantian philosophy to schooling a child, some New Englanders, excited by the idea that everyone, from birth, possessed a divine element, altered long-established pedagogy to cultivate this divine essence. They sought to replace Locke's influential psychological paradigm—which posits the mind of each child at birth as a tabula rasa, or a blank slate, upon which sensory experience writes its lessons—with the Idealists' notion that the mind has innate principles, including the religious sentiment, a view of education that requires a different pedagogy. The teacher has to help each child recognize and cultivate his internal principles. The classroom no longer was a place of rote learning, but an arena where even very young students were taught to cultivate heightened self-consciousness.

By the 1830s, prominent among the American educators moving in this direction was Amos Bronson Alcott (1799–1888). Like Brownson, he had not entered Boston's cultural hothouse until he was an adult. Born to a farming family in rural Wolcott, Connecticut, Alcott had little formal education. He was, however, an autodidact, devouring the few books of Christian piety—Bunyan's *Pilgrim's Progress* was a favorite, as was Milton's *Paradise Lost*—available to him and then progressively expanding his intellectual reach. By his mid-teens he was on the road as a peddler in western Massachusetts and New York, and in 1818 he sailed on a coastal vessel from New Haven to Norfolk, Virginia, hoping to secure work as a schoolteacher in what he regarded as the benighted

South. No positions were available, however, and he resumed peddling, traveling as far as Charleston, South Carolina.[45]

Returning to New England, between 1825 and 1828 Alcott worked as a schoolmaster in Cheshire and Bristol, Connecticut, not far from where he had been raised. Frustrated by both his school's restricted physical space and its narrow curriculum, he set out to improve both. He constructed movable desks so that the center of the room was open for group activities, and he purchased books for a school library. He broke from the common-school method of instruction by rote and varied the day's work with nature walks, physical exercises, storytelling, and directed conversation. He thought that good teaching came through the Socratic method. Most important, he believed in the innate goodness of each child whom he taught.

Alcott decided to try out his pedagogy in Boston. To move from rural Connecticut to one of the nation's largest cities was exhilarating, even if he could not immediately find a permanent position. In the interim he rubbed shoulders with other prominent reformers, including Josiah Holbrook, the father of the American lyceum movement, who boarded at the same address; and the free-thought lecturer Fanny Wright. William Ellery Channing particularly impressed him, and as he realized how Unitarianism's positive and inclusive vision of humanity accorded with his own, he began to spend more time with members of this faith.

Still footloose, though now married to Abigail May, daughter of a family prominent in New England reform, Alcott eventually accepted the offer of some Philadelphia patrons to start a school in Germantown. His stay in that region was intellectually rewarding but brief. He discovered Plato and read extensively in authors who espoused views of education or developmental psychology comparable to his own. He learned of German Idealist philosophy through Cousin's works, and his excitement only increased when he discovered Coleridge's *Aids to Reflection* with Marsh's "Preliminary Essay." But when Alcott faced financial problems at his school, he decided to return to Boston, his wife's home, where he had many friends of similar interests. When one of these, William Russell, editor of the *American Journal of Education*, told Alcott that he knew of several families interested in sending their children to a school based on his methods, Alcott moved his family north. In September 1834 he opened a "School for Human Culture" in rooms on the top floor of the Masonic Temple in Boston, the same building in which Brownson soon would commence his Boston ministry.[46]

At this point, Alcott already was a memorable figure, six feet tall and fair-skinned, with thin, straight reddish hair worn long over his ears and neck and already turning sandy blond (old age would make it white). His forehead was distinctively domed, and his mouth was large and accentuated by a long, thin upper lip. A few long furrows in his face—later very characteristic traits—already were evident. Most striking were his serene azure eyes, always seemingly fixed far in the distance—the "sky-blue man," Thoreau called him.[47] Alcott loved to talk more than listen, and his unusual language and diction were those of a man who spoke as the spirit moved him. In such venues as his Temple School or in his "conversations," he was magnetic, if also frustratingly enigmatic.

With William Ellery Channing, Boston's mayor Josiah Quincy, and Massachusetts Chief Justice Lemuel Shaw among its patrons, Alcott's school began with thirty students. Some of these children, equally divided between boys and girls and ranging in age from three to twelve years, were from the city's most prominent families. Their classroom was open and spacious, furnished with such items as Alcott believed addressed and cultivated "the imagination and heart." On pedestals in the four corners were busts of Socrates, Shakespeare, Milton, and Sir Walter Scott. On a table in front of a large gothic window was another, of "the Image of Silence," and on the opposite wall, Alcott's own table, with a curved front and small desks around it for students. Behind this stood a large bookcase filled with volumes, and a black tablet for writing. A plaster cast of Christ was set into the bookcase and "made to appear to the scholars to be just over the teacher's head," and a bust of Plato sat atop it. Alcott's assistant occupied a table near the entrance, upon which was a small figure of Atlas with the weight of the world upon his shoulders. Pictures and maps adorned the walls. The students' desks, placed around the room facing the wall (so that "no scholar need look at another" as he or she worked), had room for books, and black tablets for writing hung over them that could be swung away when other activities beckoned. A sofa near Alcott's desk, for the accommodation of visitors, completed the furnishings.[48]

The mental culture practiced at the Temple School was as novel as the room's physical space. All instruction and discipline had one end: to teach the children that they were spiritual beings closely connected to God. To this end, Alcott spent much time in Socratic dialogue, discussions initiated by either his own questions or readings from literature. He also developed the children's self-expression, both written and oral, believing that that was how they realized and shared their inherent divinity. Students kept journals in which they recorded not only their daily observations but also their internal thoughts. Grammar and spelling were less important than the flow of each student's thoughts. The parents of these scholars were also assured, however, that the instructor gave due attention to the basic skills children needed.[49]

Discipline was not neglected, for Alcott sought to mold not only each student's conscience but also his or her sense of social obligation. Thus, although he did not spare the rod, he also doled out more subtle, and unusual, punishment. For example, each day he appointed a student superintendent to oversee the conduct of the class. When the superintendent of the day observed an infraction, she reported it to the entire group, who then deliberated on the proper punishment, reinforcing a group sense of right action. If physical punishment had to be administered, with a ferule, Alcott did so outside the room, away from the other students, and only after he had clearly explained the infraction. On some occasions he made offenders administer the punishment to *him* in front of the class, which brought even the oldest scholars to tears because of their love and respect for their teacher. Particularly obstreperous behavior led to the student's removal from the class when they were enjoying a group activity such as story reading; as an alternative, Alcott simply stopped the activity so that none of the group could enjoy it, thereby instilling the notion that unacceptable behavior affected all who came into contact with it.

Alcott was fortunate to have as his assistant Elizabeth Palmer Peabody. Thirty years old and an experienced schoolteacher, she used her many contacts to forward her employer's reputation among Boston's luminaries. She had served as an assistant on Russell's *American Journal of Education* and was well known in Boston's reform circles. At first skeptical of some of Alcott's innovations, she finally was won over, and early in her tenure she began to keep a journal of the school's activities, with an eye to publishing it in order to make Alcott's reforms better known. Her *Record of a School* appeared in July 1835.

With its publication Alcott's innovative educational methods— in particular, his emphasis on the cultivation of the child's spiritual nature—became more widely known, drawing both praise and skepticism and, in some quarters, outright hostility. Channing, long Alcott's supporter, began to worry that Alcott's dialogues were too inflexible, so that students merely recited what he wanted to hear without having felt the power of God within. Channing also questioned Alcott's emphasis on self-analysis, concerned that too much introspection might inhibit rather than encourage a youngster's spiritual awakening.[50] Other critics were more severe. In the *American Annals of Education and Instruction*, William C. Woodbridge, once Alcott's supporter, called the *Record of a School* a "mingled mass of truth and error" that revealed Alcott's "strained interpretation of religion."[51] Ominously, the school began to lose income, and Peabody began her second year without yet having received any salary for her first. The new term found only a handful of new students enrolled. Alcott was unbowed, confident enough about the school's future to hire Elizabeth's sister, Mary, as another assistant, with responsibilities for the French language.

In the new term Alcott extended his conversations and initiated discussion of the life of Jesus as recorded in the Gospels, an exercise he hoped would expedite the students' awareness of their inward divinity. Again, Peabody kept a detailed record of the dialogues, which captured Alcott's habit of making apparent the sort of responses he expected. But his ideas still garnered respect, and the public was enough interested in *Record of a School* that he had Peabody issue a second edition in 1836, albeit with her clarification of some of the pedagogical methods to which more critical readers had objected.

In the interim Alcott made his way among the young Unitarians beginning to turn their denomination upside down. He was well enough known to receive an invitation to the second meeting of the Transcendental Club when it met at Ripley's, and he hosted the next meeting, at which the group discussed "American Genius—the causes which hinder its growth, and give us no first rate productions."[52] Alcott took these opportunities to publicize his students' remarkable spiritual enlightenment, and he went forward with plans to issue another volume of his dialogues. But he misjudged the suspicion that had arisen about his methods, particularly after people began to associate him with Transcendentalism.

Elizabeth Peabody had had a premonition that the public was not ready for an inside view of Alcott's tutorial in the Gospels, particularly his open discussion of physiological facts such as the Virgin birth. She registered her concerns around the same time that she tendered her resignation, in the summer of 1836, not so much over any disapproval of Alcott's theories, but because he had never paid her for her work. To Alcott's credit, he heard her objections. Naive in such matters, he took her advice only to a point: he excised potentially problematic passages from the main text but placed them in an appendix, rendering them more conspicuous. Confident in his school's future, he hired twenty-six-year-old Margaret Fuller, a remarkable young woman making her way in Transcendentalist circles, as Peabody's replacement and set her to record a second volume of his *Conversations*.

This compendium appeared at the beginning of the spring term in February 1837, and all hell broke loose. Alcott was roasted in the popular press. In the *Boston Daily Advertiser*, Nathan Hale objected to his "flippant and off hand conversation" about such serious topics as the Virgin birth and circumcision, and urged him to close his school.[53] Joseph T. Buckingham, the testy editor of the *Boston Daily Courier*, was even less restrained. He had never seen "a more indecent and obscene book," and would say nothing of its "absurdity."[54] Norton, still exercised about the controversy with his ex-student Ripley, was apoplectic. He pronounced the book "*one third absurd, one third blasphemous, and one third obscene.*"[55]

Alcott's friends tried to buoy his spirits. Emerson defended him publicly in the *Courier* (the *Daily Advertiser* would not print his letter), asking readers to give Alcott a fair hearing and not prejudge his book. Emerson also wrote him directly, confiding that he hated "to have all the little dogs barking at you, for you have something better to do than attend to them." But the public reaction was understandable, he added, for "every beast must do after his kind, and why not these."[56] Despite such support, the controversy ended Alcott's noble experiment. Over the next year the student population dwindled to the single digits, and he closed the school in June 1837.

Subsequently, Alcott gravitated to Emerson's orbit in search of support for his ideas, but it was only partially forthcoming. Having devoted much time to the education of his young daughters, for example, Alcott started a long manuscript in which he detailed their spiritual and social development. He let Emerson read it, but Emerson found it unfocused and not meriting publication. Adding fuel to the fire, Alcott's friend William Ellery Channing weighed in on his pedagogy and objected to Alcott's identification of the human soul with divinity, a cardinal doctrine at the Temple School. Alcott's depression only increased when he realized the dire financial straits in which he and his family found themselves. By the late 1830s, his educational experiment in shambles but his faith in Idealist philosophy unshaken, he refocused his agenda.

At the same time as the Temple School began to draw criticism, Ralph Waldo Emerson published, anonymously, a small book called *Nature*. It was only his second publication, following a *Historical Discourse* delivered the previous year at the town of Concord's bicentennial. *Nature* was his first published contribution to the discourse of emergent Transcendentalism, several years after people like Brownson, Ripley, and Hedge had made their debuts in print with lengthy essays in which they announced their allegiance to European Idealism as well as to a program of radical social reform. The son of William Emerson, a prominent Unitarian clergyman who officiated over Boston's historic First Church, Waldo had graduated from Harvard in 1821 but taken several years before deciding to follow in his parent's footsteps. He was ordained in Boston's Second Church in March 1829 and later that year married Ellen Tucker. What was to have been the beginning of a happy personal life, though, quickly turned tragic. Two years after their wedding, Ellen died of tuberculosis.

Even before her death Emerson had serious doubts about some points of Unitarian doctrine, precipitating his resignation from the ministry in 1832. There followed a trip to Europe, and on his return Emerson decided to make a career as a lecturer, the first Transcendentalist to do so. Tragedy struck again, in 1835, with the sudden death of his brother Edward, followed the next year by the death of his brother Charles. Emerson's only glimmer of happiness came with marriage to Lidian Jackson, even though he knew (and admitted) that she could never be to him what Ellen had.

During these troubled years Emerson joined his cousin George Ripley, Brownson, Alcott, and Hedge in their criticism of Unitarianism. Like them, he rebelled against the empiricism on which it was based, and he welcomed, via Marsh, Coleridge's *Aids to Reflection*. Moreover, on his European sojourn he had made the acquaintance not only of William Wordsworth but of the Scots essayist, historian, and reformer Thomas Carlyle, another popularizer of German thought. The two got along well, and by 1835 Emerson began to function as Carlyle's American literary agent, expediting the publication of his burlesque philosophical treatise/spiritual autobiography, *Sartor Resartus*, in the same year in which *Nature* appeared.

Emerson, however, was less versed in German philosophy and theology than other charter members of the club, for his Idealism originated more in a long-term interest in Plato and Neoplatonism, an immersion in Goethe (whom he had read in German since the 1820s), the mediation of British writers like Carlyle and Coleridge, and Sampson Reed's redaction of Swedenborgian thought. Emerson knew of Cousin, too, through the translations of the early 1830s; and he learned of Schleiermacher, Herder, and de Wette from the pages of *The Christian Examiner* as well as from his friends and classmates. Despite coming to Transcendentalism by a different route than others in his cohort, he soon began to contribute, through his writings as well as his personal example, to the group's varied intellectual program.

Emerson's difference from many of his peers was apparent from the outset, however, and did not go unnoticed. When Brownson reviewed *Nature* in the *Boston Reformer*, for example, he noted presciently that the book was "aesthetical rather than philosophical." Why then was Emerson of interest to Brownson and his friends? Because his little book touched "some of the gravest problems in metaphysical science," Brownson wrote, "and perhaps may be called philosophy in its poetical aspect."[57] The conservative Unitarian Francis Bowen, in a critical review in *The Christian Examiner*, concurred. "What novelty there is in this work," he wrote, arose "not from the choice or distinction of subject, but from the manner of treatment."[58] Elizabeth Peabody perhaps put it best: "We have said that 'Nature' is a poem; but it is written in prose."[59]

Emerson's distinctive "style" in *Nature*, this "philosophy in its poetical aspect," troubled many reviewers, for they attributed it to the influence of Continental philosophers and theologians, particularly those from Germany, whose verbal extravagance they suspected or despised. Ironically, then, Emerson, the Transcendentalist with the least firsthand knowledge of German philosophy, was tarred with the same brush. Bowen, for example, noted that although there was much worth in Emerson's little book, its effect was "injured by occasional vagueness of expression, and by a vein of mysticism that pervades the writer's whole course of thought." To peruse this book, he added, "is often painful, the thoughts excited are frequently bewildering, and the results to which they lead us, uncertain and obscure," problems that arose from Emerson's supposed infatuation with German language and thought.[60]

What did Emerson intend with his small book? When he sent Carlyle a copy within a week of publication, he described it self-deprecatingly as "an entering wedge, I hope, for something more worthy and significant."[61] Indeed, almost until *Nature*'s publication Emerson had considered it part of a larger whole. In June

1836 he wrote Hedge that he had "in solid prose" a chapter, which he called "Nature," and he wished to write another chapter "called 'Spirit.'"[62] In early September he decided to issue *Nature* as it stood.

Some critics lamented what they regarded as the book's lack of structure and coherence. The conservative Unitarian Samuel Kirkland Lathrop noted that in Emerson's writings one found "beautiful thoughts, beautiful passages, but no well-rounded, comprehensive philosophy of religion or life," no "substantial basis of faith."[63] Despite such criticism, though, Emerson clearly had a plan for his book: he deployed philosophical Idealism to open peoples' eyes to their spiritual inheritance. Hence, his pervasive metaphors of sight and blindness, which received their archetypal expression in the famous "transparent eye-ball" passage in *Nature*'s opening pages. There Emerson described the merger of the "Me" and the "Not-Me" (terms Carlyle used in *Sartor Resartus*, derived from Fries) in an ecstatic experience: "Standing on the bare ground,—my head bathed by the blithe air, and uplifted into infinite space,—all mean egotism vanishes. I become a transparent eye-ball; I am nothing; I see all; the currents of the Universal Being circulate through me; I am part or particle of God." Emerson began with the observation that "our age is retrospective," for, while "the foregoing generations beheld God and nature face to face," rather than having "an original relation to the universe," contemporaries saw "through their eyes." As a result, we live in a fallen world, even as "the ruin or blank that we see when we look at nature, is in our own eye." The book ends with the promise that if man views nature rightly, he will inhabit a new world, which "he shall enter without more wonder than the blind man feels who is gradually restored to perfect sight."[64]

Another organizing metaphor is that of the doctrine of correspondence, an attestation of Swedenborg's continuing influence on Emerson a decade after he had read Sampson Reed's *Observations on the Growth of the Mind*. Swedenborg's thought is most obvious in the fourth section of the book, where Emerson offers the following propositions to explain one of the most important uses of nature, that of "Language."

1. Words are signs of natural facts.
2. Particular natural facts are symbols of particular spiritual facts.
3. Nature is the symbol of spirit.

The first proposition derived from Emerson's belief in a primitive, universal language that originated in man's observation of the natural world. As he put it, "as we go back in history, language becomes more picturesque, until its infancy, when it is all poetry; or all spiritual facts are represented by natural symbols," and the same symbols are found to make "the original elements of all languages." Thus, "the use of natural history is to give us aid in supernatural history; the use of the outer creation, to give us language for the beings and changes of the inward creation." The relations between words and things, and things and the spirit, pervade nature, for "man is an analogist, and studies relations in all objects." When he learns to read the universe correspondentially, he sees that nature mirrors the Ideal, for there is "a necessity in spirit to manifest itself in material forms." Natural facts are thus "the end or last issue of spirit," and to know the world is to know the divine.[65]

Nature's chapter headings further indicate its general purpose and direction. In his "Introduction," for example, Emerson interrogates man's relation to nature, and asks him not to "grope among the dry bones of the past," but to realize that "the sun shines today also." But Emerson's contemporaries seemed intent on rejecting nature's manifold uses. "To speak truly," Emerson writes, "few adult persons can see nature," for most people "do not even see the sun." The true lover of nature, he claims, "is he whose inward and outward senses are still truly adjusted to each other; who has retained the spirit of infancy even into the era of manhood."[66]

As Emerson proceeds, he sets out the varied uses of nature, moving sequentially through commodity, beauty, language, discipline, Idealism, and finally, to spirit. Commodity is simply "those advantages which our senses owe to nature." Nature is firewood; it is the millstream; it provides food, clothing, and shelter. But nature is also beauty, satisfying us with its loveliness, harmony, and unity. Nature is language, too, providing man the symbols to speak about his innermost thoughts as well as to describe the world around him. Nature offers discipline, teaching what is true, beautiful, and good, for the physical laws of the universe are analogous to the great moral laws. The moral law, Emerson writes, "lies at the centre of nature and radiates to its circumference," where men exist. Nature also reflects the Ideal, for it is "made to conspire with spirit to emancipate us."[67] Finally, nature mirrors the spirit; it makes man acknowledge his relation to the Oversoul, the spiritual ether that flows through all creation. "At present," Emerson concludes, "man applies to nature but half his force." He works upon it with his "understanding" alone. He lives in it "and masters it by a penny-wisdom." He needs to understand that the "invariable mark" of wisdom is "to see the miraculous in the common." Then man feels "part or particle of God" as Me and Not-Me are reunited.[68]

Although *Nature* sold out its first edition of five hundred copies (which Emerson had subsidized) by late October, it did not make as large a stir as Brownson's or Alcott's books of the same year. For one thing, it was so unmistakably different, in language and play, that many people simply did not know what to make of it and threw it off as so much transcendental mist and moonshine. Bowen's severe review in *The Christian Examiner*, for example, and Peabody's measured endorsement in *The United States Magazine and Democratic Review* were among the only memorable contemporaneous notices in prominent journals; the venerable *North American Review* simply ignored it.

How, then, to account for Emerson's steady rise to prominence in the emergent Transcendentalist group? Brownson had one explanation. Emerson's popularity, he wrote in 1838, was accounted for "without any especial regard for his peculiar notions." There was "something in his personal manners," Brownson explained, and much about his "peculiar characteristics of style as a writer and a lecturer," and "still more to his independence, to the homage he pays to the spirit of freedom," that attracted disaffected Unitarians. It was "as the advocate of the rights of the mind," Brownson concluded, "as the defender of personal independence in the spiritual world" that Emerson won the accolades of "many young, ardent, and yet noble minds." Brownson pointedly warned the Unitarian elders, however, to show how "freedom and life can be found elsewhere than in connection with the speculations of Ralph Waldo Emerson, or to Ralph Waldo Emerson they may rest assured their pupils will resort."[69] A writer in *The Western Messenger* concurred. It was not that Emerson's readers all agree with his speculations, he explained, "but that they sympathize with his independence, manliness, and freedom."[70]

At this point in Emerson's career, his chief charisma derived from a challenge to conventional wisdom rather than for his particular wisdom itself. As significant as *Nature* subsequently proved to American literary and cultural history, as Transcendentalism developed in the mid-1830s Emerson continued to play only a secondary intellectual role, trying to make a success in his new career as a lecturer. Without pulpit or regular platform, author of a single idiosyncratic tract, he was in the wings as people like Brownson, Ripley, and Alcott played center stage. It would be two more years before he became a lightning rod for the new Transcendentalist cohort.

By year's end, 1836, a cadre of younger Unitarians had made known their displeasure with the status quo in their churches. Some, like Emerson, already were disenchanted enough to sign off; others, like Ripley and Brownson, remained within the denomination but preached a social radicalism that went far beyond what their onetime champion William Ellery Channing had counseled. When in March 1837, for example, James Walker and Francis Greenwood, in an editorial notice in *The Christian Examiner*, redefined the journal's purpose, they pointed to precisely this fact. To their satisfaction, they reported, controversies with the Trinitarians were over, but now other questions had arisen "in the public interest" on which leading members of their denomination greatly differed.[71] They wanted their journal to be a chief forum for these debates.

Recalling this period in his memoir, *The Convert*, Brownson made a similar comment. Unitarianism had "demolished" Calvinism, he observed, and "made an end in all thinking minds of every thing like dogmatic Protestantism." But now Unitarianism satisfied nobody. "It is negative, cold, lifeless," he continued, "and all advanced minds among [them] are dissatisfied with it, and are craving something higher, better, more living and life-giving."[72] The intellectual fabric was wearing thin and soon enough would have to give way, though precisely where was still an open question.

4

RELIGIOUS COMBUSTION

hroughout the antebellum period, America's Unitarian clergy were trained at Harvard, which since 1819 had assigned college faculty to instruct those who wished to prepare for the ministry. With the completion of Divinity Hall in 1826, the institution took on a more formal character and was called the Divinity College. Situated on a wide avenue about a quarter of a mile from Harvard Yard, the hall contained, in addition to thirty-seven rooms for students, a chapel, library, lecture hall, and reading room. The surrounding landscape was bucolic: behind the hall was meadowland extending all the way to Andrews Norton's home, Shady Hill, and in front there was open space that the students used for games.[1] Students followed a rigorous academic program, overseen by four faculty members responsible for courses in divinity, Hebrew and other "Oriental" languages, biblical criticism, and pastoral theology. The courses in biblical criticism were most important, for there students were introduced to the German scholarship that had transformed understanding of the scriptures. If the outside world seemed remote, the students' excitement came from debates over interpretive issues raised by foreign scholars as well as by their own faculty.

In Divinity Hall the veracity and import of Christ's miracles, as recorded in the Gospels, was a central topic of inquiry, as it was among Unitarians generally. How could Christians who believed in a rational, orderly universe overseen by a benevolent God hold that mankind needed supernatural proofs to sanction and validate faith? In other words, if God worked in rational, predictable ways, why did he have to break through the normal order of things to establish Christ's special mission in the world?

On these questions, through the early 1820s most Unitarians adhered to the "Supernaturalist" position. That is, they believed fully in the veracity of the Gospel accounts: Christ performed miracles because he was a special being endowed with extraordinary powers. Aligned against them were "Rationalists," who believed in the general thrust of the Gospel accounts but held that Christ's miracles in fact were subsequently embroidered to give more weight to his message. By the late 1820s more young Unitarians, much to their tutors' chagrin, began to espouse this latter view. Until 1835, there things stood, in the United States as well as in Europe.

In that year a young German theologian, David Friedrich Strauss, published his *Life of Jesus Critically Examined*, in which he argued that the Gospel accounts were essentially *all* mythical. After exhaustive study, Strauss concluded that little could be known of the historical Jesus because the stories of his life and death essentially were symbolic constructions based on attempts by early Christians to fit him to their messianic expectations, themselves based on earlier Jewish religious beliefs. Strauss's *Life of Jesus* exploded on the nineteenth-century religious landscape, shattering any tentative agreement to which Unitarians had come regarding the meaning of the Gospels.

The book quickly made its way across the Atlantic, where the young Unitarian divinity student Theodore Parker was one of the first to read it.[2] At the request of William Ware, then editor of *The Christian Examiner*, Parker, already widely acknowledged for his learning in German, reviewed the book for that journal. Although he was skeptical of the pantheistic drift of Strauss's religious beliefs, he still believed that the work was of "profound theological significance." He praised Strauss's bravery and intelligence in bringing before the public a matter of such great import, but he found problematic Strauss's dismissal of the entire story of Christ as myth.[3]

Among emergent Transcendentalists, William Henry Furness was one of the first to address at length this "miracles question" when he stirred his *Remarks on the Four Gospels* (1836) into the seething cauldron of liberal Christianity. Emerson's boyhood friend, Furness graduated from Harvard College in 1820 and then attended the Divinity School. In 1825 he left for Philadelphia, where for fifty years he ministered to the city's First Congregational Unitarian church. An early student of German, Furness, like other young Unitarians, found the new European exegetical scholarship liberating. His particular interest was the New Testament, and over his lengthy career he published a score of volumes that displayed the influence of the new historical criticism. Its first fruits were evident in his *Remarks on the Four Gospels.*

Furness never denied the truth of the three synoptic Gospels, for their uniformity convinced him of the veracity of the basic facts of Christ's life. But like Ripley in his "Jesus Christ, the Same Yesterday, Today, and Forever," Furness argued that Christ did not perform miracles to validate the truth of his message. Mankind believed in his teachings primarily because of their congruence with man's own internal, spiritual sense. Further, rather than claiming that Christ's deeds marked divine intervention in the physical world, Furness maintained that, given man's limited and still expanding knowledge of the physical world, he should not presume to know whether such things indeed were beyond the realm of sensory experience. For example, Furness pointed out that "the restoration of a dead man to life is not the least more wonderful than the birth of a human being."[4] Nature was so grand, so immense and unfathomable, that to doubt what Christ accomplished through it was presumptuous. Thus Furness believed in Christ's miracles as evidence of his superior moral and spiritual powers, even as he denied their necessity to prove the truth of Christ's message.

Such reasoning led Furness to a point that Emerson adumbrated in a different way in *Nature,* that miracle derives from the Latin "*miraculum,*" a wonder. "Taking the term in this sense exclusively," Furness wrote, "no one is disposed to doubt the reality of an event, solely on the score of its wonderfulness, because in this sense there is nothing that is not miraculous." The existence of an atom, he continued, is a wonder, and "the universe—all being—is miraculous."[5] Again, the point was not to question whether Christ performed wonderful deeds, but rather to acknowledge that they were tangential to the divine message that resonated in every soul.

Martin Luther Hurlburt, another Unitarian minister in Philadelphia, reviewed Furness's book for *The Christian Examiner*. He began sympathetically, praising the clergyman's belief that the synoptic Gospels were authentic narratives of Christ's life. But he resisted other parts of Furness's book with "unqualified dissent," specifically the lengthy section on "Miracles." Of late Hurlburt had noticed a growing disposition on the part of some Christians to get rid of the question of miraculous agency altogether, "as if it were a burden that embarrassed them." More specifically, there was a class of writers, epitomized by Furness, "consciously or unconsciously philosophizing away the peculiarities of the Gospel, and reducing it to a level of mere naturalism."[6] Hurlburt thus affirmed precisely what Furness attacked: the belief that "miracle" implied "a violation, or suspension, of the laws of nature."[7] He also objected to Furness's notions that because of the inherent religious sentiment, "all men are endued [sic] with miraculous powers" and that thus the mind possesses supremacy over material things. To Hurlburt this was "startling," for it supposed a sort of "sixth sense" that men possessed but were not always aware of.[8] This was precisely Furness's point. Needless to say, because of the volume's radical implications, Hurlburt did not endorse it. The journal's editor James Walker offered Furness the courtesy of a rebuttal in the next number, in which Furness unrepentantly reiterated his position, according Strauss's book a central place in Unitarians' increasingly acrimonious debates over Christ's message.[9]

The blowup came in the summer of 1838, when the graduating class of Harvard's Divinity School invited Emerson to deliver the customary discourse on the evening before commencement.[10] The previous year the college had asked him to deliver the Phi Beta Kappa address during August's festivities—after their first choice, the Reverend Jonathan Mayhew Wainwright, an Episcopalian, had declined. Emerson, who circulated in the Boston area as a Unitarian "supply" minister after his resignation from the Second Church in 1832, obliged with a lecture on the *American Scholar* that, in retrospect, has become one of his best-known writings, "our intellectual Declaration of Independence," Oliver Wendell Holmes termed it.[11] Not the least important task Emerson set himself therein was to correct what he regarded as "the extreme Eurocentrism" of many of his friends.[12] He proposed to the students that they emulate not the mere "thinker" but "Man Thinking," and urged them to honor and build on the nation's political commitment to democracy. Emerson's Phi Beta Kappa address ratified other incipient Transcendentalists' belief that the most important demand of their faith was to speak from the soul.

Emerson printed five hundred copies of the *American Scholar* at his own expense, and its circulation had a good deal to do with the divinity students' decision to offer him their podium the following year. On the evening of July 15, 1838, in Divinity Hall's chapel, Emerson addressed a small audience of six students, their families and friends, the faculty, and a few of his own friends—Ripley, Hedge, James Freeman Clarke, Elizabeth Peabody, and Theodore Parker—on challenges the new clergy faced. Harvard was represented by an imposing group: Andrews Norton, recently retired to pursue scholarship on the Gospels; Henry Ware, Sr., Hollis Professor of Divinity; his son, Henry, Jr., with whom Emerson had worked at Boston's Second Church and who had become Professor of Pulpit Eloquence and Pastoral Care; and the dean of the school, John Gorham Palfrey. Given the small audience, the occasion was not particularly auspicious for a major pronouncement on the "new views" that Emerson and his cohort were forwarding. Nevertheless, his words fractured the infant American Unitarian Association and marked his final, emphatic break with organized Christianity.

Emerson opened with an invocation to the beauty of nature, a studied parody of religious language that foreshadowed his radical critique of the sitting clergy. "In this refulgent summer," he announced, "it has been a luxury to draw the breath of life." "The grass grows," he continued, "the buds burst, the meadow is spotted with fire and gold in the tint of flowers. The air is full of birds, and sweet with the breath of the pine, the balm-of-Gilead, and the new hay." Moreover, "the corn and the wine have been freely dealt to all creatures." One is "constrained," he continued "to respect the perfection of this world, in which our senses converse."[13] Innocuous as his words sound today, his audience would have snapped to attention. Nature, Emerson was saying, is not fallen, as Christians maintained, but is itself perfect and worthy of our worship. The sacramental corn and wine are not reserved for saints alone, but are available to all who seek them. But how did this pertain to the young men about to embark on their ministry?

They had to attend to such truths and incorporate them into their preaching, for when man truly knows nature, he knows the divine spirit. "When the mind opens," Emerson said, "and reveals the laws which traverse the universe, and make things what they are, then shrinks the great world at once into a mere illustration and fable of this mind." Nature mirrors the divine and thus offers moral guidance, but "while the doors of the temple stand open, night and day, before every man, and the oracles of this truth cease never, it is guarded by one stern condition; this, namely; it is an intuition" and cannot "be received at second hand."[14] To unite with spirit through nature, Emerson claimed, is to experience the paradisiacal state of Man before the Fall.

Emerson's most radical proposition, however, was his interpretation of Christ's mission. Jesus Christ "belonged to the true race of prophets," Emerson explained, because "he saw with open eye the mystery of the soul." He clearly recognized the symbiotic relationship of matter and spirit, and understood his divinity in and through it. "Alone in all history," he continued, Christ "estimated the greatness of man."

One man was true to what is in you and me. He saw that God incarnates himself in man, and evermore goes forth to take possession of his world. He said, in this jubilee of sublime emotion, "I am divine. Through me, God acts; through me, speaks. Would you see God, see me; or, see thee, when thou also thinkest [*sic*] as I now think." But what a distortion did his doctrine and memory suffer in the same, in the next, and the following ages! There is no doctrine of the Reason which will bear to be taught by the Understanding. The understanding caught this high chant from the poet's lips, and said, in the next age, "This was Jehovah come down out of heaven. I will kill you, if you say he was a man."

In subsequent ages, however, the "idioms" of Christ's language and the "figures of his rhetoric" usurped the place of his truth, so that now churches were not built "on his principles, but on his tropes."[15]

There was more. Emerson rubbed salt into the raw wounds from the debate over miracles. Christ spoke of miracles because he believed that "man's life was a miracle," Emerson declared. But over time "the word Miracle, as pronounced by Christian churches," Emerson continued, was redefined. It became "Monster"—that is, something outside the natural order of things—and was "not one with the blowing clover and the falling rain." Here was a proposition more unsettling than anything Furness had offered, for not only did Emerson dismiss any interest in Christ's purported miracles but he also claimed that Christ enjoined man to appreciate the miracle of every moment. "Historical Christianity" failed to acknowledge this, and thus men spoke "of the revelation as somewhat long ago given and done, as if God were dead."[16] This was not the case, as a glance at the refulgent summer day proved.

Emerson also excoriated the contemporary clergy for their inability to preach from their own personal experiences. He recounted his own disappointment in a local minister (unnamed but patently Concord's Barzillai Frost) who had "sorely tempted" him to stop attending services. "A snow storm was falling all around us," he explained, but while the storm was real, the preacher was "merely spectral." "The eye felt the sad contrast in looking at him," Emerson continued, "and then out of the window behind him, into the beautiful meteor of the snow." Sadly, this clergyman had never spoken "one word that intimated that he had laughed or wept, was married or in love, had been commended, or cheated, or chagrined." He had failed dismally at "the capital secret of his profession," to "convert life into truth."[17]

How could the graduating students avoid similar failure? Go alone, Emerson directed them, and "refuse the good models, even those which are sacred in the imagination of men." "Dare to love God without mediator or veil." "Yourself a newborn bard of the Holy Ghost," he proclaimed, "cast behind you all conformity, and acquaint men at first hand with Deity." By trusting their own hearts, the young men would win the respect of their congregations and have the courage to stand up for social justice. Emerson told the young clergymen to recover true, rather than historical, Christianity. He looked, thus, "for the new Teacher" who would follow "so far those shining laws, that he shall see them come full circle; shall see their rounding complete grace; shall see the world to be the mirror of the soul; shall see the identity of the law of gravitation with the purity of the heart," for nature and spirit were so intimately linked. "In the soul," Emerson counseled, "let the redemption be sought," for "wherever a man comes, there comes revolution."[18]

An inspirational call to arms, the address also was a studied insult to the assembled clergy. Shortly after the address Francis wrote to Hedge that it had given "dire offence to the rulers of Cambridge" and raised the question of whether and, if so, how, the address should be disseminated.[19] Usually, the students themselves initiated such publication, customary for such lectures; but given the tenor of Emerson's remarks, which all the students did not endorse and by which most of the faculty were embarrassed, the decision was difficult. The students finally took the middle road and decided to print the address privately; but after Emerson revised the manuscript at the advice of friends, they published one thousand copies of *An Address before the Senior Class*. It was available in late August.

Depending on their predilection to what Emerson had already expressed in *Nature*, those who heard the address had different views of it. Cyrus Bartol was impressed; Emerson's "textless discourse" was nothing less than "the return of the Holy Ghost, with voices."[20] The young Theodore Parker called it "the noblest of all performances,—a little exaggerated, with some philosophical untruth, it seems to me, but the noblest, most inspiring strain I ever listened to." But others, he continued, differed, with one person shouting, "The Philistines be upon us," and another, "We be all dead men." Dean Palfrey, he reported, said that the part of it "which was not folly, is downright atheism."[21] The Swedenborgian Sampson Reed was also critical. He took the occasion of the third edition of his *Observations on the Growth of the Mind* to assure the public that he did not wish to be linked to Emerson's ideas. Transcendentalism, he explained, was only a step away from "sensualism" and far from the spiritual purity of Swedenborg's faith. "*Transcendentalism*," he explained, "is the parasite of *sensualism*," and he went on to characterize both as worms, poised to contaminate the beliefs that he and his fellow Swedenborgians held dear.[22]

Others were more measured. Francis told Hedge that he had heard the talk and found it "crowded with stirring, honest, lofty thoughts" but regretted that Emerson did not make "the peculiar significance of Jesus as prominent as he ought."[23] Henry Ware, Jr., wrote to Emerson the day after; he was one of those who suggested that Emerson revise it before publication. Emerson found his friend's letter filled with his usual candor and charity but insisted that, as to the doctrines expressed to the class, his "conviction" was "perfect." He believed that he owed it to his friends and colleagues to speak as he did and not "to suppress any opposition to their supposed views out of fear of offence."[24] Although Emerson had girded himself for some criticism, he did not expect what followed. For their part, the Divinity School faculty believed that he had thrown down a gauntlet.

The first attack was not long in coming. Two days after Emerson's address was available, Andrews Norton used the pages of the *Boston Daily Advertiser* to express his disgust and outrage. As an example of the vituperation to which the new views pushed an otherwise cautious man, the letter is remarkable. Significantly, Norton rang all the changes expected from one who had little sympathy for the European ideas that underlay not only Emerson's address but a whole series of recent contributions to *The Christian Examiner*. Norton waited until he was halfway through his "New School of Literature and Religion" before mentioning Emerson's publication, and he used it as only the most recent example of what for a number of years he had found so offensive in the writings of some of the younger Unitarians.

Lacing his communication with sarcasm and condescension, Norton began by observing how the current climate in literature and religion was marked by a "restless craving for notoriety and excitement." He knew where such things originated: in "ill-understood notions, obtained by blundering through the crabbed and disgusting obscurity of some of the worst German speculatists [*sic*]," which had been received "by most of its disciples at second hand, through an interpreter." In particular, he singled out as villains "that hasher up of German metaphysics, the Frenchman, Cousin"; the "hyper-Germanized Englishman, Carlyle"; and behind them all, "the veiled image of the German pantheist, Schleiermacher."[25]

The adherents of this "school," as he termed it, believed that they could discern transcendental truths by "immediate vision," and that these could not be understood unless one had similarly experienced them. In this group's writings, Norton continued, common thoughts were "exaggerated, and twisted out of shape, and forced into strange connexion"; and language was abused and "antic tricks played with it." "Inversions," he continued, "exclamations, anamalous [*sic*] combinations of words, unmeaning, but coarse and violent, metaphors abound, and withal a strong infusion of German barbarians." Most insidiously, "silly" young men and women were drawn from their Christian faith to such heretical ideas, a "disastrous and alarming" situation. Emerson's address typified all this, and it was "extraordinary and ill-boding evidence" of Unitarianism's betrayal from within.

The first response to Norton's intemperate missive came from an odd quarter. The Swedenborgian Theophilus Parsons took Norton to task, not for his arguments but for his excessively harsh tone. Whatever Norton wished to say about the European thinkers who lay behind the New Thought, Parsons observed, they were men of international standing whose reputations were not diminished by one man's rant in a provincial newspaper.[26] A few days later, in the *Boston Morning Post*, Orestes Brownson weighed in. He praised Emerson's honesty and bravery in so openly stating his views and warned that to persecute him for his ideas would only bring him more followers.

Brownson also made another telling point: Norton's notion of a unified "New School of Literature and Religion" was simply off base. He had erred in conflating two different groups of Unitarians. The Transcendentalists, whom Emerson represented, based their ideas on Carlyle's redaction of German Idealist philosophers. The Eclectics, of whom Brownson himself was an exemplar, took the most from Cousin's works. Carlyle and Cousin, he pointed out, could not be more different in their manner and goals, even if they were both indebted to German Idealism. "The Transcendentalists, so called," he wrote, "are by no means philosophers, they are either dreamers, or mere speculatists [*sic*], condemning logic, holding the understanding in light esteem." The Eclectics, on the other hand, are "a very sober and rational people," and while not Materialists, followed an "experimental mode of philosophizing," an allusion to Cousin's writings on psychology.[27] Brownson's classification proved prescient, and even more so was his sense that Emerson's theology was not that of every dissident Unitarian, nor even every Transcendentalist. He worried, for example, about Emerson's "obedience to self," for it smacked of a dangerous "egotism." "The soul's conception of God is not God," Brownson wrote, and if there was no God "out of the soul, out of the *me*, to answer to the soul's conception," then there was no God.[28]

In September, Emerson's friend and colleague Henry Ware, Jr., offered his own response in his sermon, *The Personality of the Deity*, also delivered at the Divinity School. In a measured and civil tone, he strongly reaffirmed the deity as more than a set of principles or code of laws; "Divine Personality" was central to a Christian's creed. To deny this, Ware claimed, amounted "to a virtual denial of God." If the material universe, he continued, "rests on the laws of attraction, affinity, heat, motion, still all of them together are no Deity." And if the moral universe "is founded on the principles of righteousness, truth, love, neither are these the Deity." There must be some "Being" to put these principles in action, he explained, and "to exercise these attributes." But to call such things themselves God violated "the established use of language."[29]

Emerson and Ware, for all their cordiality, were at loggerheads, for Emerson sought to startle readers into discovering the divinity within each of them. On the other hand, Ware warned that if one denied the personality of the deity, there remained no higher mind than his own, and man was left wholly to himself. Emerson simply agreed, as he did with Ware's contention that concomitantly, such a belief destroyed the possibility of any revelation "by making all truth a revelation, and all men revelers." This was precisely the thrust of Emerson's message at the Divinity School, as it had been, two years earlier, in *Nature*. And in his journals the summer before, he had anticipated Ware's criticism. "I deny Personality to God," he wrote, "because it is too little not too much." "Life, personal life," he continued, is "faint & cold to the energy of God."[30] Emerson's deity was no longer Ware's, as painful a realization as this was to Emerson's friend.

Nowhere in his sermon did Ware allude to Emerson's address, but everyone knew that he intended his talk as a rejoinder. Unfortunately, the debate did not remain so civil. When Norton received an invitation the following July from the "Association of the Alumni of the Cambridge Theological School" to speak at the First Parish Church in Cambridge at the first such meeting of the graduates (essentially on the anniversary of Emerson's speech), he fired a broadside directly at those in thrall to German philosophy. His address, *The Latest Form of Infidelity*, again put Emerson in the public eye as a chief exponent of the New Thought and ensured that hitherto he would be branded by the epithet Transcendentalist, even as the movement already was splitting into separate camps. For his part, Emerson could not understand all the attention. "It strikes me very oddly & even a little ludicrously that the good & great men of Cambridge should think of raising me into an object of criticism," he wrote Ware. Moreover, signaling his refusal to answer Norton meanness for meanness, he added that there was "no scholar in America less willing or less able to be a polemic" than he.[31]

But Norton was spoiling for a fight. Even the title of the address was a provocation, for people in the Commonwealth of Massachusetts quickly recognized the allusion to the recent celebrated case of another "infidel," Abner Kneeland, an erstwhile Baptist and Universalist minister whom Fanny Wright had converted to her Society of Free Inquirers and who, between 1834 and 1838, endured no fewer than four trials for blasphemy. In light of the confluence of Kneeland's (and Wright's) sympathies with the lower classes and Emerson's notion of the divinely empowered individual, Transcendentalist doctrine now was linked to disruption of the social as well as religious order. Further, the Massachusetts Supreme Court's conviction of Kneeland on the blasphemy charge in the spring of 1838 did not augur well for Emerson, who, if not likely to be indicted, still would be tarred as another purveyor of "infidelity."

Norton wasted no time in getting to his main point. Alumni of the Divinity School had to defend the propositions "that Christianity is a revelation by God of the truths of religion" and that "the divine authority of him whom God commissioned to speak to us in his name" was attested by miraculous displays of power.[32] Ominously, Christianity's most threatening enemies now came from within Unitarianism's ranks. They were intoxicated by foreign ideas that undermined the faith even as they pretended still to be Unitarians. The "latest form of infidelity" was distinguished "by assuming the Christian name," Norton wrote, even as it struck "directly at the root of faith in Christianity, and indirectly of all religion, by denying the miracles attesting the divine mission of Christ."[33] To deny the possibility of miracles, he bellowed, amounted to a "denial of the existence of God."[34]

For any remaining doubters, Norton appended a note consisting of "Some Further Remarks on the Characteristics of the Modern German School of Infidelity." He assaulted the vacuity of the German philosophers then in such favor among younger Unitarians. After quoting a passage from de Wette, for example, Norton exclaimed in exasperation, "The shadowy meaning of this sentence I have quoted, escapes any attempt to grasp it."[35] He also went after Schleiermacher's "system of pantheism, wrought up in a highly declamatory style, in which the language, often soars beyond meaning." To Schleiermacher, religion, he went on, is nothing but "the sense of union of the individual with the universe, with Nature, or, in the language of the sect, with the One and all." It is "a feeling," he sneered, and has nothing to do with "belief or action." Norton ended this passage by admitting his astonishment that, holding such views, on his deathbed Schleiermacher had the presumption to take the sacrament "as a Christian."[36]

Norton concluded with a lengthy note, "On the Objection to Faith in Christianity, as Resting on Historical Facts and Critical Learning." What most exercised him and other conservative Unitarians about Schleiermacher's belief in the primacy of internal religious feeling was that it discounted—indeed, made irrelevant—the education and scholarship to which scriptural exegetes had dedicated their lives. Those who undertook to influence the opinions of their fellow men on religious subjects, Norton wrote, "should have natural capacity for the office." They also should have "the requisite knowledge, of which extensive learning commonly makes a part." Moreover—here he presumably had in mind Emerson and other upstarts—such an individual must be animated by "no motives inconsistent with a love of truth and goodness, by no craving for notoriety, no restless desire to be the talk of the day, no party spirit."[37] He did not say but deeply believed that the insurgents sought nothing less than to make his scholarship, and so him, irrelevant.

Emerson was taken aback at the brouhaha and adamant not to fuel it, but by October things only worsened. In his journal he confided that "the feminine vehemence with which the A[ndrews]. N[orton]. of the *Daily Advertiser* beseeches the dear people to whip that naughty heretic [Emerson] is the natural feeling in the mind of those whose religion is external." The aim of a "true teacher," he continued, "would be to bring back men to a trust in God & destroy before their eyes these idolatrous propositions: to teach the doctrine of perpetual revelation."[38] With Emerson's continuing refusal to spar with Norton, Ripley, who had been promoting the German thinkers in a series of essays in *The Christian Examiner*, took up Norton's affront and challenge. Championing his cousin's religious views, even if they were not fully his own, Ripley hoped to consolidate the young religious reformers who so worried the infant American Unitarian Association. To engage Norton might engender such cohesion.

Ripley did not wait long to jump into the fray. His *"Latest Form of Infidelity" Examined: A Letter to Mr. Andrews Norton* bore the date September 5. He published it anonymously, as "an Alumnus of That [the "Cambridge Theological"] School," but given his sophisticated defense of German theologians, it would not have taken anyone long to recognize the pamphlet's author. Ripley spent most of his 160-page pamphlet objecting to Norton's arrogance in claiming the correctness of his own principles, when Unitarians were supposed to champion free inquiry. Norton's diatribe was particularly inappropriate, Ripley noted, because the alumni of the school to whom he spoke "neither claim authority over each others' faith, nor profess to regard uniformity of speculative opinion, as desirable, even if it were possible." The common tie that bound them, he continued, was attachment to "liberal Christianity," which they valued because "it connects the enjoyment of religion with independence of mind, and enables them to search for truth, free from human dictation." Concomitantly, he objected to Norton's uncharitable dismissal of the considerable number of Unitarians who, through their scholarly inquiries, had become convinced of the superiority of the soul's internal testimony over mere evidence of the senses.[39] Norton's haughty and dismissive tone, coupled with his self-righteous opinions on great questions of the day, was presumptuous to the worst degree and an insult to his audience.

Ripley also took his old teacher to task for his ignorance of Continental theology as well as of the German language. Spinoza was not, as Norton huffed, "a celebrated atheist," Ripley explained, nor was Schleiermacher a "pantheist" who denied the immortality of the soul. Norton believed this of Schleiermacher, Ripley continued, because he erroneously regarded one of the theologian's early works, *Discourses on Religion*, as his definitive statement of doctrine.[40] If Norton wanted to understand Schleiermacher's God, Ripley observed, he should turn to his *The Christian Faith*. Norton similarly erred in his claim that the German theologian was a member of the Rationalist or Naturalist school of scriptural interpretation, when in fact he was close to being a Supernaturalist in his understanding of Christ's role in history. Citing Schleiermacher's follower Karl Ullmann (1796–1865), Ripley made it clear that Schleiermacher's theology eventuated from a creative synthesis of Naturalism and Supernaturalism, and as such, was sui generis.

Even more damning was Ripley's indictment of Norton for his irrational and baseless fear of German theology. He embarrassed Norton by observing that even the theologians at the conservative Andover Theological Seminary evidenced a spirit of Christian liberty by engaging the New Thought, and had translated and republished it for American readers. Ripley cited approvingly the statement of two Andover professors, B. B. Edwards and E. A. Park, in their *Selections from German Literature*. "Let us see," they wrote, "how men good and true are now speculating in foreign climes, and we shall be convinced that the sky does not close in with the earth four or five miles from the spot where we happen to stand, however central that spot may be."[41]

Ripley landed a final jab when he addressed Norton's misunderstanding of de Wette. Norton had tried to impress his readers by the weight of his learning, Ripley observed; and, indeed, because of his reputation, for many his opinion carried "the weight of an oracle." Yet when Norton condemned a writer of such range and intelligence as de Wette by citing only one excerpt of twenty-one lines, and in the course of his explication made "*fourteen*" errors in translation, readers had reason to doubt his command of the language. "Knowledge of German is no merit," Ripley wrote, tongue in cheek, "but the want of it in those who undertake to expound German theology is an inconvenience."[42] Indeed!

One imagines the indignation at Norton's Shady Hill estate on the appearance of Ripley's pamphlet. To Ripley's "personal attack" Norton issued early in 1839 *Remarks on a Pamphlet Entitled "The Latest Form of Infidelity' Examined."* His riposte comprised an extended and deadening display of pedantry as he countered every charge Ripley had made. He never acknowledged, however, the real issue, whether religious feeling trumped the "facts" of Christ's miracles. Unfortunately, Ripley too was drawn offtrack, for neither did he, in his *Second Letter to Mr. Andrews Norton*, dated late in December that same year. Herein he only presented more evidence of Norton's misreading of Spinoza.[43]

What looked like a barren end to the controversy acquired new vigor when two others weighed in on Emerson's behalf. Shortly after Ripley's last barb, the young Unitarian Richard Hildreth, another Harvard graduate (1826) then editing the daily *Boston Atlas*, offered a *Letter to Andrews Norton on Miracles as the Foundation of Religious Faith* (1840). Given his peremptory tone toward Norton, it is no surprise that he published it anonymously, for his views were as novel as his tone was imperious. Hildreth did not present himself as "a dogmatist, or a mystic, a naturalist, or a pietist, a believer, or an unbeliever," he explained, but "simply in the character of a rational man—a rational man not in the German, but the English sense." Hildreth objected to Norton's attempt "to strip Religion of the transcendental and supernatural character which it has ever borne; to reduce it to the rank of natural, historical science." After all the advances in science over the past centuries, Hildreth found it remarkable that Norton would try to establish "the bare text of the Scripture as the sole source of all useful knowledge, and the science of scriptural interpretation as the only science worthy to be cultivated."[44] In other words, Norton was not rational enough.

Hildreth summed up Norton's doctrine as he had gleaned it from his recent writings. "Religion consists in knowledge, which knowledge leads to certain feelings, called Religious feelings." Further, such knowledge is only "to be attained by a critical study of the Greek and Hebrew scriptures," very difficult to understand, liable to misinterpretation, "and which in fact, have been interpreted to your satisfaction by no one but yourself." Hildreth did not stop his rudeness here. All who did not know such languages, he continued, had "nothing to do, but to look up for 'testimony'" to Norton and "meekly and faithfully" receive his pronouncements under an "awful sense of the 'responsibility'" they should incur did they dare, with their "small means of knowledge," to "suggest a difference or doubt." By Norton's rule, no one should proffer opinions on religion except those few privileged individuals, like Norton, "who are so lucky as to possess the gift of infallibility."[45] Although Hildreth went on to a distinguished career as a journalist and historian, his role in the Transcendentalist controversy began and ended with this pamphlet, which at least had the effect of further exposing Norton's arrogance to public view.

Although Ripley had effectively ended his involvement in the controversy, Norton fired one last shot across his opponents' bow. It was an anomalous pamphlet entitled *Transcendentalism of the Germans and of Cousin and Its Influence on Opinion in the Country* (1840), not his own work but a reprint of two articles from the conservative Presbyterian periodical *The Biblical Repertory and Princeton Review*, authored by J. W. Alexander, Albert B. Dod, and Charles Hodge, professors at Princeton and stalwart Trinitarians, who had originally published them early in 1839. Like their counterparts at Andover, the Princeton theologians were learned in German scholarship and philosophy, and had navigated its choppy waters to their and their charges' satisfaction. That Norton turned to those who fifteen years earlier had been his sworn enemies was a bitter irony or, perhaps, a sign of his increasing desperation.

Alexander and Dod, who authored the first of the two reprinted articles, made it clear that when they described the dangerous tendencies of German philosophy, they knew of what they spoke, not like most of the "young philosophers" in America who received their lessons by "installment," that is, through redaction in periodicals. Indeed, they were as critical of the Transcendentalists' scholarly abilities as Norton was—presumably why he republished their works.[46] The bulk of their text comprises a dismissal of Idealist philosophy from Kant through Fichte to Schelling, with Hodge, in the second installment, applying his cudgel to Hegel as well. The trio also devoted much space to a demolition of Cousin's Eclecticism. The Princetonians disdained the way that the Frenchman's philosophy "removes the God of the Bible, and substitutes in His stead, a philosophical abstraction." Cousin's "nonsense" merely "aped the German impiety," they continued, and they were distressed to see the progress that it already had made in their country.[47]

Alexander and Dod also had attacked Emerson's recent Divinity School address, for it confirmed their worst fears about the silliness that accompanied half-baked allegiance to German thought. Indeed, they hardly knew how to express "the nonsense and impiety" that pervaded the address. Rightly charting its genealogy, they called it "a rhapsody, obviously in imitation of Thomas Carlyle, and possessing as much of the vice of his mannerisms as the author could borrow, but without his genius." They also understood precisely what Emerson was saying of Christ—that "any man may now become Christ"—and lamented that there was not "a single truth or sentiment in the whole address that is borrowed from the Scriptures." Finally, they labeled Emerson's work as "the first fruits of transcendentalism in our country," and "warning evidence of the nature of the tree which has produced it."[48]

Norton's republication of these reviews was not the final volley in this pamphlet war, but by 1840 the Transcendentalist group, having rallied to Emerson's defense, began to find other ways to promulgate mutual interests. Norton's attack on Emerson had brought the former minister front and center as a chief purveyor of the New Thought, even if he declined to engage Norton directly and his overall contributions to the movement remained minimal. Francis understood how all this had occurred. In a letter to Hedge at the height of the controversy he observed that "the truth was, the fluid of malignity had been collecting a good while,—and needed but a slight point of attraction to draw it down on Emerson's head." His popularity "among the brightest young people," Francis continued, "had become very annoying to the *dei majores* [major deities] of the pulpits & the Divinity school."[49]

Emerson's increasing visibility and the new directions in which Ripley's and Brownson's ministries were taking them eventuated in a split in the emergent group over the relation of self-culture to social reform. Joining this debate was a relative newcomer to the Transcendentalists' ranks who was destined to exercise great influence on the movement. Shortly after Norton's reprint of the *Princeton Review* articles, a young minister, Theodore Parker, writing under the alias of Levi Blodgett, a "plain man," offered *The Previous Question between Mr. Andrews Norton and His Alumni Moved and Handled, in a Letter to All Those Gentlemen.*[50] Prior to this, Parker had parodied the Princeton pamphlet in a fable called "Transcendentalism" published in the liberal Unitarian journal *The*

Christian Register, but after being criticized for so blithely dismissing the opposition's arguments, he decided to respond more formally, albeit still anonymously. He also had recently published, in the July 1840 *Christian Examiner*, a lengthy, favorable review of Strauss's *Life of Christ*, in which he endorsed Strauss's method and some of his conclusions. Parker was ready to break out in a more forceful way with his own statement of where critical and unbiased scholarship on the New Testament led.

Parker was a powerful and striking presence. O. B. Frothingham, one of his first biographers, remembered him as "sturdy, strong in the arms and legs," and "with a muscular grip of the hand that knit one to him at once." His visage displayed a comparable strength of character but occasionally was "a little grim in expression." His forehead massive, Parker had piercing blue eyes, a "slightly Socratic nose" that "had the possibilities of sarcasm," and lips that curled "easily."[51] In the pulpit these characteristics made him a riveting and seemingly uncompromising presence. No one wanted to incur his wrath.

At the age of thirty, he ministered to the small town of West Roxbury, just west of Boston; Convers Francis had preached his ordination sermon, and George Ripley had given the right hand of fellowship. That was a great day for Parker, for he was from humble origins. The youngest of eleven children from a poor farming family in Lexington, Massachusetts, early on he was recognized as an intellectual prodigy. Though unable to attend classes because of his family's impoverished circumstances, he passed all his examinations at Harvard and began to prepare for the Divinity School. Beginning in 1832 he studied with Francis, then minister to Watertown, where Parker also kept a school. His mentor remembered "a young man in homely and awkward dress" who introduced himself by saying that he had heard that Francis welcomed young people to study. "I long for books," Parker said, "and I long to know how to study."[52] He attended the Divinity School between 1834 and 1836, where his intellectual gifts were so evident that Ripley invited him to attend meetings of the Transcendentalist group. He also began to publish articles in *The Scriptural Interpreter* and *The Christian Register*, where more advanced Unitarian voices could be heard. In these efforts he frequently cited de Wette, Eichhorn, Michaelis, Paulus, Herder, and other European scholars. Parker even went so far as to purchase a forty-five volume set of Herder's *Complete Works*, in German.

His forte was languages. Along with German he could read in *twenty* other tongues, including Danish, Dutch, Chaldee, and Arabic. Moved by Emerson's address at the Divinity School, he wanted to use his scholarship to buttress Emerson's case, particularly because, given Ripley's last rejoinder, he felt that the parties had strayed from the central question. Parker sought to answer this question: *"Do men believe in Christianity* SOLELY *on the ground of miracles?"* To argue his case that men should not, the "obscure" Blodgett had recourse to none other than Schleiermacher, who based his theology on a belief "IN THE EXISTENCE OF GOD" and "A SENSE OF DEPENDENCE ON HIM." These "natural and essential sentiments of the soul" were found in all religions but reached their highest expression in Christianity, Parker believed. But not in the Christianity of Luther or Calvin, or of the Unitarians or Quakers, for all those were "one-sided and false." He meant quite simply "the Christianity of Christ." "I need no miracle," Parker wrote, "to convince me that the sun shines" nor of "the divinity of Jesus and his doctrines."[53]

Parker's masquerade as the homely Levi Blodgett was short-lived, for within a few months of this publication he, like Emerson, began to make waves in Boston's frog pond. As he put it, "I intend in the coming year to let out all the force of Transcendentalism that is in me, come what will come."[54] He was well prepared to do so. Although in 1836 he had lost the Concord pulpit to another candidate, the same Barzillai Frost whose ministry Emerson pilloried in the Divinity School address, Parker was content in West Roxbury, close to his mentor Francis as well as to others involved in discussions of Unitarianism's future. In addition to meetings with the infant Transcendentalist Club, for example, Parker enjoyed gatherings of the Society of the Friends of Progress, a group centered on William Ellery Channing that included Ripley, Brownson, Alcott, Hedge, and Karl Follen.

Moreover, Parker was committed to serious scholarship. In addition to publishing scores of articles and reviews, he began to prepare a translation of C. F. Ammon's four-volume *Fortbildung des Christenthums zur Welt-religion* (1836–40) for Ripley's series, *Specimens of Foreign Standard Literature.* Parker never finished it, but by the spring of 1837 he had completed a draft of a translation of de Wette's *Critical and Historical Introduction to Canonical Scriptures of the Old Testament.* Expanded with commentary of his own, he eventually published the work in two volumes. Incubating for years, Parker's religious radicalism was everywhere evident in it. Much larger than the original and of astonishing erudition, this expanded translation provides essential background to Parker's theological development.[55]

This project confirmed his skepticism about the Bible's divine authority, for his assessment of the most recent biblical scholarship convinced him of the composite nature of many of the Old Testament books as well as of the lengthy and complex historical process that produced the Bible. Few of its books' authors or compilers could be identified definitively, and each individual book contained central passages that contradicted one another. The reader left Parker's translation of de Wette with the sense that there was no good reason to believe that the Bible was a divinely inspired (and so, a miraculously authoritative) text.

Parker republished his massive scholarly tomes twice, but disappointingly, reviewers showed little attention. He did, however, receive a sympathetic reading from his old friend and mentor Convers Francis, who wrote him that the book filled him "with astonishment at your labors and learning," and predicted that it would become a "standard work," even if not a great seller "like a novel." Francis blamed the low sales on many of the younger clergy's lack of interest in such erudition. Instead, "the cry is all for action—for doing something, not moping over books as they say."[56] Without knowing it, Francis had recorded a seismic shift among Parker's cohort, one epitomized in Orestes Brownson's ministry.

What was Brownson doing and saying immediately before and after his brief contribution to the controversy over miracles? He continued to preach to his Society for Christian Union and Progress, which Alcott and other incipient Transcendentalists frequently attended. Also, through the good offices of George Bancroft, a prominent member of the Democratic Party, he held the position of steward to the Marine Hospital in Chelsea, a sinecure that provided a generous income in the difficult years following the national financial panic of 1837. Most significantly, Brownson finalized plans for a new journal, the *Boston Quarterly Review*, which he envisioned as a mouthpiece for more advanced Unitarians. Its first issue appeared in 1838, and it grew to a circulation of one thousand and was the most popular Transcendentalist organ.

Through the mid-1830s Cousin continued to influence Brownson greatly. As the decade advanced, however, other French thinkers, most notably the French Catholic priest Félicité Robert de Lamennais—who had left the church over its recalcitrance to undertake the kind of social reform he believed the Gospels demanded—became more important to him.[57] Brownson found in the works of Lamennais a belief that liberty and democracy were closely related to Christianity, and thus that a just social system would exist only when the relationship among the three was acknowledged and acted on, in politics as well as in religion. Brownson went so far as to claim that democracy "was nothing but the political application of Christianity."[58]

A few months after Brownson's letter to Boston's daily press in defense of Emerson, he revisited the Divinity School address in a much longer review in his new periodical, clarifying his differences from Emerson. Although again praising his courage and inherent goodness, Brownson worried about the tendency to a "system of pure egotism" that ran through all Emerson's writings. He was referring to Emerson's inordinate emphasis on the soul as the center of the universe, for with self as "the center of gravitation," Brownson asked, how can man be moral? He invoked a distinction that Jonathan Edwards had made a century earlier, noting that true holiness can exist only in disinterested benevolence, that is, when man regards himself as but a part of something much greater. The individual, Brownson maintained, cannot live for himself alone. Man must "sacrifice himself for a good which does not center in himself."[59]

Neither could Brownson countenance Emerson's notion that God is nothing "but the laws of the soul's perfection" and his dis-

missal of historical Christianity, for he believed that the past continued to have meaning and that Christ was not just another prophet,
but essential to Christianity. The idea of Christ and the history of
how men have received him were essential to keep in check man's
selfishness. Brownson believed that Emerson, on the other hand,
for all his good intentions, spawned progeny whose obedience to
the moral law was questionable.

Brownson was increasingly uneasy with the self-centeredness of
Emerson's beliefs. But at least through the summer of 1840, when
he reviewed Norton's reprint of *Two Articles from the "Princeton
Review"* in his *Boston Quarterly Review*, he continued to support
the entire cohort, even though, as a writer in *The Western Messenger*
put it, Brownson and Furness had become at least as important as
Emerson to Unitarian "seekers."[60] Brownson opened this review
with a description of the "signs of the times" in the Boston area,
where he saw nothing less than a "revolution, which extends to
every department of thought and threatens to change ultimately
the whole moral aspect of our society." As in every such period,
there were those who greeted the prospect of change with open
arms and others who feared it.[61]

Brownson then detailed Norton's and Ripley's differing views of
Christianity, specifically about the meaning of Christ, and aligned
himself with those who believed that one only knew Christ's truth
through intuitive perception. Brownson also spent much time defending his favorite, Cousin, against Norton's condemnation, and
he closed with an embrace of fellow members of the New School.
So far as Transcendentalism was understood as "the recognition in
man of the capacity of knowing truth intuitively, or of attaining scientific knowledge of an order of existence transcending the reach of
the senses, and of which we can have no sensible experience," he
declared, "we are Transcendentalists." But if its critics took the
word to imply that "feeling displaced reason," that "dreaming" was
valued above reflection or "instinctive intimation above scientific
exposition," he eschewed the cognomen.[62] That was as large as
Brownson wished to make the tent.

By the beginning of the 1840s the public, reading critics such as
Bowen and Norton, ignored such fine distinctions and believed

that the Transcendentalists posed a serious threat not only to organized religion but also to the social order. Whether early in the 1840s the Unitarian vanguard would, or could, continue to develop a post-Christian theology in light of the other challenges they faced was unclear. Brownson's acute discriminations, as well as the thrust of his social criticism, suggested not. By this point Transcendentalism was becoming a many-headed Hydra.

5

CENTRIPETAL FORCES
AND CENTRIFUGAL MOTION

n the late 1830s the Boston Common, on about seventy-five acres, was one of the country's most beautiful parks. On hilly land accentuated by many unusual and beautiful trees (some planted a century earlier), it was dissected by beveled and graveled promenades that delighted Bostonians. At its head sat the imposing State House designed by the prominent eighteenth-century architect Charles Bulfinch, and across from it the Boston Athenaeum, an elegant private library founded in 1807. To the north, past Beacon Hill's fashionable residences, was a vista toward the Charles River and then west to a new Botanic Garden paid for by private subscription. In the nineteenth century an iron fence, about a mile in perimeter, surrounded the Common, the crown jewel in a city that took its open space seriously.

Tremont Street bordered this park on its south side. In the 1840s, turning on West Street and walking farther south, one came to a bustling commercial district at Washington Street, the center of, among other things, the city's burgeoning printing trade. Halfway between Tremont and Washington stood a two-story brick building, Number 13 West Street, now the site of the famed Brattle Book Shop but in 1839 a town-house residence and business occupied by Nathaniel Peabody's family. In the early 1840s this building's public rooms were a center of the emergent Transcendentalist movement.

Nathaniel was an apothecary, and his wife, Elizabeth, had run a private school. They had moved to West Street from Salem because they thought it a good business location. With them were three remarkable daughters, Elizabeth, Mary, and Sophia. Elizabeth, the oldest, had been William Ellery Channing's amanuensis, worked with Bronson Alcott at his Temple School as well as operating her own educational establishments, and was well connected to many young Unitarian intellectuals, including George Ripley and Ralph Waldo Emerson. Mary had worked for a time with her sister Elizabeth at the Temple School, and now she had her own pupils on West Street; within a few years she married the educational reformer Horace Mann. Sophia was an artist, soon smitten by one of the region's most secretive, though charismatic, intellectuals, Nathaniel Hawthorne, whom she married. At their new home, the Peabody family lived upstairs, where there also was an extra room for Mary's students. The first floor was devoted to commerce. There Nathaniel sold homeopathic drugs and—at the suggestion of the painter Washington Allston, another of Elizabeth's friends—art supplies. In the town house's front parlor Elizabeth established a foreign-language bookstore and "Foreign Library" that became a salon for the city's intelligentsia. From the same location she published books, translations of foreign texts, and titles by her patrons.

In the late summer of 1840 Elizabeth Peabody made her "debut in the mercantile world."[1] The first of its kind in Boston, her bookstore offered recent titles in English, French, Italian, German, Greek, and Latin, comprising philosophy, religion, history, and literature, among other subjects. Here one could purchase the books of such important English writers as Coleridge, Wordsworth, and Shelley; Cousin's philosophical works, George Sand's novels, and de Staël's *De l'Allemagne*; Dante and Ariosto in Italian; and Jean Paul Richter in German. She carried Alphonse de Lamartine's *History of the Girondists* and Jules Michelet's *Mémoires de Luther*, Maximilien Robespierre's *Mémoires*, and Gioacchino Rossini's *Luisa Strozzi*. Satisfied patrons also recalled such important religious titles as the French socialist Pierre Leroux's *De l'Humanité*, Benjamin Constant's *De la Religion*, and Strauss's *Leben Jesu*, and many other titles in belles lettres, including a fifty-five-volume set of Goethe's

Works in German. Peabody prided herself on handpicking her selections and worked to obtain what she needed. If a customer sought a European book that she did not carry, for example, she would try to secure it from overseas through the New York publisher John Wiley; it typically took six weeks to arrive. She also carried locally published works by her friends and customers. Her stock included, for example, Emerson's *Nature* and *Ripley's Letters to Mr. Norton*, as well as collections of short stories by her soon-to-be brother-in-law, Hawthorne.

Peabody's foreign lending library comprised close to two thousand items.[2] Her friends lent some of the books for the enterprise; others she purchased outright. She took out a five-hundred-dollar loan and invested a hefty amount—one hundred and fifty dollars—in subscriptions to foreign periodicals. On the shelves were the venerable *Blackwood's Magazine*, *The Edinburgh Review*, and the *Revue des Deux Mondes*, as well as such unusual titles as the *Annales des Sciences Naturelles* and the *Journal des Literarische Unterhaltung*. She also stocked the staple Unitarian journals: *The Christian Examiner*, Brownson's *Boston Quarterly Review*, and *The Western Messenger*. One could borrow current issues of these periodicals for a week only (one could keep the books for a month, longer if there were no requests from other subscribers), with subscription and priority in borrowing the volumes, at a cost of five dollars per year. Nonmember patrons could "hire" books for 12½ or 25 cents each, "according to their sizes," but such customers were not allowed to borrow the periodicals.

Elizabeth Peabody's rooms soon became exactly what she had hoped—in the teacher and Transcendentalist fellow traveler George Bradford's words, a kind of "Transcendental exchange."[3] William Ellery Channing, for example, was in the habit of coming to West Street in the morning to keep abreast of the latest important periodical essays. Edward Everett Hale happily recalled coming into the rooms and seeing a long counter across the parlor, all the library's books standing "on shelves in brown-paper covers."[4] Theodore Parker, a voracious reader of foreign texts, enthusiastically welcomed the business and assured Peabody that her operation "fill[ed] a vacancy, and suppl[ied] a want that has long been felt in

Boston."[5] Other regular visitors were Channing's nephew, William Henry Channing; Emerson; Fuller; the Ripleys; James Walker, now a professor at Harvard; and the young Caroline Healey, Fuller's protégée.

Presiding over this informal salon was Peabody herself, already a tad overweight (she became more so in middle age), inattentive to her dress, and famously absentminded. Thomas Wentworth Higginson remembered her as "desultory, dreamy, but insatiable in her love for knowledge and for helping others to it."[6] After a visit to "Miss Peabody's Book Room" in August 1840, the young Healey recorded how she loved to hear the proprietor talk and "to see her smile." Peabody, she continued, had "so deep learning—so youthful joyousness[,] so great experience & perfect simplicity [that] I never saw united in one character."[7] As Healey realized, despite her eccentricities—her dress and manners, "the world admit to be very outré"—Peabody was lovingly attentive to her store, for she wished it to be one "in which there were no worthless books."[8] By all accounts she kept her word, and through the 1840s—the store finally closed in 1851, when the family began to take in boarders—the bookstore and lending library remained a hubbub of activity.

The West Street address was known for other things as well. Even before the library and bookstore opened, Peabody's friend Margaret Fuller used the parlor for her renowned "Conversations." The women who attended these meetings recalled them as an epoch in their lives. At West Street, too, plans were laid for *The Dial*, from 1840 to 1844 the mouthpiece of those at the forefront of religious and social reform in Boston, as well as of those who envisioned a new day in American literature. Peabody contributed a few essays to this journal and the venue for conversation about it. From 1841 to 1843, after the publishing house of Weeks, Jordan, and Company went bankrupt, she undertook *The Dial*'s publication and handled its business affairs. She also published works by Boston's notables. One of the first titles to carry her imprint— Boston: E. P. Peabody, 13 West Street—was her friend William Ellery Channing's *Emancipation* (1840), which sold more than a thousand copies. Soon thereafter Peabody published some of her brother-in-law Hawthorne's historical tales as well as her own translation of a section of *The True Messiah* (1842) by Guillaume Oegger, a French Swedenborgian who had caught her and Emerson's attention.

Through these years Peabody's "atom of a shop" served an important purpose.[9] Against the backdrop of the well-stocked shelves at 13 West Street, disenchanted Unitarians voiced their increasingly strident criticism of the status quo and knew they would get an honest, if not always sympathetic, hearing from other customers. For a few years, united in their opposition to what they viewed as a desiccated and irrational theology, here and elsewhere the younger cohort became midwives to a whole new understanding of the spiritual life and its attendant social responsibility.

As central as Peabody's "Transcendental exchange" was to the emergent group, there were other projects, venues, and people that also served as its intellectual adhesive. Foremost among these were the quarterly journals that created a virtual community among readers throughout Massachusetts, the Northeast, and even into the Midwest and South. The prominence of *The Christian Examiner* is a case in point. From its founding in 1824 it served as the journal of record for American Unitarians, and under the editorship of James Walker it was particularly receptive to the essays and reviews of the younger Unitarians. When its leadership changed in 1839, however, it became increasingly hostile to the Transcendentalist wing of church reform. During this transition in the late 1830s and 1840s, several new periodicals offered space to those blackballed from what previously had served as their mouthpiece.

Even before the first Transcendentalist Club meeting in the fall of 1836, these individuals had considered establishing their own journal. Though now at some distance at his pastorate in Bangor, Frederic Hedge was particularly interested in such a prospect. Sarah Clarke wrote her brother in Louisville, Kentucky, where he edited another Unitarian journal, *The Western Messenger*, that the "supernal coterie" was talking of a *"Transcendental Journal."* Other names bandied about were *The Transcendentalist* and *The Spiritual Inquirer*, and named as potential editors were Hedge, Emerson,

Ephraim Peabody (recently returned from the Ohio Valley), Clarke, and Ripley.[10] Emerson even proposed to Thomas Carlyle that he immigrate to the United States to assume the periodical's editorship.[11]

In the fall of 1837 Brownson, whose commitment to social reform grew in the aftermath of the nation's severe economic depression, decided that there had been enough talk. The following January saw the first issue of his *Boston Quarterly Review*, devoted to extended discussion of religion, philosophy, and politics. As he put it in the first issue, he saw the journal's work as "effecting a reform in the church, giving us a purer and more rational theology; in philosophy seeking something profounder and more inspiring than the heartless sensualism of the last century; [and] in society demanding the elevation of labor with the loco-foco, or the freedom of the slave with the abolitionist."[12] For his first issue he recruited as contributors such friends as Parker, William Henry Channing, and the Democratic politician George Bancroft; and over the next four years he also enlisted Alcott, Ripley, Peabody, and Fuller, among others.

Brownson, however, usually contributed most of (and occasionally, all) the essays to each issue, for he used the periodical to forward his own radical views of social reform. Most memorable was his July 1840 essay, "The Laboring Classes," a scathing indictment of the condition of workingmen and -women, and a prophecy of class warfare if the situation was not remedied. With as many as a thousand subscribers before his increasing radicalism cut the number in half, the *Boston Quarterly Review* was the most widely circulated Transcendentalist organ.

Because this periodical revolved around Brownson's own social and political agenda, other Transcendentalists did not regard it as the group's vehicle. Thus, Alcott, Emerson, Fuller, and others continued to discuss another, more inclusive mouthpiece, open to serious literature as well as to essays and reviews in philosophy and religion. By October 1839, after Hedge, Parker, and Emerson were considered and dropped as candidates for its editorship, the logical choice became the brilliant and mercurial Fuller. "My vivacious friend Margaret Fuller," Emerson noted in a letter that month to Carlyle, "is to edit a journal, whose first number she promises for

1 July next." It was to be called *The Dial*, and Emerson promised Carlyle that it would give him "a better knowledge of our young people" than any he had.[13] Though Brownson, miffed that the group did not take up his offer to join his already established periodical, and Hedge, who had been drifting away from the group's theological radicalism, resisted Fuller's entreaties, most of the younger Unitarians showed interest in contributing. Fuller published the inaugural issue in July of 1840.

Emerson provided the introduction to this "Journal in a new spirit." "No one can converse much with different classes of society in New England," he continued, "without remarking the progress of a revolution" shared by those who had no "external organization, no badge, no creed, no name." Rather, they were "united only in a common love of truth, and love of its work." This new spirit, Emerson explained, affected different individuals in different ways. To some it implied reform of the state. To others, it urged "modifications in the various callings of men, and the customs of business." To yet others it opened new vistas for art and literature, and "philosophical insight." At its core, though, it was "in every form a protest against usage, and a search for principles." For such seekers the journal's editor would set *The Dial* "on the earth" to allow them to measure "no hours but those of sunshine," to apprise them of "what state of life and growth is now arrived and arriving."[14]

During its four years of publication *The Dial* comprised an unusual potpourri. Always at the mercy of what came over the transom, Fuller and, after she stepped down in 1842, Emerson assembled the journal's issues by continuing to solicit—indeed, sometimes strongarming—friends sympathetic to some aspect of the New Thought. The editors themselves supplied much copy, including such seminal pieces as Emerson's "The Transcendentalist" and Fuller's landmark of feminist thought, "The Great Lawsuit. Man versus Men, Woman versus Women." Other significant contributions came from Parker, from the poets Christopher Pearse Cranch and William Ellery Channing, and from Henry David Thoreau, who got his boost as a published writer from his appearance in *The Dial*. Surprising for the paucity of their contributions were Ripley, who became increasingly preoccupied with plans for a utopian community, and Hedge, who

continued to cultivate his connection to Unitarianism. Not unex-
pectedly, from Brownson, *The Dial* received nothing.[15]

The journal, however, never had as large a circulation as Brownson's *Boston Quarterly Review*. When Peabody, acting as business
manager for the journal, reviewed the accounts early in 1843, for
example, she realized that income was not meeting the costs of
printing, a deficit attributable to a decrease in subscriptions, then at
little more than two hundred. Outside reviews of *The Dial* continued to be mixed, but encouraged by the response to his call for assistance in the form of contributions and subscriptions, Emerson
continued to put out the journal until April of the following year.
Its demise was reported in the popular press. On May 25, for example, Horace Greeley's *New-York Weekly Tribune* reported that the
"most original and thoughtful periodical ever published in this
country" had suspended its issues.[16] Others thought differently.
Writing to his friend Convers Francis, even when the journal was
still solvent, someone as sympathetic as Parker had a more measured assessment, particularly when he considered the contents of
Brownson's journal. *The Dial*, he wrote, "bears about the same relation to the Boston Q[uarterly Review], that Antimachus does to
Hercules, Alcott to Brownson, or a band of men's maidens, daintily
arrayed in finery . . . to a body of stout men."[17] Over its four years,
however, *The Dial* recorded the Transcendentalists' remarkable
range of interests, even if any one issue did not contain enough to
make its varied constituencies think it worth the price of subscription. And, like the *Boston Quarterly Review*, for its short life *The
Dial* offered a rallying point for disgruntled Unitarians who in various ways sought to turn the world upside down.

Later in the 1840s the Transcendentalists issued other publications. In 1847, Parker, now installed in his own large, independent
church in Boston, began the *Massachusetts Quarterly Review*, which
he memorably described as "*The Dial* with a beard" and in which
he wished to center the various social reforms that preoccupied
him.[18] The journal lasted only three years, failing when its publisher went bankrupt. *The Harbinger* was more significant because
of its large subscription base. Ripley began this weekly in 1845 at
his utopian community, Brook Farm. Devoted to the ideas of
the French social reformer Charles Fourier, in 1847 this periodical

officially became the mouthpiece of the American Union of Associationists and was relocated to New York City. Although many of its pages were redactions of Fourier's complex reformist schemes, much space also was given to book reviews, poetry, the pioneering music criticism of Brook Farm member John Sullivan Dwight, and even the translation of one of George Sand's novels, *Consuelo*. Similarly committed to social reform (if not so doctrinaire in its socialism) but shorter-lived were William Henry Channing's *The Present* (1843–44) and *The Spirit of the Age* (1848–49). In different ways these journals served the interests of New England's disgruntled and idealistic Unitarians and offered forums where lively debate raged over a range of religious, philosophical, and social concerns.

Other social activities such as public lectures and less formal dialogues or "conversations" also bound together incipient reformers. The most famous of these were Emerson's lectures delivered in Boston in the mid- and late 1830s, and Fuller's Conversations, usually held at Peabody's West Street bookstore. By decade's end, Emerson, gaining more confidence each year, with sufficient success to select his own topics and, finally, entire lecture series, had established enough of a reputation as a public speaker to consider this his main occupation. The notoriety of his Divinity School address only increased his visibility, and soon his lectures became topics of wide public interest and debate.

At this point in his career Emerson was not so much imposing as magnetic. Six feet tall, long-necked, with sloping shoulders, he had dark brown hair, blue eyes, and a Roman nose which was his most prominent feature. At the podium he appeared oracular, revealing truth in finely chiseled sentences, each of which might be infinitely expanded but which he instead treated like the pieces of an artfully constructed mosaic that comprised his topic. One went to listen to Emerson, not to be entertained. If not all in attendance captured his full meaning, they still believed that they were in the presence of genius.

Between 1836 and 1838 he gave two series in Boston, a total of twenty-two lectures, on "The Philosophy of History." Late in 1838 he followed these successful offerings with another, on "Human Life," and the following season he discussed "The Present Age," an assessment of the state of social and cultural reform. Often repeated at least in part in other New England communities, these talks afforded Emerson a substantial income. Particularly in Boston, the interested public vied for tickets and for invitations to the convivial receptions that often closed the evening's entertainment. Late in his life Ripley recalled that these lectures constituted nothing less than "an era in the social and literary history of Boston, as well as in the life and culture of many individuals."[19]

Emerson was not the only Transcendentalist to venture onto the lyceum boards. His young protégé Thoreau, for example, sought to emulate him but never achieved anything like his friend's success. In 1841, Theodore Parker packed Boston's Masonic Hall and was the talk of the season. But neither Thoreau nor Parker made a living from such public appearances. Emerson, however, continued such work throughout his career, often delivering more than fifty and occasionally as many as eighty lectures a year, for a total of close to fifteen hundred over his lifetime. With such a record, he joined an elite cadre of professional speakers that included the Swiss naturalist and Harvard professor Louis Agassiz, the abolitionist and fugitive slave Frederick Douglass, and the world traveler and writer Bayard Taylor, to name only a few of the most prominent.

In the 1850s Emerson extended his itinerary, including frequent trips through New York, Ohio, and Pennsylvania, and traveling as far west as St. Louis, Des Moines, Minneapolis, and, eventually, California. Requiring him to make his own arrangements for train travel and hotel accommodations while local committees procured the halls and ensured good audiences, the work was not always easy or comfortable. In 1835, in a scene anticipating Melville's at the beginning of *Moby-Dick* when he describes the encounter of Ishmael with Queequeg at the Spouter Inn, Emerson recalled the stranger who had broken into his boardinghouse room after midnight, "claiming to share it." "But after his lamp had smoked the chamber full" and Emerson had "turned round to the wall in despair," the man "knelt down at his bedside & made in a low whisper a very long earnest prayer," which "entirely changed" the relation between the two men. "I fretted no more but respected & liked him," Emerson concluded.[20] He put up with such inconvenience because by all accounts people were eager to hear him even if they were unsympathetic to his beliefs, and he seemed genuinely to enjoy the circuit, despite its hardships. He gave much thought to his delivery, in terms of pacing as well as content; and particularly before the appearance of his first full-length book, *Essays* (1841), lectures were his primary mode of "publication." Not surprisingly, he drew this volume's contents from several of his lecture series.

At Ripley's Brook Farm, talks by community members as well as frequent and curious visitors were staple intellectual fare. Transcendentalists like Parker or Peabody offered some, but more often, particularly in the community's later years, such social reformers as Albert Brisbane and Parke Godwin, New Yorkers who represented the "associationist" community, often were heard. Another of Brook Farm's lecturers was Margaret Fuller, but she was less well known for such formal efforts than for her scintillating public Conversations, offered for several years beginning in the late fall of 1839. Conversation always had been of interest to the emergent Transcendentalist group, the most prominent examples being the periodic meetings of their "club" and Alcott's dialogues on the Gospels with his students.[21] But Fuller had something different in mind, a consciousness-raising seminar for educated women who sought to continue their education in paths trod most often by their fathers and brothers.

Fuller's father had given her the same intellectual encouragement that he provided his sons; and by the time, in her teens, that she began to circulate in Transcendentalist circles—her first and closest friend among the group was Clarke—she already was an intellectual prodigy. Her ambition and ego were large, and she quickly recognized how unusual she was. "I wish to arrive," she wrote to Clarke in 1833, "at that point where I can trust myself, and leave off saying, 'it seems to me,' and boldly feel, 'It *is* so to me.' "[22] In an attempt to engender that confidence in other women, she planned her "Conversations."

Fuller first broached her idea in August 1839 in a letter to Ripley's wife, Sophia. She envisioned a meeting each week in which attendees were repaid for the trouble of attendance by her supplying a venue where suggested topics would lead "to conversation of a better order than is usual at social meetings" where banter or gossip was the rule.[23] At Fuller's gatherings, ideas were the topics of conversation, and women gained confidence in the strength of their intellect. Her topics were ambitious: External Nature; The Life of Man; Literature; The Fine Arts; The History of a Nation, to Be Studied in Its Religious and Civil Institutions, Its Literature and Arts, and the Characters of Its Great Men.

On November 6, 1839, Fuller initiated these meetings with no fewer than twenty-five women who had subscribed to a thirteen-week series of dialogues, held on Thursday afternoons from noon until two. The group focused on Greek mythology, and Fuller's success therewith convinced her to offer a second series in the spring, on the fine arts, and another, on the same topic, in November, this time at the Ripleys' home. Peabody, who recorded abstracts of the meetings, recalled that Fuller's thoughts "were much illustrated, and all was said with the most captivating address and grace, and with beautiful modesty."[24] Not all were as entranced. Elizabeth Hoar admitted to Emerson that she liked the social dimension, adding that Caroline Sturgis, another emergent luminary among the group, became so bored at one meeting that she "quietly disposed herself to sleep on the arm of the sofa."[25]

Nineteen-year-old Caroline Healey never dozed off. Soon to emerge as one of the group's formidable intellects, at this point she was Peabody's protégée. At her urging, Healey attended Fuller's series on mythology in 1841 and remembered that she never had enjoyed anything as much. Surprised by Fuller's talking "more like a woman" than she had anticipated, as well as by her "want of grammar" when she indulged a monologue, Healey still found her more agreeable and modest than she had been led to believe. Fuller was "of an under size," the young woman recalled, and "delicately framed—with rather sharp features and light hair." Her head was small "but thrown almost wholly in front of the ears," and her forehead "of good height, her nose inclining to the Roman, and her mouth thin—and ungraceful." She also remembered Fuller's eyes as "small and gray" but with "a vivid flash," her laugh "almost child-like."[26] Others remembered her long, swanlike neck, her flowing robelike gowns, and an overall opulence that made her appear an oracle. From this point, Fuller replaced Peabody as Healey's role model, and after Fuller's premature death, in 1850, in good measure her torch for women's rights passed to this acolyte.

Positive reports of Fuller's Conversations caught the attention of men associated with the Transcendentalist group, who, always interested in more talk, enjoined her to include them. Flushed with her success, Fuller consented. The results were disappointing. Emerson recalled that on these occasions Fuller spoke well but "seemed encumbered, or interrupted, by the headiness or incapacity of the men, whom she had not had the advantage of training, and who fancied, no doubt, that, on such a question [as mythology], they, too, must assert and dogmatize."[27] Fuller did not repeat this experiment but continued her women-only classes until she moved to New York in 1844.

Fuller was not the only Transcendentalist to try her hand at this novel form of instruction. Bronson Alcott, an inveterate talker, had held such public conversations in the early 1830s and continued to do so as finances demanded. As late as 1849, recently moved back to Boston from Concord, he rented a room next to Peabody's bookstore and announced his own series—"a Course of Conversations on Man—his History, Resources, and Expectations." A ticket for all seven lectures cost five dollars, and admission to individual offerings were available at three dollars, the tickets purchasable at Peabody's bookstore next door.[28] He had enough success to offer these for a few years, and the dutiful Healey, now married to Charles Dall, attended the 1851 series, on seven contemporary New Englanders (Fuller and Emerson among the topics), sessions open to women as well as men.[29] Admittedly, these drew nothing near the attention that Fuller's efforts had a decade earlier. Both Alcott's and Fuller's discussion groups, however, served as important occasions for the emergent Transcendentalist cohort to debate timely issues.

Fuller peppered her Conversations with wide-ranging allusions to classical and foreign literature, believing such knowledge essential to a well-educated American. Ripley was of the same mind but attacked the problem differently. Beginning in 1838 he published a series of books, *Specimens of Foreign Standard Literature*, another project that bound Transcendentalists in a common purpose, in this case, of knowing the most important work of contemporary European thinkers and writers. Whom did he finally enlist as translators, and what precisely did he publish?

Ripley took the lead in the first two volumes, devoted to selections from French philosophers, *Philosophical Miscellanies, Translated from the Works of Cousin, Jouffroy, and B. Constant* (1838), which provided a solid introduction to Eclecticism. He, Brownson, and other dissident Unitarians had been much influenced by these thinkers, and in these volumes Ripley offered selections from them that he considered most significant. In his preface he also spoke to his larger ambitions for the series. He made clear that he had conceived his project with "special reference to the three leading divisions of Philosophy, History, and Theology," as well as to writings "of a popular character," including "finished specimens of elegant literature." Hitherto, the American public had been confined "too much to English books, and especially to the more recent publications of Great Britain."[30] Ripley wanted his countrymen to have a broader view; hence, his efforts on behalf of French and German writers.

Although not one of the fourteen-volume series was a runaway bestseller, the books had a respectable sale; several were reprinted, in the United States and in England, into the 1860s—James Freeman Clarke's edition of de Wette's autobiographical novel, *Theodore*, even later. As odd a potpourri as the series comprised, it typified emergent interests among not only younger and older Unitarians but among Transcendentalists themselves, split as they were into those who remained primarily interested in theological and social reform, and others who gravitated toward belles lettres. These divisions were mirrored in what, by the early 1840s, were two centers of Transcendentalist activity: one in Boston, in its churches and lecture halls; the other in suburban Concord, now easily accessible from the city by train, where Alcott, Fuller, Thoreau, Ellery Channing, and other writers (including Nathaniel Hawthorne) lived, and whose social and intellectual center was "Bush," as Emerson called his spacious home on the Lexington road. The movement that these reformers had spawned was entering a new phase, one of centrifugal expansion most evident in the proliferation of the cohort's activities along a wide spectrum of reform.

Through the 1840s, such deepening divisions among Transcendentalists became more visible. The distance between the leadership of *The Dial*—Emerson and Fuller—who valued individual spiritual growth and self-expression, and social reformers like Brownson, Ripley, and, increasingly, Parker, continued to grow. Brownson, whose mind seemed in constant evolution, had come to his radical social views by a circuitous route. The Working Men's Party and the Christian socialism of the Saint-Simonians continued to influence him. In the aftermath of the severe economic upheavals of the late 1830s and early 1840s, however, he grew more disappointed in many of his fellow Transcendentalists' seeming apathy toward the plight of the downtrodden, and found new inspiration from another group of French thinkers, particularly the social reformer Pierre Leroux.

The national economic downturn initiated by the Panic of 1837 pushed Brownson to more and more radical pronouncements. His fellow Unitarian Samuel K. Lothrop captured the shock of this upheaval of the nation's economy. "We were in the midst of peace, apparent prosperity, and progress," he observed, "when, after extensive individual failures, the astounding truth burst upon us like a thunderbolt . . . that we were a nation of bankrupts, and a bankrupt nation."[31] Brownson's analysis of the ensuing confrontation between capital and labor already was prominent in his sermon *Babylon Is Falling*, preached to his Boston congregation in 1837 and published shortly thereafter. In this powerful piece, Brownson located his contemporaries' greed and lack of charity in a cosmic drama in which divine retribution for their worship of Mammon was only a matter of time. But his lengthy piece on "The Laboring

Classes," ostensibly a review of Thomas Carlyle's recent *Chartism* (1840), in the July 1840 issue of his *Boston Quarterly Review* was of another magnitude. As powerful a piece of economic and social analysis as had appeared in the United States, it was followed by an even longer essay in the next issue of the periodical. In that piece, "The Laboring Classes—Responsibility to Party," he attempted not only to convince Americans to vote for the Democratic presidential candidate Martin Van Buren over the Whig William Henry Harrison, but also to force the Democratic Party to adopt Brownson's own radical program.[32]

In his first essay, devoting a few pages to Carlyle's pamphlet, Brownson got to the heart of the matter. In the Western world's industrial system, he claimed, workers were worse off than those in chattel slavery, for the wage laborer had "all the disadvantages of freedom and none of its blessings." As valuable property, slaves at least were properly housed, clothed, and fed, while laid-off factory operatives and other workingmen had nothing, a fact that the "hard times" of the depression brought home every day. Utterly reprehensible, then, were capitalists who perpetuated the wage system because it brought them great profit even as the true producers, the workers, suffered. "The man who employs them," Brownson wrote,

> is one of our city nabobs, reveling in luxury; or he is a member of our legislature, enacting laws to put money in his own pocket; or he is a member of Congress, contending for a high tariff to tax the poor for the benefit of the rich; or in these times he is shedding crocodile tears over the deplorable condition of the poor laborer, while he docks his wages twenty-five percent; building miniature log cabins, shouting Harrison and "hard cider."

Wage labor, Brownson concluded, "is a cunning device of the devil, for the benefit of tender consciences, who would retain all the advantages of the slave system, without the expense, trouble, and odium of being slaveholders."[33]

The great work of the age was to elevate the laborer "and to realize in our social arrangements and in the actual conditions of all men that equality of man and man" that God had established but which the nation's economic system had progressively destroyed. Brownson rejected outright what William Ellery Channing termed "self-culture." Individual self-improvement could not abolish inequality nor restore workers' rights, and it bore no relation to the whole-scale changes to the social structure that the times demanded. The entire economic system, not the reading habits of its managers, had to be changed.[34]

Christians thus had to return to the essential principles of their faith and "resuscitate the Christianity of Christ," for the "Christianity of the Church" had done its work and was powerless to do more good. Now believers had to take it into their own hands to bring the kingdom of God to earth,

> To bring down the high, and bring up the low; to break the fetters of the bound and set the captive free; to destroy all oppression, establish the reign of justice, which is the reign of equality, between man and man; to introduce new heavens and a new earth, wherein dwelleth righteousness, wherein all shall be as brothers, loving one another, and no one possessing what another lacketh.

No one, Brownson claimed, was a Christian who did not labor to reform society by molding it to God's will, a project in which the clergy no longer provided guidance. The established ministry dared not question the established social relations, he explained, lest they "incur the reproach of infidelity, and lose their standing, and their salaries."[35]

Brownson's essays ignited a firestorm of criticism and made his journal the talk of the election year, with some disgruntled Democrats even claiming that his radicalism had frightened people away from Van Buren and thus contributed to his loss. With the ensuing ascendancy of the Whig Party, the *Boston Quarterly Review* fell on hard times. In the autumn of 1842 Brownson ceased its publication, contributing essays instead to the *Democratic Review*, based in New York. By 1844, however, disappointed with that journal's editorial direction, Brownson started another periodical, *Brownson's Quarterly Review*, which ran for decades and which, even more than his previous journal, he frequently filled with his own writings. But it never attained the circulation of his earlier quarterly.

Prominent in Brownson's writings from this period was the work of Pierre Leroux, who moved him along to eventual conversion to the Roman Catholic Church. In 1841 Brownson discovered Leroux's *Réfutation de l'eclecticisme* and *De l'Humanité*, the works by which the former Saint-Simonian is best known. Brownson had long traveled toward French Christian socialism. He had read, for example, the works of the Catholic priest Félicité Robert de Lamennais and had even translated parts of his *Modern Slavery* for a Boston newspaper. Soon, other works by Lamennais appeared in English, and Brownson became familiar with *Words of a Believer* and *The People's Own Book*, in which Lamennais criticized the subjugation of the working classes and which had encouraged Brownson to offer his own thoughts on this subject.

But Leroux offered more. A few years later, his *Réfutation de l'eclecticisme* pushed Brownson away from Cousin and toward a deeper understanding of what Brownson came to call "life by communion," that is, acceptance of a traditional view of Christ's message and mission, and their commemoration in the sacrament of the Eucharist. Leroux, rejecting what he now viewed as Cousin's artificial bifurcation of philosophy and religion, championed a new "religion of humanity" based in "socialism," a term he coined in 1833. As he saw it, a culture of hyper-individualism—today we would call it a philosophical liberalism at the center of which was the protection of personal and property rights—marked the new industrial age and destroyed the possibility of social harmony. Leroux urged contemporaries to resist temptations to set themselves apart in artificially constructed social systems based on income or other artificial status markers, and instead to celebrate their connections to all human beings.

Leroux's critique of bourgeois individualism was central to Brownson's eventual rejection of Transcendentalism and his conversion to Roman Catholicism. Others in his cohort voiced similar, if more muted, criticism of the direction in which some of their friends seemed headed. Peabody, for example, was distraught at and finally repelled by Fuller's "egoism," and William Henry Channing joined Brownson as a champion of Leroux's celebration of humanity in his own socialist writings of the 1840s. But no one took the Frenchman's ideas as seriously as Brownson, who, in his devotion to the working classes, tumbled headlong into the faith that over two millennia had most emphasized communion and brotherhood. He converted to Roman Catholicism in 1844, effectually ending his career in, but not his engagement with, Transcendentalism.

Brownson's writings and example, if not his final journey to Rome, strongly affected Ripley, his initial sponsor in Boston and close friend. Since 1826 Ripley had ministered to a church near one of the wharves in southeast Boston, a location then occupied by people of the "middling class" but that soon became primarily a working-class enclave.[36] Ripley came from the clerical purple and had married into the wealthy Dana family of Cambridge. He could not but have remarked the difference between his Cambridge professors and his in-laws and those who sat in the pews of his unexceptional small stone church, for there was a great social distance between Harvard College and Griffin Wharf.

By outward markers, Ripley should have been content in his ministry. He attended to its tasks without complaint and, while not known as a charismatic speaker, enjoyed his church's confidence and approval. Moreover, residence in the city—the Ripleys lived near the church, on Chauncey Street, within walking distance of the Athenaeum and other cultural sites—allowed him contact with William Ellery Channing, Emerson, Fuller, and other intellectuals on the Boston–Concord axis, as well as the frequent opportunity to participate in the debates within the Unitarian ranks.

During his tenure, however, and particularly after the depression of 1837, Ripley became increasingly concerned about the impoverished laboring population proliferating around his church, as well as with his parishioners' apathy toward their neighbors' plight. In a powerful sermon on *The Temptations of the Times*, he warned that the great danger to the country lay in "the inordinate pursuit, the extravagant worship of wealth," based in "temptations to an excess of selfishness." Everything, he insisted, "tends to fix our regards upon ourselves and to withdraw them from others," while "a fancied independence is counted as the highest good." Convinced that he had to take action to stem this profligacy and reinstate a "deeper sense of our dependence on one another," Ripley wondered whether, given his inability to spark his flock to concerted action, he should seek another church or perhaps even leave the ministry altogether, the better to fulfill his mission to the needy.[37]

By 1840 his personal crisis had come to a head. In May he wrote his church indicating his wish to resign if they consented. For one thing, he explained, the church never had grown to its capacity of three hundred seats; and as the decade passed and the neighborhood changed its character, some parishioners had moved away, contributing to a serious financial shortfall. Further, Ripley was troubled by both the increasing conservatism that he detected in the Unitarian ranks, particularly after his debate with the truculent Norton, and by the smugness of his own congregation, who wished him to play the honorific role of "priest" but would not walk with him in the city's streets to demand social justice. Following the ordination of his young protégé John Sullivan Dwight in Northampton, Massachusetts, that May, Ripley returned to the city convinced that the ministry, so entangled financially to its constituency, would never take the lead in social reform. Still unclear about whether he should entirely abandon the ministry or seek appointment outside the Unitarian fold, in early October he penned a lengthy letter to his congregation indicating his intention to resign, an action the church long had feared.

His missive was poignant. He deprecated his own labors. Even if some of his preaching had been effective, he observed, too often there were topics of concern to him that failed to attract their attention. As a result, over time he had begun to avoid such subjects, lest he was seen to depart "from the usual sphere of the pulpit." Over time, such evasion embarrassed and depressed him, for Ripley believed that unless a minister could speak out "on all subjects which are uppermost in his mind, with no fear of incurring the charge of heresy, or compromising the interests of the congregation, he can never do justice to himself."[38]

Moreover, Ripley explained, over the decade he had been with them, things had indeed changed, particularly so in the Unitarian faith. Theological questions had given way to "a new order of ideas" that needed acting upon. He had always believed, he explained, that the essential principles of liberal Christianity made religion "to consist, not in any speculative doctrines, but in a divine life," and "established the kingdom of God, not in the dead past, but in the living present."[39] A portion of the liberal clergy now wished to act from these principles, but in doing so, they risked alienating some of their supporters and even losing their positions. Ripley had arrived at this point.

Admitting his increasing disillusionment with one segment of the Transcendentalist cohort, Ripley also made it clear that invidious social arrangements could not be addressed merely through calls for personal regeneration of the sort Emerson counseled in his writings and lectures. "The attention of some good men," Ripley wrote, "is directed chiefly to individual evils." These reformers wished to "improve private character, without attacking social principles which obstruct all improvement." Others (himself included) directed their attention to "the evils of society" and believed that "private character suffers from public sins," making it imperative to work to advance society past this point.

As he explained how he had come to his own position on these matters, Ripley provided as good a definition of Transcendentalism as any in the movement ever wrote.

There is a class of persons who desire a reform in the prevailing philosophy of the day. These are called Transcendentalists,—because they believe in an order of truths which transcends the sphere of the external senses. Their leading idea is the supremacy of mind over matter. Hence they maintain that the truth of religion does not depend on tradition, or on historical facts, but has an unerring witness in the soul. There is a light, they believe, which enlighteneth every man that cometh into the world; there is a faculty in all, the most degraded, the most ignorant, the most obscure, to perceive spiritual truth, when distinctly repented; and the ultimate appeal, on all moral questions, is not to a jury of scholars, a hierarchy of divines, or the prescriptions of a creed, but to the common sense of the race.

"These views I have always adopted," he explained, and they were "at the foundation" of all his preaching and his success as a minister. Taught "in every Protestant university in Europe" and "the common creed of the most enlightened nations," Transcendentalism, he was ashamed to say, was still miserably misunderstood and held suspect in the United States. But in it he had found his calling to preach the Gospel to the poor and give them what succor he could.[40]

At the first of the year Ripley wrote the parish another letter in which he requested dismissal in three months' time. They consented, and on March 28, 1841, Ripley delivered a moving farewell sermon, notable for its lack of rancor. It simply boiled down to this: he could dissimulate no longer. He confessed that he was "a peace man, a temperance man, an abolitionist, a transcendentalist, [and] a friend of radical reform" in social institutions, but his flock was not following him down these paths as far as he wished. He and they parted in peace, he told them, over "an honest difference of opinions."[41] Ripley's wife, Sophia, reported that there were tears flowing all around them when he ended the sermon.[42]

Ripley had no immediate prospects, but he did not lack for plans. Emerson suggested that he, Ripley, Alcott, and others combine to form a sort of Transcendentalist university in some rural town, where students would pay tuition to be taught in lectures and conversations. Nothing came of the idea. Among other reasons, it did not satisfy Ripley's pressing urge to work among the disadvantaged. More appealing was the notion of an entire community devoted to the kind of social change that Ripley envisioned. Such communities could serve as models for the society of the future, their success at all levels—economic, intellectual, social—worthy of emulation by the nation, and the world at large. But in October 1840, when Ripley broached the idea for such a community at one of the Transcendental Club's meetings, he met only a lukewarm reception. Ripley, however, was on fire. Within a month of delivering his farewell sermon, he was ready to move his family to Brook Farm in West Roxbury, only a few miles from Theodore Parker's church, to realize a new social order.

Brownson's and Ripley's vocal and visible commitment to social reform drew sustained criticism from conservative segments of the public and caused friction among the Transcendentalists. So too did some of the members' increasingly radical religious views. The most pressing problem originated with Theodore Parker, who on May 19, 1841, at the ordination of Charles Shackford in the Hawes Place Church in South Boston, delivered *A Discourse on the Transient and Permanent in Christianity*. Interestingly, he had preached the same sermon to his West Roxbury congregation only two weeks before Shackford's ordination, and it had not caused a ripple. But as he contemplated preaching it in a much more public setting— this was his first ordination sermon—he grew worried, perhaps anticipating the criticism that would follow a more public airing of his views.[43] Subsequent events proved him correct, for after he spoke at Shackford's ordination, Boston's Unitarians were in an uproar.

Parker's central point in this sermon was that "transient things form a great part of what is commonly taught as religion." For centuries, he noted, men had argued over theology and ecclesiology, and in so doing had forgotten the Christianity of Christ. Their theology stood between them and God. Indeed, he continued, "many tenets that pass current in our theology seem to be the refuse of idol temples, the off-scourings of Jewish and heathen cities, rather than the sand of virgin gold which the stream of Christianity has worn off the rock of ages."[44]

No doubt with his work on de Wette in mind, Parker also contended that current notions respecting the infallible inspiration of the Bible had no foundation in scripture. Similarly, many religions made Christianity stand on the personal example of Christ rather than on his truths, even though it was "hard to see why the great truths of Christianity rest on the personal authority of Jesus, more than the axioms of geometry rest on the personal authority of Euclid or Archimedes." In Parker's view, even if one proved that Jesus had never lived, Christianity still would exist because of its inherent truth. Christ was simply "the son of man, as we are; and the son of God, like ourselves." In him "heaven has come down to earth, or rather, earth has become heaven."[45] Christ's beauty and the mystery of Christ thus lay in the message that he was all that we can be, when we live as he did.

After the ceremony the guests adjourned for libations and dinner at Tufts' Tavern, a mile away, and all seemed well. But some attendees did not let the sermon pass unnoticed. Three orthodox Trinitarian clergymen—J. H. Fairchild of the Phillips (Trinitarian Congregational) Church, Thomas Driver of the South Baptist Church, and Z.B.C. Dunham of the Fifth Methodist Church, whom Shackford had invited as pastors of neighboring churches— recognized an opportunity to split the Unitarian ranks. Thus, they made the first parry in a duel that resulted in the sermon's notoriety. Parker's apparent unwillingness to publish his sermon led them to the bold step of writing an open letter to the *New England Puritan*, an orthodox newspaper, in which they summarized his message and challenged Parker's fellow Unitarians to speak out on his performance.

The orthodox clergymen's letter appeared in the May 28 issue of the paper; and from what they heard, Fairchild, Driver, and Dunham argued that Parker did indeed deserve opprobrium for his ideas. He had advanced sentiments so contrary to commonly accepted ideas of Christianity, they wrote, that they felt themselves "constrained by a solemn sense of duty" to inquire whether the Unitarian clergy of Boston and its vicinity sympathized with Parker.[46] Not satisfied with the accuracy of their redaction, Parker decided to publish his address, with emendations to clarify certain points to which they objected.

His enemies then jumped on the fact that his revision did not represent the sermon as he had given it. This occasioned a war of words in the Boston papers similar to that which had followed Emerson's sermon at the Divinity School in 1838. Parker thereupon issued a second edition of the *Transient and Permanent*, with an appendix that contained the "various readings" collected from a collation of the initial printed discourse with his manuscript as he delivered it in South Boston. His frustration over the controversy was evident in a letter of July 12 to Charles Miller, in which he claimed that never in his life had he written a sermon "with a deeper conviction of truth, or the good it would do in the world." Further, because the opinions in his discourse were nothing new to him, not the "thoughts of a young man but the sober deliberate convictions" of his maturity, he believed that "the end will be good."[47] This, however, did not prove to be the case.

Controversy continued through the year. In the late summer the printers Saxton and Pierce, noting the public's continuing interest in the matter, republished generous excerpts from the chief documents in the controversy as *The South-Boston Unitarian Ordination*.[48] Parker did not respond to this pamphlet, but the negative publicity had a practical effect. Many conservative Unitarian clergy were so upset with his sermon that they worried about exchanging pulpits with him, long a common courtesy in Unitarian ranks. The denomination was beginning to split at its seams.

Parker's supporters implored him to explain himself at more length, an idea he at first resisted. In late June, however, he accepted an invitation from several prominent Boston Unitarians to deliver a course of public lectures in the city, and he decided to formulate and publicize his beliefs in more extended fashion. His patrons rented Boston's old Masonic Temple on Tremont Street, the city's premier lecture hall, whose 750 seats were filled for Parker's series, subsequently published as *A Discourse of Matters Pertaining to Religion* (1842).

He had been steeling himself for such an airing of his theology. As early as 1840, he had noted in his journal that "for my own part, I intend, in the coming year, to let out all the force of Transcendentalism that is in me."[49] In the Masonic Temple he did just that, delivering five two-hour lectures in which he sought nothing less than "to recall men from the transient Form to the eternal Substance" and show them that God was alive to and in every person.[50] This was a heady suggestion, and it was no wonder that both Trinitarians and conservative Unitarians were distraught at where Parker's scholarship had led. The Reverend Samuel Osgood, for example, who sympathized with many of the Transcendentalists' views, realized into what a difficult position Parker had placed his peers. "As the Strauss of our American theology," he said in the *Monthly Miscellany*, an allusion to the German theologian whose *Life of Jesus* had caused such a stir, Parker stood "almost alone" among Unitarians. Indeed, to date, Osgood noted, no one had come to Parker's defense, so that "he is not now in any way identified with the Unitarian body."[51]

Osgood's assessment was prescient, for from this point Parker's days as a Unitarian were numbered. Loyal members of that faith still insisted that Christianity was based in a special dispensation more significant than that vouchsafed any other religion. After meeting with Parker to discuss his views, members of the Boston Association of Ministers voted to end their fellowship with him, lest their congregations think they approved of or shared his views. Parker was reduced to tears.

At this point a group of prominent religious liberals, influenced by Bostonians who supported Parker's right to preach, whatever his ideas, formed a new, independent church and convinced him to accept their call to become its minister. By 1845 he was preaching to the Twenty-eighth Congregational Society in Boston's large music auditorium, the Melodeon, which held a thousand people and on many Sundays was filled to capacity. His became one of Boston's largest churches, seven years later moving to an even more impressive edifice, the Music Hall, and provided a prominent venue from which he could speak his mind. From then on, like his friends Brownson and Ripley, Parker more and more turned his attention to pressing social issues, even as others among his cohort, notably Emerson, Alcott, and Fuller, continued to press an agenda of individual self-culture.

Writing to Frederic Henry Hedge early in 1843, Parker's friend Convers Francis summed up the complex situation among the Unitarians and provided a useful typology of its factions. "The condition of things with us in the religious world," he opined, "is anything but pleasant."

> The cauldron is kept boiling, & all sorts of materials are thrown into it. Parker lectures with great éclat to audiences of 2000 or more in Boston & Salem,—& to very large houses in other places. Among the Unitarians proper there is an old regular body, represented by some of the Boston ministers, & the Evangelical or Puritan body headed by [James Freeman] Clarke & perhaps Brownson, who aim to intensify Unitarianism by giving it more zeal & more primitive godliness. Then the Transcendentalists have another vocation.[52]

Francis's description of the factions was accurate. The next decade's challenge was whether the "Evangelical" party still had enough in common with the "Transcendentalist" wing for them to continue to work together to reform Unitarianism and, implicitly, the nation as a whole.

6

HEAVEN ON EARTH

n August 10, 1840, the "Friends of Christian Union" met in Groton, Massachusetts, a small town thirty miles northwest of Boston. In attendance were George Ripley, nearing his decision to resign his Purchase Street ministry, Bronson Alcott, and Christopher Cranch, a young Unitarian minister recently returned from the Ohio Valley. Although it was principally disciples of the millennialist William Miller who had organized the meeting, representatives of many other reformist groups attended. Ripley recalled that attendees represented "every sect, every Christian connexion [*sic*], with every variety of faith, opinion, and character," all having "a deep dissatisfaction with the religion of the age." Among the most distinctive participants were a few score "Come-outers" from Cape Cod, laypeople who had left their churches to attend to the spirit within and practice a more pure Christianity. Their rejection of doctrinal creeds and of the authority of the ordained clergy resonated with the Boston visitors so much that subsequently they adjourned with several of the Cape Codders to a nearby tavern where, as Parker put it, "we had a little convention of our own."[1]

Many of the attendees at Groton, including Parker, Ripley, and Alcott, were thrown together again in September at the second annual meeting of the New-England Non-Resistance Society at Joshua Himes's Chardon Street Chapel in Boston, a meeting called by Christian pacifists with connections to the radical abolitionist

William Lloyd Garrison. This meeting, too, was a success, so much so that after it ended, the trio met with its organizers to plan a gathering of the Friends of Universal Reform at Chardon Street that November.[2]

Persuaded to attend, Emerson, in an article he later contributed to *The Dial*, left the best record of its proceedings.

> If the assembly was disorderly, it was picturesque. Madmen, madwomen, men with beards, Dunkers, Muggletonians, Come-outers, Groaners, Agrarians, Seventh-day-Baptists, Quakers, Abolitionists, Calvinists, Unitarians, and Philosophers,—all came successively to the top, and seized their moment, if not their hour, wherein to chide, or pray, or preach, or protest.[3]

"If there was not parliamentary order," he concluded, "there was life, and the assurance of that constitutional love for religion and religious liberty" that always had characterized the United States.[4]

Reported and debated in Boston's press, the "Chardon Street Convention" gathered a cross section of New England's most committed reformers and proved a signal moment in the development of New England's intellectual life. Although the assembly took no formal action on the questions they discussed, it brought together "many remarkable persons, face to face, and gave occasion to memorable interviews and conversations, in the hall, in the lobbies, or around the doors."

Of the memorable interviews that these conventions expedited, none was more significant than that between George Ripley and Adin Ballou. Leader of a group of "Practical Christians," Ballou was contemplating the creation of a model community, plans that by 1841 eventuated in his Hopedale experiment.[5] By now also committed to the idea of working for reform in a communal setting rather than through the church, Ripley was fascinated by Ballou's project and eager to hear more.[6] He concluded that Ballou's community was too restrictive, its members required to assent to a credo based exclusively in Christianity. But the discussion fired Ripley's enthusiasm, and he immediately went forward with plans to start his own community, open to individuals of different theological views and based in egalitarian principles.

Ripley spent the late fall and winter months of 1840–41 trying to drum up support among his friends. In particular, he sought the commitment of those closely associated with *The Dial*—Emerson, Fuller, and Alcott—in hopes that their endorsement would generate widespread interest in his plan. These individuals, however, proved recalcitrant. Alcott had his own ideas for such an experimental community, "a simpler New Eden," he termed it, where, after its members had surrendered their desires for selfish gratification, they would live in harmony with the universal spirit. He doubted that any reform could occur by merely changing social arrangements.[7] Fuller, too, resisted Ripley's entreaties. She supported his plans but, like Alcott, wondered if they would bear lasting fruit. "I do not know what their scheme will ripen to," she wrote a friend, for "it is only a little better way than others." "I doubt," she concluded, "they will get free from all they deprecate in society."[8]

Ripley's siege of Emerson, who was now more widely known because of his career as a lecturer, went on for more than a month. Failing to convince him in person, on November 9 Ripley sent his cousin a long letter in which for the first time he detailed his goals for the community. He sought "to insure a more natural union between intellectual and manual labor than now exists." Toward that end, at his new community he would

> Combine the thinker and the worker, as far as possible, in the same individual; to guarantee the highest mental freedom, by providing all with labor, adapted to their tastes and talents, and securing to them the fruits of their industry; to do away the necessity of menial services, by opening the benefits of education and the profits of labor to all; and thus to prepare a society of liberal, intelligent, and cultivated persons, whose relations with each other would permit a more simple and wholesome life, than can be led amidst the pressure of our competitive institutions.[9]

He had a site in mind, in West Roxbury, where a large dairy farm would form the basis of their labor and where they also would operate a school for the children of members, and of others by tuition. Such a community would require about a $30,000 investment, raised primarily by selling shares in a joint-stock enterprise.

How did Ripley come to this particular formulation of the community's goals? One model lay in the various religious communities that dotted the country's landscape, particularly those of the Shakers, whose village at Harvard, Massachusetts, was only twenty-five miles from Boston. But with its complex theology, segregation of the sexes, and enforced celibacy, the United Society of Believers in Christ's Second Appearing did not offer much to a lapsed Unitarian, save a glimpse of the harmony possible in a community removed from entanglement in a corrupt world. More immediately influential may have been the German community of Separatists at Zoar in Ohio, which Ripley and his wife had visited in 1838 when he was on a preaching tour through the Ohio River Valley. Sophia was struck by the group's social harmony and their enjoyment of various kinds of labor, which never seemed tedious. She was enough impressed by what she saw to pen an article on Zoar for *The Dial*.[10]

One other influence on Ripley's thought arose from New Englanders' continuing interest in and engagement with European social thought. Late in 1839 James Freeman Clarke's mother, traveling in the Ohio Valley, met a young reformer named Albert Brisbane, recently returned from France, flush with ideas implanted by socialists whom he had met, particularly François Marie Charles Fourier (1772–1837), and now popularizing them in the West. On her return to Boston she shared her acquaintance's ideas about "association" with her son's friend Ripley.[11] Brisbane soon became better known. In the summer of 1840, shortly after Ripley's initial talk with Ballou in Groton, Ripley's friend Theodore Parker read Brisbane's *Social Destiny of Man; or, Association and Reorganization of Industry*, recording in his journal that he approved of the "many excellent things" in the book.[12] It is hard to imagine Parker not discussing Brisbane's ideas or sharing the volume with Ripley, who was living that summer at Charles Ellis's dairy farm in West Roxbury, just a few miles from Parker's home.

The son of a wealthy landowner in upstate New York, Brisbane emerged as the foremost American exponent of Fourier, who, beginning early in the nineteenth century, had published an eccentric yet powerful critique of Western civilization and a detailed cosmogony of what he termed "universal harmony."[13] While abroad, Brisbane had sought out the social thinker, eventually paying him for personal tutorials: he received two hour-long sessions each week, at five francs per hour, for a month and a half. His *Social Destiny of Man* was the first of several signal publications in English spawned from the master's works.

Analyzing what he regarded as man's flawed economic and social system, Fourier detailed a utopian alternative centered on model communities that he termed "phalansteries." Emphasizing development of the "harmonian man" whose desires are gratified rather than repressed, and of "attractive industry," work that satisfies one's deepest urges, Fourier promised to free Western society from wage labor and the personal alienation attendant on it. Brisbane appended his own commentaries to his translations of sections of Fourier's voluminous works, domesticating the system for American consumption by downplaying Fourier's radical critique of monogamous marriage and his wildly speculative anti-Christian metaphysics. Brisbane also lectured widely on his mentor's ideas.

With such ideas spinning through his mind, Ripley anxiously awaited Emerson's reply to his overture. Finally, on December 15, a month after Emerson had received Ripley's long missive, he wrote his friend that he could not join in the admittedly "noble & humane" enterprise. The ground of his decision, he told Ripley, was "almost purely personal." He was content with his home, the neighborhood, and the institutions in Concord around which he had built his career. More tellingly, he explained that it seemed to him "a circuitous & operose [that is, arduous] way of relieving myself of any irksome circumstances, to put on your community the task of my emancipation which I ought to take on myself."[14] Personal reform, he implied, was best accomplished in the privacy of one's closet.

Emerson had spared Ripley what he thought and said privately of his friend's plans. Earlier in the negotiation, he had admitted that he "wished to be thawed, to be made nobly mad by the kindlings [*sic*] before my eyes for a new dawn of human piety," but he simply was not "inflamed" by Ripley's plan. It was too much "arithmetic & comfort." Nor did he wish to have what amounted to, given the fairly comfortable financial circumstances of those whom Ripley had already interested in the project, "a room in the Astor House hired for the transcendentalists," a reference to one of New York City's most fashionable residences. Emerson offered his own conception of the plight of labor and his complicity in it, a passage that reveals a certain moral obliquity. "The principal particulars in which I wish to mend my domestic life," he wrote, "are in acquiring habits of regular manual labor, and in ameliorating or abolishing in my house the condition of hired menial service."[15] Evidently, Emerson neither knew much about the social problems in the neighborhood around Ripley's Boston church nor had talked with those to whom Brownson regularly ministered. To chop wood and to allow household domestics to dine with the family, as Emerson now did, would not cure Boston's social ills.

Even though no prominent Transcendentalist signed on with Ripley, by the spring of 1841 the community was a reality. Ripley had decided on the Ellis farm in West Roxbury, with which he was familiar and which was currently for sale. It comprised 170 acres, one mile northwest of West Roxbury and eight miles west of Boston.[16] The Charles River bordered it on the west, and at its northern perimeter was Pulpit Rock, a large boulder on which, in the seventeenth century, John Eliot, the "Apostle to the Indians," had preached to the native tribes. The property consisted of pasture and meadowland, some hardwood lots, and, near Eliot's Pulpit, a pine forest. The land had been used primarily for dairy farming, its surplus hay sold locally and to the Boston market. Access was from the Dedham Road, and to the left ran Palmer Brook, after which the farm later was named—Brook Farm, America's first secular utopian community. To the right of the entry was a two-and-a-half-story white clapboard building with a long ell attached to its rear, a sizable structure subsequently called the Hive. Shaded by an ancient elm tree, for years it remained the center of the community's activities. The property also included a large barn with stalls for twoscore cattle or horses. By all accounts in an idyllic setting, the farm was a place of great natural beauty, combining proximity to the city with the beauty and quiet of the countryside.[17]

By the early spring of 1841, Ripley and a handful of others were living and working at the farm, which they still rented. Their experiment, though not yet formally announced in any published prospectus, drew attention in the Boston area, and many visitors came either for the day or, as space permitted, boarded overnight, for which privilege they paid a nominal fee. Such prominent Transcendentalists as Elizabeth Peabody, Fuller, and Parker were among the first guests.

Ripley left it to Peabody to spread word of the community and its goals, which she did in a number of publications in 1841 and 1842. She based her reports on the sixteen "Articles of Agreement" to which the group attested.[18] "In order more effectually to promote the great purposes of human culture," Ripley wrote in the preamble,

> To establish the external relations of life on a basis of wisdom and purity; to apply the principles of justice & love to our social organization in accordance with the laws of Divine providence; to substitute a system of brotherly cooperation for one of selfish competition; to secure to our children & those who may be entrusted to our care the benefits of the highest physical, intellectual, & moral education which in the present state of human knowledge the resources at our command will permit; to institute an attractive, efficient & productive system of industry; to prevent the exercise of worldly anxiety by the competent supply of our necessary wants; to diminish the desire of excessive accumulation, by making the acquisition of individual property subservient to upright & disinterested uses; to guarantee to each other forever the means of physical support & spiritual progress; & thus to impart a greater freedom, simplicity, truthfulness, refinement & moral dignity to our mode of life;—We the undersigned do unite in a voluntary Association, & adopt & ordain the following Articles of agreement & Association . . .[19]

Frederic Henry Hedge (1805–90). Studied in Germany as a teenager. Instrumental in introducing German thought to the United States. For his proficiency, he was nicknamed "Germanicus" Hedge.

George Ripley (1802–80). Early advocate of German thought, including Friedrich Schleiermacher's theology. Issued *Specimens of Foreign Standard Literature* in fourteen volumes. Later resigned his ministry to found Brook Farm, a socialist community, where he advocated Charles Fourier's utopian ideas.

Orestes Brownson (1803–76). Minister-at-large to Boston's poor and a champion of the laboring classes. Founded the *Boston Quarterly Review*. Later broke with the Transcendentalists and converted to Roman Catholicism.

Harvard College (ca. 1836). Many of the men associated with Transcendentalism graduated from Harvard and entered the Unitarian ministry after attending its divinity school.

Ralph Waldo Emerson (1803–82). Best-known Transcendentalist. Championed an ethic of strong self-reliance. Renowned as a lecturer and essayist, as well as a mentor to younger men and women who gravitated to his ideas.

Bronson Alcott (1799–1888). Applied Transcendentalist ideas to childhood education at his Temple School. Founded Fruitlands, an experimental community. In the 1880s started the Concord School of Philosophy for the discussion of Idealist philosophy.

Temple School (1836). Engraving of the interior of Alcott's experimental school. Illustration in Elizabeth Peabody's *Record of a School*, an account of his pedagogy.

Elizabeth Palmer Peabody (1804–94). One of the most prominent Transcendentalist women. Alcott's assistant in his Temple School. Owner of a foreign language bookstore and lending library that became one of Boston's intellectual centers.

Henry James, Sr. (1811–82). Early advocate of Swedenborgian ideas and of Charles Fourier's utopian socialism. Father of William and Henry James.

Theodore Parker (1810–60). Prodigious scholar and linguist. Minister to one of Boston's largest liberal churches. Deeply committed to abolition and one of the "Secret Six" financial backers of John Brown's raid on Harpers Ferry.

Boston's Music Hall (ca. 1840). Home to Theodore Parker's Twenty-eighth Congregational Society, to which he delivered many of his powerful sermons against the Mexican War and slavery.

Margaret Fuller (1810–50). Most prominent Transcendentalist woman. Early advocate of women's rights. Held "Conversations" for Boston's women intellectuals. Editor of *The Dial*, the Transcendentalist journal. Reported on the European revolutions of 1848 for Horace Greeley's *New-York Tribune*.

Charles Fourier (1772–1837). French utopian socialist whose radical ideas on social organization greatly influenced George Ripley and others involved with the Brook Farm community.

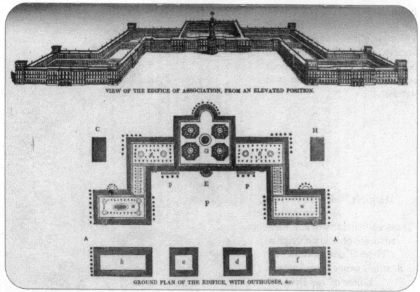

VIEW OF THE EDIFICE OF ASSOCIATION, FROM AN ELEVATED POSITION.

GROUND PLAN OF THE EDIFICE, WITH OUTHOUSES, &c.

Phalanstery (1840). Engraving of the sort of building that formed the cornerstone of Charles Fourier's utopian reform. Constructed for sixteen hundred men and women—a "phalanx"—who practiced radical economic and sexual reform. Illustration from Albert Brisbane's *Social Destiny of Man*.

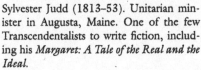

Sylvester Judd (1813–53). Unitarian minister in Augusta, Maine. One of the few Transcendentalists to write fiction, including his *Margaret: A Tale of the Real and the Ideal.*

Henry David Thoreau (1817–62). Friend and erstwhile disciple of Emerson, and contributor to *The Dial.* Sharp critic of the Mexican War and slavery. Author of *Walden,* the best-known work by a Transcendentalist.

John Weiss (1818–79). Important second-generation Transcendentalist minister. Influenced by Fichte's philosophy. Wrote *Life and Correspondence of Theodore Parker* (1864).

David Atwood Wasson (1823–87). Second-generation Transcendentalist active in the Free Religion movement and the Radical Club, organizations founded by liberal clergy disaffected from the American Unitarian Association.

Samuel Johnson (1822–82). Second-generation Transcendentalist and pioneer of the study of world religions. Wrote volumes on the religious and cultural life of India, China, and Persia.

Ripley's idealistic formulation of the community's goals called into question the moral as well as economic benefits of market capitalism and promised a more egalitarian society than the United States had yet realized. His fellow Brook Farm colleague, John Sullivan Dwight, put it this way. "Striving to love and draw near to" his neighbor, under present economic conditions man found himself in competition with him, so that one succeeds "by the other's failing." "All these individual wills," he lamented, "born for harmony" but seeking it "by private paths that lead to private ends," with private property now "the outward type and representative of individualism."[20]

In her "Plan of the West Roxbury Community" in the January 1842 issue of *The Dial*, Peabody explained the new community's organization. Brook Farm was a joint-stock company, with "subscribers"—that is, shareholders—guaranteed 5 percent annual interest on their investment and shares set at five hundred dollars each—no small amount. All members paid for room, board, fuel, lighting, and washing through directly proportionate labor, "one year's board for one year's labor; one-half year's board for one-half year's labor, and if no labor is done the whole board shall be charged," four dollars per week. Men and women were paid at the same rate, and members chose what work most appealed to them. No particular job, no matter how menial, was coerced, because all labor was "sacred, when done for a common interest." No one worked more than a ten-hour day, an enlightened idea for the time, or a six-day week. Members were guaranteed "medical attendance, nursing, education in all departments, amusements," and everyone over the age of seventy or under ten, and anyone who was sick, had free board, unless they were shareholders whose 5 percent annual interest could support them. Students of nonmembers who attended the farm's school paid on a sliding scale according to gender and age: boys over twelve paid four dollars a week for board and tuition, but girls paid five dollars (this later was equalized), and both boys and girls under this age paid three and a half dollars per week.

The community, Peabody explained, "aims to be rich, not in the metallic representative of wealth, but in the wealth itself, which money should represent," that is, "LEISURE TO LIVE IN ALL

THE FACULTIES OF THE SOUL." Thus, in addition to supplying members with food, the farm provided them with "the elegances desirable for bodily and for spiritual health"—"books, apparatus, collections for science, works of art, means of beautiful amusement"—for these should be common to all. Concomitantly, because these alone "refine the passion for individual accumulation," where all shared in the cultural resources, the "sordid passion" of selfishness would disappear. And what would pay for all this? Brook Farm promised such amenities because it would "traffic with the world at large" by marketing its surplus agricultural goods; commerce was on the increase as farms in towns surrounding Boston became essential to the metropolitan area's food supply.

By the fall of 1841 ten subscribers, the aspiring writer Nathaniel Hawthorne among them, had pledged to purchase twenty-four shares of stock in the Brook Farm Institute of Agriculture and Education. Even though all the money was not in hand, Ripley contracted to purchase the Ellis farm and an additional parcel, including another house, barn, and outbuildings, for $10,500. By March 1842 the group had completed another domicile, the Eyrey, on a foundation of huge boulders. Several hundred yards behind the Hive, it housed Ripley's library, a music room, and living quarters on the first and second floors. There were French windows on the first floor, with views over an orchard and land sloping to the Charles River on Brook Farm's western boundary.

Although in its first two years Brook Farm was not a great monetary success, its population grew from about twenty to seventy by July 1842. Unfortunately, many of these were boarders or students who, while providing important income, were not fully committed to membership. Thus, although Ripley and others of the community's prime movers felt compelled to construct new buildings to house these individuals, the whole population was not necessarily contributing to the agricultural labor of the enterprise or to the larger purpose of shared community.

As word of the institute spread in the local press as well as by word of mouth, it began to draw more and more visitors curious to see the Transcendentalists' "Kingdom of God." To accommodate this interest, Brook Farm charged overnight guests thirty-seven cents each, which included dinner, supper, and a night's lodging; and "day-trippers" were welcomed as well, gratis. A conservative estimate suggests a remarkable eleven hundred visitors a year—"of all religions; bond and free; transcendental and occidental; antislavery and proslavery; come-outers; communists, fruitists [those who subsisted on fruit alone] and flutists; dreamers and schemers of all sorts"—who brought in income but did not contribute a day's labor.[21]

In Brook Farm's first two years, those who participated in its programs, whether as members or students, were virtually unanimous in their praise of its ideals and the ways in which Ripley sought to realize them practically. Labor was shared and varied according to one's wishes, though it still fell primarily to the women to supervise the meals. Entertainment and enlightenment were available to all, with frequent picnics, evening lectures, concerts, dances, *tableaux vivants*, and an endless delight in punning and wordplay. These were not mere diversions, but went hand in hand with the effort to make Brook Farm an environment where the whole being, physical, mental, and spiritual, was cultivated.

Because Brook Farmers believed that their lofty social ideals should be inculcated early in life, the community's school, housed in the Eyrey, always was central to its purpose and quickly became its most lucrative enterprise. Abigail Morton and the English governess Georgianna Kirby oversaw the infant section (children below the age of six). Marianne Ripley, George's sister, supervised the primary classes (children between six and ten). She had some help from Sophia, who also worked with her husband in the "preparatory" school, where she taught history and modern languages and he taught mathematics and philosophy (using Victor Cousin's works as the text). Charles A. Dana heard lessons in Greek and German, with Latin and music falling to John Sullivan Dwight, who had left his Northampton pulpit after a short time to join his mentor Ripley. George P. Bradford, a young Harvard graduate, supervised classes in belles lettres. By the second year, the students in all sections numbered thirty and represented many area families who were prominent intellectually or socially. The young scholars included Emerson's nephew Frank Brown; Brownson's son Orestes,

Jr.; Parker's ward, George Colburn; Charles Sumner's younger brother, Horace; and Robert Gould Shaw, later to have a storied career in the Civil War as the leader of the Fifty-fourth Massachusetts (black) Infantry. There even were some adult learners, most prominently George and Burrill Curtis, sons of a wealthy New York banker who had heard Emerson lecture in Providence; they took such subjects as German, music, and chemistry.

Because Brook Farm, unlike Hopedale, had no religious creed, members satisfied their spiritual longings variously. Some heard Parker in nearby West Newton, while others made the trip to Boston, where they had a choice of many prominent clergy. Still others communed with Brook Farm's natural beauty or read, for Sunday was a day, one member recalled, "of recreation and enjoyment."[22] But religion was not banned on-site. Ripley, Dwight, and others often led discussions on spiritual topics of mutual interest, and visitors like Brownson and William Henry Channing could be counted on to initiate lively debate. But the true hallmark of this phase of Brook Farm's history was its genuine catholicity. As the onetime Brook Farmer John Thomas Codman recalled, there one lived in "positive harmony" with all men. When one lay down at night he could unabashedly say, "I have wronged no man. I have worked for my race" on the "grand plan" that God intended.[23] Most members and students agreed: at Brook Farm the quality of life was indeed different.

Social and cultural life went well at Brook Farm, but financially it struggled. By the end of 1842, for example, Ripley and other chief investors had to rethink its economic basis. Eager to welcome those interested in the community, Ripley had continued to construct new buildings, for which Brook Farm took out new mortgages totaling $6,300. But debt management and expenses began to outpace revenues. Some original investors, including Hawthorne, had already withdrawn and sought refund of their investment, as well as any yearly interest still owed. Around this time, proponents of Fourier's elaborate blueprint for "Association" began to gain more of a hearing in New England generally and at Brook Farm in particular.

The American reformers' infatuation with Fourier's ideas marks one of the most significant transatlantic appropriations of European thought during the 1840s. Before Brisbane's trip to France and his subsequent publication of *The Social Destiny of Man*, however, very few Americans (save Brownson, not surprisingly) had heard of Fourier. Fortunate enough to have received tutorials from the reticent master, Brisbane returned to the United States eager to convert people to Fourierism and, eventually, to build one of the Frenchman's model communities.

Fourier was a remarkable autodidact whose works ranged through sociology, psychology, economy, architecture, and philosophy. Greatly underappreciated for most of his life, when Saint-Simon's Christian socialism dominated reform efforts, Fourier struggled to publicize his ideas. Born in Besançon in 1772, the son of a successful cloth merchant, he went to school until he was sixteen and then worked in a variety of jobs—in a banking house in Lyons and a textile company in Rouen—always as a minor, and finally unsuccessful, functionary. Claiming a sizable patrimony, he invested it in the import trade in Lyon but lost it all in the aftermath of the French Revolution, which reduced him, as he put it, to "the jailhouse of commerce."[24] Never content with his work and frustrated by his inability to transcend it, he also was appalled at the monotony and waste that a free-market economy engendered.

While in a restaurant in Paris in the 1790s, he had an epiphany. Shocked to find that the price of one apple in the city could purchase a hundred in the country, he traced this economic conundrum to the inefficiency and waste of the current market system. That apple, he wrote, was one of four that changed history. "Two were famous by the disasters they caused, that of Adam and that of Paris, and two by services rendered to mankind, Newton's and my own."[25] Beginning in 1808 with his *Théorie des quatre mouvements et des destinées générales*, Fourier published a number of remarkable works, most notably his *Traité de l'association domestique-agricole*; *Le Nouveau monde industriel et sociétaire*; and *La Fausse industrie*, in which he analyzed the economic and psychological shortcomings of his age and discovered what he believed were universal laws that governed individuals' relations to one another and to God.

It is impossible to provide a synopsis of these lengthy tomes. They begin, however, from the premise that humanity had greatly harmed itself through an enthusiastic and uncritical embrace of an economic system that privileged the individual at the expense of the whole. Plotting humanity's eighty-thousand-year evolution through various stages, including its current one, defined by greed and waste, Fourier believed that humanity would progress through two more stages to a state of complete natural and spiritual "Harmony." His was an all-encompassing world program, not a mere blueprint for economic reform.

Fourier proposed that his contemporaries build and inhabit "phalansteries," cooperative communities each with 1,620 residents, in which all aspects of personal life were organized on his theory of the "passions"—that is, the instinctive, nonrational parts of the self that demand gratification. In its current state, society repressed what people most desired, contributing to existential malaise. On the contrary, in each phalanstery man's twelve basic passions would be balanced and gratified. Fourier derived his magic number of 1,620 individuals in each phalanstery from his belief that there were 810 possible personality types, given the various combinations of passions. With twice that number of people, everyone would at some time or other be attracted to (that is, wish for the good of) every other of his or her fellow phalansterians.

Each "phalanx," the group who lived in a phalanstery, thus comprised a variety of individuals in terms of backgrounds and skills, all of whose basic needs were supplied in common—provided a "social minimum" as Fourier put it—because of the increased production incumbent on cooperative labor, even as different jobs yielded different dividends, depending on their difficulty and desirability. In a phalanstery, men and women practiced "attractive industry," individuals rotating through different occupations and acquiring new skills and competence, thus sealing their interest in their fellow workers and the good of the entire unit. The end of this social engineering would be an Earth planted with two million phalansteries, connected so that nation-states, another hallmark of present vanity and selfishness, became unnecessary.

Thoughts of the age of Harmony inspired Fourier to astonishing flights of fantasy. In civilization, he claimed, the very Earth had been thrown from cosmic alignment, affecting its relation to other planets and stars. In Harmony, it would realign, and mankind would see such wondrous sights as five many-colored moons in the evening sky. Indeed, Fourier believed that celestial bodies themselves were sentient and that they copulated to create new worlds. Drawing on Franz Mesmer's notion of magnetic fluids or "aromas" that circulated in our bodies and could be therapeutically polarized through magnetism, Fourier posited an aroma circulating through culture itself that determined a people's state of development. When Earth's proper balance and sexual vitality were restored through harmonial association, disease would be unknown; the climate would warm until the far northern oceans were like the Mediterranean; new species of animals, loving and kind, would replace savage beasts; and the oceans would turn to lemonade. Even humanity's appearance would be altered as people again grew tails from their prehensile stubs and reveled in a guiltless, prelapsarian harmony. Fourier's French acolytes, as well as his American followers, downplayed these more extravagant features of his social and cosmological visions, emphasizing instead his radical economic critique so that he became best known for his theory of "Attractive Labor." But Fourier's state of Harmony cannot be understood without this spiritual component.

Until the 1850s, readers in England and the United States most frequently encountered Fourier's ideas through Brisbane's redactions. Beginning in March 1842, for example, another sanitized version of his thought was widely available. An infant Fourier Association in New York had encouraged Brisbane to proselytize through the burgeoning newspaper press. For five hundred dollars he purchased a front-page column in Horace Greeley's *New-York Daily Tribune* and for a year and a half explained and extolled Fourier's economic and social vision. As Greeley's paper gained popularity and influence, its contents were reprinted in many other papers, so that thousands of Americans (including Brook Farmers) became conversant with Fourier's ideas. When Brisbane issued some of his daily columns as a pamphlet, *A Concise Exposition of the Practical Part of Fourier's Social Science*, it sold ten thousand copies.

After the publication of *The Social Destiny of Man*, Fourier's system became a common topic of discussion among the Transcendentalists, nowhere more so than at Brook Farm, where Ripley continued to cast about for some way to improve the community's financial position. He began to require a more detailed accounting of each individual's contribution to the workforce, but to no avail. In addition, there were continued defections from the community, prompting Greeley and even Sophia Ripley to wonder if Brook Farm's membership had not become too exclusive. She "mourned" what she termed the community's "prodigality" and selfishness. "I see everywhere around me," she wrote, those who prophesy "only of themselves, casting their horoscopes, impertinently prying into their own emotions, or intoxicating themselves with the excited emotions of others." They were "wrapped and swathed in selfism [*sic*]."[26] Emerson concurred; at Brook Farm there was "no authority." Each was "master and mistress of their [*sic*] own actions— happy hapless Sansculottes" (the poorer, radicalized element of the population during the French Revolution).[27]

The community needed new and different blood. In August 1843 Ripley, who had heard much about the "Associationist" movement touted by Greeley and others, attended a convention in Albany, New York, where interested parties supported the recently announced North American Phalanx, planned for Red Bank, New Jersey. When he returned to Brook Farm, Brisbane came with him and in Boston delivered two lectures on Association. The poet Walt Whitman (himself interested in Fourier's ideas) provides a memorable portrait of Brisbane in these years. He was "a tall, slender man," Whitman recalled, "round-shouldered, chin stuck out, deep set eyes, sack-coat." Somehow or other, he concluded, Brisbane always looked as if he were attempting "to think out some problem a little too hard for him."[28] But his audiences sought to follow his cerebration. His first lecture, at the Marlborough Street Chapel in Boston, drew three hundred people, and his second talk two days later filled the building.

Pleased with his success on the platform, Brisbane also was excited by what he saw at West Roxbury. In subsequent *Tribune* columns he touted Brook Farm and encouraged artisans of all types to cast their lot with Ripley, who already had established one industry, shoemaking, to boost Brook Farm's financial resources. In the fall, two new journals committed to the Associationist movement,

William Henry Channing's *The Present* and Brisbane's *The Phalanx*, included Brook Farm among the experimental communities they praised, prompting Ripley to consider more formal association with the New York Fourierist wing, particularly so that he could solicit its wealthy backers.

Matters came to a head in late December, when Brook Farm sent representatives to a four-day convention of Friends of Social Reform at the Tremont Temple in Boston. Joining delegates from Ballou's Hopedale enterprise, the Northampton (Massachusetts) Association of Education and Industry (established by radical abolitionists), and the Skaneateles Community from rural New York (also founded by abolitionists but distinctive in prohibiting private property) were most of New England's prominent reformers: Alcott, Garrison, Brownson, and the recently escaped slave Frederick Douglass (now lecturing for the Massachusetts Anti-Slavery Society), among others. Sensing that the time was right to win converts in New England, New York–based reformers like Brisbane, Greeley, Parke Godwin, and William Henry Channing also attended. Ripley and others in the Brook Farm contingent returned to West Roxbury convinced that the community's success depended on its adoption of Fourier's economic principles, a transition they did not think would be that difficult. Shortly after the New Year, Ripley met with Brook Farm's shareholders to win approval for the plan. His task did not prove difficult, for the membership, whether or not they approved of the shift to Fourierism, understood the necessity of a change of direction.

In early January 1844 the community heard and approved a revised constitution and articles of agreement for what from that point on was called the Brook Farm Association for Industry and Education. The change reflected Ripley's decision to diversify the community's economy by taking in more craftsmen and laborers, which Greeley and Brisbane thought necessary but which irrevocably changed its membership. The new constitution reflected Fourier's scheme for the reorganization of work: a General Direction (that is, a committee of oversight), a Direction of Finance, a Direction of Education, and a Direction of Industry, with the old units of Domestic Economy and Agriculture now subsumed into this last and termed merely a "Series," another shift in the community's priorities. With this reorganization of labor into "Series" and "Groups" (Fourier's terminology), the Brook Farmers demonstrated their commitment to Fourier's notion of "Attractive Industry." In the Agricultural Series, for example, there were groups for plowing, planting, weeding, hoeing, and so on; and Brook Farm also instituted a Domestic Series and a Mechanical Series. One wit among them even proposed the "R. L. S. G.," the "rejected lover's sympathizing group."[29] But other of the basic organizing principles did not change. Interest on one's investment remained at 5 percent, and all members were still guaranteed the necessities of life and the rights to personal property and to live in family units.

No American phalanx ever grew to anything near the size Fourier envisioned. Here the Brook Farmers, like other pioneer phalansterians, followed Brisbane's suggestion—in a series of articles in the *Democratic Review* in 1842—that Fourier's principles could be put into operation in a four-hundred-member community.[30] Brook Farm, which already had a division of and reward for labor similar to what Fourier counseled, was ideally situated and suited for such an experiment. When Ripley announced the reorganization and put out a call for more participants, applications for membership soared. Six months after the publication of the new constitution, eighty-seven applicants had joined the community; and after the two-month trial stipulated in the bylaws, fifty-eight, primarily laborers and artisans rather than farmers or intellectuals, were admitted as members and accommodated into new Groups and Series. Between May 1 and September 30, 1844, Brook Farm received one hundred more applications. Clearly, the switch to Association brought new attention to the West Roxbury experiment.

The presence of a new cadre of residents and workers necessitated new physical space. By early spring, Brook Farmers had begun work on a 60' by 28' "Workshop," to house new industries; and, more ambitiously, a 175' by 40' "Phalanstery," just below the Eyrey, that would serve as the community's primary living quarters. The Workshop, behind and to the north of the Hive, comprised a carpenters' shop on the first floor, where craftsmen made sashes and blinds, while printers and artisans who made Britannia ware (silver-plated pewter) and shoes shared the second story. The community even invested in a thousand-dollar steam engine installed beneath the building to power its machinery, replacing a horse-driven mill used to turn various belt drives.

During this period of expansion, financed by loans, Ripley, Charles A. Dana, and John Sullivan Dwight continued to attend Associationist meetings throughout the Northeast and frequently held important offices, solidifying Brook Farm's position as one of the chief Associationist communities. Its prominence only increased when, after the demise of Channing's *The Present* and the increasing financial difficulties of *The Phalanx*, plans were made to transfer the organ of the American Union of Associationists from New York to Brook Farm. *The Harbinger*, as the new journal was called (in part as a pun on the French word "*fourrier*," harbinger), was first published on June 14, 1845.[31] Ripley's editorial notice spelled out its mission: "the advancement and happiness of the masses" and war "against all exclusive privilege in legislation, political arrangements, and social customs" as it strove to "promote the triumph of the high democratic faith."[32]

Encouraged by the national attention focused on his experiment, in the spring of 1845 Ripley urged and received approval for a further revision of the community's principles, and he renamed the enterprise the Brook Farm Phalanx. Not everyone approved. Amelia Russell complained that, from that point, the "poetry of our lives" vanished.[33] She recalled, among other things, how, beginning in the fall of 1845, the community fell prey to increased bickering and tension over religious services held on the premises, discussions that were exacerbated by William Henry Channing's insistence that Brook Farm stand on a solidly Christian foundation. Social friction also increased as new artisans and laborers resented what they viewed as the patronizing attitudes of the original Farmers. Complicating matters, more of Brook Farm's creditors pressed for payment or return of their original investments. Hawthorne, now living in Concord, even brought suit against his old associates. Ripley and Dana asked for financial assistance from the New York Associationists, but were rebuffed. The organization instead funneled money to the more promising North American Phalanx at Red Bank, New Jersey.

The Brook Farm Phalanx's fate was sealed on March 3, 1846, when sparks from a stove carelessly left burning in the nearly completed Phalanstery spread and within a couple of hours burned the immense building to the ground. This edifice had been started a year and a half earlier and already had consumed seven thousand dollars of Brook Farm's labor and supplies. Three stories tall, with a dining hall for several hundred people and a large lecture room on the first floor, and more than one hundred dormitory rooms and a chapel on the next two, it had become the symbol of the community's conversion to Fourier's ideas. Though members stayed on in the immediate aftermath of this tragedy, by spring they began to trickle away, some to the North American Phalanx or other experimental communities, others back to the corrupt world. Although several of the wealthier individuals who owned shares in the enterprise wrote off their losses, by summer it was clear that Brook Farm's days were numbered.

A few score of the dedicated stayed on with the Ripleys through the fall and winter, but only twelve remained the following September. In November, Ripley sold his entire library of American and foreign books to pay off creditors, a sale in its way as important for what it records of New England's intellectual life as the liquidation of the Reverend Joseph Buckminster's library thirty years earlier.[34] After this melancholy event, Ripley was reported to have told Parker (who bought many of the books) that now he knew what it was like to attend one's own funeral.[35] The Ripleys and a few others lingered in West Roxbury until October 1847, when they finally left to rejoin the world they had tried so hard to reform. Ripley went to New York, where he continued to edit *The Harbinger*, and began another career as a book reviewer for Greeley's *Tribune*. In so doing, he effectively relinquished his leadership role among New England Transcendentalists.

In 1845, with the publication of Fourier's *Oeuvres complètes*, his entire system, material and spiritual, was available to any who could read the language. Many Transcendentalists could, and their exposure to Fourier's other ideas initiated a renewed and more wide-ranging engagement with his thought, if not a rush for membership in phalanxes. Many were struck by the similarity of his spiritual ruminations to the Transcendentalists' own pronouncements on the spiritual life. Brownson, by this time disaffected from the movement and a recent convert to Roman Catholicism, observed that "Fourierism is simply an attempt to realize in society the leading principles of Transcendentalism."[36]

Despite Emerson's adamant resistance to the Brook Farm experiment, he remained genuinely interested in Fourier's worldview. In his old age, when he reviewed the important phases through which New England had moved during his lifetime, he spoke at length of Fourier and the Associationists. He was still not above lampooning some of the Frenchman's more exotic speculations—many of his contemporaries, Emerson noted dryly, had cast "sheep's-eyes" on Fourier and "his houris" (beautiful virgins who await faithful Muslim men in the afterlife) and looked forward to the time, in the reign of Attractive Industry, when all men would "speak in blank verse." But he also allowed that Fourier "carried a whole French Revolution in his head" and particularly admired his understanding of the relation of nature to spirit. "The value of Fourier's system," Emerson wrote, "is that it is a statement of such [a spiritual] order externized [*sic*], or carried outward into its correspondence in facts." Its drawback was Fourier's insistence that he himself had cracked the divine code. He left no room, Emerson lamented, for "private light."[37]

Another unusual component of Fourier's thought struck his American readers: his searching criticism of monogamous marriage. Fourier envisioned a "new amorous world," realized in the next stage of human development beyond the current "Civilization," in which men and women would stand in new relation. This speculation was of most interest to women in the Transcendentalist movement, specifically Margaret Fuller, whose *Woman in the Nineteenth Century* (1845) illustrates Fourier's strong influence, and Caroline Sturgis, another of Fuller's protégées and Emerson's good friend.

Fourier not only condemned the economic wastefulness of the isolated household but also described how destructive the individual family unit was to the physical, psychological, and sexual happiness of both men and women. In the unrepressed world of the phalanstery, all were guaranteed what Fourier termed a "sexual minimum," that is, promise of erotic fulfillment according to their inclinations and desires, a continuum that ranged from virginity or celibacy to full promiscuity. Fourier dissected and categorized love as much as any other human activity. In his brave new world, women thus had equal access not only to education and varieties of work and equal pay for it, but also to psychological and sexual gratification, freeing them from the double standard that made them repress amorous desire. Indeed, in the state of Harmony, homosexuality, polygamy, and even incest were permissible.

Careful readers of Brisbane's and Godwin's redactions understood the implication for gender relations of Fourier's elaborate taxonomy of "Passions," particularly the "Butterfly," which denoted a love of variety and change. As word got around of these more speculative parts of his system, critics were quick to paint the phalanstery as a den of iniquity. "This creature of corruption," one wrote hysterically, "which first began to crawl, lizard-like, in the filthiest dregs of Parisian infidelity, and which has never since left any thing, but its slime and venom in the track of its crawling," was now going to pollute the United States. "Human passions are to have universal, sole and undivided sway—human passions and animal appetites," he continued. "This is the nucleus of the whole system—the centre in which all its lines meet—the pivot on which all its apparatus turns."[38] Even those sympathetic to Fourier's vision could not resist a dig. Emerson was particularly severe. He opined that in the phalanstery even Saint Paul and Saint John "would be riotous." He also rather prudishly observed that to Fourier, marriage "was a calculation how to secure the greatest amount of kissing that the infirmity of human constitution admitted."[39] Clearly uncomfortable with a system based on such untrammeled freedom, Emerson predicted that the new amorous world would only be as virtuous as those who inhabited it.

Others were less skeptical. Of all Fourier's American disciples, Henry James, Sr., a Swedenborgian and devotee of Association, was least troubled by these radical views of marital reform and endorsed them publicly through a translation of the French Fourierist Victor Hennequin's *Les amours au phalanstère*, which James issued as *Love in the Phalanstery* (1849). In his preface James explained that he published the tract because contemporary sexual relations clearly demanded reform. Rather than a call to immorality, Fourier's "passional philosophy" sounded the "death-knell of our profuse prostitution and licentiousness."[40] In Harmony, men and women, unafraid of Eros, would have a newfound respect for each other.

Hennequin's tract is as remarkable a piece of reform literature as any published in the United States at that time, abjuring any explanation of Fourier's industrial and "cosmogonal" systems—the first already had its explicators and the second, although much of it "unverified by experience," Hennequin believed would eventually be verified by science—to focus on "questions of love."[41] Critics quickly condemned *Love in the Phalanstery*, however, as more evidence of the immorality toward which Association tended. One, in the *New York Observer*, wrote sarcastically that he was delighted to find someone brave enough openly to present what always was there in Fourier's voluminous works, only to go on to point out that no reader could get through the tract without being convinced that "*Fourierism* is just another name for *promiscuity*, and the doctrines of association the most corrupt and corrupting that ever were promulgated under the guise of virtue and reform."[42] In the pages of *The Harbinger*, James vigorously defended himself against such scurrilous charges and thus brought more attention to and prolonged a controversy that his fellow Associationists had long hoped to avoid.

Emerson thought to pose the important query. What, he asked, "*will the women say to the theory?*"[43] Some of them, he was surprised to learn, welcomed it. Such a powerful yet in so many ways commonsensical notion of gender relations could not but influence others beginning to speak out about women's restricted sphere. Among the Transcendentalists most affected was Margaret Fuller, who by 1843 had found her voice on the subject.

Fuller's chief contribution to the "woman question" appeared in the July 1843 issue of *The Dial* as "The Great Lawsuit. Man versus Men, Woman versus Women," which she reworked and published in 1845 as *Woman in the Nineteenth Century,* the first extended treatment of women's rights in the United States.[44] In the interim she read parts of Fourier's *Le Nouveau monde industriel et sociétaire,* and her revision and extension of the essay reveals an increasing knowledge of Fourier's works.[45] "A new manifestation is at hand," she wrote, "a new hour in the day of Man."[46] Fuller linked that glorious day to the expansion of women's economic and psychological spheres. When such a change occurred, when "every arbitrary barrier" was thrown down and "every path . . . open to Woman as freely as to Man," the world would see "crystallizations more pure and of more various beauty." Then, she continued, "the divine energy would pervade nature to a degree unknown in the history of former ages" and "no discordant collision, but a ravishing harmony of the spheres, would ensue"—Fourierist prophecy pure and simple.[47]

Fuller noted a "throng of symptoms" that denoted a contemporary "crisis in the life of Woman," that is, a time of transition between a lower and higher order, symptoms epitomized for her in the thought of three individuals. First was Swedenborg, who interpreted the past revelation and unfolded a new, and thus "approximated to that harmony between the scientific, and poetic lives of mind, which we hope from the perfect man." Swedenborg's view of woman, Fuller wrote, was "large and noble," for in his system man and woman "share an angelic ministry." The union is of "one to one, permanent and pure."[48] Her second example was Fourier. Even if some aspects of his system proved false, she observed, he still placed "Woman on an entire equality with Man" and sought to give both a sexual freedom that was the natural result of their mutual intellectual and "practical" development in the phalanstery.[49] Fuller's third inspiration was the German writer Wolfgang von Goethe, "the great apostle of individual culture," long important to her as well as to Emerson and other of their friends. If Swedenborg had made "organization and union the necessary results of solitary thought," and Fourier had prophesied that "better institutions . . . will make better men," Goethe encouraged and embodied the primacy of individual self-expression. His maxim was, "As the man, so the institutions," an apothegm that could have been Emerson's or, at this point, Fuller's. Swedenborg, Fourier, and Goethe thus each moved people "to a clearer consciousness of what Man needs, what Man can be, and [that a] better life must ensue."[50]

Fuller's epochal book influenced a wide spectrum of reformers. One was Caroline Sturgis (1819–88), her young protégée and one of Emerson's closest female friends. The daughter of wealthy Bostonians, after meeting Fuller in 1832 she began to move in Transcendentalist circles, had a brief dalliance with the poet Ellery Channing, and eventually married into the Tappan family of prominent Boston merchants. She contributed poetry to *The Dial* and remained a confidante of Fuller's and an admirer of Emerson's, with whom she had an epistolary exchange that indicates her engagement with Fourier's radical notions of love (as well as her conflicted feelings for the Concord sage).

Early in February 1845 she lent Emerson a volume of Fourier's *Oeuvres*, which he had read through, he told her, "with surprising ease, considering what courage it cost him to begin." Displaying a rather prurient cultural chauvinism, he told her that he doubted Fourier's ideas could have much effect outside of France, for his was "a French mind speaking to French minds." Still, he admired Fourier's probing social criticism and asked Sturgis if she could spare another volume as well as let him lend the current one to his friend Sampson Reed. He also assured Sturgis that, as he had learned from Fourier, he did not forget women's "loneliness & privation" in their current domestic arrangements, and he added, cryptically, "How many things are there not, my dear friend, which dear friends cannot say to each other."[51]

Sturgis's frank reply was remarkable, for she playfully chastised him. "Still seizing everything in the claws of morality, dear Waldo?" "Why may we not live like grasshoppers? Must we be so good?" "Why not wish Fourier to make the finest arrangements possible!" she continued, for as "we must eat our dinners every day, why not eat them in the best way?" She continued her assault on his repressed sensibilities with other scarcely veiled provocations. "Now our barks are stranded upon the shore or puddle about in lakes from which there is but a narrow outlet," she teased. "Would it not be better to be borne along on a wide stream where with vigorous arm we could row to every island & wild-flower that should attract us?" Invoking a Fourierist trope, she asked rhetorically, "Would there be any moralist if all were in harmony with all?" and added suggestively, "Let us learn the scales here & tune our instruments for the great symphonies."[52]

Noting that she recently had seen their mutual friends Ellery Channing and Louisa Weston, Sturgis also hoped that Emerson would "always be a good father confessor for all these young ladies & gentlemen" and allow her to see their "confessions." This was a scarcely veiled allusion to the personage, the "father confessor," whom Fourier placed in charge of arranging young lovers' relationships in the new amorous world. Tellingly, Sturgis continued, "Sometimes I can interpret them [the confessions] better than you," because Emerson did not like to "admit possibilities—all must be absolute with you, but I know very well there is something besides blue sky in the universe." Emerson's affection, she implied, if noble, remained too pure, too distant. People "think you like nothing but diamonds & feel friendless while you are their friend," she lamented, "friendless in being loved above themselves or not at all."[53] She was not alone in her frustration at Emerson's emotional frigidity. His friend Ellery Channing put it this way. "Emerson is a terrible man to deal with," he told Franklin Sanborn. "Those nearest him feel him hard and cold." "Women do not like him," Channing continued, for he "cannot establish a personal relation with anyone," even as he "can get along agreeably with everyone."[54]

Emerson's response to Sturgis displayed his uneasiness at her not so subtle hints about wanting a different relationship with him. "I am somewhat puritanical in my way of living, you will think," he told his young admirer, "but I am not in my theory."[55] A contemporary journal entry further clarifies how much Fourier's ideas about sexuality unnerved him. In his talk about women, Emerson observed, Fourier "seems one of those salacious old men who are full of the most ridiculous superstitions on the matter [of women's desires]," for in his head "it is the universal rutting season." Anyone who has lived with women, he continued, knows "how false & prurient" Fourier's ideas were, and "how chaste" women's "organization."[56] Fourier's prognostications clearly excited women like Sturgis and Fuller, but

Emerson would not walk into these woods with them. He believed that men and women were far from the virtue that made such relationships possible.

No Transcendentalist was as buffeted by utopian dreams as the ethereal Bronson Alcott, but he had a very different view of where sexual gratification fitted into his own brave new world. After the debacle of the Temple School, he had moved to Concord and held his own series of "conversations," depending as well on the largesse of friends like Emerson. Then, in 1842, again with help from Emerson and others, he traveled to England to meet a group of English acolytes centered on James Pierrepont Greaves, who shared Alcott's vegetarian diet and whose experimental school he had named Alcott House.

On Alcott's return, Emerson described the kinds of books and pamphlets his friend had brought back. "Here are Educational Circulars," he wrote, "and Communist Apostles; Alists, Plans for Syncretic Associations, and Pestalozzian Societies, Self-supporting Institutions, Experimental Normal Schools, Hydropathic and Philosophical Associations, Health Unions and Phalansterian Gazettes, Paradises within the reach of all men, Appeals to Man and Woman, and Necessities of Internal Marriage illustrated by Phrenological Diagrams." He also noted that Alcott had attended a convention of such reformers at the school and heard them debate (among other things) "reliance on Commercial Prosperity," man's right to inflict pain on another, "the reign of Love in Man instead of human Opinions," "the restoration of all things to their primitive Owner, and hence the abrogation of Property, either individual or collective" and "the Divine Sanction, instead of the Civil or Ecclesiastical authority, for Marriage."[57] Several of these ideas found their way into Alcott's subsequent utopian venture.

One English reformer, Charles Lane (1800–70), one of Greaves's disciples who arrived at Alcott House in 1841, particularly impressed Alcott. They quickly became fast friends, and soon thereafter Lane accompanied Alcott to the United States, where the two made plans for a communal experiment whose chief hallmark would be its participants' withdrawal from complicity with the corrupt world, distinguishing it from Brook Farm, whose members traded with outside communities. Alcott and Lane also were much interested in dietary and health reform as well as in versions of the associative family life. On land that Lane purchased in Harvard, Massachusetts, ten miles west of Concord, they intended to put their theories to the test.[58]

In June 1843 Lane and his son, the Alcott family, and a few others moved to Fruitlands, as they named the ninety-acre farm on the slope of Prospect Hill. The basic principles on which they based this experiment were a hodgepodge of health and reform ideas circulating in England and America, but what chiefly underlay the venture was Lane's articulation, in 1841, of what he termed "The Third Dispensation."[59] He identified the first dispensation as that of family union or "connexion by tribes." A second and higher one appealed to the "unitive principle" in man, which Lane termed "the state of union called national." But as much as this dispensation improved the first, it still did little to elevate humanity from the "narrowness" of its condition. Men and women had to find their way to a third union, the "Universal," in which they realized their shared nature and interests.[60]

Lane's lengthy letter to a prospective member regarding his and Alcott's plans to live as a "Consociate Family," subsequently published in such reform journals as the *Herald of Freedom*, the *New Age*, and in Greeley's *Tribune*, revealed the practical parameters of their plans. In order to purify themselves, members of Fruitlands sought simplicity in diet and valued "plain garments, pure bathing, unsullied dwellings, open conduct, gentle behavior, kindly sympathies, and pure minds." They also hoped to have as little to do with trade as possible because of its evil propensities, and they sought radical agricultural reform. To restore the land to its "pristine fertility," they plowed under vegetation rather than filthy animal waste. They also did not wish to drive cattle "beyond their natural and pleasurable exertion," for they regarded this as a form of abuse that elicited the "animal and bestial natures in man." Neither did they eat animal substances: flesh, butter, cheese, eggs, and milk did not pollute their table. In all these choices, Lane explained, they relied not so much on "scientific reasoning or physiological skill, as on the Spirit's dictates."[61]

Unfortunately, as at Brook Farm, these ideals were far from ever being realized. Fruitlands' land was poor, and the group's arrival in early summer meant a very late start in cultivation. They sought to practice "spade agriculture," that is, turning the soil by hand rather than using animals for plowing or cultivating, a principle on which they finally had to compromise. They abjured leather and wool, because they derived from animals, and cotton, because of its complicity in chattel slavery, so this left flax as the only alternative for clothing. When Lane visited Emerson in July, for example, Emerson wrote that his new acquaintance "was dressed in linen altogether, with the exception of his shoes, which were lined with linen, & he wore no stockings."[62] Even more impractically (and incomprehensibly), members of Fruitlands ate only "aspiring" vegetables, not those whose edible part grew underground; squash, peas, and beans were fine, but not carrots or beets. Most problematic, after a visit to the nearby town of Shirley's Shaker village, Lane was converted to their principle of celibacy, and he tried to convince Alcott to unite with that group or at least to adopt sexual abstinence at Fruitlands, something that did not sit well with Mrs. Alcott. Further, because the community's chief male members often were absent proselytizing, the burden of the work fell to her and her four daughters and contributed to her general disenchantment with Alcott's venture.

Compared with Brook Farm, Fruitlands was tiny, with never more than twelve members, all under one roof. Lane and Alcott had expected this, noting in their prospectus in *The Dial* that because they were "Pledged to the spirit alone," they anticipated "no hasty or numerous accession [*sic*] to their numbers."[63] They were more right than they knew. In addition to the Alcotts and Lane, there was the eccentric Joseph Palmer from nearby No Town (near Fitchburg), who quite literally was persecuted for his hirsute face, a rare thing at that time. Another resident was Brownson's friend Isaac Hecker, who also had been at Brook Farm and who, like his mentor, later became a Roman Catholic and the founder of the Paulist Fathers. Other of the odd assemblage (there was no common denominator among the Fruitlands group, except perhaps views more eccentric than those of the Brook Farmers) were the nudist Samuel Bower; Samuel Larned, a former Brook Farmer originally from Providence, Rhode Island, who claimed to have subsisted for a year on crackers; and Wood Abram, whose sole distinction was that he had changed his name from Abram Wood.[64]

By late fall, their small harvest was lost to an early frost, and as the Alcott women were tiring of the diet and the daily regimen of cold baths and "flesh brushing" with rough towels, the community began to disintegrate. Mrs. Alcott wanted the family to give up the experiment, and she threatened to take the children and leave. She also asked her brother, the abolitionist Samuel J. May, to stop the mortgage payments on the house and barn at Fruitlands, property he had generously subsidized. By year's end Lane left for the Shaker community, and the Alcotts, too, quit the farm. Alcott was depressed and debilitated, and a few months later he resumed family life in Concord, unable to substitute his strong attachment to the conjugal family for what Lane had envisioned as the "consociate" one needed for the "third dispensation." Emerson's assessment the previous summer had proved prophetic. "They look well in July; we will see them in December."[65]

Despite the demise of Brook Farm and Fruitlands, others among the Transcendentalists continued to proselytize for Association. William Henry Channing assumed a prominent role in the movement through founding the Religious Union of Associationists in Boston and another reformist journal, *The Spirit of the Age*. Fuller, who soon moved to New York and then to Europe, also became more deeply interested in socialism. In New York fellow traveler Greeley continued his efforts to inform the public about the direction of social reform, even reprinting the European columns of a young social theorist, Karl Marx. The Red Bank Phalanstery in New Jersey and a few other communal experiments strove to realize Fourier's vision. Eventually, Victor Considérant, one of Fourier's chief disciples, even attempted a short-lived phalanstery in the new state of Texas.

But overall, in the United States the Associationists' dream seemed ever more distant, in large measure because of the nation's enshrinement of free-market capitalism and the individualism on which it was based. Emerson spoke for his culture more than he realized when he observed that although the "world is waking up to the idea of Union," this state was attainable only "by a reverse of the methods" the Associationists counseled. "Each man being the Universe," he continued, "if he attempt [*sic*] to join himself to others, he is instantly jostled, crowded, cramped, halved, quartered, or on all sides diminished in proportion."[66] Association, for all its beauty and promise, went against what by now had become part of the American grain.

There was another reason for Association's failure to take hold in America. By 1850, Transcendentalists who disagreed with Emerson and still believed in the possibility of widespread, organized social reform were pulled into the accelerating crisis over slavery. They began to draw back from their focus on broadly humanitarian issues and gaze inward, horrified at the sin they saw at the heart of the nation. Now their writing, as well as their labors, acquired a more nationalistic cast, typified by Theodore Parker's heroic commitment to abolitionism. Before describing this pivotal development, however, it is worth considering several exemplary individuals whose activities—religious, moral, and artistic—epitomized the variety and complexity of what Transcendentalism made possible by the late 1840s.

VARIETIES OF TRANSCENDENTALISM

hrough the 1840s, Transcendentalism touched a great many individuals. There were many prime movers who worked out its implications in a variety of activities, from biblical criticism to utopian reform. But there were many others, fellow travelers who one way or another came into contact with and were affected by the New Thought. While never committing themselves fully to the movement, they were indelibly marked by it, and they illustrate its internal tensions. They may have come upon Transcendentalist ideas through attending Fuller's Conversations, hearing Brownson preach, visiting Ripley's Brook Farm, meeting with an issue of *The Dial* or *The Harbinger* at a local bookshop, or following the newspaper accounts of Emerson's latest lecture series. Some encounters were mere dalliances, fodder only for ridicule—at the expense of Alcott for his "Orphic Sayings," say, or for disgust at the Associationists' critique of marriage and at their purported licentiousness. Other encounters had more long-lasting effects: when Unitarians at Harvard's Divinity School learned of a classmate's rejection of the personal authority of Christ, setting them to reading the Higher Criticism; or when a middle-class couple wandered into Boston's Melodeon on a Sunday morning, emerging two hours later transformed to social activism by one of Parker's electrifying sermons.

Above all, Transcendentalism greatly affected young people, encouraging them to reexamine their inherited beliefs. "The key to the period," Emerson recalled, "appeared to be that the mind had become aware of itself." There was "a new consciousness," for the new generation had "with knives in their brain, a tendency to introversion, self-dissection, and anatomizing of motives."[1] O. B. Frothingham concurred. He had observed a feeling abroad "that all things must be new in the world," with the thinker called upon "to justify himself on the spot by building an engine, and setting something in motion." The first test of a truth, he declared, was its "availability."[2] In this chapter we meet four people—the businessman, mutual banking advocate, and one-time Unitarian clergyman William B. Greene; the amateur poet and lay Transcendentalist Eliza Thayer Clapp; the Unitarian minister, novelist, and poet Sylvester Judd; and the writer and natural historian Henry David Thoreau—who exemplify the various kinds of intellectual "engines" Transcendentalist ideas enabled and set in motion. Caught as much as Emerson, Parker, and others in the struggle to define Transcendentalism and its implications for American democracy, these individuals were linked by their interest in and contact with a novel view of self-consciousness that was transformative.

William Batchelder Greene (1819–78) made so strong an impression in Boston and Concord that even so severe a judge as Margaret Fuller described him as the "military-spiritual-heroico-vivacious phoenix of the day."[3] Starting in orthodox Calvinism, in just a few years Greene moved through a variety of philosophical and religious positions. An encounter with Emerson converted him to self-reliant individualism, that is, until Orestes Brownson introduced him to the Christian socialism of Pierre Leroux and, later, Philippe Buchez. From there Greene found his way to Pierre-Joseph Proudhon's "mutualism"—a system based on a belief that equal amounts of labor should receive equal pay. It was an intellectual odyssey indicative of how Transcendentalism's centrifugal force pushed individuals in ever more radical directions.[4] By the late 1840s, in an elaborate program for economic reform based in Leroux's and Proudhon's ideas, Greene rivaled even Brook Farm's Fourierists in his criticism of America's market economy and his advocacy of a general renovation of social relations.

Born in Haverhill, Massachusetts, on April 4, 1819, Greene was the son of Nathaniel Greene, a newspaper editor whose prominence in Democratic politics secured him a position as Boston's postmaster from 1829 to 1849.[5] Believing that military service was a sure way to preferment, in 1834 his father wrote to Lewis Cass, secretary of war, requesting his son's admission to the United States Military Academy at West Point. Testimonials to the application indicate the young man's preparation at several academies in Massachusetts and also, in 1833, a stay of several months in Paris with a relative and a tutor, a signal experience that whetted Greene's interest in French thought. His application was successful, and he attended West Point for two years, when he withdrew owing to poor health.

He returned to Boston to convalesce but within a year restarted his military career by volunteering for duty in the Seminole War (1835–42) then being waged in Florida. His commission supported by none other than Daniel Webster, Greene was promoted to second lieutenant, and in July 1839 he was sent to Florida, where he served for six years. He abruptly resigned, again ostensibly owing to ill health, but his own testimony, as well as that of his friend Elizabeth Peabody, indicates that he underwent a profound spiritual crisis whose resolution pushed him toward a career in the ministry.[6]

Greene joined the Charles Street Baptist Church—he had been raised in the Calvinist faith—but at the same time, perhaps at the prodding of Brownson, a family friend, he also stepped boldly into the world of the Transcendentalists, visiting Brook Farm and browsing at Peabody's West Street bookstore for a translation of Kant. Peabody was enough impressed by Greene's "different cast and method of thought" that she introduced him to her mentor, the Reverend William Ellery Channing, and soon enough Greene was visiting Emerson himself. By January 1842 Greene had published in *The Dial* and was encouraged to attend various conversations and meetings then so central to Transcendentalism's development.[7]

Later that spring, Greene again visited Emerson, probably to ask for advice about the ministry. Given his religious background, he decided to study at Newton Theological Institution, a Baptist seminary, but after reading in contemporary biblical criticism, he began to doubt the "tri-personal Godhead" and moved toward Unitarianism. In 1844 he crossed his Rubicon, the Charles River, and successfully applied to Harvard's Divinity School, where, given his theological sophistication, he was enrolled as a senior and quickly made his mark. Thomas Wentworth Higginson, his contemporary at the school and later a Unitarian clergyman and editor of *The Atlantic Monthly*, recalled him as one of the "most interesting men in the Divinity School."[8]

Greene threw himself into his studies and graduated in the summer of 1845. Married to Anna Shaw, the daughter of one of Boston's merchant princes, by autumn he preached on trial to a small Unitarian church in the rural Massachusetts community of West Brookfield, seventy miles from Boston. His liberal Christianity pleased the parish, and in October he accepted their call. James Freeman Clarke preached his ordination sermon, and Greene remained in that pulpit for five years, when he ended his pastoral relationship and also left the ministry.

Greene's publications from the 1840s and early 1850s provide another example of how Transcendentalist thought affected young clergymen reared in conservative rather than liberal Christian churches, and of how second-generation Transcendentalists received and modified the ideas of the movement's first exponents. Two major influences marked Greene's early theological development. First, he strove to reconcile the New Thought with conservative Trinitarian theology. Indeed, more than any other second-generation liberal minister, and very much as James Marsh had set out to accomplish in the 1830s, Greene strove to reconcile the relationship between Calvinism and liberal religion, and thereby illustrated the continuing influence of Calvinist theology on liberal religious reform.

Second, and probably as a result of his contact with Brownson, an old friend of his father's, he drank deeply at the well of French socialism. Even as a divinity student, he admired Buchez. Both Greene's essay in *The Dial* and his first separate publication, *The Doctrine of Life*, for example, depended heavily on this thinker's elaborately schematized notion of mankind's moral and spiritual development and, concomitantly, on his belief that human progress is predicated on certain spiritual revelations, progress recapitulated in the spiritual development of each individual.[9] Further, in Buchez as well as Leroux, Greene found strong criticism of the class divisions that characterized nineteenth-century society, which were based primarily in inequalities of property. For these French intellectuals, acquisitive capitalism, rather than marking the height of civilization, signaled mankind's continuing thralldom to its baser instincts.[10]

Greene was set on the road to these ideas by his conversion experience in Florida. In a dark night of his soul, he had realized his own helplessness in the face of God's omnipotence. As he later told Peabody, he was brought to an acknowledgment of God's sublime majesty, so that now his problem became how he might "obtain communion with the FATHER."[11] This obsession with man's helplessness in the face of God's awesome power explains why he gave so much early attention to the problem of the freedom of the will. But even as Greene's early work demonstrates a struggle with his Calvinist legacy, his exposure to Transcendentalist thought allowed him to modify his theology through the insight that a person's actions—his attempts to put himself in line with what he believes is the higher Ideal—finally *are* the religious life. As he put it, glossing Buchez, "there is no soul which does not *desire, think,* and *act*: in other words, there is no soul without *sensibility, intelligence,* and *power*." Thus, if man always has before him the proper idea of what he wants to be, Greene concluded, "he will ascend toward it."[12]

When Greene entered Newton, he had begun to organize his theology systematically and publish the results as he did so. He felt compelled to relate his new ideas to his own conservative religious background, and thus he tackled such cardinal doctrines as the Trinity, Adam's Fall, and the Atonement. He strove mightily to square his Transcendentalist notions with the Christian mysteries. In his treatment of the Atonement, for example, Greene rejected the validity of the more well-known mediatory schemes, emphasizing not that Jesus was himself made perfect through sufferings, but that "through sufferings he was made a perfect captain of salvation." In other words, in striving to emulate Christ, "the ideal man," men move toward that conformity with God that as moral beings they always seek. Greene had reflected on this as early as the winter of 1841–42, struck by a passage in William Ellery Channing's sermon *Likeness to God* (1828) as having the "whole Transcendental[ist] movement . . . wrapped up in it."[13]

While at Harvard he penned two essays for the *American Review*, an important New York publication, one a review of Emerson's *Essays, Second Series* (1844), the other on "The Bhagvat Geeta, and The Doctrine of Immortality," both of which he later incorporated with little change into a pamphlet, *Transcendentalism* (1849), an effort critical of the movement. After emphasizing that Kant's idea that an individual's sensory perceptions ultimately were erroneous because subjective, Greene examined the Transcendentalists' solution to this dilemma—to "transcend" subjective space and time. He found their reasoning confused. "When a man has cut himself off from every thing which is not himself," Greene noted, "he must find the reason of all things in himself." But, he continued, "the reason of God and the universe are not to be found in man." If one believed that it was, as Transcendentalists did, this was "a sort of human Pantheism."[14]

Despite Greene's pointed criticism of Transcendentalism's tendency to egocentrism, he dedicated his book to Emerson, whom he considered "the profoundest metaphysician, after Jonathan Edwards, which this country has ever produced." Yet he strongly objected to Emerson's understanding of how each individual soul "creates all things." This amounts to an identification of God with man, Greene wrote, and thus to an "*absorption of God in the human soul.*" To illustrate this, he quoted one of his friends, himself a pantheist, who had memorably explained the implication of such self-absorption. "I hold myself to be a leaf, blown about by the winds of change and circumstance," he told Greene, "and holding to the extreme end of the branches of the tree of universal existence." But the Transcendentalists, his friend continued, "*think themselves to be some of the sap.*"[15]

True to his Calvinist upbringing, Greene tried to preserve the notion of majestic divinity apart from man. Just as it requires a man to create a poem, it requires "a living and transcendent God, to create this transcendent poem which we call nature and man, or the visible universe." So, he continued, "the world is the thought of God," but "rendered firm and stable in its manifold relations, by the simple volition of the Divine mind." Because both the Vedas and the Gospel of John preserved this sense of divine omnipotence, Greene wanted people to focus Emerson's and other Transcendentalists' work through the lenses of such mystical texts. "Man is dependent, for the continuance of his life," Greene concluded, "upon that which is not himself."[16] To think otherwise deifies the ego in an illusory manner.

In his West Brookfield pulpit Greene continued such explorations, where the local press issued his *Remarks in Refutation of the Treatise of Jonathan Edwards on the Freedom of the Will* and his treatment of *The Incarnation*. Having satisfied himself as to man's liberty—and thus his moral accountability—in the first pamphlet, Greene turned his attention to an understanding of Christ's role in history. Rather than embracing Transcendentalist self-reliance, a hallmark of Emerson's and Fuller's understandings of the implications of Idealist philosophy, he urged communion with all humanity. Influenced by the French socialists, Greene also relied on his study of the New Testament to argue that therein "is taught the great doctrine of the mutual *solidarity* of the members of the Christian Church; and by implication, the *solidarity* of the whole human race."[17]

Greene's understanding of Man's Fall was directly related to this notion of each person's linkage to, and responsibility for, all others. When man was created, he explained, all his "passions, feelings, sentiments, and aspirations" were in harmony with "the course of universal nature." But as soon as one made his own private enjoyment the main end of his life, both the harmony of the universe and the unity of the human race shattered into "as many fragments as there were individual men, and these fragments repelled each other, for each was intensely selfish, and each cared for his own, and not for the common good." The only remedy for such sinfulness was the Incarnation, for the work of Christ, "the second Adam," was to make men "one in the bond of charity."[18]

Needless to say, such selflessness was not common in a society in which legislative fiat protected the individual's right to pursue self-interest, usually defined by the acquisition of property and profit. But Greene championed the "solidarity" with all people that Christ had typified. Borrowing an analogy from one of the pseudo-sciences of the day, Greene memorably stated his understanding of Christ's message. Although Greene knew "but little of the truth or falsehood of mesmerism," he wrote, he found it an apt metaphor for what he sought to express of man's relation to God. "As one man by a prolonged and earnest gaze," he continued, "can obtain control over another, transmitting his thoughts and feelings into the mind of the other, bringing the will of the other into complete subjection to his own, so the Father, by the might of the overpowering effulgence of his glory, magnetized our Lord, bringing him into conformity with the perfect image of his own infinite holiness." Christ in turn "magnetized" his disciples, and "these others still others," so that the succession had come down to the present day. At that very moment, he claimed, Christ's disciples could transform "the unconverted into the form and image of Christ, through the magnetism of a holy life." Seemingly unaware of the implicit elitism this analogy suggested, Greene saw himself in this apostolic succession.[19]

In West Brookfield, Greene demonstrated his commitment to this ethic of Christian mutualism through the publication of two radical economic pamphlets, *Mutual Banking* and *Equality*, which display Proudhon's influence. In these works Greene, like Fourier and his American disciples, deplored the growing distance between owner and worker, and (citing an example from Henri de Saint-Simon) noted that moneylenders were unprofitable drones in an economy to which they had no organic relation. The sudden disappearance of a thousand capitalists, he noted, would cause "a sentimental evil only, without occasioning any inconvenience to society," unlike, say, the death of fifty of the state's best surgeons. Greene thus urged the creation of "mutual banks," cooperatives not under the control of robber barons.[20]

To Greene, mutual "Love" was the only response to the inevitable strife the Industrial Revolution engendered. Because all men are brothers, they "gravitate toward the same spiritual Sun, toward the same common Father." If people were but centered fully in "INDIVIDUALISM," for Greene "a holy doctrine," they would respect the holiness of their fellow beings. Whoever contended against the rights of an individual man, he concluded, also contended against the divine, for in the indwelling of God in every human soul lay the origin and foundation of all basic human rights.[21]

Greene's legacy to American social thought thus resided in passionate sponsorship of a radically egalitarian Christian individualism that, ironically, demanded full devotion to one's fellow men and women. While virtually every other Transcendentalist, including his mentor Brownson, offered very different solutions to the growing problems between labor and capital, Greene urged both a practical cooperative movement and a Christian mysticism leavened with Transcendentalism. In his later years his thought only widened and deepened in these channels, even as his operative word remained "mutualism." Maintaining that freedom is realized only when one recognizes the divine equality of every other, he eventually moved to the Jewish mystical tradition to reinforce his belief in man's centrality to divine creation. In one of his last works, *The Blazing Star; with an Appendix Treating of the Jewish Kabbala* (1872), Greene argued that the world is "in one aspect, a poem," in another, "a logical argument." But in every respect it is "a work of art."[22] His predisposition to such mysticism marks the lasting effect of New England Transcendentalism on his unorthodox thought.

In 1848 the government functionary and aspiring writer George Wood (1799–1870) published *Peter Schlemiel in America*, a rollicking satire of contemporary American life. In the course of the novel Peter converses with a series of cultured people on topics that allowed Wood free rein to pillory the intellectual and cultural foibles of his contemporaries. Among these were Unitarianism; its stepchild, Transcendentalism; and the Fourierist movement. In the course of conversation a Mrs. Julia Smith relates how, a few years earlier, a distinguished clergyman from the city of Boston introduced her to "an entirely new set of opinions." Soon she learned from his sermons that much of what she had assumed as Christian doctrine was erroneous. As she gradually realized that the Bible was not what she had taken it to be, God's revealed word, but was only a set of myths and stories assembled over the years by apologists for their own brand of Christianity, "the Redeemer was shorn of his divinity."[23] When Wood wanted to poke the most fun at the New Englanders' extreme religious views, however, he cribbed his words from a text cited simply as "Studies in Religion," which to him epitomized fatuous Transcendentalist language.[24]

He was referring to Eliza Thayer Clapp's anonymously published *Studies in Religion*. Born in 1811 in Dorchester, Massachusetts, adjacent to Boston, Clapp lived there her whole life, never marrying.[25] Early on she moved from her orthodox faith to Unitarianism, and for many years she taught Sunday school to teenage girls. Like many others, she gradually made the transition to Transcendentalism and numbered among her close friends both Elizabeth Peabody and William Henry Channing. Describing her religious pilgrimage, she wrote, "When I was sixteen I was a belligerent Unitarian, while my friends were mild seceders from orthodoxy." "In my twenties," she continued, "when Unitarianism was in the ascendant, I was caught off into the aerial regions of Mr. Emerson and the iconoclastic zeal of Mr. Parker."[26] Believing in the ethic of self-culture popularized by William Ellery Channing and cultivated by the Transcendentalists, in her home she gave classes to young women, gratis, in history, literature, and philosophy. She read from and commented on texts and then elicited discussion, much as Fuller did. Never having sought a public life, Clapp's lasting influence came through this teaching, for which she was highly praised.

She also wrote poetry, which Emerson applauded. Its "objectiveness" most pleased him, he noted. He also admired Clapp's "fidelity of observation," for she had "a true eye" and could "see the fact as it appears," allowing her to express "some law of this Divine Life of ours." He returned her poems with comments and suggestions, and eventually published several in *The Dial*, both on Fuller's watch and his.[27]

Clapp published little else save some occasional pieces in *The Christian Register*, a Unitarian paper, and her *Studies in Religion*, the work from which Wood quoted so often. Clapp's little book, however, identified only as by "the Author of Words in a Sunday School" (the title of her book of Sabbath lessons), circulated widely among Transcendentalists. Not all of its publicity was positive, though. A reviewer for *The Harbinger* wrote that while he was prepared to read "the lofty thought and melodious utterances" of Transcendentalism's leader, Emerson, he could not stomach the "twaddle of the younger born," among whom he unfortunately numbered Clapp.[28] More positive responses came from those aligned with Transcendentalism's "individualist" wing. In a letter appended to the preface to Clapp's later *Essays, Letters, and Poems,* Hedge termed her *Studies in Religion* "a revelation." "Of all my female friends," he wrote, "and indeed of all my friends—there was none who seemed to me to possess more profound spiritual insight."[29] Not only is *Studies in Religion* one of the few extended Transcendentalist texts by a woman, it provides a superb understanding of how the Unitarian rank and file received, understood, and recycled the high intellectual philosophizing of Emerson and the other prominent Transcendentalists.

A letter of Clapp's from 1884 clarifies her earlier beliefs. "Mr. Emerson's method," she wrote, explaining her onetime predisposition to it, "as translated into practice by his ordinary disciples, was to seek the presence and authority of spiritual law in one's own consciousness" and to "consider the innermost facts of the consciousness as one in nature with God, and consequently divine in essence and infallible in its moral guidance." This analysis of consciousness, she continued, drew "to its magic circle the intuitively religious," the "more delicate and subjectively constituted moral natures, offended by the hollowness and insincerity of social forms, and the young and imaginative, to whom common life and received maxims" were "prosaic and hard." In retrospect, she grew to understand the danger of such self-reliance among those ill suited to practice it. "Hurt and disorder," she wrote, often "followed the releasing of ordinary minds and temperaments from the bondage of accredited and invested wisdom," and "the serene star of Emerson's thought was often traversed by lurid meteors," minds "assertive and dogmatic in their ignorance only." She had been one of those "caught up on the wild wings of that cyclone," and in that emotion had published her *Studies in Religion* as a testament to its power. Though by 1860, she, like Brownson, felt the want of "the rites and dogmas of Christianity" and sought the comfort and inclusiveness of a more organized church, in the 1840s she had been, as she put it, "a thorough Transcendentalist."[30]

Her *Studies in Religion* constitutes precisely what the reviewer for *The Harbinger* said, a "quotation," in an "oracular mode," of that "remarkable intellectual and moral phenomenon, New England Transcendentalism."[31] More precisely, it reflects that part of the movement represented by Convers Francis and Frederic Hedge, who, while deeply influenced by the new intellectual crosscurrents, remained firmly attached to Christianity, unlike, say, Emerson and Parker, whose beliefs moved them beyond Christianity, which they viewed as only one of many equally available, and admirable, faiths. Although Clapp had moved in that direction, and while her book showed the heady effects of conversation and correspondence with the likes of Emerson and Peabody, she is best described as a member of Unitarian's "evangelical" wing, reinterpreting Christianity in light of contemporary scriptural exegesis and Idealist philosophy.

Her chapter titles provide an index of her interests: "Spirit," "Truth," "Law and Love," "Grace," "Baptismal," "Communion," "Faith," and "Retribution," among others in the two-hundred-page book. Showing the pervasiveness of Swedenborg's influence in the 1840s, her first chapter, on the "Spirit," redacts his position on the subject. Spirit, she explains, is the invisible force behind or in everything, for the "outward is not the reality, but the form of it," the "manifestation of the inward." A star is one form of spirit, a flower is another, she continues, and the human body a third. All creation manifests spirit to the senses but finally is insufficient to satisfy man's cravings for the absolute.[32] "Every material fact," she writes, "must express some spiritual fact."[33] Simply put, as Emerson had said in *Nature*, nature is the symbol of spirit.

Clapp argues similarly in "Law and Love," in which she asks, what is meant by "Revelation"? Here, too, she was indebted to Emerson. Appearances, impressions, the sensuous, are all parts of the veil that hides us from the eternal, she observed, and whenever we are absorbed in "the transitory, the passing, by vanity, ambition, any love or mode of life that has the outward for its end and aim," so much thicker the veil. Concomitantly, those least in thrall to outward fact discern inward truth most clearly. To those who dwell in the spirit, the veil becomes transparent, and "they see truth, and tell what they see, and we receive what they tell and call it a revelation." The mistake is to think that only Moses or Jesus offer revelation, while it is available to all. "How few of us realize," Clapp writes, the constant action of "Eternal Law" and how we try to elude its "terrible Presence." Christ revealed this great law of selfless love, which mankind must try to emulate, for this was "the highest we can attain unto" and most evident "in the sense of necessity, of obligation," our service to others. To discover and serve this revelation is the reason for our existence.[34] In another chapter, Clapp elaborates Emerson's remark in *Nature* that the true mark of virtue is to see the miraculous in the simple. "Daily employments, intercourse with one's family, risings and retirings, walks and talks, meetings and partings," Clapp observed, we consider quite ordinary things, failing to recognize "that there is no such thing as common-place life or uninteresting circumstances." That which looks so common, so shopworn and dusty, in reality is divine, "an inexhaustible well of truth."[35]

Consider, also, Clapp's section on "Sonship," in which she treats Jesus. Here too the Transcendentalist influence is readily apparent. She notes, as Emerson did in his address at the Divinity School, that Jesus "is of the same race as ourselves, not a son of angels, but a son of man," so that all he could assert as actually true of himself could be true of all men. The holy life thus consists of man's "working out of him what God works in him," for there is "no limit to the son's power but the Father's revelation."[36] How shall we find out what we believe? "By noting," she replies, "that upon which we act." We may act from a "conviction" or a "sentiment" or an intuition. Whatever we term it, it constitutes the bedrock of faith.[37]

Studies in Religion constitutes a remarkable example of lay Transcendentalism. Clapp was never well known. She was no minister like Parker or reformer like Brownson; no woman's rights advocate like Margaret Fuller or mystic like Alcott. But in her youth the new views deeply touched her, and she incorporated them in moving ways into her personal belief as well as in her classes for women's edification. Late in life Clapp came to believe that Transcendentalism finally had been insufficient to carry her as far into the world of spirit as she desired. Yet it had been "a preparation, through antagonism and opposition, for a coming statement of spiritual truth as a revelation to Reason."[38] One of her friends offered the best assessment of where such reasoning took Clapp. "Miss Clapp's rare ability," she wrote, "would have enabled her to fill honorably a large public sphere," had she sought it, but she chose to live in a quiet and retired way. Her personal influence, however, was "very distinctly felt as a stimulus to intellectual and moral growth by the circle that drank from her unfailing spring of inspiration."[39] *Studies in Religion* thus testifies to how powerfully Transcendentalist ideas influenced even the commonest of lives.

Margaret Fuller initially dismissed Sylvester Judd's novel, *Margaret: A Tale of the Real and Ideal* (1845), but she changed her mind. Then living in New York, Fuller apologized in Greeley's *New-York Daily Tribune* for the "stupidity" of an earlier brief notice of Judd's effort. Now that she had read it more carefully, she found it "full of genius, profound in meaning, and of admirable fidelity to Nature in its details." Her friends, she added, concurred. They drew "from it auspicious omens, that an American literature is possible even in our day."[40] *Margaret* offers another illustration of how Transcendentalism fertilized the Unitarian mind and nurtured remarkable intellectual fruit. When the book was reissued later in the century, a writer for the *Springfield Republican* claimed that Judd's novel was, without doubt, one of "the manifold utterances" of Transcendentalism.[41]

Judd was born in Westhampton, Massachusetts, in 1813 and was raised, as Greene and Clapp had been, in a religiously conservative household. Educated at nearby Hopkins Academy, he entered Yale College and after his graduation in 1836 taught at a private academy in the Worcester County, Massachusetts, town of Templeton. This small hill-country community comprised a sizable population of Unitarians as well as orthodox Christians. Exposed to liberal Christianity by some of his new friends and neighbors, Judd realized soon enough, as he wrote to his sister-in-law, that though he had been "employed by the Orthodox party," he had become "too liberal." That May he began to attend the local Unitarian services and wrote in his journal that he loved to worship "in Nature's temple" whose "dome is the sky, whose pillars are the mountains."[42]

Moving to Northampton, Massachusetts, Judd prepared a lengthy manuscript called his "Cardiagraphy," an analysis of his "heart" in which he strove to come to grips with his conflicted religious state. In it he explained that, while many of his friends found him changed, in his deepest self he remained the same, having in view the great end of doing good to man and glorifying God.[43] What had changed, however, was his acceptance of consciousness as the "primary, incontrovertible, unequivocal source" of spiritual evidence. Consciousness was nothing less than "the eye of the soul." Anything that contradicted its testimony was false, including the stringent Calvinist faith in which he had been raised. Through the eye of his soul Judd saw a beautiful, not a fallen, world, and men and women who were good, not irretrievably lost to sin. His soul had "burst from its prison-house," and he walked forth "buoyant with freedom, upwards towards its God." He had found his way to Transcendentalism.

In the late summer of 1837 Judd entered Harvard's Divinity School and was in Cambridge when Emerson delivered his Phi Beta Kappa address, although we do not know if he heard it. In Judd's second year of study Emerson delivered his notorious address to the graduating class at the Divinity School, and it is inconceivable that Judd could ignore the rancorous debate that ensued. He soon met the great Channing, whose soul he found "full of great thoughts, great plans of progress, reformation, and Christianization," and he also became a close friend of the brilliant but eccentric Jones Very, tutor of Greek at Harvard, whose *Essays and Poems* (1839) Emerson helped to publish.[44] An exemplary student, Judd used his Harvard years not only to prepare for the Unitarian ministry but also to widen his reading. He knew his Carlyle and Coleridge, followed the Norton-Ripley debate, and, like other young men at the Divinity School, learned German and borrowed books by Fichte, Hegel, and Schelling from the college library. On Visitation Day in June 1840, he was chosen as one of two speakers for his class, and he addressed the gathering on "The Uses of Intellectual Philosophy to the Preacher," presaging his career as a minister and writer.[45]

That summer, Judd was called to a Unitarian church in Augusta, Maine, where the nearest person in the same intellectual orbit was Frederic Henry Hedge, in nearby Bangor. Like Hedge, Judd considered himself one of the "Evangelical Unitarians" and proselytized for what he termed the "Birthright Church," an open church into which every person is born, just as he is born into a family and a community, and to which he owes allegiance and from which he receives benefits like the sacraments.[46] In his role as moral leader of the community, Judd also encouraged reform, taking special interest in the temperance movement as well as the work of the American Peace Society. He did his good work locally and remained in the Augusta ministry until his death, in 1853.

Judd is remembered for his literary output, especially the novel *Margaret: A Tale of the Real and Ideal, Blight and Bloom; Including Sketches of a Place Not Before Described, Called Mons Christi*, which the Boston publishers Jordan and Wiley issued in 1845 in an edition of one thousand copies, half of which Judd subsidized. The book was intended, he wrote his friend the Reverend Edward Everett Hale, "to promote the cause of liberal Christianity" and "give body and soul to the divine elements of the gospel." The novel was about Christ, he continued, and "him it would restore to the church, him it would develop in the soul, him it would enthrone in the world." Judd designed the book to show how a life in Christ led one to the causes of "peace, temperance, and universal freedom."[47] It was also, he wrote, a "New England book," designed to "embody the features and improve the character of our favorite region." What was more, it would "fill a gap, long left open in Unitarian literature,— that of imaginative writings," and as such be of some use in the hands of the clergy, in families, and in "Sunday-school libraries."[48] Judd also clearly envisioned his work as a contribution to the small stock of American regional fiction, a genre pioneered by James Fenimore Cooper and Catharine Maria Sedgwick. No novelist published with more vaunted hopes.

Judd's novel tells the story of the eponymous Margaret, a country girl unencumbered by artificial religion or philosophy, open to the genial influences of the natural world, which speak to her intuition. She is, in other words, a young, unconscious Transcendentalist, reading the lessons of nature at every step, making the right decision because she follows her conscience. Margaret lives in the backwoods, at "the Pond," with the family of Didymus Hart, to whom she had been brought at a young age by one of their sons, Nimrod, following the death of her parents and to evade the machinations of an evil grandfather. Among the Harts, and particularly under the tutelage of their second son, Chilion, Margaret flourishes, even as she encounters more and more of civilization's corruptions, including her neighbors' harsh Calvinist faith. Because of her natural piety she resists attempts to bring her to the "true" faith, although she is moved by descriptions of the remarkable Jesus, about whom she has had a moving dream that marks her movement into Unitarianism, though she cannot yet name it. In memorable passages Judd provides vivid pictures of what it is like to grow up untrammeled by society, and he ends the first section, "Childhood," with Margaret on the verge of adolescence.

The second part, "Youth," finds Margaret in her teens, still resisting attempts to win her to the orthodox fold even as she pays the penalty for so doing. One day she meets a Mr. Evelyn, who, recognizing her as a troubled though pure soul, speaks to her of his religion. Evelyn is Unitarian, his theology perfectly congruent with what hitherto had been unspoken, though everywhere evident, in Margaret's life. His words, filled with Transcendentalist-inspired appreciation of nature and its relation to spirit, deeply move his young tutee, as does his sense of Christ as the ultimate Transcendentalist, who preached the divinity of all men and the miracle of quotidian existence.

In the final section, "Womanhood," which Judd narrates in epistolary form, Margaret and Evelyn, now her husband, regenerate the community by inculcating the ethic of Transcendental Christianity: a white cross on the summit of nearby "Mons Christi" marks the reformation. Importantly, Judd did not imagine such societal transformation as an Associationist experiment, but rather as the triumph, in each individual, of the Christian doctrine of love. As remarkable a utopian vision as any presented by Brisbane, Ripley, or Alcott, Judd's Mons Christi most resembles William Henry Channing's Christian socialism and Elizabeth Peabody's "Glimpse of Christ's Idea of Society."[49] Mons Christi, that is, exists because the inhabitants of the village have recognized the centrality of Christ and the inherent goodness of the human heart. *Margaret*, Judd hoped, might help to initiate just such a transformation on a large scale, making Mons Christi more influential than Brook Farm ever could be.

No brief redaction captures the intellectual and emotional richness of this novel; it was indeed all that Judd had hoped. And it enjoyed a measurable degree of success. In 1851, for example, Judd published a revised two-volume edition, eliminating passages that some critics found "vulgar"; this emended version was reissued as late as 1882. Also, F.O.C. Darley, one of the country's premier book illustrators, was "so much struck with the graphic delineations of the book, and their truly American character," that he produced an elegant oversize portfolio of engravings, *Compositions in Outline . . . from Judd's "Margaret"* (1856), of scenes and characters from the novel, speaking to his, and his publisher's, sense of its significance.[50] *Margaret* was also heralded not only "as a record of great ideas and sentiments" but also as being "among the few good books of the age." One critic recognized how effectively Judd dispensed with religious cant, and how sincerely and accurately he depicted "the deep and universal spirit of Christ." The book's immediate and chief practical work, one reviewer wrote, is that it "contemplates social advancement and reform." And in this vein, "we recognize a higher truth in it than in any other writings that have come under our notice, which advocate the reorganization of society," a slap at the Associationists' pipe dreams.[51]

Writing in *The Christian Examiner*, another Unitarian, Frederic Dan Huntington, criticized the "unnaturalness and stiffness," as well as the vulgarity and "low life," of the first part of the novel, but he was pleasantly surprised that such imperfections later vanished, when "earnest thoughts were uttered and earnest sympathies are engaged." We do not often meet, he wrote of the third section, "with finer illustrations and statements of the nature, character and real mission of Christ, and the significance of the Gospel."[52] James Russell Lowell, reviewing Henry Wadsworth Longfellow's

Kavanagh: A Tale a few years later, compared it to *Margaret* and effusively praised the latter as a major contribution to the nation's literature. He termed Judd's novel "the most emphatically American book ever written."[53]

Other critics saw his book as limited, abrupt, and lacking in artistry, but perhaps the most unusual notice was Brownson's in *Brownson's Quarterly Review*, where he used the novel as the occasion for a long essay on how "Protestantism Ends in Transcendentalism." Admitting that he had not even read the book but had relied on a "Protestant lady's" redaction (perhaps Margaret Fuller's, in the *Tribune*), Brownson, now a Roman Catholic, classified the work "under the general head of Transcendentalism." It was not just that *Margaret* was a "weak and silly book," but that it counseled an excessive and dangerous self-reliance that led to solipsism. Brownson's main point was that no Protestant, "as a Protestant," had a right to censure the book, for though one might affect "a great contempt of Transcendentalism, and horror at its extravagance and blasphemy," it was based on nothing less that that on which Protestantism was founded, the right of private judgment over external authority in matters of faith. To Brownson, Transcendentalism was not a simple "Yankee notion" peculiar to New England, but "the dominant error of our times." In books like Judd's, he concluded, it "reaches its termination, exhausts itself, and can go no farther; for there is no farther." Transcendentalism, he declared, "is the last stage this side of NOWHERE."[54]

Such criticism did not discourage Judd, who in 1850 published two other ambitious works. The first was *Philo: An Evangeliad*, a highly allegorical, long, blank-verse narrative, which he began in 1845. In a letter, Judd explained this poem's purpose as an attempt to see if liberal and rational Christianity comprised epic and heroic elements. The poem also asks whether, "in this very sensible and sound age of ours, imagination must needs [*sic*] be inactive, and awed by philosophy, utility, and steam." If *Margaret* was "a Christian consummation in a single neighborhood," he continued, *Philo* "is the same for the land at large, and the whole world."[55] In its one major notice, in the *North American Review*, Andrew Preston Peabody noted such ambitions but repeated some of the criticisms of *Margaret*. Peabody also acknowledged that Judd was too familiar with the best in literature "not to have the canons of good taste at his easy command." If he "will make himself their master, there are no laurels too high for his reach."⁵⁶

In his third literary effort, *Richard Edney and the Governor's Family, a Rus-Urban Tale* (1850), Judd turned to the contemporary novel of manners, even as he again illustrated the redemptive potential of character. It narrates Edney's move from the Maine countryside to the city of Woodlyn (Augusta, Maine), where he is challenged by the moral ambiguity incumbent on the Industrial Revolution, in this case, vast, recently constructed sawmills. In anticipation of the rags-to-riches tales soon popularized by Horatio Alger, Edney, by dint of moral and physical courage, finds favor with the governor's family and eventually wins his daughter. The book champions the work ethic of the farmer and artisan against the shrewd manipulations of the new capitalists. Much indebted to Emerson's notion of self-reliance and its frequent oversimplification into the platitude that a man is what he chooses to make of himself, *Richard Edney* acknowledges that liberal religion was entering a new phase, one defined more by attention to external character than to inward soul. In this novel there is no Mons Christi, only Richard's pluck and timely visits from Lady Luck.

Literary and intellectual historians debate whether Judd should be numbered among the Transcendentalists, but anyone attentive to the degree to which nature and conscience influence his central characters has no trouble answering in the affirmative. Judd's time spent among Channing, Emerson, and others pushed him beyond the conservative Unitarianism typified at Harvard. One cannot imagine, for example, someone saying of Andrews Norton, as they did of Judd, "Nature was to him the revelation and embodiment of Divinity itself."⁵⁷ Rusticated in northern New England, far from the city whose teachers had changed his life, he dedicated his ministry and career as an author to the lessons then—and continuously—learned from Transcendentalism.

Although now most often associated with New England Transcendentalism, through the 1840s Henry David Thoreau (1817–62) was only an apprentice in the movement. A native of Emerson's

Concord, he grew up in middling circumstances, his father a pencil maker, his mother taking in boarders to supplement the family's meager income. He entered Harvard College at sixteen and graduated the year Emerson gave the Phi Beta Kappa address. At college he took four semesters of German, and one summer he enlisted Orestes Brownson to tutor him in the language; it remained a lifelong passion, but like Margaret Fuller, he gravitated more to Goethe than to the Idealist philosophers. Thoreau also excelled in classics, later completing and publishing translations from the Greek and Latin. After graduation, with his older brother John, he took up school teaching in his hometown.

Through this period Thoreau came more and more under Emerson's influence and thus within Transcendentalism's expanding orbit. In 1840 he attended one of the final meetings of the Transcendental Club, held at Emerson's home, and his older friend solicited his writings for the projected *Dial.* "Aulus Persius Flaccus," an essay on the Roman satirist, as well as examples of Thoreau's own verse, appeared in the journal's early issues, under Fuller's editorship. In March 1841, Ripley, recognizing his friend's strong practical bent, asked him to join the fledgling Brook Farm enterprise. Sympathetic to many of the group's goals, Thoreau finally decided against it, declaring in the privacy of his journal that he would "rather keep bachelor's hall in hell than go to board in heaven."[58] That summer, Thoreau moved into Emerson's "Bush" as handyman and housekeeper to the now-increasingly absent Emerson, whose lecture career was taking off. Thoreau was an intimate of the household, Lydian's confidant, and for all intents and purposes Emerson's protégé.

The year 1842 held great personal losses for Thoreau and Emerson, with the death early in January of Thoreau's beloved brother John from tetanus and of Emerson's adored five-year-old son, Waldo, of scarlet fever within the same month. Grief tore at and changed both men. All that saved them was their renewed faith in the rightness of nature and their dedication to their work. For Thoreau this involved the pen, for he had decided to become a writer and lecturer, like his older friend, who the year before had published his first substantial book, *Essays,* and was traveling throughout New England and New York on the lyceum circuit.

Since his graduation, at Emerson's instigation, Thoreau had kept a journal, a storehouse of his thoughts and observations, as well as where he worked out preliminary drafts of his essays. When in May 1843 Emerson convinced him to travel to Staten Island to live with his brother, William Emerson, and tutor William's children, Thoreau took the opportunity to show some of his writing to the city's many publishers and editors. He quickly found, however, that his Boston connections did not get him far in the nation's publishing hub, which already was beginning to center on emergent literary celebrity. He also was disappointed to learn that, given the glut of writers, many of the journals, including the important *Knickerbocker*, paid contributors little or nothing. As he put it in a letter to his mother, "My bait will not tempt the rats,—they are too well fed."[59] Thoreau did, however, meet interesting people, most of them connected in some way to either Emerson or George Ripley and his socialist experiment at Brook Farm. These included William Henry Channing, about to commence his journal *The Present*; the Fourierist Albert Brisbane, whom Thoreau described as looking "like a man who has lived in a cellar, far gone in consumption"; Horace Greeley, two years into his editorship of the *New-York Daily Tribune*; and Henry James, Sr., deeply into Swedenborgianism.[60]

At the suggestion of his friend Hawthorne, Thoreau paid a visit to John L. O'Sullivan at *The United States Magazine and Democratic Review* and showed him his review of German utopian John Adolphus Etzler's recently reprinted tract, *The Paradise Within the Reach of All Men*, which the editor wanted him to revise because, as Thoreau wrote Emerson, he objected "to my want of sympathy" with the Associationist movement, which O'Sullivan supported.[61] Thoreau obviously felt encouraged, however, and he soon enough turned out "The Landlord," a somewhat nostalgic piece about tavern keepers, given that the metropolis now was overrun with boardinghouses. O'Sullivan published it and, the next month, printed his revised review of Etzler as well.[62]

This was the extent of Thoreau's fortune in the city. He hated urban life: "The pigs in the street," he wrote Emerson, "are the most respectable part of the population."[63] After only six months—he had been prepared to stay in New York two years—he returned to Concord. From this period his "Natural History in Massachusetts"; two travelogues—"A Walk to Wachusett" and "A Winter Walk"; and his lengthy review of Etzler comprise his major accomplishment prior to the publication of *A Week on the Concord and Merrimack Rivers* (1849), a memorial to his brother recording a two-week boating trip they once had taken. These pieces indicate how his association with Emerson and other Transcendentalists affected his subsequent literary and philosophical development.

Thoreau's review of Etzler's *The Paradise Within the Reach of All Men, Without Labor, by Powers of Nature and Machinery: An Address to All Intelligent Men* sheds light on the contemporary debate within Transcendentalism over the merits of Associationist-based reform. Indeed, Emerson's suggestion that Thoreau review the work—originally printed in Pittsburgh in 1833 and reprinted in London in 1842, where his friend Alcott encountered it—no doubt related to Emerson's own struggle over whether to join Brook Farm. Given Thoreau's eminently practical bent—he had worked in the family pencil factory as well as being a carpenter and surveyor— Emerson considered his young friend ideal to assess Etzler's scheme to harness nature on "scientific" principles, toward the reorganization of society.

Etzler was a German immigrant who had settled in the United States in 1831. Caught in the utopian fervor that swept Europe in the early decades of the nineteenth century, as well as in the heady advances in technology that already had brought such remarkable inventions as steam power, electromagnetism, and daguerreotypy, he believed his mission was to develop new technology whose use would return Earth to a paradisiacal state. He sought financial backers— among them the prominent communitarian George Rapp, leader of the Harmonites in Ohio—for an experimental community near Cincinnati. When this effort failed, Etzler moved to Pittsburgh to edit a German-language newspaper, and he published *The Paradise Within the Reach of All Men*, an odd tract that combined his interests in technological innovation and messianic speculation.

Because his ideas crossed Fourier's at several points, particularly in his advocacy of social reform based in planned communities, in 1840 he attended the Fourier Society of New York's celebration of their namesake's birthday. There he met, among other Association-ists, C. F. Stollmeyer, publisher of Albert Brisbane's *Social Destiny of Man*, who thereupon boosted Etzler's writings and inventions—including his "naval automaton," a ship that was directed by wave power. By 1844, disappointed that nothing had come of his grand plans in the United States, Etzler moved to England, where Hugh Doherty and other Associationists took up his utopian ideas and extravagant inventions. There Etzler continued his ambitious brainstorming. He founded a Tropical Emigration Society to plant one of his projected communities in Venezuela; when this idea fell through after a breakdown in negotiations with the country's leaders, he moved to the island of Trinidad, projecting colonies on floating tropical islands in the Caribbean. By this time, however, he had lost the interest of all but the most loyal of his American acolytes.

In addition to being enthralled by technology—he came to the United States with a group led by John A. Roebling, who later built the Brooklyn Bridge—Etzler had been inspired by Hegel's deterministic philosophy, believing that there were reasons for all that had happened and would happen, explanations the rational man could anticipate and act on to hasten a secular millennium. Thus, in *The Paradise Within the Reach of All Men* he argued that if mankind properly harnessed nature, within ten years the vast, rude American wilderness would blossom into an immense garden. Leveling mountains, creating or draining lakes, constructing roads and canals, covering the ocean with floating islands bearing gardens and palaces: men would accomplish all this by the application of mind to matter. In this new world, because of the land's limitless bounty, work would not be drudgery, and men and women would spend their time creating and living in the ideal community, labor-saving inventions restoring the lost paradise.[64]

Such millennial dreams were shared by a wide range of reformers and religious prophets, but Thoreau, eminently practical, would have nothing to do with them. He rightly compared Etzler's vision to Fourier's and found the German's schemes one of "the signs of the times," a veritable "transcendentalism in mechanics." Certainly Etzler's vision of a world liberated from the drudgery of labor resonated in Thoreau, who believed that humanity spent too much time getting a living rather than living life itself. "How meanly and grossly do we deal with nature!" he exclaimed. But Etzler did not have a full understanding of nature. The wind, the tides, the waves, sunshine—in Etzler's fertile brain these were the keys to man's transformation of the earth into a new Garden of Eden, with all labor now reduced, Thoreau wrote sarcastically, "to a short turn of some crank." But what, Thoreau asked, about that "crank within," the "prime mover in all machinery?" That is, how did one harness each person's "divine energy"? Here Thoreau recurred to Emersonian Transcendentalism. We must "first succeed alone," he maintained, before "we may enjoy our success together." The chief fault of Etzler's plan was the same as that at the heart of Fourier's schemes, he sought "to secure the greatest degree of gross comfort and pleasure merely." He "paint[ed] a Mahometan's heaven," a pleasure palace, and neglected the most important point, that internal "moral reform" must come before any millennium.[65]

While admiring Etzler's desire to make nineteenth-century life something more than it was, Thoreau maintained that for all their supposed practicality, his schemes would do little to transform life unless men's hearts first were changed. Sounding much like a Unitarian minister, Thoreau counseled men to stoke "the heat of love." Love "can warm without fire, feed without meat, clothe without garments, and shelter without roof" and thus "make a paradise within which will dispense with a paradise without."[66] So much for Fourier's and Etzler's incessant calculation and ratiocination! Men had to discern and harness higher laws.

And Thoreau knew where to find them, something that Emerson had intuited when he gave his young friend his first major assignment. Thus, in his brief introduction to Thoreau's "Natural History of Massachusetts" in *The Dial*, Emerson explained how he had begged his friend to "lay down the oar and fishing line, which none can handle better, to assume the pen."[67] The result, "Natural History of Massachusetts," was indeed such a promise of his future achievement, and it exemplifies Thoreau's gift of discerning the import of the natural world in ways that his contemporaries, even friends like Emerson or Hawthorne, rarely countenanced.

Taking as his occasion seemingly mundane scientific reports, Thoreau opened the essay with a moving meditation on the restorative powers of nature. "Surely," he wrote, "joy is the condition of life," for "the spruce, the hemlock, and the pine will not countenance despair." "Think of the young fry that leap in ponds," he reminded his readers, "the myriads of insects ushered into being on a summer evening, the incessant note of the hyla [tree frog] with which the woods ring in spring, the nonchalance of the butterfly carrying accident and change painted in a thousand hues upon its wings, [and] the brook minnow stoutly stemming the current."[68] Compared to these, the din about religion, literature, and philosophy heard in contemporary pulpits, lyceums, and parlors was unimportant. Close observation of nature mattered, Thoreau submitted, and if the reports under review (error-strewn though he found them) brought us closer to it, so much the better.

In this essay Thoreau also anticipated several powerful passages in his masterpiece, *Walden* (1854). At one point, for example, in his discussion of the birds of Massachusetts, he comments on the "Great Northern Diver" (common loon), describing its "game" on a pond as it tries to escape being cornered by someone in a boat, a premonition of his lengthy passage on the same creature in "The Ponds" section of *Walden*. At another juncture he notes how "the foliate structure is common to the coral and the plumage of birds, and to how large a part of animate nature," anticipating the famous "railroad-cut" passage in the "Spring" chapter of that book, when he sees in the thawing sandbank the same images of the life force, and he understands, as he puts it, that "vegetation has been made the type of all growth."[69] By this point, in other words, Thoreau already saw in the intricacy of nature the universal laws that underpin all life.

"Let us not underrate the value of a fact," Thoreau wrote in his final paragraph. "It will one day flower in a truth." The true "man of science," he continued, did not learn "by inference and deduction, and the application of mathematics to philosophy, but by direct intercourse and sympathy" with nature.[70] This discovery of universal law attendant on the quotidian facts of nature, and the ability to translate this knowledge into memorable prose, hereafter became Thoreau's hallmarks.

The results of Thoreau's gift are apparent in less-restricted ways in his two travel essays from this same period, when he was not bound to the format of a review. "A Walk to Wachusett" recounts his and his friend Richard Fuller's four-day trip to the mountain of that name, thirty-five miles from Concord, that dominates the central Massachusetts landscape and offers grand views of its larger sister, Mount Monadnock, forty miles northwest, in New Hampshire. Walking through the cool woods of Acton and Stow, just west of Concord, the pair rested in the highlands at Lancaster, looking longingly westward at their destination, and spent the night at a tavern at Stillwater, a village in the western part of Sterling, four miles from the base of the mountain. Early the next morning they were on its summit, nineteen hundred feet above Princeton and three thousand feet above sea level, not an immense height, yet making them feel a "sense of remoteness," so "infinitely removed from the plain" did they seem.[71]

They enjoyed looking to other mountain ranges, the Berkshires and Green Mountains to the west, the White Mountains to the north, and they even arose early enough to watch the sun rise from the sea. By noon they were descending to spend the night in the nearby town of Harvard. Evincing what became his trademark ability to draw truths from natural facts, Thoreau noted that even on the dusty road they endeavored to "import a little of that mountain grandeur." "We will remember," he wrote, "within what walls we live, and understand that this level life too has its summit" and that there is "elevation in every hour, as no part of the earth is so low that the heavens may not be seen from, and we have only to stand on the summit of our one hour to command an uninterrupted horizon."[72] The lines typify Thoreau's trademark eloquence.

So, too, the language of "A Winter Walk," for on a journey even closer to home, out from town the morning after a deep snowfall, Thoreau manages to elicit the beauty of newly fallen snow as it transforms the common landscape. Culled from his journal, his descriptions evoke synesthetically the serenity and purity in the aftermath of a storm. "Every decayed stump and moss-grown stone and rail," he writes, "and the dead leaves of autumn, are concealed by a clean napkin of snow." A cold and searching wind "drives away all contagion, and nothing can withstand it but what has a virtue in it," so that whatever we meet in the cold, we "respect for a sort of sturdy innocence, a Puritan toughness."[73] "In this lonely glen," he observes, "with its brook draining the slopes, its creased ice and crystals of all hues, where the spruces and hemlocks stand up on either side, and the rush and sere wild oats in the rivulet itself, our lives are more serene and worthy to contemplate."[74] This was a paradise far from Etzler's, for the wonders of technology were superfluous.

In March 1845 Thoreau borrowed an ax and began to clear tall white pines on acreage that Emerson had purchased on Walden Pond, a mile from Concord's center. On July 4 he moved into a cabin he had built on the land, and he remained there for two years, two months, and two days, "to transact some private business with the fewest obstacles," as he put it.[75] While at Walden Pond he continued his long-standing rituals of daily walking and writing, filling page after page in his various notebooks and his journal. He also mined these to assemble a draft of his first book, *A Week on the Concord and Merrimack Rivers*, which after much revision he published.

In these years he also continued to oscillate in Emerson's rainbow, but over time he thought of himself as more Emerson's equal and less his disciple, a split that widened in the 1850s. Emerson was a hard taskmaster. "I am very familiar with all [Thoreau's] thoughts," Emerson wrote in his journal. "They are my own quite originally drest." "But if the question be," he continued, "what new ideas has he thrown into circulation, he has not yet told what that is which he was created to say."[76] But during the previous decade Emerson clearly regarded Thoreau as a valuable addition to the stable of young minds he had assembled in Concord, the young man's essays being proof texts of Emerson's "Self-Reliance." Thoreau was, Caroline Dall recalled, "in his own person a powerful refutation of the theories of the Socialists."[77]

These four examples indicate that by the mid-1840s Transcendentalism was a pulsing, magnetic current, drawing many different people into it and subsequently freeing them to work in various innovative ways, indelibly marked by their contact with the ideas that characterized the movement. Greene, Clapp, Judd, and Thoreau are not so much extraordinary as exemplary. One could easily replace them with other individuals for whom Transcendentalist ideas provided comparable draughts of inspiration. Further, by this time, in the popular mind, Transcendentalism, no matter how much its representatives denied it, had assumed a fairly stable, if not fully describable, identity. People knew what to expect, for example, when they went to hear a sermon by Parker or sat down to read an essay of Emerson's.

These four also point up the increasingly visible fractures within the Transcendentalist movement, between disciples of Emerson, empowered by his enshrinement of the self-reliant individual, and those who, following Brownson's and Ripley's lead, found in Idealist philosophy the grounding for a truly egalitarian society. By the late 1840s, with the country plunged into war with Mexico and increasingly preoccupied with the issue of slavery, Transcendentalism changed even more as the transatlantic ideas that had proved the group's main inspiration seemed less immediately relevant. The European democratic revolutions of 1848 briefly kept alive dreams of a transatlantic cadre of intellectuals whose humanitarian ideals might transform the world. After 1850, however, New England's radicals, whether proponents of self-culture or advocates of broad social reform, were left alone with America. Transcendentalism's rich intellectual garden began to bear different fruit.

8

SELF AND SOCIETY

y the mid-1840s, with the increasing furor over the extension of American slavery into newly acquired Western Territories and widespread social upheaval in Europe, social reform was everywhere the subject of endless talk, if not always action. Thus, Emerson's March 3, 1844, lecture, "New England Reformers," at Amory Hall in Boston, was timely. He was invited by a group of Come-outers, who believed that everyone should be free to hold whatever religious views he pleased and that one's faith should eventuate in action on behalf of the less fortunate. Hence their interest not only in ecclesiastical reform but also in matters of diet and health and in issues of social justice such as prison reform and antislavery. In the late winter and spring of 1844 one could not find a more radical meeting in Boston. Emerson joined a series of prominent speakers, including the abolitionists William Lloyd Garrison and Wendell Phillips; the communitarians Adin Ballou, the founder of the Hopedale Community, and Charles Lane, Bronson Alcott's associate at Fruitlands; and, at Emerson's suggestion, the young contrarian Henry Thoreau.[1]

Amory Hall, which the group began to rent in January 1844, stood at the corner of Washington and West streets in Boston, just down the block from Elizabeth Peabody's bookstore and lending library. The Society at Amory Hall scheduled twelve Sunday lectures, at 10:30 a.m. and 7:30 p.m. Presentations were not repeated, but consisted of separate talks (or longer ones in two parts), usually by the same speaker, with the afternoon hours devoted to discussion on previously announced topics. Donations or subscriptions to the whole series were solicited but not required; in any event, the Society did not have any trouble making ends meet. Garrison, labeled the "chief Priest" by one opposition paper, presented on the first two Sundays as well as on the last, and addressed the group not, as one might expect, on abolition, but on "Worship," the "Priesthood," and "The Conditions and Rights of Women," subjects that indicate the linkage in his mind (as well as in the minds of his listeners) of other sorts of reform to the pressing question of slavery.[2] Emerson's contribution to the series epitomized a version of the Transcendentalist ethos based on uncompromising self-reliance by now closely identified with the speaker. By no means, however, was his the ruling ethos, for many Transcendentalists questioned the efficacy of such self-reliance in light of the magnitude of the Mexican War, European revolutionary upheavals, or the horrors of slavery, causes that pitted communities and great aggregates of interests against one another.

Emerson's courteous if somewhat tongue-in-cheek advice on how to initiate social change provided an answer of sorts. He began by noting how New England recently had witnessed manifold signs that the impulse to reform society had fallen away from "the church nominal" and had reappeared in various societies (like that at Amory Street) composed of "ultraists, of seekers, of all the soldiery of dissent."[3] Without a touch of irony he listed the more unusual initiatives—dietary and agricultural reform of the sort instituted at Bronson Alcott's Fruitlands, for example, as well as assaults on the institution of marriage (with Fourier's speculations in mind). To these he added homoeopathy, hydropathy, mesmerism, and phrenology. Beyond the "petulance" and "puerility" of such efforts, Emerson saw greater problems.

In the reformers' haste to do away with the old, he observed, they often did not adequately prepare "to affirm and to construct," for they were satisfied to eradicate an evil without consideration of what should take its place. "Society gains nothing whilst a man, not himself renovated," attempts to renovate things around him, with the "disgusting result" of vanity or hypocrisy. Further, to be swept up too exclusively in one category of reform could make an individual morally obtuse. Emerson was adamant about the ill effects of such "partiality." To focus solely on one moral evil elided the fact that "the wave of evil washes all our institutions alike," so that one could not afford to waste one's time in such exclusive attacks. "The street is as false as the church, and when I get to my house," he continued, "or to my manners, or to my speech, I have not got away from the lie."[4]

Just as problematic as this moral obliquity and partiality was the reformers' increasing reliance on "association" to combat social injustice, the approach Hedge, Ripley, and others advocated. Emerson applauded such intentions, admitting that Brook Farm and the Northampton Association of Education and Industry were comprised of "men and women of superior talents and sentiments." Over time, however, he feared that the communities might become asylums for those who had "tried and failed" in the world. Friendship and association were fine, as long as one realized "that no society can ever be so large as one man." In relying too much on others, a person becomes a fraction of himself. There simply can be "no concert in two," Emerson declared, "where there is no concert in one."[5]

Here is the heart of Emerson's belief about reform: only after an individual experiences the paradise within can he join with others, similarly enlightened, to restore the outer paradise. Only then would institutions, comprised as they were of discrete individuals, change. Admittedly, men and women at work together appeared to accomplish more when they met as equals. But reform remained only cosmetic unless this union was "inward." It did not consist merely in external covenant, for those who banded together in an imperfect state were, on all sides, "cramped and diminished" in proportion. "The union," he concluded, "must be ideal in actual individualism."[6]

This belief in radical individualism, articulated so powerfully in Emerson's *Essays* (1841) and *Essays, Second Series* (1844), was at the heart of his Transcendentalism. In "New England Reformers," the final essay in his second volume, he reiterated his profoundly democratic sense that "the net amount of man and man does not vary."

The new world that reformers seek, Emerson urged, would not arrive because "we drink water, we eat grass, we refuse the laws, we go to jail." Such activities were in vain if the heart was not pure. The new world would not arrive until each obeyed his or her genius, "the only liberating influence."[7]

In the six years between the publication of his address to the Divinity School and the appearance of *Essays, Second Series,* Emerson had moved from being a little-known lightning rod for the movement's religious eccentricity to center stage as its chief proselytizer for an imperial self. He did so primarily through his career as a public lecturer, popularizing a compelling ethic of self-reliance in a prophetic mode that made auditors believe they were in the presence of genius. He also gathered around him in Concord a coterie of likeminded young seekers who welcomed his attention and gained from his sponsorship. Emerson's success in this could be measured by his mounting critics. The Unitarian patriarch William Ellery Channing, for example, observed to Elizabeth Peabody that, had Frederic Henry Hedge become more a presence in Transcendentalism, he might have introduced it in such a way that "it would not have become identified with the extreme Individualism" by then indelibly associated with it. Channing also observed that the danger that beset Transcendentalists was that they sometimes mistook "their individualities for the Transcendent."[8] Even the young Caroline Healey found parts of Emerson's thought problematic. Reading *Essays* shortly after the book appeared, she liked such pieces as "Compensation" and "History" but found what he had to say about self-reliance "extravagant and unsafe." More unusually, she appears not even to have read *Nature* until 1846, even though she had been traveling in Transcendentalist circles for years.[9] The seemingly willful obscurity of some of Emerson's writings prompted another criticism of Transcendentalism, that its adherents were narcissistic and self-indulgent. Francis Bowen criticized "the insufferable arrogance of the new school, and their anxiety to place themselves apart from the mass of mankind." He also noted that with them, "originality has become the cant of the day."[10]

Behind such criticism lay Emerson's belief (expressed emphatically in "New England Reformers") in the primacy of individual consciousness, that is, in the erection in every mind, as the conservative clergyman Simeon Doggett rightly characterized it, of "the standard of truth and right, and hence for every one to do what is right in his own eyes."[11] Emerson codified this version of the self in his first two books of essays. Coupled with his frequent lecture series in Boston, as well as his individual appearances in cities and towns throughout the Northeast, for many people these books, assembled from Emerson's journals and lectures, typified American Transcendentalism, even as others in the group insistently condemned the egotism to which his ideas led.

In *Essays* the pivotal essay was "Self-Reliance," in which Emerson praised the individual who learns "to detect and watch that gleam of light which flashes across his mind from within, more than the lustre of the firmament of bards and sages." Self-reliance, then, is nothing less than the willingness "to believe that what is true for you in your private heart is true for all men." This inner voice, however, Emerson observed, grows "faint and inaudible" the more mankind becomes wrapped in social bonds. "Society," he noted, is nothing more than a "joint-stock company, in which the members agree, for the better securing of his bread to each shareholder, to surrender the liberty and culture of the eater," a transparent dig at the Brook Farm experiment. Thus, "whoso would be a man, must be a nonconformist."[12]

Emerson understood what such ideas implied, but he was supremely confident of their correctness. He recounted how one friend, on hearing him question, "What have I to do with the sacredness of traditions, if I live wholly from within?" observed that "these impulses might be from below, not from above." Emerson calmly replied, "They do not seem to me to be such; but if I am the Devil's child, I will live then from the Devil," for no law was sacred to him but that of his own nature. Even more problematic was Emerson's sense of what such beliefs implied for the nature of social reform. "Do not tell me," he wrote, "as a good man did to-day, of my obligation to put all poor men in good situations," for "are they *my* poor?" As to "miscellaneous popular charities; the education at college of fools; the building of meeting-houses to the vain end to which many now stand; alms to sots, and the thousand-fold Relief Societies," he confessed that he sometimes gave a "dollar" but did not really expect it to do any good in any larger way.[13] So much for the work of Brownson and Parker!

Emerson maintained that greater self-reliance would "work a revolution in all the offices and relations of men; in their religion; in their education; in their pursuits; their modes of living; their association; in their property; in their speculative views." Reformers, he continued, might "summon conventions and vote and resolve in multitude," but God would "deign to enter and inhabit you" only by "a method precisely the reverse." Man would be strong and prevail when he threw off all foreign support and stood alone. "Is not a man better than a town?" he asked rhetorically. When one asserts his "Will," he concluded, one chains "the wheel of Chance" and is free of worry over its revolutions. "Nothing can bring you peace but yourself," he concluded. "Nothing can bring you peace but the triumph of principles."[14]

Other essays in the collection buttressed such ideas. "The Over-Soul" spoke to that divine current that flows through intuition and directs one's morality, and "Compensation" posited a world always in perfect balance, even though on occasion one might think that the cosmic scales were weighted against one. Further, this collection of essays identifies not only the Emerson who resisted Ripley's and Alcott's appeals to join their communitarian ventures, but also the person who provided a culture in the midst of upheaval—the factory, the railroad, the steamboat, the daguerreotype, and the telegraph, among other inventions irrevocably changing notions of space and time—a way to cope with the attendant change and confusion. On the lecture platform and in the press Emerson provided tools through which Americans could adapt to their novel condition, neither resisting nor condemning it.

Although *Essays, Second Series* was the work of a man chastened by experience (the title of the book's greatest essay), it still demonstrated Emerson's belief in the individual will to prevail, albeit in a universe that he could not fully mold to his wishes. Having lost his five-year-old son and Henry Thoreau's brother within the span of a few weeks at the beginning of 1842 (and the death of his first wife, Ellen, a decade earlier, from which he never fully recovered), he had good reason to question whether "compensation" really kept things in cosmic balance.

"Experience" comes early in the volume, and it marked Emerson's mature understanding of the delicate relationship between individual "power" and universal "form." In the epigram to the essay he names the "lords of life" that he will subsequently elucidate, those inescapable facts that bind us, as the Lilliputians did Gulliver, as we struggle to achieve happiness. What is man to do about them? Meet life head-on, he counsels, without expectation, and take the "potluck of the day." "I am thankful for small mercies," Emerson writes. "To fill the hour,—that is happiness; to fill the hour and leave no crevice for a repentance or an approval." This, from the man who eight years earlier had urged each individual to build his own world! Now, "to finish the moment, to find the journey's end in every step of the road, to live the greatest number of good hours, is wisdom." Moreover, consciousness, the center and glory of *Nature* and "Self-Reliance," now was mankind's bane, for "the discovery we have made that we exist" was nothing less than "the Fall of Man."[15]

When people asked, then, why he did not "realize" his world in the way he once had prophesied, he urged "patience and patience," for "we shall win at last." We till our gardens, he explains, eat our dinners, discuss household with our wives, and think nothing of such things, while they are in fact to be savored. "Never mind the ridicule, never mind the defeat," he tells us; "up again old heart!" For there "is victory yet for all justice."[16] In Emerson's world, the individual prevailed, even if the castle he built lacked final grandeur. Reviewing several volumes of Emerson's works in 1850, Theodore Parker understood his friend's accomplishment. "Mr. Emerson is the most American of our writers," he proclaimed, for "the idea of America" appeared in him "with great prominence." What idea? That of "personal freedom, of the dignity and value of human nature, the superiority of man to the accidents of a man."[17]

Emerson championed the empowered individual, the self-reliant genius for whom conscience was the highest law. But other Transcendentalists lamented how much such self-regard obscured the

Transcendentalists' response to social problems. Elizabeth Peabody had another word for it, "egotheism," which she used in characterizing her disappointment in the tendency of much Transcendentalist thought. The problem with viewing the world as Emerson did was that people "deified their own conceptions; that is, they say that their conception of God is all that men can ever know of God." She recognized this as early as 1838, when she was at Emerson's home as he revised his Divinity School address for publication. She noticed a passage that he had not delivered—as he explained, "merely for want of time." In it he had warned, she wrote, "against making a new truth a fanaticism," which, perhaps, had it been published, "would have saved many a weak brother and sister Transcendentalist from going into the extreme of *ego-theism*." "Too soon," she remembered Emerson writing, "we shall have the *puppyism* of pretension looking down on the head of all human culture; setting up against Jesus Christ every little *self* magnified."[18] Emerson obviously recognized that his ideas might lend themselves to uses other than those that he wished.

Peabody, much closer in her religious views to her mentor William Ellery Channing, concluded that when one held such self-centered views as Emerson did, "faith commits suicide" and the individual, not realizing that there is "beyond our conception, inconceivable Power, Wisdom, and Love," becomes self-centered. "Man," she urged, "proves but a melancholy God" in comparison to the divine being whom she still worshipped.[19] A reviewer in Greeley's *Tribune* was even more severe. After hearing Emerson speak on "The Transcendentalist" in his series on "The Times," the correspondent lamented Emerson's insistence that a Transcendentalist should not labor "for small objects, such as Abolition, Temperance, Political Reforms, &c." "So we would ask Mr. Emerson," he wrote indignantly, "whether the Poverty, Ignorance and Misery of the Human Race and the devastated and neglected conditions of the Globe are not objects great enough to arouse the Philosopher of the Transcendentalist School to action."[20] Emerson's friend Henry James, Sr., baldly stated the criticism. "The curse of our present times, which eliminates all their poetry," he observed of his contemporaries' resistance to socialism, is the "selfhood imposed on us by the evil world," a project in which some Transcendentalists were undeniably complicit.[21]

Despite such criticism, through the 1840s Emerson commanded his side of the Transcendentalist barricade, enlisting Alcott; Fuller; the Salem, Massachusetts, poet and eccentric Jones Very; and a host of younger admirers like Thoreau, Ellery Channing the younger, Charles King Newcomb, and Caroline Healey in a program of self-culture that revolved more around literature than social reform. But if Emerson held this intellectual vantage, other of his colleagues in the Transcendentalist circle were not ready to relinquish their dreams of an American democracy based in social harmony. For these individuals, selfless work for humanitarian reform was at the heart of Transcendentalism's promise.

One of the most vocal of these individuals was Theodore Parker. In the wake of the controversy over his *Discourse on the Transient and Permanent in Christianity* and *Discourse of Matters Pertaining to Religion* he had been ostracized from fellowship with other Unitarian clery in the Boston Association of Ministers. In the midst of these difficulties, he and his wife, Lydia, spent a year abroad to recuperate from the heated attacks on his ministry. Before he returned to the United States in the fall of 1844, he had met Charles Dickens and Thomas Carlyle, the philosophers Cousin and Friedrich Schelling, and such giants of scriptural history and exegesis as Strauss, Johann Neander, E. W. Hengstenberg, and the great de Wette, a translation of whose commentary on the New Testament had been published by Parker. He also took time to learn about the ecclesiastical and civil governments of the various countries he visited, knowledge that, upon his return, influenced his notion of American democracy and its destiny.

His sermons before Boston's Twenty-eighth Congregational Society, over which he was formally installed on January 4, 1846, were little short of electrifying. Peabody, long an admirer, recalled that when she heard Parker deliver his "A Lesson for the Day," the "deep music of his earnest voice" moved her as she had seldom been moved. "I want you to hear Parker preach now," she told

John Sullivan Dwight, for "he has got on fire with the velocity of his spirit's speed—& the elements melt in the fervent heat of his word." In short, she wrote, "He is a son of thunder."[22] Peabody's young friend, Caroline Healey, agreed. Present one evening when Emerson and others were discussing Parker, she was disappointed that no one captured what she felt for her new friend. "I had it on my lips to say," she explained, that "'every word falling from Mr. Parker's lip is a battle ax—it cleaves—a skull.'"[23]

What message did Parker so powerfully proffer? From the time of his first difficulties with the Boston Association to his assumption of his new pulpit, he had been traveling a road from religious radicalism to much more committed social and political involvement. Rather than adhere to Emerson's notion of self-reliance and the personal empowerment it promised, Parker was influenced by Schleiermacher's sense of man's cosmic dependence. God is not what we are, but what we *need* to make our lives whole, and one way to realize this is through selfless devotion to God's creation. For Parker, this meant a commitment to social action. Now he found a new circle of supporters, having painfully lost so many friends and admirers in the controversy over his religious radicalism. He consorted with the likes of prison reformer Samuel Gridley Howe; educational reformer Horace Mann; and abolitionist Joseph May, a disciple of Garrison's. Through May, he also befriended the Whig politicians Charles Sumner and Josiah Quincy, and others in the party sympathetic to abolition. Concomitantly, Parker moved toward a more vocal antislavery position, a journey hastened by the country's annexation of Texas early in 1845 in what many regarded as a ploy by Southern states to extend slave territory.

Parker's sermons at mid-decade reflected his new orientation. Gone were the detailed exegeses of thorny scriptural passages and the well-reasoned defenses of his ecclesiastical prerogatives. Instead he addressed the causes of crime and poverty in Boston, the selfishness of the merchant class, the immorality of the war with Mexico, and, ever more commonly, the agenda of the antislavery movement. By 1847, with his close friend Ripley now reviewing books for Horace Greeley's *Tribune*, and Brownson marginalized by his increasingly fervent Catholicism, Parker had become the social conscience of the Transcendentalist movement.

A look at a few of his chief sermons from this period indicates how far he had spun from Emerson's orbit. Several of these, preached in the Melodeon in 1846 and 1847 on social conditions in Boston, bear comparison to Brownson's fiery essays and sermons at the beginning of the decade. Most remarkable was Parker's astute analysis of the complicity of the wealthy in tearing the city's frayed social fabric. He understood that the problems of the poor—their seemingly inexorable descent into crime, drunkenness, and prostitution—were caused as much by the complacency of the comfortable as by any personal faults. In other addresses he took up such subjects as the "perishing" and the "dangerous" classes in Boston, linking the urban poor and the criminal to society's general neglect of the conditions that spawned them. With a large body of statistics recently prepared by the city at his command, Parker painted a dark picture of the city's steady decline into social chaos. What was needed to remove the cause of all this, Parker reminded his audience, was simply "the application of Christianity to social life." "I look to you to do something in this matter," he told his congregation. "I look to you to set an example of a noble life, human, clean, and Christian," not debasing the poor, but uplifting them.[24]

Parker's rage at his contemporaries' acquisitiveness was unbounded. "Love of money," he trumpeted in 1849, "is out of proportion to love of better things—to love of justice, of truth"; and wealth was "often made the end to live for; not the means to live by."[25] Condemning in turn tavern keepers and the popular, sensationalist press for their contribution to the city's moral quagmire, he implored his hearers to realize that "we are all brothers, rich and poor, American and foreign; put here by the same God, for the same end, and journeying towards the same heaven, and owing mutual help."[26] He urged his auditors to join in organized politics to stay the city's decline.

The battles against intemperance, and for prison reform and universal education, could be won only when Christians took control of corrupt political parties. Pointing to the election of 1848 in which Whig candidate Zachary Taylor had defeated Democratic nominee Lewis Cass and Free-Soil aspirant Martin Van Buren in a hard-pitched contest, Parker approvingly observed that "the last election has shown us what resolute men can do." He cited the efforts of all the parties—"what meetings they held, what money they raised, what talent was employed, what speeches made, what ideas set forth," toward the end that virtually everyone's vote was solicited. When public-spirited men, Parker concluded, turned their attention "to reforming the evils of society, with such a determined soul, what evil can stand against mankind?"[27] In Parker's moral calculus, Emerson's right-minded individual still mattered, as long as he worked through concerted political activity to realize the good society.

In the mid-1840s Parker threw in his lot with the Whig Party, linked to it as he was through Sumner and Quincy. At this time the nation was preoccupied with the extension of slaveholding territory, specifically the annexation of Texas and the subsequent war with Mexico, to which Parker was bitterly opposed. His *Sermon of War*, preached at the Melodeon in June 1846, as well as his *Sermon of the Mexican War*, delivered two years later at the conflict's conclusion, marked his growing indignation at the social evil of slavery as well as his continuing belief in the power of American democracy as an engine for the nation's good.

In his *Sermon of War*, Parker could hardly contain his outrage at politicians' blatant instigation of armed conflict for their own self-serving ends. He lambasted his Massachusetts countrymen's silence when President Polk declared war, and he was even more outraged when, after the governor called for volunteers, the church and the press still did nothing. Hitting his fellow citizens where he knew it hurt, he asked if they realized the toll the battles would take on their purses. He was speaking in a city, he bellowed, "whose most popular Idol is Mammon, the God of God; whose Trinity is a Trinity of Coin!" And even though the fighting was thousands of miles from Boston, the price of their stocks had fallen, the rates of their insurance were altered, and their commodities waited on the docks, unshipped.[28] Add to this economic disruption the immense waste of goods and property, and the terrible loss of human life that accompanied the conflict, and one knew the true dogs of war.

Parker was speaking not only to Americans but to Christians. "Aggressive war is a sin," he reminded them, "a corruption of the public morals." It was a "practical denial of Christianity; a violation of God's eternal law of love."[29] What blinded his countrymen to this evident truth? "The eyes of the North are full of cotton," he told his audience, "they see nothing else, for a web is before them; their ears are full of cotton, and they hear nothing but the buzz of their mills; their mouth is full of cotton, and they can speak audibly but two words—Tariff, Tariff, Dividends, Dividends." Northern politicians closed their eyes as long as more money was to be made, and as a result, the "nation's neck now invites a tyrant."[30] Finally, Parker reminded them that war, horrible as it was, was not the worst calamity that could befall a nation. "It is far worse to lose all reverence for right, for truth, all respect for man and God; to care more for the freedom of trade than the freedom of men; more for a tariff than millions of souls." Look at your rulers, he told his audience, "and see your own likeness!"[31]

Parker and other opponents of the Mexican War were shouting into the wind; and when the conflict ended two years later, he sarcastically assessed his congregation's putative gains. When the war began, he recalled, "there was a good deal of talk about it here; talk against it." But, Parker observed wryly, "as things often go in Boston," it ended in talk, as many men "diligently set themselves to make money out of the war and the new turn it gave to national affairs."[32] He again mentioned the war's cost in monetary and human terms, more than he could have predicted two years earlier, when he had prayed that the conflict would be brief. Parker's anger was palpable. "I wish," he said,

all of this killing of 2,000 Americans on the field of battle, and the 10,000 Mexicans; all this slashing of the bodies of 24,000 wounded men; all the agony of the other 18,000, that have died of disease, could have taken place in some spot where the President of the United States and his Cabinet, where all the Congress who voted for the war . . . the controlling men of both political parties, who care nothing for this bloodshed and misery they have idly caused, could have stood and seen it all; and then that the voice of the whole nation had come up to them and said, "This is your work, not ours ... We have trusted you thus far, but please God we never will trust you again."[33]

Slavery was "the blight of this nation," he told the assembled, "the curse of the North and the curse of the South" and, whether they acknowledged it or not, the reason for which the war was fought. Slavery hindered commerce, manufacture, and agriculture, he added, and it "confounds your politics" and silenced the "ablest men." It had robbed three million people of "what is dearer than life" and prevented the welfare of seventeen million more. "You ask, O Americans, where is the harmony of the Union?" Parker knew the answer. "It was broken by slavery." A good man had to speak out and vote against the slave power.[34]

The timbre of Parker's voice was not Emerson's. By the mid-1840s Parker wanted political and social change and did not depend on self-culture to initiate it. Conscience might make one realize what political party to support, but thereafter one effected change through organized pressure. By 1850, at the vanguard of the abolition movement, he set aside his projected history of religious thought and began to work tirelessly to realize his ideal of a democratic America. He was not much interested in the Associationists' dream of international cooperation and union. The country's unique moral problem of slavery now demanded all his attention.

In 1849, when Elizabeth Peabody introduced her new project, a journal called *Aesthetic Papers*, she had explicitly in mind the division between self and society epitomized by Emerson on the one hand and Parker on the other. Gallantly she tried to broker a peace between them. In her quarterly she wished to assemble, she proclaimed, on the "high aesthetic ground," writers of different schools. In particular, she hoped that her journal would bring together "the antagonistic views of Philosophy, of Individual and Social Culture, which prevail among the various divisions of the Church, and of the Literary and Scientific world." Reacting to the increased divisiveness in the Transcendentalist as well as the Unitarian folds, she sought "a white radiance of love and wisdom" from "the union of many-colored rays," to cultivate "an harmonious intellectual and moral life in our country."[35] Tellingly, *Aesthetic Papers* failed after one issue.

One contributor to Peabody's journal was Henry Thoreau, who like Parker was outraged at the Mexican War. But if Parker's response was a call to organized political action, Thoreau's came in a different key, modulated not only by his friend Emerson's sense of individual sovereignty but also by Thoreau's interest in the New England nonresistance movement, whose advocates included abolitionist William Lloyd Garrison. Still living in his cabin on Walden Pond when the Mexican War broke out, Thoreau refused to pay his poll tax, which he considered a levy that directly connected him to the nation's hostilities. As a result of his infraction he was locked overnight in Concord's jail, until someone paid the pittance for his release. His gesture, however, was destined to become much more significant, for as the war raged, he worked up a lecture on the subject of "Resistance to Civil Government," which he first delivered at the Concord Lyceum early in 1848. In the spring of 1849 Elizabeth Peabody, casting about for submissions to her periodical, solicited it. The essay appeared that summer and became the journal's most famous contribution. In 1866 it acquired the moniker "Civil Disobedience," by which it has subsequently been known.

The piece had a long incubation. Shortly after Thoreau's incarceration, for example, in his journal he recorded his outrage at the war. "There probably never were worse crimes committed since time began than in the present Mexican war," he wrote, yet the public had not and probably never would learn what "reckless villain" had fathered them, because so many people were complicit. One had to be master of his own actions, Thoreau continued in an Emersonian pitch, for "any can command him who doth not command himself." He held out little hope for the counsel of the likes of Parker or Ripley. "Countless reforms are called for," he observed, "because society is not animated or instinct enough with life, but like snakes I have seen in early spring—with alternate portions torpid & flexible—so that they could wriggle neither way."[36] The problem with society was that its individual constituents did not assume control over their relationship to the state.

Thoreau was nothing if not a man of action, and in his lecture he counseled just that, individual acts of resistance against a government whose policies he found immoral. "How does it become a man to behave toward this American government to-day?" he asked. "I answer that he cannot without disgrace be associated with it." As Thoreau saw it, to do nothing stripped away one's humanity and made a citizen part of the government's well-oiled machine. The only proper action for a decent man was to make his life a "counter friction to stop the machine," for men should be "men first, and subjects afterward." "It is not desirable to cultivate a respect for the law," he intoned, "so much as for the right."[37]

Like Parker, Thoreau recognized that too many people who claimed to oppose slavery never took concrete action to combat it, because it affected their purses. There were thousands, Thoreau declared, "who are *in opinion* opposed to slavery and to the war, who yet in effect do nothing to put an end to them; who, esteeming themselves children of Washington and Franklin, sit down with their hands in their pockets. And say they do not know what to do . . . What is the price-current of an honest man and patriot to-day?"[38] His main complaint with the political process that Parker championed was that it took too long and became a substitute for decisive, direct action. "Unjust laws exist," Thoreau observed. "Shall we be content to obey them or shall we endeavor to amend them, and obey them until we have succeeded, or shall we transgress them at once?" Men thought that they had to persuade the majority to agree with them before such laws could be changed, but in refusing to act, they compounded the evil. Even worse, because people were silent, the government never saw the error of its ways. Why didn't it encourage citizens to be on the alert to point out its faults? he asked. "Why does it always crucify Christ, and excommunicate Copernicus and Luther, and pronounce Washington and Franklin rebels?"[39] Why, but because the majority of its citizens would rather do nothing, for expediency.

Thoreau dared to challenge the Massachusetts government by not paying his poll tax. With, say, a highway levy he had no quarrel, for he used the roads as much as others. But with regard to the Mexican War he wanted it clear that he disagreed with the state.

"I simply wish to refuse allegiance," he explained, and "to withdraw and stand aloof from it effectually." He did so because he firmly believed that "any man more right than his neighbors, constitutes a majority already." "I know this well," he continued, "that if one thousand, if one hundred, if ten men whom I could name,—if ten honest men only,—aye, if *one* HONEST man, in this state of Massachusetts, *ceasing to hold slaves*, were actually to withdraw from his copartnership, and be locked up in the county jail therefor [*sic*], it would be the abolition of slavery in America." Why? It mattered not "how small the beginning may seem to be," he explained, for "what is once well done is done for ever."[40] Men and women had to act with integrity, no matter what the cost.

In this essay Thoreau took Emerson's Romantic individualism to new heights and integrated it practically into ethics. Man's conscience constituted the higher law, and only the state that recognized this was worthy of man's allegiance. There never would be a really free and enlightened state, he explained, until it recognized "the individual as a higher and independent power, from which all its own power and authority are derived, and treats him accordingly."[41] This was not the case in the era of Clay, Webster, and Calhoun, consummate politicians all; nor was it yet the case with someone like Parker, who still believed in the political system. But Thoreau's call to conscientious individuals to wash their hands of complicity in a government that supported slavery was a cry to arms that would resonate more and more in the next decade. In 1854 he devoted an entire book to argue against a wrongheaded and immoral economy that drove just such immoral aspirations.

If by the mid-1840s Thoreau's understanding of the scope and importance of social issues had greatly increased, so, too, had Margaret Fuller's, particularly after the autumn of 1844, when she left Boston for New York to work as the book reviewer for Horace Greeley's *New-York Tribune*. Fuller had accepted her new position after a series of personal disappointments in New England. She recently had relinquished editorship of *The Dial* because of ill health and disappointment in the periodical's shrinking subscription base.

She also was frustrated by Emerson's inability to respond to, or even understand, her emotional needs, something she had in common with her friend Caroline Sturgis.[42] At this point Greeley, whose wife had attended several of Fuller's Conversations, recruited her for his *Tribune*, which over the three years that he had owned it had grown into a newspaper with an astonishing 50,000 subscribers (by the mid-1850s its circulation topped 300,000).

The notion of writing for such a large audience appealed to Fuller, though she initially was wary of Greeley's offer, for the city dailies were not known for their sophistication. He assured her, however, of his sincerity in publishing a paper that, while appealing to the masses, would elevate their taste in literature, art, music, science, religion, and reform. Greeley had bought the *Tribune* to bring culture to the people, and he very much wanted Fuller as part of the experiment.[43] She accepted, overseeing his paper's "literary" department, writing three essays a week at a salary of five hundred dollars a year, and over the next four years she contributed more than 250 pieces, most over the byline "*"".[44] In her very first assignment—a review of Emerson's *Essays, Second Series*—she ruminated on what she had left behind in Concord and Boston, and on her relationship to this author. She was not afraid to present an objective view of his reputation; and thus, after granting his undeniable influence as a lecturer, she fairly, and acutely, detailed the criticism against him.

Emerson always had faced charges of willful obscurity, she observed, and of "an inclination, at times, to subtlety at the expense of strength." But more troubling, given her own disappointment in fostering a more intimate relationship with him, was his "inadequacy" to represent the human heart's "full vocation and its deeper needs." Emerson was undoubtedly a man of ideas, she continued, "but we want the ideal man also; want the heart and genius of human life to interpret it, and here our satisfaction is not so perfect."[45] Once closely identified with Emerson's ethic of self-reliance, Fuller was beginning to understand how it worked against the creation of deep interpersonal relationships.

In her columns Fuller brought precisely this "heart and genius of human life" to her observations, and her attempts in this vein plunged her more and more into reformist circles. Thus, while she took seriously her position as book reviewer, she also used her front-page columns (previously occupied by Albert Brisbane) to educate readers in significant political and social issues. Her interests centered on the city's institutions for the criminal and the indigent, the plight of the slave, and the expansion of woman's sphere. Her engagement with these topics marked an important transition in her career. As editor of *The Dial* she had worked to inculcate an interest in literature and poetry. Since her early twenties she had admired German writers, particularly Goethe.[46] Her first published books were translations of the correspondence between Bettina von Arnim and the canoness Günderode, and Johann Peter Eckermann's *Conversations with Goethe*, in Ripley's series. Now employed by Greeley, whose proclivities toward politics and reform dominated his newspaper, and having recently read Fourier's works in the original (rather than in Brisbane's or Godwin's sanitized versions), Fuller moved beyond Emerson's cerebral and self-centered response to reform.

Her largest arena was that of women's rights. The achievement of remarkable women throughout history had preoccupied her at least since her Conversations, which often centered on this topic. Her seminal feminist statement, however, "The Great Lawsuit. Man versus Men, Woman versus Women," published in one of the last numbers of *The Dial* and subsequently expanded into *Woman in the Nineteenth Century*, assured her primacy in the women's rights movement. There was much in that book that derived from the Unitarian virtue of self-culture and the Emersonian ethic of self-reliance, for she maintained that woman, in other words, is "a child of the spirit" as much as man.[47]

She also insisted on the uniqueness of principles identified by social custom as "feminine" but which were present in different degrees in both women and men. "Male and female," she wrote, "represent the two sides of the great radical dualism." But in fact, "they are perpetually passing into one another." "There is no wholly masculine man," she continued, "no purely feminine woman."[48] But, most importantly, the feminine had to be melded with more "masculine" qualities to form a whole person. "The growth of Man is two-fold," she explained, "masculine and feminine."[49] The trouble with marriage as it currently existed was that man "did not clearly see that Woman was half himself; that her interests were identical with his; and that, by the law of their common being, he could never reach his true proportions while he remained in any wise shorn of hers."[50]

But Fuller's analyses were as much economic and social as psychological. She sharply criticized women's subordinate position in marriage and their exclusion from work that provided more economic independence as well as personal satisfaction. "Let them be sea-captains, if they will," she exclaimed. It was not "the transient breath of poetic incense" that a woman wanted, she continued, for one could get that from a lover. Nor was it "money" or "notoriety," either. Rather, what woman needed was not to rule but "as a nature to grow, as an intellect to discern, as a soul to live freely and unimpeded, to unfold such powers as were given her."[51] Instead, all around her Fuller saw women content as objects of "masculine" desire and confined to a domestic sphere in marriages that provided no opportunity for the independence in which she herself had been nurtured.[52]

Once in New York, Fuller became acutely aware of the position of workingwomen and the poor, and she was motivated to publicize their plight. She was led in this direction by her renewed friendship with William Henry Channing, who, after spending time in New England proselytizing for the Associationists, had returned to New York to minister to a small church of reform-minded parishioners.[53] Never fully in the Fourierist camp, he had developed more completely his notion of "Christian Union," a fervent, millennial faith put to the use of redressing the world's social ills.[54] For him and his followers, Christian love, and labor in its spirit, would initiate a more egalitarian society. His was an activist congregation to whom he emphasized a Christian's obligation to work for the good of neglected or alienated segments of the population: the poor, the mentally ill, the imprisoned, immigrants, and slaves; and he celebrated Christ as chief among reformers. By 1847 he melded these ideas into what he termed the Church of Humanity.

Channing held many leadership positions in the city's reform movements and had been a founder of the New York Prison Association. Under his auspices, Fuller gained entry for an inside look at conditions. She also renewed contact with Georgianna Bruce, an English reformer and Brook Farm member now relocated to the city, who in turn introduced her to Eliza Farnham, superintendent of the women inmates at Sing Sing, the New York state prison at Ossining on the Hudson River. As a result, shortly after taking up her tenure at the *Tribune*, Fuller began to alternate her literary reviews with starkly realistic descriptions of some of the city's hitherto invisible social institutions.

Even before she started work at the *Tribune*, in October 1844, she had visited Sing Sing and interviewed the women prisoners, a practice usually prohibited. With Channing accompanying her and boarding nearby with the prison chaplain, Fuller stayed overnight inside the prison with Farnham. Allowed to speak with several of the women prisoners, she found that even the most incorrigible were "decorous" in their conduct and "frank in their conversations," reminding her of her "Boston Classes," that is, of the women in her Conversations.[55] She shared with the inmates her concern for woman's plight—she was revising what would become *Woman in the Nineteenth Century*—and some were enough moved to ask for private interviews. She was much impressed by how Farnham's "gentle and intelligent treatment" already had ameliorated the inmates' conditions, and she promised to speak with them individually when she returned. She also took the unusual step of writing directly to some, assuring them that she already had apprised others of their condition and encouraging them to read the books that "some of the ladies of Boston" would soon send at her request.[56]

Fuller's visit to Sing Sing moved her deeply, and she alluded to it in her "Thanksgiving" *Tribune* column, issued in the late fall of 1844. Using as her occasion the quintessential New England holiday, Fuller reminded her readers that "if charity begin at home, it must not end there" but rather extend to "the great circle of humanity," so many of whom had less to be thankful for at that season. Wherever the "impulse of social or political reform darts up its rill through the crusts of selfishness, scoff and dread arise and hang like a heavy mist above it," she observed. She took much heart, however, from a recent meeting to organize "an Association for the benefit of Prisoners," where among other things a participant read of the positive effect musical activities had had on prisoners in

France. Fuller was forcibly reminded, she wrote, of her recent experience at Sing Sing, when female prisoners joined in singing a
"choral[e]" that described "the last thoughts of spirit about to be
enfranchised from the body" with the refrain "All is well." They
sang it so gently and resignedly, she recalled, that the good spirit of
the music had penetrated them; she hoped that the spirit of "religious sympathy," too, might take hold as efforts increased for their
moral instruction.[57] The following June, in an appeal for support of
an "Asylum for Discharged Female Converts" to protect recently
released prisoners from the city's manifold temptations to vice, she
reminded her readers of the comfort in which they lived and urged
them to consider the sights that she had seen. "If only a released in-
mate had a place of refuge," she implored, some precious soul
might be saved from "unwilling sin, unutterable woe."[58]

Of equal concern was an even larger population, the city's indigent, who lived either on the streets or in almshouses. She was thun-
derstruck at the immense contrast between magnificent wealth and
dire poverty in New York, a situation that inspired some of her most
moving columns. In a brief essay on the "Prevalent Idea that Polite-
ness is too great a Luxury to be given to the Poor," for example, she
related the story of an impoverished boy berated by an upper-class
woman on a ferry. Fuller was outraged at the matron's presumption
and "vulgarity." Reflecting on how often the rich condescended to
the less fortunate, Fuller inveighed against such instances of "insolent rudeness or more insolent affability founded on no apparent
grounds, except an apparent difference in pecuniary position."[59]

This callous hauteur reached its peak in the city's indifference to
those who fell from working poverty into true pauperism and thus
depended on private charity or the public dole. Fuller addressed the
plight of these unfortunates in "Our City Charities" after a visit to
several of the city's institutions for the indigent. "The pauper establishments that belong to a great city," she wrote, admonished readers
of "stern realities" that had to be looked at so that people would
learn of what use they could be to the less fortunate. Visiting in turn
the Bellevue Alms House, the city's Farm School for children, the
Asylum for the Insane, and the penitentiary on Blackwell's Island,
Fuller succinctly characterized conditions and needs at each.[60]

She found the Alms House cleaner and more comfortable than she had expected, for example, but she lamented the lack of opportunities for "suitable and sufficient employment," save gardening and sewing. Ever aware of the topic to which she had devoted her most recent book, she noted how sorry she was, in the institution's hospital, "to see mothers with their newborn infants exposed to the careless scrutiny of male visitors." This sensitivity to the need for an individual's privacy and self-respect runs all through Fuller's New York writings.

More disturbing was the insane asylum. There the space was insufficient for its population, with twice as many patients housed than the building could accommodate. Fuller compared the institution unfavorably to another in the city, Bloomingdale, under the enlightened supervision of Pliny Earle, a doctor with a special interest in treating the mentally ill. There, she noted, people were the objects of individualized treatment, with attendants taking into account different "shades of character and feeling" among the inmates; there, too, the accommodations were "nicely kept up" and "decorum preserved." The asylum's administration took care to show the insane "in every way that they felt no violent separation betwixt them and the rest of the world, and might easily return to it." At the city asylum, by contrast, the inmates "crouched in corners," she wrote, and "had no eye for the stranger, no heart for hope, no habitual expectation of light."

All this paled, however, before what Fuller found at Blackwell's Island, where the city's hardened criminals were sequestered. In comparison to Sing Sing, conditions were abysmal, and she hoped that the enlightened administration of the New York State institution could be replicated at the penitentiary. Fuller particularly lamented the want of proper matrons—indeed, of any matrons—to care for the seven hundred women incarcerated there. Worse still, the entire institution lacked any organizing principle, save "the punishment of fault." The penitentiary needed, she urged, a classification and division of the prisoners according to the nature of their crimes; instruction, "practical, oral, and by furnishing books which may open entirely new hopes and thoughts" to the inmates; and a sanitary system, which would promote "self-respect, and through health and purity of body, the same in mind."

She closed by noting that in New York "there is wealth enough, intelligence, and good desire enough, and surely, *need enough*" to effect the necessary reformation of such institutions and make them models for those in other cities. But because the administrators of such reformatories were entangled in the political patronage system, she despaired of immediate change. "It is a most crying and shameful evil," she wrote, "that the men and measures are changed in these institutions with changes from Whig to Democrat, from Democrat to Whig." People like Earle and Farnham, not political hacks, should be the ones under whose charge the unfortunate were rehabilitated. Week after week Fuller alerted readers to the social injustice so rampant in the city but from which they too often shielded their eyes, and her columns constitute an early form of municipal exposé that reached its height in the muckraking journalism at the turn of the twentieth century.

Like many in Greeley's circle, Fuller also was exercised by the horror of American slavery, and in her columns she indicted politicians that supported it. Significantly, however, she resisted the notion that communitarian association was the answer to the country's ills. Rather, following her friend Channing's lead, she appealed to her readers' Christian conscience. Institutions themselves—the almshouses, asylums, and prisons—were not the problem. Personal ignorance perpetuated the misery seen on the city's streets. To live the Gospel of Christ implied a profound brother- and sisterhood that would initiate a social and spiritual millennium. That Fuller had moved to such a position after her long sojourn in Emerson's orbit testifies to New York's indelible impact on her. There she could not avert her eyes from suffering, as she could in Concord or at Brook Farm. Awakened to the inequalities that gave the lie to America's purportedly egalitarian society, she subordinated her transcendent ego to her social conscience.

When the opportunity arose for Fuller to sail to Europe to report on the unfolding democratic revolutions, she jumped at the chance, eager finally to visit the Continent and to see how other nations welcomed freedom, equality, and brotherhood. Beginning in the

1830s, Transcendentalists periodically had come into contact with European émigrés who had fled the Continent. Europe's freedom fighters had watched Greece achieve independence from the Ottoman Empire in 1827 and were inspired as well by both the Belgian Walloons' success against the Dutch and the Italians' challenges to Austrian Hapsburg rule. The next to strike for their freedom were the Poles, but their insurrection, commenced in November 1830 and lasting over a year, was decisively and savagely crushed by Czar Nicholas I. Those who could, escaped. Among them were such prominent individuals as the poet Adam Mickiewicz, the composer Frédéric Chopin, and the Hungarian philologist Karoly (Charles) Kraitsir. For many of these exiles, France was their destination; a few hundred, aided by the Massachusetts reformer Samuel Gridley Howe, made their way to the United States, determined to keep alive their dreams for a free Poland.[61]

Howe had interested many of his Transcendentalist friends in these wars for European liberation. Trained as a physician, he had served with the Greek rebels for six years in their fight against Turkey and now threw himself into the Polish cause. He raised money in Boston that he personally delivered to the exiles—along with two flags "from the youth of Boston"—in Paris, where he remained for several months as chairman of the newly established Polish National Committee. He was joined by such prominent Americans as Samuel F. B. Morse and James Fenimore Cooper, who likewise had raised funds in the United States. They aided Kraitsir's and others' attempts in 1833 to obtain land grants in America so that émigrés could resettle. Like that of the Greeks a few years earlier, the cause of the Poles captured the Americans' imagination because they believed that their own Revolution half a century earlier served as the inspiration for such republican movements in Europe.

Among the émigrés, Kraitsir was important to the Transcendentalists through Elizabeth Peabody's sponsorship of his novel philological and pedagogical ideas. Subsequent to his attempts to obtain land grants, Kraitsir had established a foreign-language school in Maryland and in 1840 was named professor of modern languages and history at the University of Virginia. Not finding Charlottesville, or the South in general, to his liking, particularly because of slaveholding, he moved to New England and found himself under Peabody's wing. He was not the first émigré whose cause she had espoused. The same year, Joseph Podbielski, another pedagogue, boarded with her and convinced her of the importance of Josef Bem's chronological charts for teaching world history. Peabody crusaded to have public schools adopt his published grids, overlaid with colors and shapes, to learn by decade the succession of important events. Over the next few years she elaborated on his work with her own researches into ancient history to make the charts more all-encompassing.

Kraitsir's method of teaching languages was even more influential. In 1845 he lectured in Boston on the philosophy of language, positing a universal vocabulary based on the sounds the vocal organs could produce. If Bem's charts organized the complex history of the world into manageable form, Kraitsir offered nothing less than proof of mankind's primal unity. Peabody was fascinated. She published his pamphlet *The Significance of the Alphabet*, in which he announced his radical ideas, and in 1847 he boarded with her family on West Street.[62] In 1849, after a trip to Europe, Kraitsir returned to West Street, but embroiled in a nasty custody suit with his wife in which Peabody futilely intervened, by 1851 he moved to New York. There in 1852 he published his *Glossology: Being a Treatise on the Nature of Language and on the Language of Nature*. What Peabody found compelling in Kraitsir's system was his search for and presumed discovery of that phantom of uniformity for which the nineteenth century yearned, a unity that demonstrated how, beneath their temperamental and cultural differences, men in fact were one.[63]

While Peabody was involved in the sponsorship of such immigrant pedagogues as Podbielski and Kraitsir, by the late 1840s Fuller had become even more directly involved in the European struggles. In 1846 her friends the philanthropists Marcus and Rebecca Spring invited her to accompany them to Europe as a tutor to their twelve-year-old son, and Greeley agreed to pay her—he advanced her $125—for periodic travel reports. Between 1846 and 1850 she filed thirty-seven dispatches from the Continent (twenty-four from Italy alone during the height of its revolution), a rich archive of how one American understood her country's example to other nations struggling toward democracy. Moreover, in Europe her interest in utopian socialism, whetted by her reading in Fourier and her experiences in New York and now tempered by her first-hand experience among European intellectuals and their émigré friends, was transformed into deep sympathy with the revolutionary agenda.

The Springs and Fuller first toured England, where she met Wordsworth and Carlyle, visited her acquaintance Harriet Martineau, and met Giuseppe Mazzini. Living in exile since 1837 and already planning his return to Italy, Mazzini filled Fuller's mind with his mystical understanding of nationhood and of an individual's need to subsume himself in it. Neither did the travelers neglect Europe's social conditions: they visited mechanics' institutes in the factory cities of Manchester and Liverpool, a coal mine in Newcastle, and ironworkers in Sheffield. By mid-November 1846 the group moved on to Paris, Fuller carrying letters of introduction from Mazzini to many French intellectuals. In that city she met, among others, the writer George Sand (Mme Dudevant); the Catholic abbé Félicité Robert de Lamennais, and the socialist and onetime Saint-Simonian Pierre Leroux; and such prominent followers of Fourier as Victor Considérant, Hugh Doherty, an Irish socialist and translator of his works, and Clarisse Vigoureux, another follower. Most important, Fuller also encountered the exiled Polish poet Mickiewicz, who advocated strong nation-states as well as women's rights. He became Fuller's intimate friend and prophesied that her mission was to contribute to the deliverance of the Polish, French, and American women, all the while encouraging her to think more about herself and her sexual needs.

Psychologically, to Fuller, Europe was like a strong, healthy tonic. "Had I only come ten years earlier," she lamented to her friend Caroline Sturgis, for "now my life must ever be a failure, so much strength has been wasted on obstructions which only came because I was not in the soil most fitted to my nature."[64] On meeting Mickiewicz, she wrote Emerson that she found him "the man I had long wished to see, with the intellect and passions in due proportion for a full and healthy human being," a comment that must have given Emerson pause, given Fuller's frustrating attempts for him to see her in just this way.[65] But besides fulfilling her lifelong dreams about art, literature, and romance, Fuller's travels also deepened her sense of the significance of national culture and destiny to which Mazzini had awakened her. She understood that she was witnessing an impending large-scale social crisis caused by the inequalities in wealth that the present political regimes tolerated. With her eyes opened to Europe's social ills, she saw more clearly her own nation's failures, which she blamed on "the selfishness or stupidity" of those who opposed "an examination of these subjects."[66]

Early in 1847 the Springs' traveling party crossed the Alps into Italy, where under the new pope, Pius IX, the hope for liberty for and the union of the various Italian principalities grew. Among his first acts, for example, Pius IX freed many political prisoners who had agitated for such reform. Here Fuller again encountered the charismatic Mazzini, who, encouraged by the pope's policies, had returned from exile to lead efforts to liberate and unify the various city-states. Fuller found herself in the middle of heated political activity, swept up with enthusiasm for the patriots' cause. She also had a newfound appreciation of what socialists brought to the table. Writing from Rome to her friend Channing in May 1847, Fuller told him that art was no longer important to her. "I see the future dawning," she prophesied, and "it is in important aspects Fourier's future," melded with Mazzini's quasi-religious understanding of the necessity of individual sacrifice for the nation.[67]

By 1848 the Continent was on fire with revolutionary zeal. Early that year, citizens of Palermo rose against Ferdinand II, who ruled Sicily and Naples, and he quickly capitulated to their demands by granting a constitution. French workers and students deposed the corrupt and insensitive Louis-Philippe and declared a republic overseen by poet Alphonse de Lamartine. Inspired by these successes, other liberation movements broke out in Prussia, Austria, Spain, Ireland, Romania, and Denmark. The powerful Prince Metternich of Austria fled his country, and Frederick William IV of Prussia was forced to allow the election of a popular assembly in the city-states he oversaw. In Hungary, Louis Kossuth led his people against the Hapsburg monarchy. Back in the United States, these revolutions were greeted with goodwill and followed with great interest, none more so than those in France and Italy. When the Springs decided to continue on to Germany, Fuller, excited over the Italian freedom fighters' prospects, stayed on in Rome.

She had another reason to do so. When she first arrived, in May 1847, she met a twenty-six-year-old Italian patriot, the Marchese Giovanni Ossoli, under the dome of St. Peter's. By December 1847, as throughout Europe the republicans' dreams rose, Fuller was pregnant with his child, and in May she retreated to the hills of Abruzzi to await the birth. There she also continued work on a book-length history of the Italian revolution, a project that grew from her dispatches to Greeley. Their son, Angelo Eugene Philip Ossoli, was born early in September, and in November, Fuller left him with a wet nurse and returned to Rome to rejoin her husband, now a member of the pope's Civic Guard. She found herself in the heart of revolution. But throughout Europe the uprisings failed. By 1849, foreign troops attacked the Holy City, quashing the resistance and restoring the papacy. Everywhere liberation movements collapsed under assault from entrenched powers. The republican moment had passed.

The several months of reports Fuller filed with Greeley remain among the best eyewitness accounts of the rise and fall of the Roman Republic. "I have been engrossed, stunned almost, by the public events that have succeeded one another with such rapidity and grandeur," she wrote her friend Channing. "It is a time such as I always dreamed of, and for long secretly hoped to see."[68] She faithfully read newspapers from around the Continent to keep apprised of events in other countries, and she corresponded with European friends who could provide her new information. "I rejoice to be in Europe at this time," she wrote, "and shall return possessed of a great history."[69]

She was particularly moved that Italians viewed their battles as an extension of the principles of freedom for which her countrymen had fought and secured for the entire American people, even as she lamented Americans' ignorance and lack of interest in political and social developments on the Continent, a fact that she blamed on their crass materialism. In one column, on "Old and New World

Democracy," she reminded her readers that the same arguments against the emancipation of Italy were used against the emancipation of American slaves, "the same arguments in favor of the spoliation of Poland as for the conquest of Mexico." America, Fuller concluded scornfully, was "no champion of the rights of men, but a robber and a jailer . . . her eyes fixed, not on the stars, but on the possessions of other men."[70]

Whereas America was "spoiled by prosperity, stupid with the lust of gain, soiled by crime in its willing perpetuation of Slavery, shamed by an unjust war, noble sentiment much forgotten even by individuals, the aims of politicians selfish or petty, the literature frivolous and venal," in Europe a nobler spirit was struggling, a spirit that cheered and animated hers. As she had promised, she transformed her dispatches into a book manuscript, declaring, "Here things are before my eyes worth recording, and, if I cannot help this work, I would gladly be its historian."[71] But the siege of Rome made it dangerous for the Ossolis to remain. The family—she and Ossoli now were married—moved to Florence, where Fuller unsuccessfully sought out an English publisher for her history. No matter. She remained confident in what she had written: "If I cannot make any thing out of my present materials," she wrote her friends, "my future is dark indeed."[72]

The Ossolis decided to leave in the summer of 1850, on an ill-fated voyage. The choice of a sailing ship rather than a newer, more reliable steamship was dictated by Fuller's always precarious financial condition. Even before leaving the Mediterranean, the captain died of smallpox, and the first mate assumed command for the Atlantic crossing. In sight of land, off Fire Island, New York, in a full hurricane, the mate miscalculated his position and drove the *Elizabeth* onto a bar, where hours spent being battered by the high seas finally broke the vessel. There were some survivors, but the Ossolis were not among them. Only their son's body was recovered, along with some of their belongings, but not the manuscript.

It is difficult to say what sort of greeting awaited Fuller and what she would have done once she resettled. Letters from friends strongly suggest their discomfort with Ossoli—not an intellectual, as most of them were. Such personal considerations aside, however, it would have been even more difficult for Fuller to deal with the increasingly virulent and volatile political situation in her home country. With the passage of the Fugitive Slave Law, part of the infamous Compromise of 1850, those who had nourished dreams of shared progress with the nations of Europe toward more freedom and equality were brought face to face with what Fuller had seen in Rome as she contemplated her nation's shortcomings.

The triumphal American tour of Louis Kossuth, leader of the abortive Hungarian revolution, who arrived in New York in 1851 from exile, was telling. Greeted by immense crowds wherever he went, he nevertheless symbolically marked the end of America's fascination with European republicanism. As he traveled throughout the country trying to garner support for his country's revolutionary cause, Whigs and Democrats North and South divided over whether the nation should consider the kind of foreign intervention he urged.[73] The United States had its own problems, and in the next decade that meant turning from Europe to face the internal demon, slavery.

9

THE INWARD TURN

zra Stiles Gannett, editor of *The Christian Examiner* between 1843 and 1849, had a good vantage point from which to survey the intellectual terrain contested by New England's liberal Christians. Reviewing Unitarianism's development at mid-decade, he admitted that Transcendentalism had affected the denomination "with a meteor-like rapidity." The movement had captivated or deluded some and frightened or puzzled others, "who looked on and said nothing." But since then it had declined "with a slower and more equal descent, to the point where we may expect its harmless explosion." He concluded, "Our mention of it is but the making up of yesterday's journal."[1]

Gannett's confident dismissal of Transcendentalism's influence was not just wishful thinking, for by 1850 something had indeed changed. Not that public intellectuals like Emerson or Parker had lost influence, for their reputations only grew in the 1850s. But the coherence and focus of the movement was dissipated, so that to brand someone a Transcendentalist no longer meant what it had in 1840. For one thing, the group's participation in transatlantic intellectual discourse had progressively contracted, Fuller's untimely death its most emphatic and tragic marker. Her acolyte Caroline Dall put it simply. "I do not think that I am mistaken," she said in the 1880s, "that what is meant by Transcendentalism perished with Margaret Fuller."[2] But the demise of Brook Farm, New England's most ambitious Fourierist experiment, also contributed, as did disillusionment with the failure of Europe's democratic revolutions of 1848. Fragmented into different camps depending on their orientation toward reform, New England Transcendentalists, who for two decades had eagerly embraced Continental ideas to help them understand and address their nation's—and mankind's—shortcomings, became preoccupied with issues they believed were unique to the United States, chief among them the curse of slavery. "The agitation against slavery," O. B. Frothingham recalled, "had taken hold of the whole country; it was in politics, in journalism, in literature, in the public hall and parlor."[3]

Predictably, after the Treaty of Guadalupe Hidalgo that closed the Mexican War, there was renewed debate over the extension of slavery in the newly acquired territories. Matters came to a head in 1849, when California asked for admission to the Union as a Free State. As Northern abolitionists gained more public support and Whigs threatened to pass more stringent antislavery legislation, Southerners became increasingly worried and bitter, so much so that some began to think that, should the antislavery North have its way, the Southern states should withdraw from the Union. To avert this, in September 1850, after bitter debate, Congress, under the leadership of Senators Henry Clay and Stephen A. Douglas, passed a set of measures subsequently known as the Compromise of 1850.

Its provisions were complex and divisive enough to require their being taken up individually rather than in an omnibus bill. California entered the Union as a Free State. The new territories of New Mexico and Utah were established without mention of slavery, their citizens to decide the matter when they applied for full statehood. The slave trade was outlawed in the District of Columbia, but slaveholding was not. Disputed boundary claims of Texas into western areas of the United States subsequently incorporated into New Mexico were settled by the cession of these lands to the federal government, for a ten-million-dollar payment to Texas.

Most importantly, Fugitive Slave Laws were made much more draconian, giving Southern slave owners unprecedented powers to recover runaways from Free States. Any citizen who aided escaped slaves or inhibited federal authorities from recovering them was subject to a prison term of up to six months and a thousand-dollar fine. Slaves were not entitled to trial by jury and when apprehended were arraigned in federal court where a United States judge or commissioner heard the claimant's case for recovering his "property." A slave's testimony was not admitted; and a written affidavit, rather than the personal testimony of the owner, was all that was required as proof of ownership, opening the way for bounty hunters to undertake the sordid task of returning runaways. Finally, there was no appeal of the judge's or commissioner's decision.[4]

Particularly dismaying to many Northerners, the great Whig senator from Massachusetts, Daniel Webster, had thrown his considerable influence behind the compromise measures and on March 7, 1850, he delivered an impassioned speech in which he urged passage of the bills to preserve the Union. Webster's actions outraged Emerson, who had become increasingly concerned about slavery and drawn into abolitionist circles.[5] For years he had admired the immensely gifted and charismatic senator, whom he once termed "a natural Emperor of men" who was "the triumph of the understanding," but which in him was "undermined & supplanted by the Reason for which yet he is so good a witness."[6] But early in the 1840s, as the sectional crisis heated up, Emerson began to worry that Webster was currying too much favor with Southern interests.

By the end of the decade, his view of Webster had become darker, as the senator continued to truckle to Southerners, presumably to further his chances for the presidency. "Webster has never done any thing up to the promise of his faculties," Emerson observed in 1849.[7] Such criticism was mild, however, compared with Emerson's disgust after Webster's March 7 speech. "'Liberty! liberty!' Pho! Let Mr[.] Webster for decency's sake shut his lips for once & forever on this word," Emerson exclaimed in his journals. "The word *liberty* in the mouth of Mr. Webster sounds like the word *love* in the mouth of a courtezan [*sic*]."[8] Emerson spewed his rancor not only at Webster but at Massachusetts citizens who had not resisted more forcefully the provisions of the Fugitive Slave Law. "No man can look his neighbor in the face," Emerson wrote. "We sneak about with the infamy of crime in the streets, & cowardice in ourselves and frankly once and for all the Union is sunk[,] the flag is hateful[,] & will be hissed."[9]

The Fugitive Slave Law marked a turning point in Emerson's involvement with organized reform, particularly the abolition movement. As much as he enjoyed the lecture platform, he was uncomfortable with public debate. But by the early 1840s, with the question of Texas statehood—and thus of the expansion of the slave power—looming, he began to accept invitations to speak on the issue of slavery, an activity that increased after Webster's defection.

One of Emerson's most significant forays into this arena occurred in the summer of 1844, when the Concord Female Anti-Slavery Society asked him to deliver an address on the tenth anniversary of the abolition of slavery in the British West Indies. The occasion was unusual, for although there were many strong advocates of antislavery in Concord—including Emerson's own wife, Lidian, and Henry Thoreau's mother, Cynthia—abolition itself was not universally popular.[10] When a heavy rainstorm the day before the occasion washed out plans to have Emerson speak on the grounds of Hawthorne's residence at the Old Manse, he cast about for another venue, only to discover that no local church would open its doors to the event. His young friend Thoreau thereupon procured the courthouse, and when the sexton of the First Church meetinghouse refused to ring its bell (the usual summons for important community gatherings), Thoreau himself pulled the belfry rope to raise a crowd. This was superfluous, however, for that same day Concord was the site of the Middlesex County antislavery fair, which drew participants from the whole region, assuring Emerson a large audience.

Emerson took the occasion seriously. He prepared by reading Thomas Clarkson's definitive *History of the ... Abolition of the African Slave Trade* as well as James Thome and J. H. Kimball's *Emancipation in the West Indies*, works that contained graphic descriptions of slave owners' abuses. He particularly admired England for voluntarily abolishing the peculiar institution on the grounds of reason, despite the considerable economic interests involved. Like the United States, England ended the slave trade in 1807. Realizing that this had done little to aid the plight of those already enslaved, however, they continued to debate the matter until the populace saw that abolition was the only enlightened alternative.

Finally, in May 1833, Lord Stanley, minister for the British colonies, introduced into the House of Commons a bill for emancipation. To placate the planters for the loss of their labor force, it included a provision that the black population of the islands would be registered as apprentices for a set number of years, giving their masters three-fourths of their profits but now enjoying the rights and privileges of freemen. At the end of their terms of apprenticeship, they and their children were permanently manumitted. In short, after August 1, 1834, slavery was "utterly and forever abolished" in the British Empire.[11]

The greatest obstacle to this glorious accomplishment, Emerson told his audience, had been that the British were "shopkeepers, and have the timidities of that profession." Americans, their children, were similar. "We peddle, we truck, we sail, we row, we ride in cars, we creep in teams, we go in canals—to market, for the sale of goods," he observed. All that Americans cared about was keeping the customer contented, supplied with good sugar, coffee, tobacco; and if toward that end there resulted "a few unpleasant scenes on the coast of Africa? That was a great way off," Emerson said sarcastically. If anyone mentioned the "homicide, madness, adultery, and intolerable torture" that accompanies slavery, Americans "let the church bells ring louder, the church organ swell its peal, and drown the hideous sound." The sugar cultivated by slaves "was excellent; nobody tasted blood in it." The coffee, too, "was fragrant; the tobacco was incense; the brandy made nations happy; the cotton clothed the world."[12] In England, however, honest men and women had not overlooked the abominable system on which these luxuries were based. In 1834 the British had made the right decision. Would Americans do the same?

Most appalling to Emerson were laws in South Carolina, Georgia, and Louisiana that allowed white citizens of these states arbitrarily to detain free black sailors, cooks, and other menial workers visiting their ports on merchant vessels and, if their jail costs (often exorbitant to discourage payment) were not met, to sell them into slavery. On this issue Emerson was a states' rights man, demanding that citizens of Massachusetts, white or black, be given the protection to which they were entitled by the United States Constitution.

It astonished him that the Massachusetts government took no action in such cases. "The Governor of Massachusetts is a trifler; the State-house in Boston is a playhouse; the General Court is a dishonored body: if they make laws which they cannot execute." If Massachusetts did not have the power to defend its own people and its own shipping, because it had delegated it to the federal government, he asked, did it not have representation in that government? "I may as well say what all men feel," Emerson concluded, "that whilst our very amiable and very innocent representatives and senators at Washington are accomplished lawyers and merchants, and very eloquent at dinners and caucuses, there is a disastrous want of *men* from New England."[13]

He also praised the accomplishments of Caribbean blacks who in the aftermath of emancipation had risen to occupations and positions of authority throughout the islands. This was not the case in the United States, where descendants of Africans were precluded any opportunity to be a white person's equal. This only reflected on the moral bankruptcy of American white society, however, for "the civility of no race can be perfect whilst another race is degraded." It was a doctrine common to both the oldest and the newest philosophy: that one man cannot injure another "without a sympathetic injury" to all.[14]

Over the next several years Emerson gave other antislavery addresses, on the Fourth of July in the nearby town of Dedham in 1846, for example, and at an antislavery convention in Worcester in the summer of 1849 attended by more than five thousand delegates from all over New England. Then came the Compromise of 1850, and with it the harsh truth that by federal statute Massachusetts had to comply with the Fugitive Slave Law. That spring Emerson accepted an invitation from some of his townsmen to speak on this issue, an occasion precipitated by the capture and rendition in Boston of the runaway slave Thomas Sims. In this speech, fired by months of rumination on Webster's treachery, Emerson spoke as one transformed. As he put it in the first paragraph of his speech, "The last year has forced us all into politics."[15]

He who in 1836 had counseled "Build therefore your own world" now awakened every morning to a political reality that pained him throughout the day. The very landscape seemed robbed of its beauty, and he even had trouble breathing because of the "infamy" in the air. But the notorious law seemed not to have the same effect among his fellow citizens. Emerson was surprised to find that among "presidents of colleges and professors, saints and brokers, insurers, lawyers, importers, manufacturers," there was not "an unpleasant sentiment, not a liberal recollection, not so much as a snatch of an old song for freedom" that intruded on their passive obedience to the new statutes. The only good thing to come from them was that they "had the illuminating power of a sheet of lightning at midnight." They showed the truth about America to those willing to see.[16]

Most despicable, all seemed excused by allegiance to "party," that is, to politics. "Nothing proves the want of all thought," Emerson seethed, and "the absence of standard in men's minds more than the dominion of party." Here were "upright men, *compotes mentis*, husbands, fathers, trustees, friends, open, generous, brave, who can see nothing in this claim for bare humanity and the health and honor of their native state, but canting fanaticism, sedition, and 'one idea.'" Because of such preoccupation, he continued, the wealth and power of Massachusetts were thrown into "the scale of the crime." Boston, which Emerson's friend Oliver Wendell Holmes had called the "hub of the universe," was nothing less than the slave master's "hound."[17]

Emerson now came to the same conclusion Thoreau had over the Mexican War. "An immoral law," Emerson declared, "makes it a man's duty to break it, at every hazard." He was disappointed that moral outrage had not moved his fellow citizens to civil disobedience. "I thought," he said, "that all men of all conditions had been made sharers of a certain experience, that in certain rare and retired moments they had been made to see how man is man." "I thought," he continued, "that every time a man goes back to his own thoughts, these angels receive him, talk with him, and, that, in the best hours, he is uplifted in virtue of this essence, into a peace and power this world cannot give."[18] Emerson had believed, in other words, that men would be directed to oppose slavery by instruction from the transcendent Reason. Now he knew otherwise. They had to be shocked into disgust and action by an encounter with the horror of slavery, directly embodied in the likes of Thomas Sims and vicariously by words like Emerson's.

After outlining other grounds on which Massachusetts citizens should resist the new law—how could a law be enforced that fines pity, he asked, or that could not be executed by good men?—Emerson made his larger point. "Every person who touches this business is contaminated," he claimed. He also repeated his indictment of Webster, angrily noting that "the one eminent American of our time, whom we could produce as a finished work of nature," had deserted the cause of righteousness. Webster's fault, Emerson now realized, was that the great senator thought that government existed for the protection of property rather than to ensure the good of all its citizens. Indeed, nothing seemed more hypocritical than the bluster about the preservation of the Union by which supporters of the Compromise defended their vote. What was the Union "to a man self-condemned, with all sense of self-respect and chance of fair fame cut off, with the names of conscience and religion become bitter ironies, and liberty the ghastly mockery which Mr. Webster means by that word?" What must people do? "One thing is plain," Emerson declared. "We cannot answer for the Union" but have to keep Massachusetts "true" by resisting the law's provisions.[19]

Shortly after the passage of the Kansas-Nebraska Act and four years after Webster's speech, Emerson revisited it in an address delivered at an antislavery meeting at the Tabernacle, on Broadway in New York City. Introduced by Stephen Douglas, this act left to popular sovereignty—that is, the settlers' votes—the question of whether slavery would be allowed in these two new territories. It was viewed by antislavery forces as another capitulation to the Southern cause, and Emerson linked it to the earlier and much-despised Compromise of 1850. He stated his continuing discomfort with speaking to public questions. "It seems like meddling," he said, "or leaving your work." Public events, however, caused him to feel the necessity to turn to the public arena. Even though Webster had been dead for two years, his perfidy had brought on the Fugitive Slave Law, so that no one in the Free States could escape complicity with slavery, a situation now exacerbated in the Kansas-Nebraska territories.[20] This same month, another runaway, Anthony Burns, had been arrested in

Boston, causing the largest uproar yet among antislavery supporters. Burns's hearing and subsequent efforts to free him traumatized the community and intensified support of the abolitionists' cause.

Through the decade, Emerson continued to work at literary projects, publishing *Representative Men* in 1850 and *English Traits* six years later, neither of which, oddly, contained any of his antislavery writings. Like any moral person, he obviously was deeply moved by the slaves' plight and had weighed in against the immorality of the plantation system, but he could hardly have been termed a leader among abolitionists. At this point another Transcendentalist stepped into the fray. Antislavery advocates sought and received Emerson's support in the decade's subsequent ideological battles, but it was Theodore Parker, "our Savonarola," as Emerson called him, who most galvanized Massachusetts citizens against the continuing erosion of their, and all Americans', liberties.[21] The Fugitive Slave Law had pushed Emerson into antislavery politics, but it made Theodore Parker one of the nation's most prominent abolitionists.

Since the mid-1840s Parker had become progressively more involved in various reform activities, particularly for Boston's poor and institutionalized, and with the start of the Mexican War he had begun to devote much attention to the slavery question, too. But with Webster's defection and the subsequent passage of the various bills that constituted the Compromise of 1850, like other reform-minded New Englanders, he was greatly radicalized. Parker was engaged with all the great reform movements of his time—"peace, temperance, education, the condition of women, penal legislation, prison discipline, the moral and mental destitution of the rich, the physical destitution of the poor." None had broken in "upon the settled order of his life" or become "a dominant factor in his experience." However, his biographer continued, "it was different with antislavery reform."[22]

Parker was outraged by the annexation of Texas and the outbreak of the Mexican War, but his sermons on these topics had been based more on his support of the peace movement and a condemnation of United States imperialism than on a settled disposition against slavery. Although as early as 1841 he had preached against the peculiar institution, he did not publish a major antislavery statement until 1848, his open *Letter to the People of the United States . . . Touching the Matter of Slavery*, primarily a socioeconomic analysis of the slave system. Yet while he devoted the majority of the letter to matters like the "Effects of Slavery on Industry" and "Law and Politics," fact-filled arguments about how slavery undermined the nation's prosperity and growth, he concluded with a broad moral indictment. "American slavery," he wrote, "is the greatest, foulest wrong which man ever did to man; the most hideous and detested sin a nation has ever committed before the just, all-bounteous God—a wrong and sin wholly without excuse."[23]

The passage of the Fugitive Slave Law and the ensuing attempts to enforce it in Boston moved Parker to his life's work. Assuming the chairmanship of the executive committee of the Vigilance Committee, established in the late 1840s to oversee the welfare of runaway slaves in the area and to come to their defense when attempts were made for rendition, Parker became one of the three or four best-known antislavery activists of the decade, a position established through his virulent polemics against the Fugitive Slave Law and the South, and his sheltering of runaways. His colleagues on the executive committee included Wendell Phillips, Samuel Gridley Howe, and the attorney Charles Mayo Ellis. Parker despised Northerners' complicity with the law and spoke against it on any occasion. Thus, in May 1850, before the New England Anti-Slavery Convention in Boston, Parker condemned the moral bankruptcy of the nation's politicians—and in particular those from Massachusetts—evident in their defense of the recent Compromise, and he starkly simplified the moral issue before all Americans. The question of most consequence was not whether the Union should be preserved, but "whether freedom or slavery is to prevail in America." All else paled in comparison, and Parker was confident that in this matter, abolitionists were "on the side of God."[24]

Soon thereafter two fugitives, William and Ellen Craft, Parker's parishioners, were pursued. After he married them formally at an African American boardinghouse in the city, the couple escaped to

England, bearing his letter of introduction to the prominent English Unitarian clergyman James Martineau. But theirs was only a prelude to other attempts at rendition in the cradle of American liberty. Shadrach Minkins came next, fortuitously rescued by a crowd of supporters and sent on his way to Canada. Then Thomas Sims was arrested for disturbing the peace—he was defending himself in an assault—delivered to his pursuers, and put aboard a vessel bound for Savannah. Boston was electrified, and the authorities were so alarmed that three hundred policemen guarded the jail in which Sims was kept. Parker was so involved in Sims's plight that one of the abortive plans hatched for his rescue—an attempt to board the Savannah-bound vessel from another boat to steal him from captivity—was planned in his own study. Parker's words were leading to direct and, by federal law, sometimes illegal action.

In a sermon delivered at the Melodeon on a day of fast and humiliation, Parker spoke on "The Chief Sins of the People," using the occasion of Sims's imprisonment to castigate the city for allowing this outrage. In the United States, he claimed, a historic love of individual liberty was being eroded by inordinate love of wealth. This selfishness, Parker observed, was now "the most obvious and preponderate desire in the consciousness of the people," having grown exponentially in the past half century, particularly among those whom he called the "controlling" class. With them, he continued, "everything gives way to money, and money gives way to nothing, neither to man nor to God." Parker had moved from ratiocination to an emotional appeal for public action against the Fugitive Slave Law. Money, he declared, "is master now, all must give way to it," and "the church, the State, the law, is not for man, but money."[25]

Parker also objected to the fact that there was a false idea afoot that people were morally bound to obey any law until it is repealed, when in fact the law of God always took precedence over any "statute of an accidental president unintentionally chosen for four years."[26] Tired of the division between the two great sects in Christendom—"the churches of Christianity, and the churches of commerce"—Parker urged ministers to stop bowing to the moneyed interests and to speak out against the injustice of the Fugitive Slave

Law and slavery in general. Invoking the region's hallowed memory of the Revolutionary generation, Parker asked their descendants to support the same ideals and so to speak out against the party in power. "Resist, then, by peaceful means," he urged, "not with evil but with good. Hold the men infamous that execute this law, give them your pity, but never give them your trust, not till they repent." What if nothing changed? Should one support the Union at all cost? If men continued to enforce the Fugitive Slave Law, Parker opined, "I do not know how soon it will end; I do not care how soon the Union goes to pieces. I believe in justice and the law of God," he continued, and that "ultimately the right will prevail."[27] "America," he exclaimed, "thou youngest born of all God's family of States!"

> Thou art a giant in thy youth, laying thine [*sic*] either hand upon either sea; the lakes behind thee, and the Mexique [*sic*] bay before. Hast thou too forgot thy mission here, proud only of thy wide-spread soil, thy cattle, thy corn, thy cotton, and thy cloth? Wilt thou welcome the Hungarian hero [i.e., Louis Kossuth], and yet hold slaves, and hunt poor negroes through thy land? Thou art the ally of the despot, thyself out-heathening the heathen Turk. Yea, every Christian king may taunt thee with thy slaves. Dost thou forget thine own great men—thy Washington, thy Jefferson, forgot thine own proud words prayed forth to God in thy greatest of prayer? Is it to protect thy wealth alone that thou hast formed a State? And shall thy wealth be slaves? No, thou art mad. It shall not be.[28]

Yet Parker knew how difficult effecting such change would be.

The following year, on the anniversary of Sims's incarceration, Parker spoke on "The Boston Kidnapping," venting his anger at the outrageous actions of his city's elected officials in handing Sims over to the bounty hunters to return him to a life of misery. The twelfth of April, he warned, would be the anniversary of a great crime, and of a great sin "against the law of God wrote in human nature."[29] Neither did it escape Parker that ironically, Sims landed in Georgia on April 19, the day of the battle of Lexington and Concord. "Some of you had fathers in the battle of Lexington," he told his auditors, "many of you relations," and some kept "trophies from that day," won on the battlegrounds. He then dramatically raised a shredded coat. "Here is a Boston trophy from April 19, 1851," he said. "This is the coat of Thomas Sims," worn on April 3, when he was captured. "Sims did not give his liberty easily," Parker continued dramatically. "See how they rent the sleeve away" and tore the coat to "tatters." "Will Boston be called on again to return a fugitive?"[30] If so, he asked, how would elected officials and citizens conduct themselves?

They found out, two years later, with the case of Anthony Burns. In late May 1854 Burns, returning from his work in a clothing shop in Brattle Street, was jailed on a trumped-up charge of burglary. This was a ruse to take him into custody, for when he was brought to the courthouse, his master, a Virginia plantation owner, who thereupon asked for his rendition, confronted him. The Vigilance Committee quickly went into action and secured the city's historic Faneuil Hall for a meeting on the evening of May 26. Several thousand people attended.[31]

The meeting's organizers intended to rally the crowd to overwhelm the courthouse the next morning and carry off the prisoner, but they were unable to control the increasingly agitated attendees. Finally, when word came that some of Boston's African American population already were marching on the courthouse to free Burns, Faneuil Hall erupted in chaos, many participants immediately rushing to join the march. Thomas Wentworth Higginson, a young Worcester, Massachusetts, Unitarian minister in the city for the Vigilance Committee's meetings, already was at the site and took the lead in battering down the building's stout doors; when they finally gave way, he was one of the first inside. But Burns was well protected, and after much fighting—one person, James Batchelder, a watchman at the courthouse, was killed and Higginson himself gashed on the face—the liberators were driven back. Disarray spread with word that someone had been killed.

The next morning, shaken U.S. commissioner Edward Loring resumed the hearing on Burns's fate, and despite much legal maneuvering by Richard Henry Dana and other attorneys on the

Vigilance Committee, on June 2 Burns was delivered to his master and returned to a Virginia plantation. At Parker's urging, Boston's population turned out along the route to protest the city's shame, wrapped their homes with black crepe, and tolled the bells of the various meetinghouses. Because of their part in stirring up the crowd at Faneuil Hall and at the courthouse, he, Wendell Phillips, Higginson, and four others were indicted for "obstructing, resisting, and opposing the execution of the law," with a trial set for April 1855. The stakes in the battle to end slavery had risen significantly since Thoreau was jailed overnight for not paying his poll tax.

On June 4, 1854, in the immediate aftermath of the assault on the courthouse, Parker preached on "The New Crime against Humanity" and indicted citizens for abandoning the ideals of the Revolutionary generation by selling their souls to Mammon. "You remember the meeting at Faneuil Hall, last Friday," he said, when even the words of his friend Wendell Phillips, "the most elegant words yet spoken in America in this century, hardly restrained the multitude from going, and by violence storming the Court House." What stirred them, he asked? "It was the spirit of our fathers—the spirit of justice and liberty in your heart, and in my heart, and in the hearts of us all." Moreover, the reason why there was not even more outrage at the Fugitive Slave Law in general and the Burns case in particular was because slavery allowed cunning men to secure money and political power.[32]

A month later he again made these charges, in a sermon on "The Dangers Which [*sic*] Threaten the Rights of Man in America." In America, he told his auditors, "money is the great object of desire and pursuit." The money standard measures everything, Parker continued, for "Mammon is a profitable God to worship—he gives dinners!" The nation was at a crossroads, he warned, with this chief question before it: "Which shall prevail—the idea and fact of Freedom or the idea and the fact of Slavery?" Given his countrymen's complicity in the slave system—New England's mills, after all, needed Southern cotton—he worried that liberty might fail. "Was it for this the pilgrims came over the sea?" he asked. "Does Forefathers' Rock assent to it?" Was it for this that the New England clergy prayed and John Eliot carried the Gospel to the Indians?

"Today," Parker concluded, "America is a debauched young man, of good blood, fortune, and family, but the companion of gamesters and brawlers; reeking with wine; wasting his substance in riotous living; in the lap of harlots squandering life which his mother gave him." Would he return to Mother Liberty, or would he perish?[33]

Conspicuous by its absence in this and all the passionate sermons and addresses he gave in the aftermath of Burns's rendition is any mention of the plight of the slaves themselves. With the exception of a gesture to writers like Harriet Beecher Stowe, Parker rarely laced his addresses with graphic descriptions of slavery's horrors. Instead, he condemned the institution as profoundly un-American, a system whose values did not belong in a nation founded on sacred principles of freedom of conscience and individual liberty. The corrupting power of slavery on the nation's values most concerned him. Time after time, he lamented their betrayal by politicians, North and South, who for pecuniary gain sacrificed the lofty ideals on which the nation was founded. This invocation of the Founding Fathers not only played well in Boston, the cradle of the American Republic, but also moved the many others sympathetic to the cause of antislavery.

Arrested late in November 1854 for his role in instigating the attack on the courthouse to free Burns, Parker genuinely feared imprisonment, and in his journal he recorded what he would do in that eventuality: compose a sermon per week, he noted, to be read in the Music Hall and printed the following week. He also would prepare a volume of sermons from old manuscripts, write his "Memoirs," and return to work on his "Historical Development of Religion."[34] But the occasion never came. His lawyers and the lawyers for the other defendants successfully argued that the indictments were flawed. The district attorney, Commissioner Benjamin F. Hallett, dismissed all charges, telling Parker, "You have crept out through a knot-hole this time." Parker retorted, "I will knock a bigger hole next time."[35] Parker subsequently published a two-hundred-page account of his actions in the Burns affair, *The Trial of Theodore Parker for the "Misdemeanor" of A Speech in Faneuil Hall Against Kidnapping . . . with the Defence*, a tour de force of legal and ecclesiastical reasoning as well as of moral indignation, peppered with contempt for those in Boston—particularly Commissioner Loring—who so eagerly complied with the Fugitive Slave Law.

Parker soon made good on his promise to Hallett through his support for a "free" Kansas, that is, his encouragement of New Englanders and others sympathetic to the antislavery cause to settle in the new Western Territories to prevent the South from acquiring more legislative power. Opposed by "border ruffians" from Missouri, a slave state, who likewise flooded the area with immigrants to gain support for their own position, antislavery settlers soon were at war. Parker opposed the idea of popular sovereignty because it overrode the Compromise of 1820, and after South Carolinian Preston Brooks viciously beat Massachusetts senator Charles Sumner on the Senate floor for his incendiary speech, "The Crime against Kansas," Parker was virtually apoplectic.

In one of two speeches before the American Anti-Slavery Society in New York on May 7, 1856, an event at which Garrison introduced him as "a very excellent fanatic, a very good infidel, and a first-rate traitor," Parker spoke on the "Present Crisis in American Affairs."[36] Just a few days earlier a contingent of forty-five people, some of them his parishioners, had embarked for Kansas with twenty "Sharp's rifles," ready to keep Kansas from the hands of the Southerners.[37] The United States, Parker observed, now comprised two different populations, once united, but in the last two generations "so diverse in their institutions, their mode of life, their social and political aims" that now they were not only unlike but hostile. Citizenship still bound them together, "but no moral union makes the two one." And they were on a collision course in Kansas.[38]

Once again Parker presented the question in practical rather than moral terms. The battle is for Kansas, he proclaimed. "Shall it be free, as the majority of its inhabitants have voted; or slave, as the Federal Government and the slave power" have determined "by violence" to make it? Would Kansas be a place for the Northern workingman or the Southern plantation owner? Would slavery spread all over the United States and root out freedom from the land? Americans could still end this crime against humanity by ballots, he observed; but "wait a little, and only with swords and with blood can this deep and widening blot of shame be scoured out from the continent."[39]

Parker was by now moving down a more and more radical path, obsessed that the United States was at a crossroads in its brief history. He shelved his long-anticipated work "The Historical Development of Religion," which promised to set a new standard for comparative studies, and more and more turned to the nation's internal political problems. His deep involvement in the Kansas-Nebraska question eventually brought him in contact with another radical abolitionist, not a clergyman or a politician, but a Connecticut-born tanner and wool merchant named John Brown, just back from the territories.

Parker met Brown in Boston in 1857, introduced by Franklin Sanborn (1831–1917), a young schoolteacher in Concord who, after graduation from Harvard, had attached himself to Emerson and other Transcendentalists and entered enthusiastically into various reform movements. Sanborn had just met Brown, whose three eldest sons had moved to the Kansas Territory to augment the antislavery population and who in 1855 had joined them, answering their request for weapons by delivering them himself. Brown was already well known in abolitionist circles. In 1848 he had shared with Frederick Douglass his dream of founding a community for runaway slaves in the vastness of the Allegheny Mountains; Douglass was the first to call him "Captain."

Outraged by Brooks's brutal caning of Sumner in the Senate chamber, as well as by recent violent actions of proslavery settlers in Kansas—in May 1856, for example, a group had sacked the capital of Lawrence, destroying a newspaper office and other buildings and killing two men—Brown retaliated in kind. Shortly after the attack on Lawrence he and some of his supporters seized and brutally killed five proslavery settlers at Pottawatomie Creek. More fighting ensued, and proslavery militias took prisoner two of Brown's sons. In a battle in which Brown and a small number of antislavery settlers held their own against three hundred "bushwhackers" from Missouri at Ossawatomie, another of his sons was killed. To compensate for these heartbreaking losses, Brown won the release of his two captured children and valiantly continued his resistance in the territory. Throughout the antislavery North he became a hero, "Ossawatomie Brown."[40]

In November, Brown returned to New York (where he had left his wife and younger children on his farm in North Elba) and New England to raise money for guns and supplies for the Kansas settlers. He introduced himself to Sanborn. Brown sought to raise and equip a small army—one hundred strong—to protect the Kansas settlers and make occasional forays into Missouri, where the proslavery militias were based. For this he needed thirty thousand dollars and two hundred rifles.

Ignited by his enthusiasm and vivid accounts of actions already undertaken in the new territory—by all accounts, Brown was nothing if not spellbinding and convincing—Sanborn consented to help and thereupon introduced him to Samuel Gridley Howe as well as to Parker, who hosted a reception for him. Garrison and Wendell Phillips were both skeptical of Brown's Old Testament demeanor and eagerness to resort to violence. Howe and Parker, however, were won over. Also present was the wealthy Medford, Massachusetts, merchant, George Luther Stearns (1809–1867), a strong backer of the Emigrant Aid Company and the Massachusetts State Kansas Committee, groups that bankrolled antislavery emigrants in Kansas. Brown so impressed Stearns that out of his own pocket he paid for two hundred handguns for Brown's militia.

When the New England contingent of the Kansas Aid Society, a national group based in Chicago, agreed to give Brown the rifles he wanted as well as five thousand dollars, Brown's plan was well under way. Continuing his solicitations, in early March, Brown found himself at Sanborn's home in Concord, where he was introduced to the town's literary lions. He met both Emerson and Thoreau and soon enough was engaged to lecture at the Town House, where he drew an appreciative audience but again met with only small, courteous contributions. Taken all around, his New England trip had not been overly lucrative. He thereupon penned a bitter "Farewell" to some of his New England supporters, a missive that moved Stearns so much that he gave Brown a seven-thousand-dollar letter of credit against his own account, a sum that put the Captain back into operation.[41] By August, with political matters in Kansas stabilizing in favor of the antislavery party, Brown began to develop his quixotic plan to attack a federal arsenal in Virginia, liberate and arm the local slave population, and continue such forays throughout the South.

He stopped in Rochester, New York, to apprise Douglass of his plan, but even given his host's willingness to liberate the slaves by force, he met with considerable skepticism. Brown then apprised his strongest backers, swearing them to confidentiality, of a grand strategy for freeing the slaves, the details of which he did not yet share. New York abolitionist Gerrit Smith wanted Brown's New England coterie to meet at his home in Peterboro, New York, outside Rochester—Brown was afraid of being seen in Boston—but Stearns, Howe, Parker, and Higginson chose not to go. Sanborn did, however, and on February 22, an auspicious holiday, he heard Brown's plans for attacking a Virginia arsenal, freeing and arming the slaves on several nearby plantations, and establishing a government in the liberated area on the basis of a constitution he had already prepared. Brown asked Smith and Sanborn and, through them, their friends, for at least eight hundred dollars to carry out his plans.

On Sanborn's return to Boston, he shared details of this plot with Higginson, Parker, and Howe; Brown himself took it up with his large backer, Stearns. Parker was intrigued but wanted to hear from Brown in person. This time he took the risk, and on March 4 in a Boston hotel he met those who, with the addition of Smith, thereafter would comprise the "Secret Six," individuals who had been apprised of, and morally and financially supported, Brown's attack on the federal arsenal at Harpers Ferry, Virginia. Parker the Transcendentalist, along with two second-generation members, Higginson and Sanborn, had come this far in his radicalism. Over the next few months, coconspirators in what proved one of the most infamous episodes leading to the Civil War, they assiduously raised money among their friends for what they euphemistically termed a new "experiment" to free the slaves.

The rest is history. Delayed by the machinations of Hugh Forbes, an unstable confidant who knew of Brown's larger plan and had worked Washington's corridors warning against him, Brown finally attacked the arsenal. Forbes's warnings in Washington, though, had less to do with the assault's outcome than did the small number of recruits and the failure of Brown's actions to foment a wider rebellion. With his force decimated and Brown himself wounded, in a few days he and the remainder of his militia were captured and tried, and the majority of them, Brown included, were executed. Documents found in his home in North Elba implicated the Secret Six, of different minds about whether Brown should have struck when he did. Writing to his brother William a few days after Brown's capture, Emerson provides a sense of how worried he and his friends were about the conspirators' fate. These "bushels of letters," he noted, showed Brown's "extensive relationships with many northern supporters" and "have naturally alarmed some of his friends in Boston."[42]

One of the most famous and strident voices for abolition, Parker was virtually silent during this traumatic period, but not because he was intimidated. By 1858 he realized that he had tuberculosis. On his doctor's advice, early the next year he and his wife left for Cuba and Santa Cruz in the Caribbean, a warmer climate where he might better cope with the disease. From there they sailed to Europe and settled in Rome, where he eagerly followed news of Brown's plight. Writing to the prominent abolitionist Francis Jackson late in November, Parker reiterated what he had come to believe—that men held against their will have a natural right to kill everyone who seeks to prevent their liberty, and that it was a natural duty for freemen to do for the enslaved all that they have a right to do for themselves. "Brown will die, I think," Parker wrote, "like a martyr, and also like a saint."[43]

A continent away, Parker was beyond the reach of United States law, if in failing health, but the remainder of the Secret Six had much to worry about. Sanborn absconded to Canada, a retreat that upset supporters like Emerson who thought that he should repent and argue Brown's case. After a prominent Boston attorney opined that none of the Six could be indicted for treason if they had not taken part in the act itself, Sanborn returned to Concord by the day of Brown's execution, taking part in services organized by his sympathizers. Fearing prosecution, Stearns and Howe also had left the country and did not return from Canada until after Brown's execution. Gerrit Smith was confined in a Utica, New York, lunatic asylum, committed for "mental collapse" shortly after the attack on Harpers Ferry. This left Higginson. After planning various unrealistic attempts to rescue Brown from federal authorities, he returned to Worcester. He felt betrayed by his fellow conspirators, none of whom confessed to having been involved in Brown's grand "experiment," and he thought that they had not done enough to ensure the raid's success. With the threat of subpoena from a congressional committee looking into the raid, the conspirators squabbled about what to do and say. Higginson and Sanborn were the only ones actually summoned to testify, but none were ever prosecuted. Parker died in Florence on June 10, 1860. Recriminations about loyalty to Brown and his grandiose plans, which he had based on a belief that he had obeyed the voice of his conscience, preoccupied the survivors for their lifetimes.

Although in Concord Brown had little success drumming up support for his plans, many townsmen were sympathetic to the antislavery cause, some eventually drifting into the camp of the radical abolitionists. Anticipating what Brown and others already knew, Emerson admitted that he was "glad to see that the terror at disunion and anarchy is disappearing," for the price of the slaves' freedom might demand just that.[44] After Brown's death, on December 2, he and other Concord citizens planned an appropriate memorial, work in which Henry Thoreau took the lead. To avoid inciting the crowd, the speakers—Emerson, Alcott, Sanborn, Thoreau, and a few others—agreed to keep the service solemn rather than make it a call to political action. Emerson read Brown's last words; Alcott recited a church service for the death of a martyr; and Sanborn performed a dirge he had written for the occasion. After a few brief remarks, Thoreau read some poems, including Sir Walter Raleigh's "The Soul's Errand" and his own translation from Tacitus.[45]

The Thoreau family long had been considered "advanced" in their abolitionist views, and through the 1850s Henry continued to reflect and speak out on slavery, particularly after the Anthony Burns case. On July 4, 1854, he spoke in Framingham, Massachusetts, at a mass meeting for abolitionists called by Garrison, on "Slavery in Massachusetts," an address widely reported in the local press.[46] Even more powerful was his "Plea for Captain John Brown," delivered in Concord on October 30, 1859, as the insurgent languished in prison. Because Concord's community remained split over the propriety of Brown's actions, the town selectmen would not allow anyone to ring the meetinghouse bell to summon townspeople to the lecture. Once again, as he had done a decade earlier for Emerson's address on the anniversary of the West Indian emancipation, Thoreau performed the task himself.

He devoted much of his speech to Brown's character rather than to a defense of his actions in Kansas and at Harpers Ferry; Thoreau believed that Brown's ideals, rather than his violent actions, were most important. Like Emerson, he made much of Brown's Revolutionary heritage and praised him as "by birth and descent a New England farmer," one who had not gone to Harvard but to "the great university of the West, where he sedulously pursued the study of Liberty." Thoreau also linked him to the Puritans of Cromwell's day, "men of simple habits, straightforward, prayerful; not thinking much of rulers who did not fear God." But above all, Thoreau noted, he was "a man of rare common sense and directness of speech, as of action; a transcendentalist above all, a man of ideas and principles."[47]

Not an admirer of the popular press, Thoreau admitted that for days after the raid on Harpers Ferry he had read all the newspapers but never encountered a "single expression of sympathy" for Brown and his men. Everywhere he found the words "misguided," "wild," "insane, "crazed," "deluded." But Brown was a superior being. "No man in America," he continued admiringly, "has ever stood up so persistently and effectively for the dignity of human nature," and in that way Brown was "the most American of us all."[48] More remarkable was Thoreau's admission that he understood how one could be driven to draw blood over the slavery issue. "A man may have other affairs to attend to," he admitted, and he "did not wish to kill nor [*sic*] to be killed," but he could foresee "circumstances in which both these things would by me be unavoidable." The federal government was in thrall to the slavery interests, and for an American to keep his decency, he might have to act as Brown had done, striking a blow, like the men of 1776, for freedom. Thoreau did not doubt Brown's significance. "Some eighteen hundred years ago Christ was crucified," he continued, and "this morning, perchance, Captain John Brown was hung. These are the two ends of a chain which is not without its links."[49]

Thoreau's address was enthusiastically received, and he soon had invitations to repeat it elsewhere, which he did at Boston's Tremont Temple on November 1, after Frederick Douglass had canceled because of his own complicity in Brown's plans. The lecture was sold out and reported in all the Boston papers, some favoring it, others condemning it as wildly fanatic. Two days later, at the request of his good friend H.G.O. Blake, Thoreau again reprised the lecture, with great success, at Washburn Hall in Worcester. He also prepared another address, "The Last Days of John Brown," for a commemoration at Brown's home in North Elba on July 4, 1860, which he could not attend. R. J. Hinton, the secretary of the meeting, introduced and read the paper, to much praise: "Mr. Thoreau's voice," one report of the event proclaimed, "was the first which broke the disgraceful silence or hushed the senseless babble with which the grandest deed of our time was met."[50]

At Thoreau's funeral, in 1862, his friend and erstwhile mentor remembered his praise of Brown. "Before the first friendly word had been spoken for Captain John Brown," Emerson said, Thoreau "sent notices to most homes in Concord that he would speak in a public hall on the condition and character of John Brown, on Sunday evening, and invited all people to come." Representatives of both the Republican committee and the abolitionist committee advised him not to do so, thinking it premature and his words potentially inflammatory and detrimental to their causes. Thoreau replied, Emerson told the mourners, "'I did not send to you for advice, but to announce that I am to speak.'" In many ways, not the least in his single-minded devotion to conscience, Thoreau was cut from the same rugged homespun as Brown. As he had said of Brown, so Emerson said eloquently of Thoreau: "No truer American existed."[51] When James Redpath brought out his *Echoes of Harper's Ferry* (1860), a collection of essays and addresses on Brown, he commemorated Brown's relation to Concord, the cradle of liberty, by dedicating the volume to Thoreau, as well as to Emerson, Phillips, and other "Defenders of the Faithful."[52]

All that was left was the final conflagration, which neither Parker nor Thoreau lived through but which Emerson, Brownson, Ripley, Peabody, and others of the Transcendentalist cohort survived. The year 1860 brought accelerating crises, as Abraham Lincoln, the presidential candidate of the infant Republican Party, was elected over a split Democratic Party—the Southern wing nominating John C. Breckinridge and the Northern, Stephen Douglas. The South Carolina militia's attack on Fort Sumter in Charleston Harbor on April 12 was the spark everyone had awaited, with anticipation or dread.

To this point, Emerson continued his efforts for abolition, but his spirit took a severe blow when his good friend Parker, long an inspiration, died. Invited to speak at his memorial, Emerson declined, sensitive to the distance between his friend's heroic and long-term engagement with antislavery and his own halting entrance onto that stage. "Our differences of method & working," Emerson wrote to the memorial committee, "[were] such as really required and honored all his [Parker's] catholicism and magnanimity to forgive in me."[53] In the privacy of his journal he was even more candid. "I can well praise him at a spectator's distance, for our minds & methods were unlike—few people more unlike," a tacit admission of the fractures within the Transcendentalist party.[54]

To his credit, as the war drew closer, Emerson did not shy away. In January 1861 he accepted Wendell Phillips's invitation to speak at the annual meeting of the Massachusetts Anti-Slavery Society at the Tremont Temple in Boston. Phillips and James Freeman Clarke, the latter now head of his own independent church in Boston and emerging in his own right as an important antislavery spokesperson, joined him on the platform. The meeting was large and rowdy, with pro-Union advocates, who feared that inflammatory rhetoric might encourage secession, vociferous in their disapproval of Emerson's condemnation of the South's moral corruption. When he declared that if the Union were broken, it would only be because of the re-calcitrant slaveholders' "barbarism," he sent the assembly into chaos. The pro-Union crowd continually interrupted his speech with cat-calls and offensive slogans, finally causing Emerson to stop while police cleared the building. This was not his usual reception, but it indicated how divided the Massachusetts citizenry had become over the escalating sectional crisis.[55]

In the early months of the war, particularly after the Union de-feat at the first Battle of Bull Run, Emerson joined the debate among Northerners over whether there should be immediate eman-cipation, even as President Lincoln held out for preservation of the Union. As the war continued its brutal course, Emerson was invited to lecture at the Smithsonian Institution, an opportunity he could not refuse, for it provided an opportunity to meet and speak before many of the nation's most important politicians, including the pres-ident, whom he met twice and lobbied to emancipate the slaves. On January 31 Emerson gave his lecture, "American Civilization," a revision of an address he had delivered in Boston several months earlier.

He minced no words. Taking as his starting point the nobility of all voluntary labor, no matter how menial, he observed, "now here comes this conspiracy of slavery,—they call it an institution. I call it a destitution." Because of the slave system, he continued, Ameri-cans had attempted to hold together two states of civilization, a higher one, in which "labor and the tenure of land and the right of suffrage" were defended; and a lower state, in which "the old mili-tary tenure of prisoners or slaves, and of power and land in a few hands, makes an oligarchy." All the facts—economical and moral—were on the side of emancipation, but people in power did not have the courage to take the next, necessary step. Civilization, Emerson proclaimed, demanded emancipation. It is "a principle; everything else is an intrigue."[56]

Emerson played the pragmatist. Unless the North took the affir-mative step of emancipation, war would only preserve the Union in its present corrupt state and not ensure the triumph of any larger ideal. Emerson called on Lincoln to act. The power of emancipation, Emerson continued, would alter "the atomic social constitution of the Southern people," for they intended to keep out white labor, particularly German and Irish immigrants, because it would cost them wages. Emancipation, he proclaimed, at one stroke would elevate the poor whites of the South and identify their interest with those of the Northern laborers.[57] In September 1862, when Lincoln finally acted, Emerson rejoiced to a Boston audience, "Our hurts are healed; the health of the nation is repaired." And if Lincoln's action did not "promise the redemption of the black race," he continued, it at least "relieve[d] it of our opposition." For that he, as well as other of his friends, thought the war worth fighting.[58]

But with the war raging, what work was left for the circle, of whom Emerson now was the center, so many of whom had sacrificed their other interests—philosophical, literary, philanthropic, and theological—to this all-consuming national tragedy? In 1849, after the debacle at Brook Farm, George Ripley moved to New York to work at Greeley's *Tribune*, and after Fuller's death he became the literary editor of the paper. Although he supported the Free-Soil candidate, John Frémont, in the presidential election of 1856, after his defeat, Ripley had withdrawn from politics. He did not think that violence was the way to destroy slavery, and falling back on the French thinkers who had so influenced him, he was willing to await the march of social progress to end the evil. If enough antislavery immigrants settled in the South, he thought, eventually proslavery forces would be defeated in each state and change effected through the legislative system. Ripley supported the North during the conflict, of course, but he thought that even with the South's defeat, one had to work with Southerners to realize a lasting peace. Not on record about the Secret Six, he probably would have found his friend Parker's involvement quixotic at best.[59]

Brownson's case was different. By the 1850s he had been a devout Roman Catholic for a decade—indeed, one of the American church's chief intellectual voices—and lived in New York, where he joined his old Transcendentalist friends in lamenting the increase in slave territories and the South's attempts to gain even more. For many years a staunch member of the Democratic Party, after the Supreme Court's decision in the Dred Scott case in 1857, Brownson drifted toward the new Republican Party, even though he was slow to relinquish his long-standing support of states' rights. Chief Justice Roger Taney's ruling that Dred Scott, a slave then living in

Missouri who had sued for his freedom because he had lived in Free States and territories, was not a citizen (implying as well that no African American could be) and so could not bring suit, so outraged Brownson that he moved to the party of Lincoln. In *Brownson's Quarterly Review* he continued to argue for the unity of the races and the inherent dignity of each person, and he lambasted Southerners for trying to enlarge their political base. Although these views were not popular with all his Catholic readers, he continued to advocate the notion that the war was not only to preserve the Union but to effect full emancipation.[60] By 1861, the impending crisis thus preoccupied virtually all surviving Transcendentalists, even though none served in battle.

But what was the long-term effect of this turn away from the kinds of intellectual and social engagement that hitherto had so clearly defined the Transcendentalist movement? When the war was over, where would the energy flow? After the North's victory, what work remained for the circle of which Emerson now was the de facto center, if almost by default? One thing is clear. Because of the Transcendentalists' confrontation with the internal demon of slavery, their vision for cultural and social renewal became more nationalistic and less concerned with the universal humanitarianism that hitherto had defined the faith of so many of them. A few among the second generation continued to dream of a new kind of social harmony, but with the North's triumph, industrial capitalism only increased its hold on the nation. The self-reliant entrepreneur was man of the hour, and the Gilded Age was Emerson's, as he was canonized as America's philosopher.

10

FREE RELIGION AND

THE DREAM OF A COMMON HUMANITY

eviewing his life in *Cheerful Yesterdays* (1898), Thomas Wentworth Higginson devoted a chapter to "The Birth of a Literature," in which he chronicled the rise of the "*Atlantic* circle" who wrote for *The Atlantic Monthly* and its longtime publisher, Ticknor and Fields. This group was typified, he continued, by Emerson, the novelist Nathaniel Hawthorne, the abolitionist and poet John Greenleaf Whittier, the genial essayist Oliver Wendell Holmes, and poets Henry Wadsworth Longfellow and James Russell Lowell, "to name only the six most commonly selected as representatives." These embodied a truly national literary culture, Higginson claimed. What "saved this circle from becoming a clique and a mere mutual admiration society," he continued, "was its fortunate variety of temperaments." A contributor to the magazine from its inception as well as a friend of all the parties whom he named, Higginson was in a position to know.[1]

In the 1860s *The Atlantic* was still a new publishing venture. A decade earlier the author and abolitionist Francis Henry Underwood, a native of the small western Massachusetts hill town of Enfield, had conceived of a monthly magazine, comparable to *Harper's Magazine*, devoted to the literature and culture of Boston and its environs, more lively and au courant than the stuffy *North American Review* and more wide-ranging than *The Christian Examiner*. In 1857 Underwood convinced Phillips, Sampson and Company to undertake the venture, and he lined up as supporters and potential contributors Emerson, Longfellow, Holmes, Lowell, and others. The first issue of *The Atlantic: A Magazine of Literature, Art, and Politics* appeared late that same year, Lowell its first editor and Underwood offering stalwart assistance for several years. In 1859, after Phillips, Sampson failed, the publisher William Ticknor bought the journal and transferred the editorship to his business partner, James T. Fields. Thereafter the firm used the journal as virtually a house organ to tout its own authors (including Higginson). At its inception *The Atlantic* was pro-Union and antislavery and, once the war had begun, solidly behind Lincoln.[2]

Given Emerson's prominence on Higginson's list, one might expect that other Transcendentalists would find a home in the new periodical, but such was not the case. Ironically, the 1850s, which saw the Transcendentalists' inward turn, also produced the most highly regarded American literature to date, but most of it related only indirectly to Emerson's and, to a lesser degree, Margaret Fuller's encouragement of belles lettres. By most standards, the Transcendentalists' lasting literary achievement was limited to Emerson, Thoreau, and Walt Whitman (a special case), a reminder that the movement's most important influence lay elsewhere. And while the literary achievement of these Transcendentalists resulted from attempts to reconcile long-standing interests in self-culture with the bumptious nationalism that dominated the 1850s, in the cases of other great writers from the period, particularly Hawthorne, Herman Melville, and Harriet Beecher Stowe, it issued from their challenge to the New England Idealists' cosmic optimism.

Consider, for example, Emerson's *English Traits* (1856), in which he used his recent trip to England and the Continent, in the signal years 1847–48, as the occasion to meditate on the Old World and the New. Herein he did not stress cross-fertilization so much as America's direct cultural inheritance from the mother country. "If there be one test of national genius universally accepted," he continued, "it is success; and if there be one successful country in the universe for the last millennium, that country is England."[3] He also admired, in his chapter on "Manners," England's enshrinement of domesticity, the "taproot[,] which enables the nation to branch wide and high," rooted as it was in the sanctity of private property.[4]

Coupled with an unwavering common sense that issued in "strong earthy expression" rather than airy symbol and metaphor, the English emphasized "fact" in a way that permanently marked their, and their ex-colonies', character.[5]

Emerson was aware of how accurately these same traits now were viewed as American, as Alexis de Tocqueville had noted in his influential *Democracy in America*. Emerson thus linked his fulsome praise of England to a belief that the United States had inherited its virtues. This Anglophilia accounts for his implicit devaluation of France's and Germany's contributions to the world's social construction: England had been successful because it did not fall into the mire of French socialism or wander aimlessly in the labyrinth of German philosophy. Albion's gift to the New World thus consisted of simplicity and clarity, virtues that fitted well with the Market Revolution, rather than the moral complexity and ambiguity that characterized Hawthorne's and Melville's great works.

Thoreau's *Walden* (1854), arguably the literary masterpiece of the Transcendentalist movement, similarly embodies a love affair with America as the writer struggles to square his devotion to conscience with the republican ideals on which the nation was founded. An American Everyman, Thoreau mixes the water of Walden Pond with that of the Ganges and slashes the weeds in his bean field like a soldier fighting the Trojan War. For Thoreau, God culminates in the present moment of each person's life and transforms all aspects of that life into acts of devotion. Content to be in and of the world rather than to transcend it, in his great book Thoreau moved Emerson's lessons in new directions and, describing the results in his crystalline prose, offered what became the culmination of Transcendentalism's literary phase.

But Thoreau, from whom one might have expected more good writing, died of tuberculosis at a tragically young age. His friend Ellery Channing, although a promising poet, never approximated the bard Emerson envisioned in his essay "The Poet" (1843), nor did such male representatives of the sentimental genre as Longfellow, Lowell, or Holmes. That left Walt Whitman, who filled Emerson's description of an American bard more than any other, but his Transcendentalism was not so much a deep intellectual substratum but simply another layer to the complex social and imaginative life that eventuated in *Leaves of Grass* (1855). Tellingly, he initially won Emerson's praise but resisted gravitation into his orbit, something that tended to short-circuit promising careers unless one eventually broke free from Emerson's magnetic field, as Thoreau did in *Walden*. To Emerson, Whitman was just another aspiring author, no more or less interesting, finally, than a handful of other young writers whose careers he boosted. When, in subsequent editions of his book, Whitman included homoerotic and otherwise sexually explicit verse, Emerson lost interest.

Thus, through the 1870s Emerson remained the patriarch of American letters, for European visitors a wonder of the Western world as well known as Niagara Falls and the Lowell mills, but his best work was behind him. *The Conduct of Life* (1860), published on the eve of the war, is his only satisfying book from his later career, and after 1865 he settled more and more into his newly assumed role as the country's de facto philosopher in chief, his essays old and new used to justify the economic order. Other first-generation Transcendentalists simply dropped from the literary radar screen. Ripley labored in New York, serving the republic of letters with reviews for Greeley's newspaper and then turning his attention to the *New American Cyclopædia*, the many volumes of which he edited with his old Brook Farm friend Charles A. Dana. Brownson wrote endless polemics and book reviews for *Brownson's Quarterly Review*, now essentially a church organ. Peabody busied herself with the kindergarten movement, which she worked tirelessly to popularize in the United States, and with Native American rights. Hedge moved back to the Boston area, serving several terms as president of the American Unitarian Association and finally as a professor of ecclesiastical history and (later) of German at Harvard.

Where did this leave younger, second-generation Transcendentalists who, like their mentors, had been swept up in the sectional crisis and survived? Though little remarked, these younger figures, many trained at Harvard Divinity School in the 1840s and 1850s, were not in the least retiring; and they kept philosophical Idealism and its moral implications in the public eye long after the war. What was the relationship of these younger Transcendentalists to this

"Atlantic group," and what were their contributions to the subsequent cultural moment, what George Santayana termed the "Genteel Tradition," of which they were representative? More generally, how significant was the afterlife to Transcendentalist ideas and ideals beyond their widespread diffusion in a watered-down Emersonianism, which for three decades had shaped New England's intellectual discourse?

Theirs were very different intellectual battles from those their precursors had waged. Giving credence to Emerson's notion of the timeless conflict between opposed philosophical views, in the postbellum period American intellectuals again divided into the two contending parties, Materialists and Idealists. Now, however, the former marched under a banner emblazoned with the names of Auguste Comte, Charles Darwin, and William Graham Sumner rather than with that of John Locke, while their opponents struggled to maintain consciousness at the center of philosophical inquiry and to buttress ethical imperative in the face of what they regarded as amoral scientific materialism. In the post–Civil War period their contributions to other aspects of American intellectual discourse remained vital, if less remarked, particularly among those who kept alive a dream of a common humanity based in the irreducible equality of all souls.

The most unusual group of these Idealists surfaced in the 1850s, not in Concord or Boston, but half a continent away, in Cincinnati and St. Louis. The Ohio group centered on John B. Stallo, whose *General Principles of the Philosophy of Nature* (1848) offered American readers a sophisticated introduction to Hegel's philosophy.[6] Joining him in his admiration for the German philosopher were social reformer Peter Kaufmann, Transcendentalist fellow traveler Moncure Conway, and socialist August Willich, whose lectures and writings illustrate the various uses to which Hegelian Idealism could be put.[7] Kaufmann, for example, drew on Hegel's notion of how, over time, contested truth resulted in social amelioration, while Conway used the philosopher to interrogate the supernatural basis of faith, positing a belief in miracles as simply a stage to a higher form of religion. Willich, a champion of the laborer, eventually found his way to Hegel's followers, Ludwig Feuerbach and Karl Marx, powerfully grounding his critique of market capitalism in historical dialectic.

Stallo's contributions to the proliferation of Hegel's ideas were manifold. For one thing, he elaborated the philosopher's belief that thought is fundamentally identical with the universe, itself God's self-revelation. Not surprisingly, given the congruence of this concept with Transcendentalism, Stallo's book became well known among certain New England intellectuals. Parker, who knew his Hegel, reviewed it for his *Massachusetts Quarterly Review* and called it "a grand, solid book" and "altogether the best thing upon the profound subject to which it relates that has ever appeared on this side of the water."[8] In his journals, Emerson redacted Stallo's *General Principles*, a book that exerted considerable influence on his subsequent understanding of history. Indeed, Stallo, one scholar writes, was "the most persistent influence to keep Emerson's mind occupied with German thought."[9]

By the late 1850s American interest in Hegel had shifted to St. Louis, where William Torrey Harris (1835–1909), a Connecticut native who emigrated to the West after dropping out of Yale, gathered around him a group of German émigré intellectuals committed to German Idealism.[10] Bronson Alcott's conversations on Platonism as well as his ideas on education had whetted Harris's philosophical interests; in Cincinnati he both taught in and administered the public school system, and was an early advocate of the kindergarten movement. In 1858 Harris met Henry C. Brockmeyer, a Prussian immigrant to the Mississippi Valley who made and lost a fortune in tanning and shoe manufacture. An autodidact, Brockmeyer subsequently devoted himself to reading and discussing philosophy and politics. He introduced his new friend to Hegel's thought, which he had discovered in the selections that Frederic Henry Hedge offered in his *Prose Writers of Germany* (1848). After the Civil War, Harris and Brockmeyer organized the St. Louis Philosophical Society, devoted to the popularization of Hegelian philosophy. When convenient, Stallo and Willich made the trip downriver for meetings.

Hegel provided these men with a way to understand such large-scale events as America's rapid economic development and the recent trauma of war. In their view, to date, the United States occupied the highest step of humanity's progress, even as, given the dialectical nature of history, the country was still evolving, for good or ill. The St. Louis Hegelians sought to align themselves with its future course. They also appreciated the philosopher's proposition that spirit continuously manifests itself in the world, providing a way for humanity to ground philosophical abstractions in experience. Like their counterparts in Ohio, the St. Louis Hegelians lamented the growing tendency to privilege fact over consciousness, a tendency responsible for the country's descending spiral into philosophical materialism.

Given Harris's conversion at Alcott's hands, these midwesterners also were much interested in Transcendentalism, and they invited both Emerson and Alcott to lecture in St. Louis. They particularly admired the New Englanders' longtime advocacy of spiritual self-consciousness, as well as their notion of God's eternal presence in the world, concepts they married to Hegel's philosophy. To forward the group's agenda, in 1867 Harris founded the *Journal of Speculative Philosophy*, a mouthpiece for American Hegelianism that he edited until 1893. In addition to carrying many of his essays, the journal included work by Alcott, Emerson, and several prominent younger Unitarians, as well as pieces by such budding philosophers as Charles Sanders Peirce and William James. The influence of the St. Louis Hegelians, however, never extended far beyond the rarified world of philosophical debate. Mounting a systematic challenge to Comte's Positivism and Darwinian thought, they never extended their influence enough to redirect the nation's priorities.

Other direct inheritors of the Transcendentalists deployed philosophical Idealism in different ways. The oldest member to emerge as a major voice of postwar Transcendentalism was Cyrus Bartol (1813–1900), who had published his first important work, *Discourses on the Christian Spirit and Life*, in 1850 but whose influence within the group was minimal until after the Civil War. O. B. Frothingham remembered him as "a soaring mind enamored of thoughts on divine things, inextricably caught in the toils of speculation." His Transcendentalism, Frothingham concluded, "had a cast of its own," for Bartol was a transitional figure.[11] He graduated from Bowdoin College in 1832 and Harvard Divinity School in 1835, and attended many of the early meetings of the Transcendentalist Club. However, after he began a pastorate at Boston's West Church in 1837 that continued until 1884, he made a concerted effort to escape Emerson's and Parker's force fields, worshipping a more personal Christian deity than they allowed and remaining loyal to the mainstream Unitarians—he voted, for example, with ministers who sought to exclude Parker from their pulpits. In his theology the West Church minister thus recalls Frederic Henry Hedge, another long-lived first-generation Transcendentalist stalwart who distanced himself from Emerson and Parker even as he continued to inflect his Unitarianism with Transcendentalist ideas.

In *Discourses on the Christian Spirit and Life*, Bartol proclaimed Christ's unique dispensation. "He is not, in the phrase of the day, a 'representative man,'" Bartol noted (a nod to Emerson's recent book, *Representative Men*), "but representative of deity." "The world recedes not from him, but approaches him. He seems in the future, not in the past. He transcends all our transcendentalism."[12] Bartol also shied away from the ecumenical embrace of the world's religions that characterized Parker and, in less theological and intrusive ways, Thoreau. Mankind should not let the Bible, Bartol urged, "be classed with other books of inferior quality, lower proof, of different import and from a different source," for it had "a divinity possessed by no Koran, by no oriental documents, which with their strange names decorate of late the fond speech of some, by no teachings of pagan sages, or proverbs of nations."[13]

After the Civil War, in good measure because of his continuing advocacy of intuitionist beliefs, Bartol became a major voice among radical Unitarians, some of whom (though he was not among them) formally organized in 1867 as the Free Religious Association. This group coalesced after 1865, when Henry W. Bellows organized a National Conference to unite American Unitarians and, in the debate over the group's principles, succeeded in keeping the phrase

"Lord Jesus Christ" in its constitution's preamble, effectively eliminating from membership more broad-minded clergy. Hedge and Clarke joined him in this effort, for like Bellows, they supported a "confessional" denomination, that is, one associated with a Christian creed.

At the conference's second meeting, in 1866, disaffected Unitarians reopened the confessional question but again were defeated, prompting some of them to meet a few months later in Boston at Bartol's elegant Beacon Hill home to discuss their own association. By their third meeting their number had grown to thirty, primarily clergymen and a few lay leaders, and they finally agreed on a constitution for an organization to express their diverse views. Much debate centered on the question of whether, if one advocated "free religion," one should organize at all.[14] Their Free Religious Association, they declared, thus would promote the interests of "pure religion," encourage "the scientific study of theology," and "increase fellowship in the spirit."[15]

Thirty-seven members subsequently signed the document and elected O. B. Frothingham their first president. Despite his initial enthusiasm, however, Bartol was not among them, probably because, an unreformed intuitionist, he objected to the constitution's emphasis on the "scientific" basis of theology as well as subscription to an overarching statement of principle.[16] Hedge, too, demurred, committed to the American Unitarian Association and uneasy with the emphasis on science. "The only element in which religion can thrive and be a power in society," he opined, "is an element of mystery and faith." "The world of knowledge and the world of faith," he wrote in 1867, "are principally distinct."[17]

The Free Religious Association was never numerically large. However, it exercised considerable influence on American church history, for it erected a spacious tent under which those uncomfortable with the confessional emphasis of the American Unitarian Association met to share ideas. Bartol remained an important contributor to the ongoing religious debates that engaged the membership, but he also founded, in 1867, the Radical Club, to promote unfettered discussion of subjects of interest to freethinkers. This group had no formal membership requirements and at one time or

other in its thirteen-year history numbered among its attendees virtually all of Boston's prominent intellectuals.[18]

In a contemporary essay, on "Radicalism," Bartol explained the
relation of the Free Religious Association to the Radical Club. Some
radical Unitarians chose not to join the Free Religionists, he explained, because they had neither talent nor relish for what amounted
to a new sect. They loved free thought, "coveted no personal publicity, and would not put their principles in any conventional gear."
The Radical Club, he explained, was "against any final wording" of
a person's faith.[19] Its principles were simple and broad: "It denies to
affirm, clears the way to travel, vetoes less than it signs, and tears
down to build. Its affirmation is, Spirit takes in all."[20] In support of
the club's premises, he invoked the controversial Trinitarian Congregationalist, the Reverend Horace Bushnell, who worshipped a
deity that the believer could approach through the medium of language but never know entirely. Bushnell could "swallow" all creeds,
Bartol explained approvingly, for he saw "the centre of the target
they all hit." No word, he continued, sufficed to describe God, so
people had to use many, "as a surveyor his triangular series for a
measure." When "*love*" repeated and overworked sounds sentimental, Bartol explained, we use "*truth*"; and the designation "*Allah* is
refreshing when *God* has become trite."[21] Members of the Radical
Club agreed.

The surest mark of Bartol's continuing Transcendentalism was
his acknowledgment of the eternal presence of the spirit in the
world. In a scientific age, he wrote, in which everything had to be
clearly observed, conceived, and described, mankind could not
"overlook what no sphere of definition can include." There was no
strict definition possible for even the meanest thing, he continued,
for there was something transcendent "in the origin and orbit of
every particle, and a conscious infinity in the soul they serve." In
short, God is present throughout creation.[22]

Proponents of science promised to prove the idea of God, he
continued, but in their materiality provided "but a coroner's in-
quest over the dead," never the living spirit. Bartol cared not if
deity was personal, for this in no way negated his inward sense
of divine presence. God's personality was not mankind's raised to

the highest power, he explained patiently, "but ours is his reduced to the lowest terms." Science could not find a deity external and separate from the worshipper, but such was revealed daily in "our conscience and heart," where the true proof lay.[23] Unthreatened by new scientific and technological advances, Bartol insisted on the interpenetration of the worlds of matter and spirit, even as he strenuously resisted capitulation to materialism alone.

Other, younger members of Bartol's religious circle met the challenge of Positivism in various ways, some by returning for more draughts at the sources of philosophical Idealism. Among these was Thoreau's classmate John Weiss (1818–1879), who graduated from the Divinity School in 1843 and spent several months at the University of Heidelberg. From Worcester, Massachusetts, grandson of a German Jew and son of a barber, at Cambridge Weiss quickly found his way into the Transcendentalist circle. After completing his theological studies, he succeeded his friend Convers Francis in the pulpit in Watertown but four years later was forced to resign because of his increasingly radical abolitionist views. He moved to a Unitarian church in New Bedford, where he remained until 1859, when ill health made him relinquish that pulpit. In 1862 Weiss returned to the Watertown church and ministered there through the decade. Closely associated with radical Unitarianism, he was a founder of the Free Religious Association and a member of the Radical Club.

Parker's activism greatly influenced Weiss. One of his earliest published sermons, for example, treated the Anthony Burns affair; and after 1854 he traveled more and more in the great abolitionist's orbit, a debt he repaid a decade later with his two-volume *Life and Correspondence of Theodore Parker* (1864), long the definitive biography. This memorial solidified his position as a key figure among second-generation Transcendentalists, and his many essays in *The Radical* and *The Christian Examiner* provide an index of progressive Unitarian thought.

Bartol left the most revealing portrait of Weiss. His ethnicity was evident, his friend recalled, and "soft lines of manly beauty enclosed

his olive-colored oriental features, and his fluent, half-feminine form."
He never was vigorous, and in middle age his figure was "so thin
and sepulchral" that he seemed to have just risen from the grave.
Indeed, he looked so weak that Parker was once reputed to have
judged him a "doomed man." But this "strangely blended tender-
ness and strength," Bartol continued, served him well in the pulpit,
for it "issued in the singularity of his voice," so mellow "that no
woman's utterance could exceed, and among men was beyond
compare."[24]

Weiss was an equally effective writer. In 1871 he published an
ambitious book of essays, *American Religion*, that revealed a worthy successor to Parker in trying to consummate, in the wake of the
Darwinian revolution, a viable marriage between science and religion. It also was a telling artifact of the inward turn that marked
Transcendentalism in the 1850s, for more than any of his contemporaries Weiss emphasized America's unique social conditions and
their relation to emergent theology. In the book Weiss was clearly
indebted to Fichtean Idealism, for he resurrected the study of the
relationship between mind and universe all but forgotten during
the 1850s and 1860s. Weiss accurately identified, for example, the
population's aversion to serious philosophical inquiry as a major
factor contributing to the saccharine culture of the Gilded Age. "A
great deal of American literary and religious striving," he wrote,
"runs to sentimentalism because the fatigue of discovering the
order of the world" was too great for citizens so obsessed with
progress and gain. He proposed a return to German Idealism—he
had, after all, studied at Heidelberg—so that mankind might discern the relation between natural and spiritual things. This identity
of mind with universe underpinned Weiss's theology, which he
termed "theistic naturalism."[25]

He had a dynamic understanding of the relationship of world to
spirit, and he believed that such a religious vision was particularly
suited to America, from its origins a country blessedly free of
"priestcraft." Colonizing of a new world, he wrote, allowed an experiment on a continent where every man could have his religion
"like air, gratis, by opening the window." With its political democracy, the United States provided the ideal location to base religion

in the sacredness of the individual, as God had intended. Each person, Weiss wrote, is sacred by virtue of the "organic fellow-feeling that moral and spiritual truth has for itself wherever it is found"; hence, mankind's need to tolerate—nay, embrace—all people of all faiths. This was the basis of an American religion. His countrymen, he counseled, had to cultivate "the natural affinity which demands and secures the service of each individual for the other, and prompts the sacrifices of the republic."[26]

Fichte would have approved of Weiss's individualism. There was nothing outside of the individual, Weiss declared, for consciousness is all that one can know. There is nothing beyond the phenomena that we embrace and apprehend.[27] Knowing this, an individual recognizes the same in all others and thus respects all humanity. This was Weiss's dream of America's gift to the world: a true, all-encompassing, nonjudgmental democracy.

If each person is so miraculous, self-contained, and sacred, what then is the divine? Weiss used the phrase "Divine Immanence," what Emerson had termed the "Oversoul." God was simply *everything*, Weiss declared, the whole of life, the whole of history, the whole of science and religion, "an immeasurable Presence, holding the roots of every sweet or noxious thing." Further, this was the source of all moral law. "Immanence," Weiss continued, "is in all intuitive comprehension of all principles, or it is in none. It exists in all characteristic excellencies, or it exists in none."[28]

Thus, Weiss loyally carried Emerson's standard of individual consciousness into the postbellum period, shoring Idealism against both the amorality of the new science and the rapacious market economy. Fichte's chief American representative, Weiss was convinced that the project of his generation was to establish as the bedrock of a genuinely inclusive American faith "some necessary truths that express real organic relations between the finite and the infinite."[29] Toward that end, Bartol recalled, Weiss always had been "earnest." If some were troubled by his unusual temperament, "so like a rustling changeable silk, or an opal flashing with many hues," still, he loved truth and was "as steady as a drill-sergeant at his post." Weiss's courage never shifted or flinched, Bartol concluded.[30] To him, consciousness was supreme, and the scientific materialism of the Positivists but the lantern show of their minds.

If Weiss continued to champion the pure Idealism that had so inspired the first-generation Transcendentalists, David Atwood Wasson (1823–87) cultivated a mystical sense of unity everywhere revealed in the universe that links him to the young Emerson. Another minister present at Bartol's during planning for the Free Religious Association, Wasson, like his host, never formally joined the group but often spoke at its meetings and contributed to *The Radical* and its intellectual successor, *The Index*.[31] He was born in Brooksville, Maine, son of a shipbuilder, and raised in an isolated, orthodox religious environment. He was a hardy child until his eighteenth year, when a fight with a bully during "the political contest of 1840" left him with a painful spinal injury that progressively crippled him. After a prolonged period when he was bedridden and in pain, he attended Phillips Academy in Andover, Massachusetts, and in 1845, Bowdoin College, a logical choice for someone of his background. In 1849 he entered the Bangor Theological Seminary, a conservative seminary second in reputation only to Andover, to pursue his goal of the ministry.

Around this time, Wasson encountered Carlyle's *Sartor Resartus*. As one of his biographers puts it, to Wasson, Carlyle's "freedom of mental action, the sincerity, the hatred of pretence, the passion for spiritual light, the faith in the soul, came like a breath of inspiration." Transcendentalism was in the air, and he "was swept by it towards divinity."[32] He was never the same. When he left Bangor two years later, he was ordained over an orthodox church in Groveland, Massachusetts, but he ran into difficulties because of his increasingly liberal religious views, particularly his belief that regeneration and salvation were not gifts of faith, but were obtained by "intelligent moral culture and spiritual development."[33] His preaching satisfied the congregation, that is, a majority of the parishioners, but not the church members, who controlled the organization, and on their complaint a council of neighboring churches urged Wasson's dismissal.

Shortly thereafter he met Higginson, ministering in nearby Newbury, who lent him books and introduced him to fellow Unitarians. Wasson's intellect grew exponentially—in natural history, in Swedenborg's doctrines, and in the German language. When Higginson took a leave from his new parish in Worcester, Massachusetts, Wasson substituted for him and after his return remained as his colleague. Wasson's chronic ill health, however, prevented him from settling long in one location. There followed a year and a half in Concord, after extended hydropathy for his painful spine, and then a year in Medford, as the houseguest of George Luther Stearns, abolitionist and member of the Secret Six. In the early 1860s Wasson preached to much acclaim as far west as Cincinnati and also in Boston-area churches, most notably at Parker's Music Hall; and in May 1865 that congregation, finding him a worthy successor to their recently deceased minister, installed him over the Twenty-eighth Congregational Society.

His biographer remembered him as one of the finest minds of his generation—"clear, sinewy, delicate, careful, well furnished." His preaching was not "effusive, glittering, wordy, or 'eloquent.'" Rather, it was "compact, full of movement for thoughtful listeners, but demanding close attention, unconventional, original, [and] free from the commonplaces of the pulpit."[34] But Wasson was also a harsh judge of what he took as others' weaknesses. He complained of the unfinished character of Emerson's compositions, for example, and detected in him "a disposition to catch the common ear by the point of his sentences" rather than through closely reasoned argument.[35] For his part, Emerson approved of this sharp new voice among the faithful and loomed large behind Wasson's theological pronouncements.

It was Theodore Parker, however, who influenced Wasson's understanding of the clergy's central role in reform, making all the more significant his installation over Parker's Twenty-eighth Congregational Society, when Wasson delivered his own sermon, on *The Radical Creed*. Clearly honored by his selection, he assured the assembled—"the most radical religious society in America"—of his commitment to their founders' ideals.[36] He described his belief in a *"supernatural"* God, as opposed to a *"preternatural"* or "*contranatural*" one. "The supernatural is God; the supernatural is the only Reality," Wasson explained, while nature was "the form under which Reality condescends to be seen by the physical eye."[37] Wasson also weighed in, as his predecessor had done, on the ongoing debates over Christ's miracles. He explained that belief in a supernatural God precluded the kinds of events most Christians thought of when they used the word "miracle." One could only believe in preternatural miracles if one held that nature was "an opaque screen or wall between God and man, sundering and hiding them from each other," a notion, he concluded, "the spawn of a materialistic mock philosophy."[38] Rather, miracle implied the constant revelation of God to man, through nature.

Wasson believed that the church was a spiritual community with distinctive bonds. "My life is distinct," he explained, but not separate from someone else's. Men are not merely "tagged together by fate and natural necessity; by one's liability to take infection from another; by your need of some one to make your coat, and the like." Rather, the bond of unity was "a root of faithfulness," as "soul is fertilized by soul; inspiration goes with a true communion; God is implicated in the relationship between man and man." He separates himself from heaven, Wasson explained, who separates himself "in love, in interest, in spiritual fellowship," from his fellow man.[39]

One of Wasson's later essays, "Unity," opens a particularly large window on his readjustment of Transcendentalist ideals to the exigencies of the Gilded Age. Here he explores the notion that underneath the world's seemingly illimitable variety, there is unity, which science helps us to know. Though the mind sees everywhere what it takes to be contradictions, rival "egotisms and dogmatisms," contending "quarrels and opinions," the heart demands that they be resolved and finally testifies that they are. This desire for and discovery of the unity of all is the religious element in man. Religion, Wasson concluded, is simply the soul's attraction to this oneness. Toward that

> unity which enfolds and saturates the all; toward the eternal wholeness, which has neither parts nor wants; toward that ineffable centrality, which rounds in and includes the circumference; toward that which is all-in-itself, and all-in-all to that

which is not itself; toward this eternal rest and sufficiency of oneness, the heart, the soul, the centrality of man tends with a transcendent attraction.[40]

"Unity" or "Over-Soul" returns man to his wholeness, his oneness, with the natural world.

Acknowledgment of this oneness shapes the moral life, and the person who recognizes it realizes that "love and equity alone make unity," while selfishness is divisive, and egotism "insular." What humanity has to realize is its hunger for wholeness. This is the atonement, the at-one-ment, a doctrine found in virtually every religion. This is our "God-manhood," the spiritual nature of man "in which God abides, and ever reproduces himself." In every man, Wasson continued, this spiritual nature tries to realize itself wholly, and "as you ally your will with it, and give it effect in your bosom, you enter upward into a union with absolute life and Godhead, you enter outwardly into a unity with all humanities, all souls, all immortalities, now and evermore."[41] There was no more eloquent or compelling argument for brotherhood than that which science could help reveal.

"What do I think of Wasson?" the great Harvard psychologist and philosopher Williams James was asked shortly after Wasson's death. "I look upon him as one of the great instructors of mankind." And so Wasson's essays reveal. Through his particular understanding of the supernatural, Wasson had achieved unity, his friend Stearns reported, "the one complete cosmopolitan mind of his time."[42]

Such mysticism had pushed first-generation Transcendentalists toward recognition of their contemporaries' equality in the spirit, whatever their gender, but the dreams of radical women's rights advocates like Fuller were sidetracked with the onset of the Civil War. Among the second-generation Transcendentalists, what became of Fuller's pioneering work, particularly her call for economic and psychological freedom for women? Caroline Healey Dall (1822–1912), one of Bartol's parishioners whose wealthy family lived on Beacon

Hill, assumed her mantle. At eighteen she had wandered into Elizabeth Peabody's bookshop and fallen under Transcendentalism's spell. While still in her teens she placed essays in religious periodicals, and in 1849, five years after her marriage to the Unitarian minister Charles Henry Appleton Dall, she published a collection of *Essays and Sketches*.[43] She attended Fuller's Conversations and heard Parker lecture, including his series that eventuated in *A Discourse of Matters Pertaining to Religion*. His calls to social action moved her to begin to teach Sunday school classes to Boston's urban poor, and she frequently attended to her students' material and medical needs as well.

Dall's world fell apart in 1855, when her husband left the family as a missionary to Calcutta, work he continued for thirty-one years with only brief visits home, until his death. She essentially was widowed and thrown on her own resources. She had written on women's issues even before Charles left, particularly for *The Una* (1853–55), the first periodical devoted entirely to the women's movement and which for almost a year she coedited with its founder, Paulina Wright Davis.[44] After her husband's departure, Dall threw herself into the nascent women's movement and rapidly became a well-known and powerful speaker and writer on the subject, worthy successor to Fuller, who always had fascinated her and about whom she wrote at length.

Dall's radical social and political views already were displayed in her first book, dedicated to her father, who disapproved of some of its contents, a reaction that hurt her deeply. "He had read it steadily through," she recorded in her diary, but said that the article on the "Sabbath" should have been left out, "that on Reforms would do me no credit—nor that on the [Mexican] War—[and that] nobody would buy the book but abolitionists."[45] He did not object to Dall's essays on the rights of women, on which, oddly at this point, she still held fairly conservative views.

That soon changed, however, and in later work the influence of Fuller's *Woman in the Nineteenth Century* is patent. In 1860, in her *Historical Pictures Retouched*, a collection of essays and "fancies," most of which had appeared in *The Una*, Dall spoke at length of Fuller's importance to her. Dall called *Woman in the Nineteenth*

Century "doubtless the most brilliant, complete, and scholarly statement ever made on the subject." Counting Fuller with other such pioneers for women's rights as Mary Wollstonecraft and Madame de Staël, she lamented how "very far from Margaret's is the standard of noble truth, of womanly aspiration, of literary culture, which satisfies the demand of society now."[46] The memory of Fuller was a constant stimulus to endeavor, Dall said elsewhere, and if she had to characterize her in two phrases, they would be "Truth-teller and Truth-compeller." Something in her presence, Dall continued, tore away all disguises, for there was "an electric power to her womanhood, which claimed the inmost being of every one with whom she came in contact."[47]

Dall's father had educated her as a son, allowing her to range freely in languages, philosophy, theology, and other subjects usually reserved for young men preparing for college, an upbringing remarkably similar to Fuller's. Dall later recalled that early on she knew well where her natural sphere of work lay. Could she have had a theological education, she wrote, or "had even the paths of the ministry been open to women," she had every reason to believe that she would have become a "settled minister."[48] In her early *Essays and Sketches*, in treating woman's place, like Fuller she longed for the time when "a finished education" would be every woman's birthright, the respect of the other sex "her legitimate inheritance," a woman of any rank would be able to obtain a livelihood for herself or her children "without overtasking the generosity of man," and she would no longer find herself, even for a moment, "a tool or a plaything."[49] Such changes would improve men as well as women, for by putting women on equal educational and economic footings, men would find their relationships to them more meaningful.

Dall extended this argument in lectures delivered in the late 1850s and published in 1860 as *"Woman's Right to Labor"; or, Low Wages and Hard Work; in Three Lectures* and again in her magnum opus, *The College, The Market, and the Court; or, Woman's Relation to Education, Labor, and Law*—except for Fuller's treatise the most important work from the early period of the American women's movement. Dedicated to suffragette Lucretia Mott, Dall's book was an ambitious attempt to speak to the complex connections among systems of education, labor, and law that kept women subordinate. Writing with more clarity than Fuller, Dall stitched essays from three different series of lectures she had delivered, and she offered them now in a format "popular in form and low in price." "I believe," she declared in the book's preface, in "the elevation of woman through education, which is development; through labor, which is salvation; through legal rights, which are only freedom to develop and save,— as part of the mission of Jesus on earth, authorized by him, inspired of God, and sure of fulfillment as any portion of his law."[50] Her work on behalf of her sisters became her divine mission.

Although Fuller was sophisticated in historical matters, Dall's book was of a different order, a set of related quasi-sociological treatises buttressed with fact and example. She included much, for example, from her own firsthand experience with Boston's working poor, including their frequent descent into prostitution, and offered as well a prospectus, "The Opening of the Gates," describing which professions were beginning to welcome women. Even more pathbreaking was her detailed treatment of the history of law as it pertained to women, from the French legal system and English common law to a lengthy section on the current American jurisprudence on inheritance and divorce. How could a woman have a right to life, she wrote, who never consented to laws which may deprive her of it? How could she have a right to liberty, "whose person, if not yet in custody, almost inevitably becomes so" when she married, for with that act she lost her own earnings, could make no valid contract, and was "taxed without representation"? How could she have a right to happiness if she was deprived of the custody of her own person, of the guardianship of her children, of the right to devise or share her property?[51]

In an appendix, she assembled examples of the progress that had been made for women in education, labor, and law since she first had given her course of lectures. She never lost interest in statistically charting such gains, and later she became active in the American Social Science Association, founded in 1865 by Franklin Sanborn and others to forward reform in such areas as the treatment of prisoners and the insane, the plight of the urban poor, and the civil service, long corrupt. In 1895, for another of these groups, the Society for

Philosophical Inquiry, she lectured on "Transcendentalism in New England," an invaluable retrospective of the movement.[52]

More than Elizabeth Peabody, who in the postbellum years wandered in a maze of reform activities, from kindergarten education to Native American rights, Dall centered herself and became the most prominent, and effective, second-generation Transcendentalist devoted to women's rights. She and Peabody stayed in contact, but the older woman never was as outspoken on the subject and often chided her erstwhile protégée for what she regarded as her indiscretion in proselytizing for the cause.

In February 1859, for example, Peabody took Dall to task for her comments about Horace Mann's presidency of Antioch College, the first to admit women with men. Evidently, Dall had suggested in a lecture that Mann had not been as open to women's rights as some assumed, and Peabody jumped to her late brother-in-law's defense. "I thought the lecture in which you spoke of him in so bad taste that it would be an argument against women's education," she wrote. Peabody also mentioned that she had heard of Dall's plan to lecture "upon *labour*" and that she was "going to make *painful statements* [a reference to her plan to treat prostitution]," so that Peabody would not attend "with a gentleman by [her] side." "I do feel," she sniffed, "that the natural sphere of woman is above the slough of human nature."[53]

Peabody also frequently raised the issue of Dall's role in the organized women's rights movement, whose direction and tactics Peabody often questioned. For once, however, she was quite complimentary. "I do not like conventions of women for Women's Rights—as you know," she wrote Dall. "I did not when I first heard of them & would not sign the first call that was made." But, she continued, in a recent convention over which Dall had presided, she had liked her "action & speech."[54] At this event Dall had behaved with much decorum, prompting Peabody to comment that she thought the speaker thus would win many converts to the positions she advocated. She also approved Dall's *Woman's Right to Labor*, admitting that her book was "better than lectures" and would "penetrate beyond the reach of a single voice & be read & reread & cannot fail to awaken attention."[55]

More frequently than not, though, Dall and Peabody went their separate ways. Like her eminent predecessor Fuller, Dall believed that the chief obstacle to a realization of Emerson's imperial self, regardless of gender, resided not so much in the new science as in the bonds of social and economic convention. Not surprisingly, given Dall's radicalism, other prominent women's right advocates such as Elizabeth Cady Stanton and Susan B. Anthony, who focused their activities on women's political empowerment, did not bring Dall into their inner circle. Thus, as with her much-admired predecessor, Dall's immediate influence was not as great as it should have been.

If Fuller was Dall's presiding genius, Theodore Parker, the student of world religions, was Samuel Johnson's. Born in Salem, Massachusetts—his father a physician and his mother a member of one of the town's prominent families—Johnson (1822–82) graduated from Harvard in 1842 and entered its Divinity School. A classmate remembered him as striking: tall, with a "warm and rich complexion" and long black hair, always walking "with a swinging gait," the head thrust forward "as if in quest of some object . . . before him in the distance."[56]

Johnson excelled in Greek, which he began under Jones Very, another Salem native and a poet in whom Emerson took an interest. Unfortunately, Very had to relinquish his classes during Johnson's freshman year, when he was institutionalized after insisting that he was under the inspiration of the Holy Spirit, a claim met unsympathetically. When Very showed Emerson some verse supposedly written at the Spirit's behest, for example, the Concord sage quipped, but "cannot the spirit parse & spell?"[57] With Very on leave, Johnson took modern languages—French from Henry Wadsworth Longfellow, recently appointed as professor of Romance languages, and German, for his divinity studies.

Some of Johnson's professors introduced him to the New Thought, and he immediately responded to the Transcendentalism in the air.[58] His biographer noted that the cast of his mind was intuitive rather than logical, and thus he was "a transcendentalist by nature, a born idealist." Johnson, he continued, "sought spiritual

truths by direct vision, not by any process of induction; by immediate inward experience, rather than by inference from outward
experience." Moreover, in these years his Transcendentalism, later
"a carefully-weighted *rationale of thought*," was more "a nature, a
perception, a sentiment, an inward, unargued [*sic*] faith" that soon
assumed a "*mystical* phase." His fellow divinity student and closest
friend, Samuel Longfellow, for example, cited a letter in which Johnson spoke of his mystical sense of an "All-Filling Presence" as a
"centre-*soul*" that "not only floats around, but actually *is* all things,
is ourselves."[59]

Seniors at the Divinity School preached gratis in neighboring
churches as part of their apprenticeship, and Johnson was initiated
at Alvan Lamson's liberal church in Dedham and then in the West
Roxbury church, with which Parker recently had cut his ties when
he settled over Boston's Twenty-eighth Congregational Society.[60]
Johnson approved of Parker's radical theology and supported his
right to fellowship with other Boston-area churches, but this position eventually cost the young man opportunities for permanent
settlement. In 1846, for example, he began to minister (although
he never was formally called) to the newly formed Harrison Square
church in Dedham, only to lose the pulpit within the year because
of his radical political and antislavery views.

Johnson next began to preach to a Unitarian congregation in
Lynn, Massachusetts. When, a year later, in 1853, they asked him
to remain permanently, he accepted on the condition that they
change their name to that of a "Free Church," because he never
formally identified himself as Unitarian. They agreed and also allowed him to eschew both ordination—he believed that the inward
call to preach and the outward call of those who wished to hear him
comprised the formal seal of his ministry—and the administration
of sacraments. For seventeen years Johnson preached a "natural religion," which, as he explained it, was simply "another name for
truth, freedom, piety, righteousness, [and] love."[61] He attended
the meetings at Bartol's to plan the Free Religious Association but
never formally joined the organization. He occasionally spoke before it, however, and published essays in *The Radical*.[62] He also lent
his voice to the antislavery and temperance causes.

Johnson remained with the Lynn Free Church until a bad fall and ensuing disability forced his resignation. In his farewell address he related how, when once asked to what religion he belonged, he replied, "You shall count me nowhere; but you shall exclude me nowhere. I will have the freedom of all times and all hearts; but I will, of my own motion, take on no special bonds, and wear the special labels, of none."[63] He remained loyal to that definition, maintaining that all religions had inherent worth and dignity that allowed their adherents to overcome life's manifold trials, and whose study made him appreciate the commonality beneath various faiths' seemingly contradictory versions of the divine.

Johnson's major contribution to postbellum Transcendentalism did not come in theology, but in religious anthropology, specifically his monumental *Oriental Religions and Their Relation to Universal Religion*, with separate volumes on India, China, and Persia. As early as 1854 he had given lectures in Salem that were the germ of his scholarship in comparative religion; as he explained to Samuel Longfellow, he had been "putting the Oriental Lectures into a more sermonic form, to awake, if possible, some desire for a broader culture in the people." He later termed his project an attempt to demonstrate "the Universality of Religious Ideas."[64] The complexity of Johnson's effort was tremendous, for he read assiduously the work of "scholars, linguists, [and] travelers, in German, French, and English." He published his first volume, *India*, in 1872 and *China* in 1877. *Persia*, uncompleted at his death, was prepared for the publisher in 1885 by his brother-in-law.[65]

Longfellow accurately assessed these pioneering works, indebted as they were to Johann von Herder's notion that a people's religious beliefs were closely linked to their cultural identity. Johnson, his friend noted, not only explained "the mythologies, theologies, and worships of these Eastern nations" but also "held religion to cover, or at least to grow out of, or be modified by, all the national life of the peoples," work that necessitated chapters on government, education, science, and society.[66] Johnson based his massive work on what he considered scientific principles and termed it "a contribution to the Natural History of Religion."[67] Influenced by the rise of social Darwinism, he believed that men's religious beliefs progressed through various stages. This development was natural, Johnson explained, and proceeded "by laws inherent and immanent in humanity."[68] Most important, in these works Johnson treated Christianity as just one faith among many, itself moving through evolutionary changes.

The "Universal Religion" toward which mankind tended, Johnson wrote (in a vein reminiscent of Eclecticism), could not be "any one, exclusively, of the great positive religions of the world." Rather, it had to comprise what was best in each.[69] Thus, he did not write as an apologist or advocate of Christianity or of any other distinctive religion, but as one "attracted on the one hand by the identity of the religious sentiment under all its great historic forms, and on the other by the movement indicated in their diversities and contrasts toward a higher plane of unity, on which their exclusive claims shall disappear." The time had arrived for mutual interchange of religious experience between the East and the West, for which neither was fully prepared but which was "indispensable to the advancement of both forms of civilization."[70] Johnson penned his volumes to help mankind attain this noble dream of an inclusive faith.

Sadly, for all his efforts to categorize beliefs still little known in the West, Johnson's heroic scholarship met with little popular or scholarly success. Roberts Brothers, the firm to which he first brought his manuscript on India, turned it down as too polemical and theological.[71] Making minor changes, he submitted it to James Osgood and Company, who also found it too argumentative but agreed to publish it if Johnson paid close to sixteen hundred dollars toward its production. He did, but two years after its publication a mere fifty copies had been sold. His second volume, *China*, fared no better. Criticized by scholars for the author's reliance on Western scholarship rather than on primary sources, and his problematic claim to study religion in a scientific manner, neither *India* nor *China* made as large an impact as Johnson wished.

It did not help that, the year before *India* appeared, James Freeman Clarke had published *The Ten Great Religions* (1871), his own treatment of the world's various faiths, which proved immensely popular, going through no fewer than nineteen editions. Clarke was the popular minister to Boston's Church of the Disciples, established in 1841 and meeting in the Melodeon, where Parker's church had begun. As early as 1857 he had published a review essay in *The Christian Examiner* on "Comparative Theology of Heathen Religions" that demonstrated his interest in cross-cultural matters, and in 1867 Harvard appointed him lecturer on non-Christian religions at the Divinity School.[72] The following year in *The Atlantic Monthly* he began to issue some of the essays that eventually became his book on the subject.[73]

What differentiated Clarke's work from Johnson's was his staunch Unitarianism. Although much involved with antebellum Transcendentalism and a lifelong friend of Margaret Fuller's, Clarke never left the denomination, and he remained an important player in the American Unitarian Association. Thus, when he came to discuss, say, the "Oriental" religions that Johnson explored, he subordinated them to Christianity, viewing them as indicative of various stages through which humanity passed before it arrived at Christianity, the universal religion. A less threatening (and admittedly more readable) book than any of Johnson's, *Ten Great Religions* proved immensely influential into the early twentieth century and solidified Clarke's position as one of the nation's major Unitarian voices.

Despite the disappointing reception of his works, Johnson was not bitter. When he resigned his pulpit in Lynn, he gave an eloquent valedictory to his Free Church. He was proud, he stated, that in all his years with them, he had repudiated denominational religion and never sought to build an ecclesiastical institution for transmitting personal and local interests from generation to generation. His goal had been simple: "to make the place where I stand a centre for the freest communication of thought and faith, of stimulus to public and private duties, to fearless inquiry according to conviction and conduct according to conviction."[74] Given Johnson's receptivity to and interest in the universal human impulse to believe, Theodore Parker would have welcomed his commitment as well as his scholarship, even as the majority of his contemporaries, beginning to experience a great wave of immigration from eastern and southern Europe, were content to maintain theirs as a Christian nation.

The year after O. B. Frothingham published *Transcendentalism in New England* (1876), the *Radical Review* carried Samuel Johnson's lengthy essay on the same topic, which, when it was reprinted in a book of his essays, *The Atlantic Monthly* singled out for particular praise. "America," the anonymous reviewer wrote, "has furnished no other statement at once so full and compact of this philosophy."[75] Johnson aimed his essay at recent "materialists" who, he believed, underestimated the import of Transcendentalism to current philosophical debates. Far from finding Idealism obsolete in light of scientific materialism, he presented it as "the primal condition of knowing, the transmutation of sense-impressions by original laws of mind, whose constructive power is not to be explained or measured by the data of sensation." Mind, he continued, "is obviously the exponent of forces more spontaneous and original than any special product of its own experience." All that we know is ideas, he insisted, "yet not as unrealities," for it was man's recognition of them as reporting objective truth that made them the root of all knowledge.[76]

Johnson insisted on the centrality of consciousness to religious belief. By an intuition of God, he wrote, he did not mean "a theological dogma or a devout sentiment," nor " '*a* God,' Christian or other." Rather, he meant a "presumption of the infinite as involved in our perception of the finite, of the whole implied by the part, of substance behind all phenomena, and of thought as of one nature with its object."[77] Intuition comprised the recognition of the inevitable step beyond experience or observation by which man lived and grew. The Positivists' miscalculation in their war against the Idealist method was thus in their erroneous divorce of science from the internal sense of the unlimited and universal. If science were to account for the infinite, Johnson believed, it had to recur to Transcendentalism, which posited universal principles for mankind's acquisition and comprehension of supernal knowledge.[78]

The St. Louis Hegelians, Bartol, Weiss, Wasson, Dall, and Johnson, each in his or her own way, promulgated this same religious principle, directly inherited from antebellum Transcendentalism, even as they eschewed the moniker. They continued to insist that faith was, finally, beyond external proof. But so insisting, they failed to capture the public's imagination enough to redirect America's moral direction from selfishness to selflessness. The future lay with those who acknowledged the world of the spirit but also, in their embrace of science, explained faith as, at best, a pragmatic proposition.

11

TOWARD THE GENTEEL TRADITION

n 1876 Edmund C. Stedman, New York author and prominent member of the city's Independent Liberal Church, republished in book form an essay on his minister Octavius Brooks Frothingham that he had first issued in the popular periodical *The Galaxy*. Stedman's reason for so doing, explained publisher George Haven Putnam in an introductory note, was because the growing interest "in the purport and influence of what are known as Radical ideas" demanded notice of the life and teachings of the man "who, more probably than any other American, is the representative and apostle of the liberal faith." Frothingham, Stedman believed, was the one in whom the now-legendary Theodore Parker's ideas and ideals were most expanded and developed.[1]

Putnam noted one difference, however. While Parker had "stormed traditionalism in its stronghold, Boston," a provincial city, Frothingham's field was "the world as represented in a metropolis," New York, where a cult of celebrity had risen around certain personages. Frothingham, much more than Parker, had become someone to "see," his church visited each week not only by loyal followers but by crowds of curious visitors who wished to acquaint themselves with the characteristic men and places of the city. Among New York's clergy, only the Reverend Henry Ward Beecher, in Plymouth Church, Brooklyn Heights, drew a larger gallery.[2]

Stedman left a memorable description of Frothingham in his pulpit. After moving from smaller venues, his congregation had leased a large hall, the Masonic Temple, at the corner of Twenty-third Street and Sixth Avenue. As befits Masonic architecture, it had a high ceiling resting upon two rows of imposing pillars that led to a semicircular recess from which Frothingham spoke. Religious services began at 10:45 a.m. on Sundays, when the doors were closed for an organ voluntary and hymn, followed by a reading, usually from Moncure Conway's *Sacred Anthology*, a collection of sacred texts from the world's religions.[3] Deacons reopened the doors for latecomers, who swarmed to available seats in time for a prayer in which Frothingham recalled the sacred ties of human brotherhood. After another hymn, the doors were opened again for a final rush of people who arrived for the sole purpose of hearing the sermon.[4] The hall held a thousand auditors.

Frothingham then rose for the sermon. He was not so much imposing as striking in "temperament and person," a representative, Stedman thought, of the "purest New England type." He was "sinewy but light and graceful," his parishioner recalled, and had a clear-cut face, an intellectual forehead, a "large unarched New England nose," and a pointed chin, all suggestive of "equally[,] the most delicate refinement and the sturdiest polemical vigor." Also distinctive was his delivery, for although Frothingham carefully prepared his address, he did not read but spoke it extempore, each week a virtuoso performance. He preached not on a biblical text, but on an announced theme that was cleverly woven throughout his sermons which, Stedman contended, were almost without a modern counterpart. There was no other preacher with a spirit more eloquent and imaginative, yet who relied "so utterly upon the force of reason in his teachings" and made his discourses so intellectually satisfying.[5]

Most important, while profoundly reverential, Frothingham reversed the method of the evangelical preachers, trying to reach "the heart through the brain—through the perceptive, reasoning, and aesthetic faculties." More logically organized and synthetic than Emerson's sermons, Frothingham's were as poetical and riveting. Every face was directed toward him, Stedman explained, "young and old hang upon his lips," anxious not to lose a word. When he was finished, people felt that they had been "subjected to a certain mental tension," watching "his free and fine intellect at play," and they left the hall well nourished on spiritual food that "carries its own digestion."[6] More than anyone else in the 1870s, Frothingham shone Transcendentalism's light into the moral and spiritual darkness of the Gilded Age.

Stedman was correct: Frothingham was a New Englander through and through. His family were first generation Puritan settlers; and his father, Nathaniel Langdon Frothingham, had ministered to Boston's First Church, on Summer Street, from 1815 to 1850, succeeding William Emerson, Waldo Emerson's father.[7] During the Transcendentalist ferment, the elder Frothingham remained a conservative Unitarian, taking the lead in Parker's trial for "heresy"; but his son, after graduating from Harvard in 1843, entered the Divinity School and became a disciple of the New Thought. Among his classmates were Samuel Longfellow, Thomas Wentworth Higginson, and Samuel Johnson. Before his graduation in 1846 Frothingham far surpassed what his father had found objectionable in Parker's theology.[8]

Frothingham's first pastorate was in Salem's North Church, where his views soon met with resistance from more conservative Unitarians. He had been fertilized through contact with Parker, who not only awakened his social conscience but introduced him to the Higher Criticism of Ferdinand Christian Baur, a disciple of Schleiermacher. At this point, in theology Frothingham was a nondenominational theist who rejected the need for any external assurances of faith. When he added to this his increasingly strident indictment of slavery, the congregation bristled. After preaching an inflammatory sermon on the rendition of Anthony Burns, in which he indicted fellow Christians for tolerating and excusing slavery, Frothingham's position became tenuous.

In 1855 the Unitarian Society in Jersey City, New Jersey, on the recommendation of the influential Henry W. Bellows of All Souls Church in New York, expressed interest in his candidacy, and Frothingham accepted their call. But he again was disappointed, for this church, too, was lukewarm to his radical views. He cast about for another position, and Bellows again lent support, this time for a position in the city. In 1859 Frothingham moved to a new Unitarian society, the city's third (the other two overseen by Bellows and Samuel Osgood). He remained there for two decades, eventually redefining it—though it cost him the support of Bellows and Osgood—as an "Independent Liberal Church" rather than as Unitarian. In this venue Frothingham preached a powerful theism that posited man's inherently spiritual nature, even as he remained skeptical of what precisely one could say about "God."

For twenty years he regularly published articles and reviews in *The Christian Examiner*. These reveal deep reading and sophistication in theology as well as in the Higher Criticism, and he often was attacked for the severity—some said the honesty—of his assessments. This journal was the official voice of Unitarianism, and its editor, George E. Ellis, often sparred with Frothingham over his submissions before publishing them.[9] By 1865 Frothingham had moved even farther from his father's generation's understanding of Unitarianism, to a more skeptical faith buttressed both by intuition and experience, a "scientific theism" with no special dependence on the person of Christ or any other religious leader. He found his voice in this new pitch through the Free Religious Association, which he helped organize and lead in its early years.

When the rump of radical Unitarians meeting at Cyrus Bartol's home enlisted Frothingham in their deliberations, they made a wise move, for as one participant said, Frothingham's name on their roster was "worth a thousand men."[10] He always insisted on free inquiry in spiritual matters, without any dogmatic fetters. Members of the Free Religious Association thus accepted any and all personal creeds as individual statements of belief that might themselves comprise theism, agnosticism, or even atheism. Further, they held that even in its most liberal manifestations, traditional Christianity was bankrupt because it did not make room for the claims of scientific materialism. The Free Religious Association did, even as its members kept intuitive religion in play.

Later in life Frothingham recalled his ambitions for this organization. He believed that all the world's religions were on equal footing and assumed man's inherent spiritual nature. Universal, too, was a tendency to worship, which led to the movement's chief foundation, a "pure Theism" in which members contemplated the progressive "elevation of all mankind to the dignity of children of the Highest," a sentiment in accord with Frothingham's commitment to Hegelian philosophy and its emphasis on "Becoming," as well as to sociologist William Graham Sumner's theory of social evolution.[11] Fervently democratic and respectful of each individual soul, Free Religionists did not fear or resist the latest scientific postulates but greeted them as new information for their spiritual journeys. Frothingham remained the leader of this dynamic group until 1876, publishing essays and reviews in *The Radical*, *The Index*, and *North American Review* as well as a series of books and pamphlets that made him one of the most prolific of the new generation of religious thinkers.

His fullest and most influential statement of the new religion was *The Religion of Humanity* (1873), reprinted several times and widely regarded as a benchmark of the Free Religion movement. Herein Frothingham incorporated what most distinguished the modern age—a belief in "Natural Science"—into a meaningful religion. All around him he saw "primeval faiths" disintegrating under "the chemical influence of this quick and subtle [*sic*] Naturalism." Even Unitarianism was affected, but although his father's generation had integrated this "naturalism" into their "understanding and affections," they had left "the reason, the conscience, and the soul, under the dominion of traditional beliefs and instituted forms," the result a hybrid religion, Janus-like, with one foot in each world. "Unconscious, as pioneers always are," he wrote, "of the idea that defined their own positions, allowing inconsistent elements to lie side by side among the first principles of its thought," the old Unitarians "struggled between the upper and nether millstones of Nature and Grace."[12]

Frothingham, however, discerned that the spirit of God has its workings "*in and through human nature*," and this became the basis of his "religion of humanity." In this system of belief "the inspiration of the moral sentiments, the divine character of the heart's affections, the heavenly illumination of the reason, [and] the truth of the soul's intuitions of spiritual things" took their places among "the axioms of theological thought." In countless ways, a deeper understanding of nature complemented the supernatural. Revelation, for example, was "the disclosure of truth to the active and simple reason." Inspiration was the "drawing of a deep breath in the atmosphere of serene ideas." Regeneration was "the bursting of the moral consciousness into flower." Miracle was not a suspension or violation of law, but "the fulfillment of an untraced" one. Christ's humanity proved his divinity, and so "the child of human nature is the true son of God." All that man considered divine was part of the natural order. Thus, the new "Liberal Church" had a rational method of attaining truth that demanded "the harmony of principles—the orderly sequence of laws," just as science did. Finally, this religion of humanity was particularly appropriate to the United States and its faith in democratic institutions, for such belief had "confidence in the human nature that is in man," while "the word Liberty is always on its lips."[13]

What organized the material world, in other words, flowed as well through the spiritual, a sentiment Frothingham shared with Emerson.[14] "Will the irresistible grace," Frothingham wrote lyrically, "which makes the orbs of the solar system dance to their spheral [*sic*] music cause no lyric movement among the members of the human family?"[15] To him, God was not a personality, but the organizing power in nature. Humanity itself was an extension of divinity, an idea that Auguste Comte, in his own formulation of a "religion of humanity," had rejected. Although Comte, Frothingham wrote, believed in the solidarity of mankind, he erroneously dismissed the spiritual element, concentrating instead on "a mechanical arrangement of outward apparatus," without soul. Those who championed the new radical religion understood the eternal place of soul in humanity and embraced it, rejecting Comte's "scientific chimera."[16]

Most remarkable was Frothingham's sense of a "Christ of Humanity," by which he meant the conglomerate human race, the sum of all its parts. Believing that God existed as an "Unsearchable One," men and women yearned for inspiration by a God-Man. For Frothingham, however, "nothing less than all the humanity there is in the race meets the conditions of a doctrine of incarnation." "A perfected humanity," he continued, "would not more than express the Absolute in the form of qualities; a perfected humanity, comprised of living men and women regenerate and happy; and surely nothing less than all the completed humanity there is will furnish anything approaching to a relatively adequate expression of it." The Christ of Humanity was, then, "*the human element in mankind.*"[17]

Thus, the historical Jesus was not the Christ. Rather, he was no other than "the greatest souls among themselves, the best they knew, whether the best were near or far off." Such people in history were "transfigured and translated," and others conjured with their names. Jesus, Frothingham concluded, was precious for what he represented rather than for what he was. "He glorified common qualities; he set the seal on principles that all share; he made illustrious the spirit of goodness that has its lowly, retired shrine in every heart." He was the symbol "of that essential human nature which is the Messiah cradled in the bosom of every man."[18] In Frothingham's schema, man's calling was to mankind, for in it was his humanity and his divinity.

Frothingham remained in New York until 1879, when, developing health problems, on the advice of doctors he retired to Boston. He became the unofficial memoirist of the Transcendentalist movement, a role he had long prepared for. In 1874 he published a *Life of Theodore Parker*, more readable than Weiss's unwieldy compendium, and soon thereafter a biographical account of the abolitionist *Gerrit Smith* (1878). In his retirement he prepared *George Ripley* (1882) for Charles Dudley Warner's prestigious *American Men of Letters* series; a *Memoir of William Henry Channing* (1886); a collection of David A. Wasson's essays with a lengthy biographical introduction (1889); a memoir of his father, *Boston Unitarianism, 1820–1850* (1890); and his own *Recollections and Impressions, 1822–1890* (1891). Frothingham had become, de facto, both the movement's historian and, through his own contributions to "Radical" religion, its seer, true to the first generation's dream of a common humanity united by an inherent spiritual principle.

In this light, however, his magnum opus, *Transcendentalism in New England: A History* (1876), published the same year as Stedman's encomium to him, is oddly elegiac. Here if anywhere one should look to understand in what, among second-generation

Transcendentalists, the movement's legacy consisted. But for someone with friends among the most vital successors to first-generation Transcendentalists, Frothingham approached the period as though it were only a memory kept alive by a few septuagenarians like Emerson and Bronson Alcott, eviscerated of its early force rather than existing as a living faith. Frothingham observed that as "a form of mental philosophy," Transcendentalism "may have had its day." At any rate, he continued, it was "no longer in the ascendant," for everywhere it was being "suppressed by the philosophy of experience, which, under different names," was taking possession of the speculative world. Frothingham admitted that he "was once a pure Transcendentalist," warmly sympathetic to the movement's aspirations, and "an ardent admirer of transcendental teachers," by which he meant an admirer of Emerson's belief in the primacy of individual consciousness, but now he had moved on to a new understanding of the religious life, one that, while still championing the universality of religious experience, made room for faith's personal dimension, which might include appreciation of the very science so lamented by many of his peers.[19]

For all his praise of younger Radical Club colleagues like Weiss and Wasson, Frothingham worried that as proponents of pure Idealism, they could do little to halt that philosophy's eclipse. In the 1830s and 1840s, he explained, the Transcendentalists' opponents had been literalists, dogmatists, and formalists. Now they were Positivists. Transcendentalists turned Radical Club members, denying the relevance of science to religion, were embattled like the "holders of a royal fortress" facing overwhelming insurgents or "the king and queen of France" looking out "on the revolution from their palace at Versailles." They—Frothingham did not include himself—would fight "admirably to the last," he wrote, but would be defeated. Transcendentalism, Frothingham concluded, had been "an episode in the intellectual life of New England; an enthusiasm, a wave of sentiment, a breath of mind that caught up such as were prepared to receive it, elated them, transported them, and then passed on,—no man knowing whither it went."[20]

Some cognoscenti begged to differ. The New York Unitarian clergyman and erstwhile Transcendentalist Samuel Osgood took issue with the author's characterization of the movement as a thing of the past. He suggested that the group's very success in spreading its ideas now made their philosophy seem less visible and relevant. "The sect of Transcendentalists has disappeared," he wrote, "because their light has gone every where."[21] If by this he meant that American culture had simply absorbed the group's most distinctive thought, its deification of the individual, he was correct.

Bronson Alcott, too, thought differently from Frothingham and, still deeply committed to Idealist philosophy, refused to surrender the field. In 1879, with his friend the St. Louis Hegelian William Torrey Harris, he founded the Concord Summer School of Philosophy and Literature, an annual institute whose lecturers and discussants kept the subject of consciousness front and center.[22] Each summer from fifty to one hundred participants—college professors and students, schoolteachers, writers, theologians—from all parts of the country descended on Hillside Chapel on Alcott's Orchard House grounds to address their generation's chief philosophical challenge, the spread of materialism.

Always more committed to Plato than to Hegel, a position that had made his visits to the St. Louis Hegelians uncomfortable, Alcott presided over the four- to- six-week sessions as their patron saint. After a stroke in 1882, he relinquished leadership of the school to Harris and Franklin Sanborn, who administered it until Alcott's demise, in 1888. But despite the considerable intellectual firepower on display—lecturers included, besides Alcott and Harris, Emerson, Higginson, Hedge, Sanborn, William Henry Channing, the former Brook Farmer and social reformer Ednah Cheney, and David A. Wasson—their utter refusal to entertain any arguments from science doomed the school to final irrelevance, a judgment typified by Caroline Healey Dall's confident dismissal of Alcott in her lecture on Transcendentalism. "Although he was prominent in the public eye," she wrote, and "did more than anyone to bring ridicule upon the movement, he had no significant influence."[23] With Alcott's passing, Transcendental Idealism as the antebellum generation knew it disappeared as a viable faith. Frothingham viewed himself as a harbinger of a different kind of religion, the first genuinely to merge the world and the spirit.

In 1911 George Santayana lectured at the University of California on "The Genteel Tradition in American Philosophy" and described a country ruled by "two mentalities." One was "a survival of the beliefs and standards of the fathers, the other an expression of the instincts, practice, and discoveries of the younger generation." American philosophy, that is, was compounded of a Calvinism that oscillated "between a profound abasement and a paradoxical elation of the spirit," and a cosmic optimism, typified by Transcendentalism, in which the sense of sin had evaporated and nature was "all beauty and commodity." "If you told the modern American," Santayana said, "that he is totally depraved, he would think you were joking," for he "is convinced that he always had been, and always will be, victorious and blameless."[24]

Santayana described how Transcendentalism fitted into this scheme. He understood it as a point of view rather than a creed. Transcendentalism, he said, was "systematic subjectivism." "It studies the perspectives of knowledge as they radiate from the self," for knowledge is "always seated here and now, in the self of the moment," while "the past and the future, things inferred and things conceived, lie around it." They cannot be "lighted up save by some centrifugal ray of attention and present interest, by some active operation of the mind."[25] His assessment is extraordinarily apt, for just such a dependence on consciousness linked Emerson, Brownson, and Ripley in the 1830s to Frothingham and his cohort in the 1880s. But child of the new era as he was, Santayana also observed that Transcendentalist logic, "the method of discovery for the mind," had been transformed into "the method of evolution in nature and history" and, so "abused, became transcendental myth." What had begun as a conscientious critique of knowledge was turned into a "sham system of nature." We must, the great twentieth-century philosopher urged, distinguish sharply "the transcendental grammar of the intellect" from the "various transcendental systems of the universe, which are chimeras."[26]

Santayana identified Emerson as one who had best understood Transcendentalism as a mode of seeing. "He was a cheery, child-like soul, impervious to the evidence of evil." He practiced the transcendental method in all its purity, opening his eyes to the world every morning "with a fresh sincerity, marking how things seemed to him then." Nature, according to Emerson, was precious because it was man's own work, a mirror in which he looks at himself and says, "What a genius am I. Who would have thought there was such stuff in me?"[27] "To reject tradition and think as one might have thought if no man had existed before," Santayana wrote elsewhere, "was indeed the aspiration of the Transcendentalists."[28]

Here Santayana captured the problematic egotism at the heart of Emersonian thought as well as the dangerous solipsism it could encourage if one believed that the individual himself is separate from what he sees. This led to the elevation of liberal principles of selfhood into precisely the kind of dogmatism against which Emerson warned. Concomitantly, and crucially for those who urged social reform, if one privileged the self in this way, why should one break from his protective shell to serve the needs of others?

Santayana inherited the nineteenth-century Idealist tradition and transformed it, not by an adherence to Transcendentalist method, but from a willingness to subject it to critical analysis, salvaging what he could. In this work he found a fellow traveler and generously accorded him primacy in the effort. William James, his Harvard colleague, also struggled to come to terms with what his father's friend Emerson had bequeathed to the Genteel Tradition. James, particularly in his examination of religious experience, Santayana observed, "gave a sincere and respectful hearing to sentimentalists, mystics, spiritualists, wizards, cranks, quacks, and impostors" because he believed that any of these might have something to teach him. But trained as he was in physiology, he also represented the new scientific mind. For James, Santayana wrote, "intelligence is no miraculous, idle faculty, by which we mirror passively any or everything that happens to be true, reduplicating the real world to no purpose." Rather, it "has its roots and its issue in the context of events." Intelligence is "one kind of practical adjustment, an experimental act, a form of vital tension," and "does not essentially serve to picture other parts of reality, but to connect them."[29]

Reality, then, was never only of mind but rather the interaction of life with it. Frothingham's scientific theism, with its respect for the varieties of religious experience, led, finally, to this: a world in which each person makes his own truth from what works for him. James termed it Pragmatism. Emerson called it "Experience." With its ascension, the other half of the Transcendentalists' dream, of a common humanity committed to social justice, fell by the wayside. If truth is what an individual finds congruent with his experience rather than a deeply shared social ideal, individualism triumphs, as it did in the Gilded Age and beyond. This was the Transcendentalists' lasting legacy, for better or worse. They were, if nothing else, great optimists.

NOTES

PREFACE

1. J. A. Saxton, "Prophecy—Transcendentalism—Progress," *Dial* 2 (July 1841), 101.

2. Orestes Brownson, review of John William Draper's *History of the Conflict Between Religion and Science*, *Brownson's Quarterly Review* 4th ser., 3 (April 1875), 158.

3. Cyrus Bartol, *Radical Problems* (Boston: Roberts Brothers, 1872), 73.

4. Ralph Waldo Emerson, "The Editors to the Reader," *Dial* 1 (July 1840), 2–3.

5. James Freeman Clarke, *Autobiography, Diary, and Correspondence* (Boston: Houghton, Mifflin, 1891), 133.

6. Charles Dickens, *American Notes for General Circulation*, 2 vols. (London: Chapman and Hall, 1842), 1:133.

7. Higginson, "Sunny Side," *Part of a Man's Life* (Boston: Houghton, Mifflin, 1905), 12.

8. Ibid.

9. Henry Adams, review of O. B. Frothingham's *Transcendentalism in New England: A History*, *North American Review* 123 (October 1876), 471.

10. Francis Bowen, *Critical Essays: On a Few Subjects Connected with the History and Present Condition of Speculative Philosophy* (Boston: H. B. Williams, 1842), 7.

11. "J," "R.W.E.," *Arcturus* 1 (April 1841), reprinted in Philip F. Gura and Joel Myerson, eds., *Critical Essays: On American Transcendentalism* (Boston: G. K. Hall, 1982), 21.

12. Ralph Waldo Emerson, *Journals and Miscellaneous Notebooks*, eds. William H. Gilman et al., 16 vols. (Cambridge: Belknap Press of Harvard University Press, 1960–82), 8:211.

13. Saxton, "Prophecy," 87.

14. Octavius Brooks Frothingham, *Transcendentalism in New England: A History* (New York: G. P. Putnam's Sons, 1876), v–vi.

15. Frederic Henry Hedge, one of the Transcendental coterie, did so in an article on Samuel Taylor Coleridge in *Christian Examiner* 14 (March 1833), 119–20. But see chapter 2, note 54, below.

16. The phrase was the Reverend William Ellery Channing's in a sermon (1838) of that title. On the Market Revolution see Charles G. Sellers, *The Market Revolution: Jacksonian America, 1815–1846* (New York: Oxford University Press, 1991).

INTRODUCTION: LOCATING THE "LIKE-MINDED"

1. Joel Myerson, Daniel Shealy, Madeleine Stern, eds. *Selected Letters of Louisa May Alcott* (Boston: Little, Brown and Company, 1987), 126–28.

2. James Elliot Cabot, *A Memoir of Ralph Waldo Emerson*, 2 vols. (Boston: Houghton, Mifflin, 1887), 1:249.

3. Caroline Healey Dall, *Transcendentalism in New England: A Lecture* (Boston: Sold by Roberts Brothers, 1897), 16.

4. William Henry Channing, in *Memoirs of Margaret Fuller Ossoli*, eds. R. W. Emerson, W. H. Channing, and J. F. Clarke, 2 vols. (Boston: Phillips, Sampson and Company, 1852), 2:14.

5. "J," "R.W.E.," *Arcturus* 1 (April 1841), reprinted in Philip F. Gura and Joel Myerson, eds., *Critical Essays on American Transcendentalism* (Boston: G. K. Hall, 1982), 20–21.

6. Orestes Brownson, review of *Two Articles from the "Princeton Review,"* *Boston Quarterly Review* 3 (July 1840), 270.

7. *Memoirs of Ossoli*, 2:15.

8. Noah Porter, "Transcendentalism," *American Biblical Repository*, n.s., 8 (July 1847), reprinted in Gura and Myerson, *Critical Essays*, 36.

9. Francis Bowen, "Locke and the Transcendentalists," *Christian Examiner* 23 (November 1837), 176, 184. Also reprinted in Bowen's *Critical Essays: On a Few Subjects Connected with the History and Present Condition of Speculative Philosophy* (Boston: H. B. Williams, 1842).

10. "Senex" [Theodore Parker], "Transcendentalism," *Christian Register* 25 (April 1840), reprinted in Gura and Myerson, *Critical Essays*, 4. The pamphlet in question was *Two Articles from the Princeton Review* (Cambridge: John Owen, 1840).

11. Charles Mayo Ellis, *An Essay on Transcendentalism* (Boston: Crocker and Ruggles, 1842), 11.

12. Ibid., 19.

13. Ibid., 71.

14. Ibid., 23–24.

15. Ibid., 72; and J. A. Saxton, "Prophecy—Transcendentalism—Progress," *Dial* 2 (July 1841), 87. This is an ambitious attempt to trace the history of Transcendentalism, as worthy of study as Ellis's or Murdock's offerings.

16. James Murdock, *Sketches of Modern Philosophy, Especially Among the Germans* (1842; New York: M. W. Dodd, 1844), chapter xv, passim.

17. Murdock probably took this approach because of the recent publication of several of Cousin's works in George Ripley's *Specimens of Foreign Standard Literature*; see chapter 2, note 2, below.

18. Murdock, *Modern Philosophy*, 179.

19. Ibid., 181.

20. Perry Miller made this point in his seminal *The Transcendentalists: An Anthology* (Cambridge: Harvard University Press, 1950), 8.

21. Murdock, *Modern Philosophy*, 177.

22. Octavius Brooks Frothingham, *Transcendentalism in New England: A History* (New York: G. P. Putnam's Sons, 1876), 302, 136–37.

23. William C. Gannett, *Ezra Stiles Gannett: Unitarian Minister in Boston, 1824–1871* (Boston: Roberts Brothers, 1875), 198.

24. George Ripley in George Ripley and George P. Bradford, "Philosophic Thought in Boston," in Justin Winsor, ed., *The Memorial History of Boston*, 4 vols. (Boston: J. R. Osgood and Company, 1881), 4:305.

25. Francis Bowen, review of Emerson's *Nature*, *Christian Examiner* 21 (January 1837), 380.

26. Ralph Waldo Emerson, "The Transcendentalist," in *Collected Works of Ralph Waldo Emerson*, vol. 1, *Nature, Addresses, and Lectures; Historical Introduction and Notes by Robert E. Spiller; Text Established by Alfred R. Ferguson* (Cambridge: Harvard University Press, 1971), 201.

27. Ibid., 201, 203.

28. Ibid., 204–205.

29. Ibid., 208.

30. Ibid., 209–10.

31. Ibid., 211.

32. Ibid., 216.

33. Robert N. Hudspeth, ed., *The Letters of Margaret Fuller*, 6 vols. (Ithaca: Cornell University Press, 1983–94), 2:108.

34. B. B. Edwards and E. A. Park, *Selections from German Literature* (Andover, Mass.: Gould, Newman & Saxton, 1839), 4.

35. Hudspeth, ed., *Letters of Fuller*, 2:135.

36. Joseph Henry Allen, *Our Liberal Movement in Theology* (Boston: Roberts Brothers, 1882), 71.

37. Frothingham, *Transcendentalism in New England*, 115, 106.

1: SEARCHING THE SCRIPTURES

1. On Buckminster's importance see Lawrence Buell, "Joseph Stevens Buckminster: The Making of a New England Saint," *Canadian Review of American Studies* 10 (Spring 1979), 1–29.

2. See William Bentley, *Diary*, 4 vols. (Salem, Mass.: Essex Institute, 1905–14), 4:112 for a description of the event.

3. The best biography of Stuart is Jon H. Giltner, *Moses Stuart: The Father of Biblical Science in America* (Atlanta: Scholars Press, 1988). The sale is described at pp. 8–9.

4. Moses Stuart, "The Study of the German Language," *Christian Review* 6 (1841), 457.

5. William C. Gannett, *Ezra Stiles Gannett, Unitarian Minister in Boston, 1824–1871* (Boston: Roberts Brothers, 1875), 63.

6. On the background to early American Unitarianism, see Conrad Wright, *The Beginnings of Unitarianism in America* (Boston: Starr King Press, 1955).

7. For the development of nineteenth-century American Unitarianism, see Daniel Walker Howe, *The Unitarian Conscience: Harvard Moral Philosophy, 1805–1861* (Cambridge: Harvard University Press, 1970).

8. I have written about this subject at more length in *The Wisdom of Words: Language, Theology, and Literature in the New England Renaissance* (Middletown, Conn.: Wesleyan University Press, 1981); and "The Transcendentalists and Language: The Unitarian Exegetical Background," in Joel Myerson, ed., *Studies in the American Renaissance, 1979* (Boston: Twayne Publishers, 1979), 1–16.

9. John Locke, *Essay Concerning Human Understanding*, ed. Russell Kirk (Chicago: Gateway, 1956), 132, 137, 141, 172.

10. Giltner, *Moses Stuart*, 9.

11. Edward Everett, review of Goethe, *North American Review* 4 (January 1817), 217–62.

12. Ralph Waldo Emerson, "Historic Notes on Life and Letters in New England," *Lectures and Biographical Sketches* (1883), in *Complete Works of Ralph Waldo Emerson*, Edward Waldo Emerson, ed., 12 vols. (Boston and New York: Houghton, Mifflin, 1903–04), 10:312.

13. Elisabeth Hurth, "Sowing the Seeds of 'Subversion': Harvard's Early Göttingen Students," in *Studies in the American Renaissance, 1992* (Charlottesville: University Press of Virginia, 1992), 93.

14. Orie William Long, *Literary Pioneers: Early American Explorers of European Culture* (Cambridge: Harvard University Press, 1935), 120–21.

15. Caroline Healey Dall, *Transcendentalism in New England: A Lecture* (Boston: Sold by Roberts Brothers, 1897), 14–15.

16. Karen Kalinevitch, "Turning from the Orthodox: Emerson's Gospel Lectures," *Studies in the American Renaissance, 1986* (Boston: Twayne Publishers, 1986), 105, n. 11.

17. Ronald A. Bosco and Joel Myerson, *The Emerson Brothers: A Fraternal Biography in Letters* (New York: Oxford University Press, 2006), 96.

18. For a good biographical notice see William Sprague, *Annals of the American Pulpit*, 9 vols. (New York: Robert Carter and Brothers, 1859–69), 8:538–47.

19. See Thomas Albert Howard, *Religion and the Rise of Historicism: W.M.L. de Wette, Jacob Burckhardt, and the Theological Origins of Nineteenth-Century Historical Consciousness* (Cambridge, Eng.: Cambridge University Press, 2000), 71–76.

20. George Washington Spindler, *The Life of Karl Follen: A Study of German-American Cultural Relations* (Chicago: University of Chicago Press, 1917), passim, esp. 71, 85, 98, 122, 142.

21. Andrew P. Peabody, *Harvard Reminiscences* (Boston: Ticknor, 1888), 117.

22. *Life, Letters, and Journals of George Ticknor*, 2 vols. (Boston: J. R. Osgood and Company, 1876), 1:352.

23. Sprague, *Annals*, 8:547.

24. Moses Stuart, *A Commentary on the Epistle to the Hebrews*, 2 vols. (Andover, Mass.: Mark Newman, 1827–28), 1:v.

25. Joseph Buckminster, *Sermons by the Late Rev. J. S. Buckminster, with a Memoir of His Life and Character* (Boston: John Eliot, 1814), 167.

26. On Norton see Lillian Handlin, "Babylon est delenda—The Young Andrews Norton," in Conrad Edick Wright, ed., *American Unitarianism* (Boston: Massachusetts Historical Society, 1989), 53–85; and Howe, *The Unitarian Conscience*, 299–303. Howe also treats Ware's appointment to the Hollis Chair; see pp. 4–5.

27. Jaazariah Crosby, in Sprague, *Annals*, 8:432.

28. Ibid.

29. Orestes Brownson, review of *Two Articles from the Princeton Review*, *Boston Quarterly Review* 3 (July 1840), 269.

30. George Ripley in George Ripley and George P. Bradford, "Philosophic Thought in Boston," in Justin Winsor, ed., *The Memorial History of Boston*, 4 vols. (Boston: J. R. Osgood and Company, 1881), 4:299.

31. Henry A. Pochmann, *German Culture in America: Philosophical and Literary Influences, 1600–1900* (Madison: University of Wisconsin Press, 1957), 128–31.

32. Moses Stuart, *Letters to the Rev. Wm. E. Channing, Containing Remarks on His Sermon, Recently Preached and Published in Baltimore* (Andover, Mass.: Flagg and Gould, 1819), 11.

33. On Stuart's use of these critics see Giltner, *Moses Stuart*, 45–55.

34. Moses Stuart, *Letters to Channing* (1819), reprinted in *Miscellanies* (Andover, Mass.: Allen, Morrill, and Wardlaw, 1846), 156–57.

35. Emerson quoted in Elizabeth Palmer Peabody, *Reminiscences of the Rev. William Ellery Channing, D.D.* (Boston: Roberts Brothers, 1880), 371.

36. Andrews Norton, *An Inaugural Address, Delivered Before the University of Cambridge, August 10, 1819* (Cambridge: Hilliard and Metcalf, 1819), 18–20.

37. Andrews Norton, *A Statement of Reasons for Not Believing the Doctrines of the Trinitarians* (1819, rev. 1833; Boston: American Unitarian Association,

1859), 162. Norton had first responded to Stuart in two reviews in the *Christian Disciple* for 1819 and later expanded one of the pieces into *A Statement of Reasons*, which he continued to revise until it reached its final form in 1833.

38. Norton, *Statement of Reasons*, 138, 149, 148.

39. Orville Dewey, *Autobiography and Letters* (Boston: Roberts Brothers, 1883), 44.

40. On Marsh see Peter Carafiol, *Transcendent Reason: James Marsh and the Forms of Romantic Thought* (Tallahassee: University of Florida Press, 1982).

41. James Marsh, review of Stuart's *Commentary on the Epistle to the Hebrews*, *Quarterly Christian Spectator* 1 (1829), 147, 116.

42. See Hurth, "Harvard's Early Göttingen Students," 105, n. 7, for Everett's translation of Herder's *Introduction to the Old Testament*, dated 1818.

43. See Jerry Wayne Brown, *The Rise of Biblical Criticism in America, 1800–1870: The New England Scholars* (Middletown, Conn.: Wesleyan University Press, 1969), 50, n. 14.

44. George Ripley, review of Herder's *Sammtliche Werke*, *Christian Examiner* 19 (May 1835), 178, 183, 172.

45. For Peabody's interest in language see Philip F. Gura, "Elizabeth Peabody and the Philosophy of Language," *ESQ: A Journal of the American Renaissance* 23, 3rd qtr. (July 1977), 154–63.

46. Elizabeth Peabody, "Spirit of Hebrew Poetry," *Christian Examiner* 16 (May 1834), 174–75. This was the first of three essays on biblical criticism that Peabody published in subsequent numbers of the journal. She had intended a total of six, but the editor, Andrews Norton, had "cut off untimely my little series," as she later wrote Orestes Brownson. Norton, she later explained, "was opposed to a series on any one subject" and did not even "condescend" to read the other three pieces "because, as he said, I must needs be incompetent to the subject from want of learning." See Elizabeth Palmer Peabody to Orestes Brownson [ca. 1840] in Bruce A. Ronda, ed., *Letters of Elizabeth Palmer Peabody: American Renaissance Woman* (Middletown, Conn.: Wesleyan University Press, 1984), 248; and Elizabeth Palmer Peabody, *Reminiscences of the Rev. William Ellery Channing, D.D.*, 145.

47. Peabody, "Spirit of Hebrew Poetry," 175–76.

48. Kalinevitch, "Emerson's Gospel Lectures," 89.

49. Ralph Waldo Emerson, "The Lord's Supper," *Miscellanies* in Emerson, *Complete Works*, 11:10–11, 21. Also see Elisabeth Hurth, "William and Ralph Waldo Emerson and the Problem of the Lord's Supper: The Influence of German 'Historical Speculators,'" *Church History* 62, no. 2 (June 1993), 190–206.

50. Ralph Waldo Emerson, "Divinity School Address," in *Collected Works of Ralph Waldo Emerson*, vol. 1, *Nature, Addresses, and Lectures; Historical Introduction and Notes by Robert E. Spiller; Text Established by Alfred R. Ferguson* (Cambridge: Harvard University Press, 1971), 81, 93.

2: REINVIGORATING A FAITH

1. George Ripley to Convers Francis, January 17, 1837, in Mathew David Fisher, "A Selected, Annotated Edition of the Letters of George Ripley, 1828–1841" (Ph.D. diss., Ball State University, 1992), 98–100.

2. The series comprised Ripley's *Philosophical Miscellanies, translated from the French of Cousin, Jouffroy, and B. Constant, in two volumes* (1838); John Sullivan Dwight's *Select Minor Poems, translated from the German of Goethe and Schiller* (1839); Margaret Fuller's *Conversations with Goethe in the Last Years of His Life, translated from the German of Eckermann* (1839); William Henry Channing's *Introduction to Ethics, Including a Critical Survey of Moral Systems, translated from the French of Jouffroy, in two volumes* (1841; for some reason, these are listed next in the numbering of the series, although their publication date precedes the next title); Cornelius C. Felton's *German Literature, translated from the German of Wolfgang Menzel, in three volumes* (1840); James Freeman Clarke's *Theodore; or, the Skeptic's Conversion. History of the Culture of a Protestant Clergyman, translated from the German of De Wette, in two volumes* (1841); Samuel Osgood's *Human Life; or, Practical Ethics, translated from the German of De Wette, in two volumes* (1842); and Charles Timothy Brooks's *German Lyric Poetry. A Collection of Songs and Ballads, translated from the best German Lyric Poets* (1842).

3. George Ripley to James Marsh, February 23, 1838, in John J. Duffy, ed., *Coleridge's American Disciples: The Selected Correspondence of James Marsh* (Amherst: University of Massachusetts Press, 1973), 192–93. As an indication of Ripley's catholicity, he asked Leonard Woods, Jr., a professor at the conservative Bangor Theological Seminary in Bangor, Maine, to translate some of the work of the German biblical scholar August Twesten; see Ripley to James Marsh, February 23, 1838, in Duffy, *Coleridge's American Disciples*, 211.

4. George Ripley to James Marsh, October 17, 1840, ibid., 240.

5. Marsh first published his translation of *The Spirit of Hebrew Poetry* in *The Biblical Repertory*, a journal edited by Charles Hodge of Princeton and then in book form in 1833.

6. James Marsh, "Ancient and Modern Poetry," *North American Review* 6 (July 1822), 106, 123–28.

7. Ibid., 123.

8. Peter Carafiol, *Transcendent Reason: James Marsh and the Forms of Romantic Thought* (Tallahassee: University of Florida Press, 1982), 127.

9. James Marsh, review of Stuart's *Commentary on the Epistle to the Hebrews*, *Quarterly Christian Spectator* 1 (March 1829), 147.

10. James Marsh, "Preliminary Essay," in Samuel Taylor Coleridge, *Aids to Reflection* (Burlington, Vt.: Chauncey Goodrich, 1829), xiv.

11. Ibid., xxv.

12. Ibid., xxxix.

13. See Coleridge, *Aids to Reflection*, 260, Marsh's note.

14. Marsh, "Preliminary Essay," viii; and Coleridge, *Aids to Reflection*, 261.

15. Karl Follen, cited in Roland V. Wells, *Three Christian Transcendentalists: James Marsh, Caleb Sprague Henry, Frederic Henry Hedge* (New York: Columbia University Press, 1943), 18.

16. James Freeman Clarke, *Autobiography, Diary, and Correspondence* (Boston: Houghton, Mifflin, 1891), 39.

17. James Marsh to Henry J. Raymond, March 1, 1841, in Duffy, *Coleridge's American Disciples*, 256. Raymond later worked for Horace Greeley on *The New Yorker* and the *Tribune*. As an undergraduate he had been Greeley's agent in northern New England. See ibid., 247, notes 1 and 3.

18. Charles Follen to James Marsh, April 14, 1832, in Duffy, *Coleridge's American Disciples*, 128. The editor of Marsh's letters notes that although he never published a translation of Fries, a manuscript text of lectures survives, with an inscription on the cover indicating it is a translation of Fries's *Logic*. See Duffy, *Coleridge's American Disciples*, 128, n. 7; and ibid., 138; and Joseph Torrey, *The Remains of the Rev. James Marsh, D.D. Late President and Professor of Moral and Intellectual Philosophy, in the University of Vermont; with a Memoir of His Life* (Burlington, Vt.: Chauncey Goodrich, 1845), 118.

19. See John W. Rogerson, *W.M.L. de Wette, Founder of Modern Biblical Criticism: An Intellectual Biography* (Sheffield, Eng.: Sheffield Academic Press, 1992) for the best biography.

20. J. D. Morell, *An Historical and Critical View of the Speculative Philosophy of Europe in the Nineteenth Century* (1841; New York: R. Carter & Brothers, 1847), 596.

21. Ibid., 598–601; quotations from 600 and 601.

22. Fries presented these ideas in his important *Wissen, Glauben, und Ahnung* (Jena: J.C.G. Göpfert, 1805).

23. Morell, *Historical and Critical View*, 666 and note.

24. On de Wette's reception in the United States, see Siegfried B. Puknat, "De Wette in New England," *Proceedings of the American Philosophical Society* 102, no. 4 (August 1958), 376–95.

25. Wilhelm M. L. de Wette, *Theodore; or, The Skeptic's Conversion. History of the Culture of a Protestant Clergyman*, trans. James Freeman Clarke, 2 vols. (Boston: Hilliard, Gray, and Company, 1841), 1:15.

26. Ibid., xxxi.

27. Ibid., 76–77.

28. Moses Stuart, *Letters to the Rev. Wm. E. Channing, Containing Remarks on His Sermon, Recently Preached and Published in Baltimore*, reprinted in *Miscellanies* (Andover, Mass.: Allen, Morrill, and Wardlaw, 1846), 81–82.

29. George Ripley to James Marsh, February 23, 1838, in Duffy, *Coleridge's American Disciples*, 210.

30. Ibid.

31. *Philosophical Miscellanies, translated from the French of Cousin, Jouffroy, and B. Constant*, trans. George Ripley, 2 vols. (Boston: Hilliard, Gray, and Company, 1838), vol. 1.

32. William H. Channing, *Introduction to Ethics, Including a Critical Survey of Moral Systems*, translated from the French of Jouffroy, 2 vols. (Boston: Hilliard, Gray, and Company, 1841), 2:xv–xvii.

33. *Philosophical Miscellanies*, 1:29.

34. Ibid., 1:32–33.

35. Ibid., 1:37.

36. Orestes Brownson, "Recent Contributions to Philosophy," *Christian Examiner* 22 (May 1837), 181–217; and William Henry Channing, "Skepticism of the Present Age," ibid. 25, no. 3 (November 1838), 137–57.

37. James Murdock, *Sketches of Modern Philosophy, Especially Among the Germans* (1842; New York: M. W. Dodd, 1844), 177, 179. Victor Cousin, *Introduction to the History of Philosophy. Translated from the French by Henning Gotfried Linberg* (Boston: Hilliard, Gray, Little, and Wilkins, 1832).

38. Ralph Waldo Emerson, *Journals and Miscellaneous Notebooks* (hereafter JMN), eds. William H. Gilman et al., 16 vols. (Cambridge: Belknap Press of Harvard University Press, 1960–82), 5:455.

39. Ralph Waldo Emerson, "The American Scholar," in *Collected Works of Ralph Waldo Emerson*, vol. 1, *Nature, Addresses, and Lectures; Historical Introduction and Notes by Robert E. Spiller; Text Established by Alfred R. Ferguson* (Cambridge: Harvard University Press, 1971), 68.

40. James John Garth Wilkinson, *Emanuel Swedenborg: A Biography* (Boston: O. Clapp, 1849), 75. Another good contemporary biography is Nathaniel Hobart, *Life of Swedenborg: with Some Account of His Writings* (Boston: Allen and Goddard, 1831).

41. Ralph Waldo Emerson, "Historic Notes on Life and Letters in New England," *Lectures and Biographical Sketches* (1883), in *Complete Works of Ralph Waldo Emerson*, Edward Waldo Emerson, ed., 12 vols. (Boston and New York: Houghton, Mifflin, 1903–04), 10:311–12.

42. Wilkinson, *Swedenborg*, 86.

43. On Reed see Clarence P. Hotson, "Sampson Reed, a Teacher of Emerson," *New England Quarterly* 2 (April 1929), 249–77; and Kenneth Walter Cameron, *Young Emerson's Transcendental Vision* (Hartford: Transcendental Books, 1971), 285–87, for a list of his articles in the *New Jerusalem Magazine*.

44. Ralph Waldo Emerson to William Emerson, September 29, 1826, in *Letters of Ralph Waldo Emerson*, eds. Ralph L. Rusk and Eleanor M. Tilton, 10 vols. (New York: Columbia University Press, 1939–95), 1:176. Reed's book was reviewed in *Christian Examiner* 3 (January 1826): 418–26.

45. Sampson Reed, *Observations on the Growth of the Mind* (Boston: Hilliard and Metcalf, 1826), 13.

46. Ibid., 22–24.

47. Ibid., 24.

48. Wilkinson, *Swedenborg*, 261.

49. Sampson Reed, *Observations on the Growth of the Mind* (rev. ed., 1838; reprint, Boston: O. Clapp, 1841), vi.

50. Theophilus Parsons, "Transcendentalism," *New Jerusalem Magazine* 14 (December 1840), reprinted in Philip F. Gura and Joel Myerson, eds., *Critical Essays on American Transcendentalism* (Boston: G. K. Hall, 1982), 16.

51. Emerson, JMN, 7:322.

52. Ibid., 8:182–83.

53. Ralph Waldo Emerson, *Collected Works of Ralph Waldo Emerson*, vol. 4, *Representative Men; Historical Introduction and Notes by Wallace E. Williams; Text Established and Textual Apparatus by Douglas Emory Wilson* (Cambridge: Harvard University Press, 1987), 75, 68.

54. George Willis Cooke, *A Historical and Biographical Introduction to the "Dial,"* 2 vols. (1902; reprint, New York: Russell and Russell, 1961), 1:17.

55. Caroline Healey Dall, *Transcendentalism in New England: A Lecture* (Boston: Sold by Roberts Brothers, 1897), 15. With a letter ca. 1840 to Orestes Brownson, Elizabeth Peabody included an essay written around 1826 but not published in which she used "the word *transcendentalism*," which she had not seen elsewhere "except in Coleridge's friend [*The Friend*]"; see Elizabeth Palmer Peabody to Orestes Brownson [ca. 1840], in Bruce A. Ronda, ed., *Letters of Elizabeth Palmer Peabody: American Renaissance Woman* (Middletown, Conn.: Wesleyan University Press, 1984), 248. The essay was one of a series of six on the Hebrew scriptures, three of which had been published in the early 1830s in *Christian Examiner*, that she wanted Brownson to publish in his *Boston Quarterly Review*; see chapter 1, note 46, above.

56. Henry A. Pochmann, *German Culture in America: Philosophical and Literary Influences, 1600–1900* (Madison: University of Wisconsin Press, 1957), 144; Henry David Gray, *Emerson: A Statement of New England Transcendentalism as Expressed in the Philosophy of Its Chief Exponent* (1917; reprint, New York: Frederic Ungar Publishing Co., 1958), 188.

57. Cyrus Bartol, *Radical Problems* (Boston: Roberts Brothers, 1872), 70.

58. Frederic Henry Hedge, "Swedenborg," *Christian Examiner* 15 (November 1833), 196.

59. Ibid., 218.

60. George Ripley, "Professor Marsh's Translation of Herder," *Christian Examiner* 18 (May 1835), 172.

61. George Ripley, "Herder's Theological Opinions and Services," ibid. 19 (November 1835), 180–81.

62. Ibid., 195–96.

63. George Ripley, "Schleiermacher as a Theologian," *Christian Examiner* 20 (March 1836), 1, 2, 4.

64. Morell, *Historical and Critical View*, 617.

65. Patrick W. Carey, ed., *The Early Works of Orestes A. Brownson*, 5 vols. to date (Milwaukee: Marquette University Press, 2000–), 3:2.

66. Clarke in de Wette, *Theodore*, 1:xvi.

67. Orestes Brownson, "Cousin's Philosophy," *Christian Examiner* 21 (Septem-

ber 1836), 33–64; "Recent Contributions to Philosophy," ibid. 22 (May 1837), 181–217; "Benjamin Constant," ibid. 17 (September 1834), 63–77.

3: TRANSCENDENTALISM EMERGENT

1. Samuel Eliot Morison, *Three Centuries of Harvard, 1636–1936* (Cambridge: Harvard University Press, 1936), 268–72, for a description of the bicentennial festivities.

2. Ralph Waldo Emerson to Frederic Henry Hedge, July 20, 1836, *Letters of Ralph Waldo Emerson* (hereafter LRWE), eds. Ralph L. Rusk and Eleanor M. Tilton, 10 vols. (New York: Columbia University Press, 1939–95), 2:29.

3. James Elliot Cabot, *A Memoir of Ralph Waldo Emerson*, 2 vols. (Boston: Houghton, Mifflin, 1887), 1:244–45.

4. Joel Myerson, "A Calendar of Transcendental Club Meetings," *American Literature* 44, no. 2 (May 1972), passim.

5. Ralph Waldo Emerson, *Journals and Miscellaneous Notebooks* (hereafter JMN), eds. William H. Gilman et al., 16 vols. (Cambridge: Belknap Press of Harvard University Press, 1960–82), 5:194.

6. Myerson, "Calendar," 197–207.

7. Ralph Waldo Emerson, "Historic Notes on Life and Letters in New England," *Lectures and Biographical Sketches* (1883), in *Complete Works of Ralph Waldo Emerson*, ed. Edward Waldo Emerson, 12 vols. (Boston and New York: Houghton, Mifflin, 1903–04), 10:322.

8. Sterling Delano, *Brook Farm: The Dark Side of Utopia* (Cambridge: Harvard University Press, 2004), 26.

9. Perry Miller, *The Transcendentalists: An Anthology* (Cambridge: Harvard University Press, 1950), 106, termed 1836 the annus mirabilis of the movement.

10. Brownson mentions Follen, along with Schleiermacher and Constant, in the preface to *New Views of Christianity, Society, and the Church* (Boston: J. Munroe and Company, 1836). See also Charles Follen, *Religion and the Church* (Boston: J. Munroe and Company, 1836).

11. Ripley to Bancroft, September 20, 1837, in Siegfried B. Puknat, "De Wette in New England," *Proceedings of the American Philosophical Society* 102, no. 4 (August 1958), 384.

12. Orestes Brownson to George Bancroft, September 12, 1836, in Daniel R. Barnes, "An Edition of the Early Letters of Orestes Brownson" (Ph.D. diss., 1970), 122.

13. Henry F. Brownson, *Orestes A. Brownson's Early Life* (Detroit: Henry F. Brownson, 1898), 90–91.

14. For example, Brownson reviewed his *New Views* and *Charles Elwood* in the journal; see *Boston Quarterly Review* 1 (1838), 1–27; and ibid. 3 (1840), 258–60.

15. Isaac Hecker, "Dr. Brownson in Boston," *Catholic World* 45 (July 1887), 466.

16. Noah Porter, "Transcendentalism," *American Biblical Repository*, n.s., 8 (July 1842), reprinted in Philip F. Gura and Joel Myerson, eds., *Critical Essays on American Transcendentalism* (Boston: G. K. Hall, 1982), 40.

17. On Tuckerman see Daniel Walker Howe, *The Unitarian Conscience: Harvard Moral Philosophy, 1805–1861* (Cambridge: Harvard University Press, 1970), 246–55; and Conrad Edick Wright, "Saving a Soul: Joseph Tuckerman and the Final Days of Sylvester Colson," Massachusetts Historical Society, *Proceedings* 104 (1992), 110–22.

18. Orestes Brownson, *The Convert*, in Brownson, *The Works of Orestes A. Brownson, collected and arranged by Henry F. Brownson*, 20 vols. (Detroit: T. Nourse, 1882–1907), 5:82–83.

19. See John Weiss, *Discourse Occasioned by the Death of Convers Francis, D.D.* (Cambridge: privately printed, 1863) for a good assessment of this important Unitarian.

20. Orestes Brownson, "Benjamin Constant on Religion," *Christian Examiner* 17 (September 1834), 64.

21. Ibid., 70.

22. Orestes Brownson, *New Views of Christianity, Society, and the Church* (Boston: J. Munroe and Company, 1836).

23. Ibid., 11–13.

24. Ibid., 55.

25. Ibid., 64–65.

26. Ibid., 86–87.

27. Ibid., 91–94.

28. Ibid., 115.

29. James Walker, "Editorial Notice," *Christian Examiner* 22 (March 1837), 128–29.

30. Brownson, *The Convert*, in *Works*, 5:93.

31. The modern biography of Ripley is Charles R. Crowe, *George Ripley, Transcendentalist and Utopian Socialist* (Athens: University of Georgia Press, 1967).

32. Octavius Brooks Frothingham, *George Ripley* (Boston: Houghton, Mifflin, 1882), 45.

33. George Ripley in *Philosophical Miscellanies, translated from the French of Cousin, Jouffroy, and B. Constant*, 2 vols. (Boston: Hilliard, Gray, and Company, 1838), 1:278.

34. George Ripley, review of Friedrich Lücke's "Recollections of Schleiermacher," *Christian Examiner* 20 (March 1836), 3–4. A year earlier, in the *Biblical Repository and Quarterly Observer*, Moses Stuart had offered the first American translation of any of Schleiermacher's work in his "On the Discrepancy between the Sabellian and Athanasian Method of Representing the Doctrine of the Trinity" (5, no. 18 [April 1835], 265–70).

35. Ripley, "Schleiermacher," 4.

36. George Ripley, *Discourses on the Philosophy of Religion, Addressed to Doubters Who Wish to Believe* (Boston: J. Munroe and Company, 1836), iv.

37. Ibid., 9–11, 35.

38. Ibid., 59.

39. George Ripley, "Martineau's *Rationale of Religious Inquiry*," *Christian Examiner* 21 (November 1836), 228.

40. George Ripley, "Schleiermacher as a Theologian," *Christian Examiner* 20 (March 1836), 35–36.

41. Ripley, "Martineau's *Rationale*," 249–51.

42. Ibid., 253–54.

43. Andrews Norton, [Letter to the Editor,] *Boston Daily Advertiser*, November 5, 1836, p. 2. In Joel Myerson, ed., *Transcendentalism: A Reader* (New York: Oxford University Press, 2000), 160–62.

44. George Ripley, [Letter to the Editor,] *Boston Daily Advertiser*, November 9, 1836, p. 2. In Myerson, *Transcendentalism*, 163–67; and Perry Miller, *The Transcendentalists*, 160–63.

45. The modern biography is Frederick C. Dahlstrand, *Amos Bronson Alcott, an Intellectual Biography* (Madison, N.J.: Fairleigh Dickinson University Press, 1982).

46. Alcott later approvingly heard him preach there, and shortly thereafter the minister moved in with the Alcott family, for Abigail kept boarders to supplement her husband's income.

47. Odell Shepard, *Pedlar's Progress: The Life of Bronson Alcott* (Boston: Little, Brown and Company, 1937), 235.

48. The description of the school is taken from Elizabeth Palmer Peabody, *Record of a School, Exemplifying the General Principles of Spiritual Culture* (Boston: Russell, Shattuck and Company, 1836), 1–2.

49. Ibid., 2–25.

50. Elizabeth Palmer Peabody, *Reminiscences of the Rev. Wm Ellery Channing, D.D.* (Boston: Roberts Brothers, 1880), 356–57.

51. [William Woodbridge,] "Record of a School," *American Annals of Education and Instruction* 5, no. 10 (October 1835), 477–78.

52. Myerson, "Calendar," 200.

53. [Nathan Hale,] "Conversations with Children on the Gospels," *Boston Daily Advertiser and Patriot* 42 (March 21, 1837).

54. [Joseph T. Buckingham,] "Alcott's Conversations on the Gospels," *Boston Daily Courier* 12 (March 29, 1837).

55. See LRWE 7:278, n. The statement was published by Joseph T. Buckingham in his editorial comment in the *Boston Daily Courier* in early April 1837: he attributed the words to a "clergyman at no great distance from Boston." Alcott's copy of the paper identifies this person as Norton.

56. Ralph Waldo Emerson to Bronson Alcott, March 24, 1837, in LRWE 2: 61–62. See also Charles Lane, *The Law and Method of Spirit-Culture: An*

Interpretation of A. Bronson Alcott's Idea and Practice at the Masonic Temple, Boston (Boston: J. Munroe and Company, 1843).

57. Patrick W. Carey, ed., *The Early Works of Orestes A. Brownson*, 5 vols. to date (Milwaukee, Wis.: Marquette University Press, 2000–), 3:76.

58. Francis Bowen, review of Emerson's *Nature, Christian Examiner* 21 (January 1837), 377.

59. *United States Magazine and Democratic Review* 1 (February 1838), 319.

60. Francis Bowen, "*Nature*," 371, 378; and "Locke and the Transcendentalists," *Christian Examiner* 23 (November 1837), 193.

61. Ralph Waldo Emerson to Thomas Carlyle, September 17, 1836, in Joseph Slater, ed., *The Correspondence of Emerson and Carlyle* (New York: Columbia University Press, 1964), 149.

62. Ralph Waldo Emerson to Frederic Henry Hedge, July 20, 1836, in LRWE, 2:30.

63. Thornton Kirkland Lathrop, ed., *Some Reminiscences of the Life of Samuel Kirkland Lathrop* (Cambridge: John Wilson & Son, 1888), 65.

64. Ralph Waldo Emerson, *Nature*, in *Collected Works of Ralph Waldo Emerson*, vol. 1, *Nature, Addresses, and Lectures; Historical Introduction and Notes by Robert E. Spiller; Text Established by Alfred R. Ferguson* (Cambridge: Harvard University Press, 1971), 10, 7, 43, 45.

65. Ibid., 17, 19.

66. Ibid., 7, 9.

67. Ibid., 11, 26, 30.

68. Ibid., 42, 43, 44.

69. Brownson, *Early Works*, 4:51–52, from the *Boston Morning Post*.

70. "Ralph Waldo Emerson and the New School," *Western Messenger* 6, no. 1 (November 1838), 46.

71. James Walker and Francis Greenwood, "Editorial Notice," *Christian Examiner* 22 (March 1837), 135.

72. Brownson, *The Convert*, in *Works*, 5:75–76.

4: RELIGIOUS COMBUSTION

1. See Octavius Brooks Frothingham, *Recollections and Impressions, 1822–1890* (New York: G. P. Putnam's Sons, 1891), 26–30; Conrad Wright, "The Early Period (1811–1840)," in George Hunston Williams, ed., *The Harvard Divinity School: Its Place in Harvard University and in American Culture* (Boston: Beacon Press, 1954), 21–77.

2. He got it from Henry Walker, minister to Charlestown, Massachusetts, in 1836 or 1837; see John Weiss, *Life and Correspondence of Theodore Parker*, 2 vols. (New York: D. Appleton & Company, 1864), 1:122.

3. Theodore Parker, "Strauss' *Life of Jesus*," *Christian Examiner* 18 (July 1840), 273–316.

4. William Henry Furness, *Remarks on the Four Gospels* (Philadelphia: Carey, Lea, and Blanchard, 1836), 151, 157. Ripley's sermon is excerpted by Perry Miller in *The Transcendentalists: An Anthology* (Cambridge: Harvard University Press, 1950).

5. Furness, *Remarks on the Four Gospels*, 146.

6. Martin Luther Hurlburt, "Remarks on the Four Gospels," *Christian Examiner* 22 (March 1837), 103–104.

7. Ibid., 107.

8. Ibid., 111–12.

9. William Henry Furness, "The Miracles of Jesus," *Christian Examiner* 22 (July 1837), 283–321.

10. *Letters of Ralph Waldo Emerson* (hereafter LRWE), eds. Ralph L. Rusk and Eleanor M. Tilton, 10 vols. (New York: Columbia University Press, 1939–95), 2:147.

11. Oliver Wendell Holmes, *Ralph Waldo Emerson* (Boston, New York: Houghton, Mifflin, 1885), 115.

12. Robert D. Richardson, Jr., *Emerson: The Mind on Fire: A Biography* (Berkeley: University of California Press, 1995), 263–64.

13. Ralph Waldo Emerson, "Divinity School Address," in *Collected Works of Ralph Waldo Emerson*, vol. 1, *Nature, Addresses, and Lectures; Historical Introduction and Notes by Robert E. Spiller; Text Established by Alfred R. Ferguson* (Cambridge: Harvard University Press, 1971), 76.

14. Ibid., 76, 80.

15. Ibid., 81.

16. Ibid., 81, 84.

17. Ibid., 85–86.

18. Ibid., 89, 90, 91, 93.

19. Convers Francis to Frederic Henry Hedge, August 10, 1838, in Guy R. Woodall, "The Record of a Friendship: The Letters of Convers Francis to Frederic Henry Hedge in Bangor and Providence, 1835–1850," *Studies in the American Renaissance, 1991* (Charlottesville: University Press of Virginia, 1991), 34.

20. Cyrus Bartol, *Radical Problems* (Boston: Roberts Brothers, 1872), 68.

21. Theodore Parker to George E. Ellis, August 7, 1838, in Octavius Brooks Frothingham, *Theodore Parker: A Biography* (Boston: J. R. Osgood and Company, 1874), 106.

22. Sampson Reed, *Observations on the Growth of the Mind* (1826; Boston: O. Clapp, 1838), vii.

23. Woodall, "Letters of Francis to Hedge," 34.

24. Ralph Waldo Emerson to Henry Ware, Jr., July 26, 1838, LRWE, 2:146–50.

25. For Andrews Norton's diatribe, see *Boston Daily Advertiser*, August 27, 1838.

26. Theophilus Parsons, *Boston Daily Advertiser*, August 30, 1838.

27. Patrick W. Carey, ed., *The Early Works of Orestes A. Brownson*, 5 vols. to date (Milwaukee, Wis.: Marquette University Press, 2000–), 4:47–52.

28. Orestes Brownson, "Mr. Emerson's Address," *Boston Quarterly Review* 1 (1838), 504–12; "Norton on *The Evidences of Christianity*," ibid. 2 (1839), 87, 112.

29. Reprinted in Joel Myerson, *Transcendentalism: A Reader* (New York: Oxford University Press, 2000), 250–60.

30. Ralph Waldo Emerson, *Journals and Miscellaneous Notebooks* (hereafter JMN), eds. William H. Gilman et al., 16 vols. (Cambridge: Belknap Press of Harvard University Press, 1960–82), 5:471, 467.

31. Ralph Waldo Emerson to Henry Ware, Jr., October 8, 1838, LRWE, 2: 166–67.

32. Andrews Norton, *A Discourse on the Latest Form of Infidelity* (Cambridge: John Owen, 1839), 4–5.

33. Ibid., 9, 11.

34. Ibid., 11.

35. Ibid., 40–41.

36. Ibid., 44.

37. Ibid., 61.

38. Emerson, JMN, 7:110–11.

39. George Ripley, *"The Latest Form of Infidelity" Examined: A Letter to Mr. Andrews Norton* (Boston: J. Munroe and Company, 1839), 3, 5, 12–13.

40. Ibid., 132.

41. Ibid., 142.

42. Ibid., 150.

43. George Ripley, *Defence of "The Latest Form of Infidelity" Examined: A Second Letter to Mr. Andrews Norton* (Boston: J. Munroe and Company, 1840), 84.

44. Richard Hildreth, *Letter to Andrews Norton on Miracles as the Foundation of Religious Faith* (Boston: Weeks, Jordan, and Company, 1840), 3–4.

45. Ibid., 8–9.

46. J. W. Alexander, Albert B. Dod, and Charles Hodge, *Two Articles from the Princeton Review* (Cambridge: John Owen, 1840), 10–11.

47. Ibid., 63.

48. Ibid., 67–68, 69.

49. Woodall, "Letters of Francis to Hedge," 37.

50. It is conveniently reprinted in Joel Myerson, *Transcendentalism: A Reader*, 261–80.

51. Frothingham, *Theodore Parker*, 581–82.

52. John Weiss, *Discourse Occasioned by the Death of Convers Francis, D.D.* (Cambridge: privately printed, 1863), 67.

53. Levi Blodgett (Theodore Parker), *The Previous Question between Mr. Andrews Norton and His Alumni Moved and Handled, in a Letter to All Those Gentlemen* (Boston: Weeks, Jordan, and Company, 1840), 4, 15, 18.

54. Theodore Parker, Journal, ca. May 27, 1840, quoted in Dean Grodzins,

American Heretic: Theodore Parker and Transcendentalism (Chapel Hill: University of North Carolina Press, 2002), 199.

55. Wilhelm M. L. de Wette, *A Critical and Historical Introduction to the Canonical Scriptures of the Old Testament / from the German of Wilhelm Martin Leberecht de Wette; translated and enlarged by Theodore Parker,* 2 vols. (Boston: C. C. Little and J. Brown, 1843).

56. Gary A. Collison, "A Critical Edition of the Correspondence of Theodore Parker and Convers Francis, 1836–1859," 2 vols. (Ph.D. diss., Pennsylvania State University, 1979), 2:302–303.

57. Two of Lamennais's books were particularly important to Brownson, his *Paroles d'un croyant* (1834) and *Le Livre du people* (1837), both of which were translated and published in Boston, as, respectively, *The Words of a Believer* (1834) and *The People's Own Book* (1839).

58. Carey, ed., *Early Works of Orestes A. Brownson,* 4:425–26.

59. Ibid., 4:123–25.

60. "Ralph Waldo Emerson and the New School," *Western Messenger* 6, no. 1 (November 1838), 46.

61. Carey, ed., *Early Works of Orestes A. Brownson,* 5:253–54.

62. Ibid., 5:297.

5: CENTRIPETAL FORCES AND CENTRIFUGAL MOTION

1. Elizabeth Palmer Peabody to William Ellery Channing, July 10, 1840, cited in Megan Marshall, *The Peabody Sisters: Three Women Who Ignited American Romanticism* (Boston: Houghton Mifflin, 2005), 393. On Peabody's library specifically see Leslie Perrin Wilson, "'No Worthless Books': Elizabeth Peabody's Foreign Library, 1840–1852," *Publications of the Bibliographical Society of America* 99, no. 1 (2005), 113–52.

2. Elizabeth Palmer Peabody, quoted in George Willis Cooke, *A Historical and Biographical Introduction to the "Dial,"* 2 vols. (1902; reprint, New York: Russell and Russell, 1961), 1:148. For the catalog see Madeleine Stern, "Elizabeth Palmer Peabody's Foreign Library," *American Transcendental Quarterly* 20, supplement (1973), 5–12.

3. George P. Bradford in George Ripley and George P. Bradford, "Philosophic Thought in Boston," in Justin Winsor, ed., *The Memorial History of Boston,* 4 vols. (Boston: J. R. Osgood and Company, 1881), 4:329, n. 1.

4. Edward Everett Hale, *A New England Boyhood* (Boston: Little, Brown and Company, 1900), 248.

5. Theodore Parker to Elizabeth Palmer Peabody, July 1, 1840, cited in Marshall, *Peabody Sisters,* 393.

6. Thomas Wentworth Higginson, *Cheerful Yesterdays* (Boston: Houghton, Mifflin, 1898), 86.

7. Helen R. Deese, ed., *Daughter of Boston: The Extraordinary Diary of a Nineteenth-Century Woman* (Boston: Beacon Press, 2005), 19.

8. Elizabeth Palmer Peabody to Samuel Gray Ward, September 13, 1841, cited in Bruce A. Ronda, *Elizabeth Palmer Peabody: A Reformer on Her Own Terms* (Cambridge: Harvard University Press, 1999), 186; and Helen R. Deese, ed., *Selected Journals of Caroline Healey Dall*, in Massachusetts Historical Society, *Collections* 90 (2006), 69.

9. Higginson, *Cheerful Yesterdays*, 86.

10. Joel Myerson, "A Calendar of Transcendental Club Meetings," *American Literature* 44, no. 2 (May 1972), 32.

11. Ralph Waldo Emerson to Thomas Carlyle, March 12, 1835, in Joseph Slater, ed., *The Correspondence of Emerson and Carlyle* (New York: Columbia University Press, 1964), 119.

12. [Orestes Brownson,] "Introductory Remarks," *Boston Quarterly Review* 1 (January 1838), 6.

13. Emerson to Carlyle, March 18, 1840, in *Correspondence of Emerson and Carlyle*, 261; and April 21, 1840, ibid., 269.

14. [Ralph Waldo Emerson,] "The Editors to the Reader," *Dial* 1 (July 1840): 1–4.

15. See Joel Myerson, *The New England Transcendentalists and the Dial: A History of the Magazine and Its Contributors* (Rutherford, N.J.: Fairleigh Dickinson University Press, 1980), passim.

16. Ibid., 98.

17. Theodore Parker to Convers Francis, December 18, 1840, in Gary L. Collison, "A Critical Edition of the Correspondence of Theodore Parker and Convers Francis, 1836–1859," 2 vols. (Ph.D. diss., Pennsylvania State University, 1979), 1:203.

18. Thomas Wentworth Higginson, *Margaret Fuller Ossoli* (Boston: Houghton, Mifflin, 1884), 161.

19. George Ripley in Winsor, *The Memorial History of Boston*, 4:304.

20. Ralph Waldo Emerson, *Journals and Miscellaneous Notebooks* (hereafter JMN), eds. William H. Gilman et al., 16 vols. (Cambridge: Belknap Press of Harvard University Press, 1960–82), 5:272.

21. See Lawrence Buell, *Literary Transcendentalism: Style and Vision in the American Renaissance* (Ithaca: Cornell University Press, 1971), 77–101.

22. Margaret Fuller to James Freeman Clarke, ca. May 20, 1833, in Robert N. Hudspeth, ed., *The Letters of Margaret Fuller*, 6 vols. (Ithaca: Cornell University Press, 1983–94), 1:182.

23. Margaret Fuller to (Sophia Ripley?), August 27, 1839, ibid. 2:86–89.

24. *Memoirs of Margaret Fuller Ossoli*, eds. R. W. Emerson, W. H. Channing, and J. F. Clarke, 2 vols. (Boston: Phillips, Sampson and Company, 1852), 1:330.

25. Elizabeth Hoar to Ralph Waldo Emerson, March 27 [1841] in Myerson, "Mrs. Dall Edits Miss Fuller: The Story of Margaret and Her Friends," *Papers of the Bibliographical Society of America* 72 (1978), 191.

26. Deese, *Daughter of Boston*, 20.

27. *Memoirs of Ossoli*, 1:347–48.

28. Odell Shepard, *Pedlar's Progress: The Life of Bronson Alcott* (Boston: Little, Brown and Company, 1937), 423.

29. Deese, *Daughter of Boston*, 137–42.

30. [George Ripley,] *Philosophical Miscellanies, translated from the French of Cousin, Jouffroy, and B. Constant*, 2 vols. (Boston: Hilliard, Gray, and Company, 1838), 1:vii.

31. Samuel K. Lothrop, "Existing Commercial Establishments," *Christian Examiner* 22 (July 1837), 398.

32. "The Laboring Classes" is found in its entirety in Patrick W. Carey, ed., *The Early Works of Orestes A. Brownson*, 5 vols. to date (Milwaukee, Wis.: Marquette University Press, 2000—), 5:298–327.

33. Ibid., 5:306–08.

34. Ibid., 5:310–12.

35. Ibid., 5:321–23.

36. See Octavius Brooks Frothingham, *George Ripley* (Boston: Houghton, Mifflin, 1882), 38, a letter from Ripley to his mother.

37. George Ripley, *The Temptations of the Times* (Boston: Hilliard, Gray, and Company, 1837), 12, 9.

38. [George Ripley,] *A Letter to the Congregational Church in Purchase Street by Its Pastor* (Boston: Printed, Not Published, by Request, for the Purchase Street Church, 1840), 5. Also available in Frothingham, *Ripley*, 63–91.

39. Ripley, *A Letter*, 7, 24.

40. Ibid., 25–26, 28.

41. George Ripley, *A Farewell Discourse, Delivered to the Congregational Church in Purchase Street, March 28, 1841* (Boston: Freeman and Bolles, 1841), 18–19.

42. Frothingham, *Ripley*, 92–93.

43. Theodore Parker, *A Discourse on the Transient and Permanent in Christianity; Preached at the Ordination of Mr. Charles C. Shackford, in the Hawes Place Church in Boston, May 19, 1841* (Boston: Printed for the author, 1841). The sermon is available in Perry Miller, *The Transcendentalists: An Anthology* (Cambridge: Harvard University Press, 1950), 259–84. Parker's journals and letters for the few months preceding the sermon's composition point to deep reading in German theologians like Strauss, in whose work he found the very title of the sermon. See Strauss, "Über Vergängliches und Bleibendes im Christenthum" ("On Transience and Permanence in Christianity"), which Parker knew by 1839; and Dean Grodzins, *American Heretic: Theodore Parker and Transcendentalism* (Chapel Hill: University of North Carolina Press, 2002), 242.

44. Theodore Parker, *A Discourse on the Transient and Permanent in Christianity; Preached at the Ordination of Mr. Charles C. Shackford, in the Hawes Place Church in Boston, May 19, 1841*, 2nd ed. (Boston: Printed for the author, 1841), 8–9, 12.

45. Ibid., 15–16, 21.

46. *The South-Boston Unitarian Ordination* (Boston: Saxton and Pierce, 1841), 3–6.
47. Parker, *Transient and Permanent*, 2nd ed., 4. Theodore Parker to Charles Miller, July 12, 1841, Massachusetts Historical Society.
48. *South-Boston Ordination*, 2.
49. John Weiss, *Life and Correspondence of Theodore Parker*, 2 vols. (New York: D. Appleton and Company, 1864), 1:155.
50. Theodore Parker, *A Discourse of Matters Pertaining to Religion* (Boston: C. C. Little and J. Brown, 1842), 5, 7.
51. Samuel Osgood, review of Parker's *Discourse, Monthly Miscellany* 7 (August 1842), 145–50.
52. Convers Francis to Frederic Henry Hedge, January 24, 1843, in Guy R. Woodall, "The Record of a Friendship: The Letters of Convers Francis to Frederic Henry Hedge in Bangor and Providence, 1835–1850," *Studies in the American Renaissance, 1991* (Charlottesville: University Press of Virginia, 1991), 44–45.

6: HEAVEN ON EARTH

1. Dean Grodzins, *American Heretic: Theodore Parker and Transcendentalism* (Chapel Hill: University of North Carolina Press, 2002), 225–28, gives the best account of this, citing from Parker's manuscript diary.
2. *The Liberator*, October 30, 1840.
3. Ralph Waldo Emerson, "Chardon Street Convention," in *Lectures and Biographical Sketches*, in *Complete Works of Ralph Waldo Emerson*, ed. Edward Waldo Emerson (Boston and New York: Houghton, Mifflin, 1903–04), 10:351–54.
4. Ibid., 10:352.
5. See Edward K. Spann, *Hopedale: From Commune to Company Town, 1840–1920* (Columbus: Ohio State University Press, 1992).
6. This meeting between Ripley and Ballou is detailed by Butler Wilmarth, one of Ballou's supporters; see William H. Fish, *Memoir of Butler Wilmarth, M.D.* (Boston: Crosby, Nichols, 1854), 88–89.
7. Frederick C. Dahlstrand, *Amos Bronson Alcott, an Intellectual Biography* (Madison, N.J.: Fairleigh Dickinson University Press, 1982), 184–85.
8. Margaret Fuller to William Henry Channing, March 29, 1841, in Robert N. Hudspeth, ed., *The Letters of Margaret Fuller*, 6 vols. (Ithaca: Cornell University Press, 1983–94), 2:205.
9. Printed in Octavius Brooks Frothingham, *George Ripley* (Boston: Houghton, Mifflin, 1882), 307–308.
10. Sophia Ripley, "Letter," *Dial* 2 (July 1841), 122–29.
11. Joel Myerson, *New England Transcendentalists and the "Dial": A History of the Magazine and Its Contributors* (Rutherford, N.J.: Fairleigh Dickinson University Press, 1980), 200.

12. Albert Brisbane, *Social Destiny of Man; or, Association and Reorganization of Industry* (Philadelphia: C. F. Stollmeyer, 1840); Grodzins, *American Heretic*, 218.

13. See Charles Pellarin, *Life of Charles Fourier* (New York: W. H. Graham, 1848); and Carl Guarneri, *The Utopian Alternative: Fourierism in Nineteenth-Century America* (Ithaca: Cornell University Press, 1991).

14. Ralph Waldo Emerson to George Ripley, December 15, 1840, *Letters of Ralph Waldo Emerson* (hereafter LRWE), eds. Ralph L. Rusk and Eleanor M. Tilton, 10 vols. (New York: Columbia University Press, 1939–95), 2: 368–71.

15. Ralph Waldo Emerson, *Journals and Miscellaneous Notebooks* (hereafter JMN), eds. William H. Gilman et al., 16 vols. (Cambridge: Belknap Press of Harvard University Press, 1960–82), 7:407–408; and Emerson to Ripley, December 15, 1840, LRWE, 2:370. Regarding Emerson's servants' resistance to his plans for them see Emerson to William Emerson, March 30, 1841, LRWE 2:389.

16. The best descriptions of Brook Farm are in Sterling Delano, *Brook Farm: The Dark Side of Utopia* (Cambridge: Harvard University Press, 2004).

17. See ibid., particularly chapter 1.

18. Peabody's descriptions are "The Community at West Roxbury," in the *Monthly Miscellany of Religion and Letters* 5 (August 1841), 113–18; "A Glimpse of Christ's Idea of Society," *Dial* 2 (October 1841), 214–28; and "Plan of the West Roxbury Community," ibid. 2 (January 1842), 361–72.

19. Delano, *Brook Farm*, 64–65.

20. John Sullivan Dwight, *A Lecture on Association, in Its Connection with Education* (Boston: Benjamin H. Greene, for the [New England Fourier] Society, 1844), 3, 5.

21. John Thomas Codman, *Brook Farm: Historic and Personal Memoirs* (Boston: Arena Publishing Company, 1894), 79–81.

22. See "The Hopedale and Brook Farm Communities," *The American Socialist* (June 22, 1876), 102.

23. Codman, *Brook Farm*, 177–78.

24. Jonathan Beecher, *Charles Fourier: The Visionary and His World* (Berkeley: University of California Press, 1985), 56. Beecher's is the standard biography.

25. Charles Fourier, *Oeuvres complètes*, 12 vols. (Paris: Éditions Anthropos, 1966–68), 10:17; also cited in Jonathan Beecher and Richard Bienvenu, eds., *The Utopian Vision of Charles Fourier: Selected Texts on Work, Love, and Passionate Attraction* (Boston: Beacon Press, 1971), 1.

26. Sophia Ripley to Ralph Waldo Emerson, July 5, 1843, cited in Delano, *Brook Farm*, 121–22.

27. Emerson, JMN, 8:392.

28. Walt Whitman, "New York Dissected, V. Street Yarn," *Life Illustrated*, August 16, 1856, reprinted in *New York Dissected*, eds. Emory Holloway and Ralph Adimri (New York: R. R. Wilson, 1936), 129.

29. Marianne Dwight, *Letters from Brook Farm, 1844–1847*, ed. Amy L. Reed (Poughkeepsie, N.Y.: Vassar College, 1928), 84.

30. Albert Brisbane, "On Association and Attractive Industry," *United States Magazine and Democratic Review* 10 (June 1842), 566.

31. In an unpublished lecture on Fourier, George Ripley explained this pun; see David A. Zonderman, "George Ripley's Unpublished Lecture on Charles Fourier," *Studies in the American Renaissance, 1982* (Boston: Twayne Publishers, 1982), 207.

32. "Editorial Notice," *Phalanx* 1, no. 23 (May 23, 1845), 354–55.

33. Amelia Russell, "Home Life of the Brook Farm Association," *Atlantic Monthly* 42 (July–December 1878), 458–66 and 556–63; Henry W. Sams, *Autobiography of Brook Farm* (Englewood Cliffs, N.J.: Prentice-Hall, 1958), 220–21.

34. See *Catalogue of a Select Private Library . . . to Be Sold at Public Auction . . . November 5, 1846* (Boston: Alfred Mudge, 1846).

35. Grodzins, *American Heretic*, 496.

36. Orestes Brownson, "Transcendentalism, or the Latest Form of Infidelity," *Boston Quarterly Review* 2 (July 1845), 310.

37. Ralph Waldo Emerson, "Historic Notes on Life and Letters in New England," *Lectures and Biographical Sketches* (1883), in *Complete Works of Ralph Waldo Emerson*, 10:331, 333.

38. Donald C. M'Laren, *Boa Constrictor or, Fourier Association Self-Exposed as to Its Principles and Aims* (Rochester, N.Y.: Printed by Canfield & Warren, 1844), 13, 17.

39. Emerson, JMN, 9:50; "Historic Notes on Life and Letters," *Complete Works*, 10:333.

40. Victor Hennequin, *Love in the Phalanstery*, trans. Henry James (New York: DeWitt and Davenport, 1849), v–vi.

41. Ibid., 2.

42. *New York Observer*, October 7, 1848, p. 162.

43. Emerson, JMN, 9:100.

44. Fuller's essay is in *Dial* 4, no. 1 (July 1843), 1–47.

45. Margaret Fuller to Orestes Brownson, January 28, 1844, in *Letters of Fuller*, 3:174–75.

46. Margaret Fuller, *Woman in the Nineteenth Century* (1845; reprint, New York: W. W. Norton, 1971), 20, 33.

47. Ibid., 37.

48. Ibid., 122–23.

49. Ibid., 123–24.

50. Ibid., 124–25.

51. Ralph Waldo Emerson to Caroline Sturgis, February 1, 1845, LRWE, 8:5–6.

52. Ibid., 8:4–5, note 13.

53. Ibid.

54. Franklin B. Sanborn, *Recollections of Seventy Years*, 2 vols. (Boston: R. G. Badger, 1909), 2:349.

55. Ralph Waldo Emerson to Caroline Sturgis, February (?) 8(?), 1845, LRWE, 8:8.

56. Emerson, JMN, 9:191.

57. Ralph Waldo Emerson, "English Reformers," *Dial* 3 (October 1842): 227–28, 242. *The Alist; a Monthly Magazine of Divinity and Universal Literature*, edited by Francis Barnham. The title comes from "the Hebrew title of God, *Alah*"; see *Dial* 3, 233, note.

58. Ibid., 237; on Fruitlands see Richard Francis, *Transcendental Utopias: Individual and Community at Brook Farm, Fruitlands, and Walden* (Ithaca: Cornell University Press, 1997).

59. Channing reprinted this essay in the *Present* 1 (1843): 110–21 in English Fourierist Sophia Chichester's translation.

60. Ibid., 110–11.

61. Lane's letter is also found in Clara Endicott Sears, *Bronson Alcott's Fruitlands, comp. by Clara Endicott Sears; with Transcendental Wild Oats, by Louisa M. Alcott* (Boston: Houghton Mifflin, 1915), 41–52, from which I cite it, p. 44. Also see "The Consociate Family Life," *New Age* 1 (November 1, 1843), 120; *New-York Daily Tribune*, September 2, 1843; and *Herald of Freedom*, September 8, 1843.

62. Emerson, JMN, 9:26.

63. Charles Lane, "Fruitlands," *Dial* 4, no. 1 (July 1843), 135–36.

64. See Sears, *Fruitlands*, passim.

65. Emerson, JMN, 8:433.

66. Ibid., 8:250–51.

7: VARIETIES OF TRANSCENDENTALISM

1. Ralph Waldo Emerson, "Historic Notes on Life and Letters in New England," *Lectures and Biographical Sketches* (1883), in *Complete Works of Ralph Waldo Emerson*, ed. Edward Waldo Emerson, 12 vols. (Boston and New York: Houghton, Mifflin, 1903–04), 10:308, 311.

2. Octavius Brooks Frothingham, *Transcendentalism in New England: A History* (New York: G. P. Putnam's Sons, 1876), 105–06.

3. Margaret Fuller to Ralph Waldo Emerson, November 9, 1841, in Robert N. Hudspeth, ed., *Letters of Margaret Fuller*, 6 vols. (Ithaca: Cornell University Press, 1983–94), 2:251.

4. The standard account of French influence on American Transcendentalism is Walter L. Leighton, *French Philosophers and New-England Transcendentalism* (Charlottesville: University Press of Virginia, 1908).

5. The main biographical sources for Greene are George Willis Cooke, *A Historical and Biographical Introduction to the "Dial,"* 2 vols. (1902; reprint, New

York: Russell and Russell, 1961), 2:117–28; and Joel Myerson, *New England Transcendentalists and the Dial: A History of the Magazine and Its Contributors* (Rutherford, N.J.: Fairleigh Dickinson University Press, 1980), 155–56. Also see Philip F. Gura, "Beyond Transcendentalism: The Radical Individualism of William B. Greene," in Conrad Wright and Charles Capper, eds., *The Transient and Permanent in American Transcendentalism* (Boston: Northeastern University Press, 2000), 471–96.

6. Elizabeth Palmer Peabody, *Reminiscences of the Rev. William Ellery Channing, D.D.* (Boston: Roberts Brothers, 1880), 435–45.

7. Ibid., 435.

8. William B. Greene, [*The Incarnation,*] *A Letter to the Rev. John Fiske, D.D.* (West Brookfield, Mass.: Merriam and Chapin, 1848), 20; and Thomas Wentworth Higginson, *Cheerful Yesterdays* (Boston: Houghton, Mifflin, 1898), 106.

9. On Buchez see especially D. G. Charlton, *Secular Religions in France, 1815–1870* (London: Oxford University Press, 1895), 182–84; Edward Berenson, *Populist and Left-Wing Politics in France, 1830–1852* (Princeton: Princeton University Press, 1984); and François-André Isambert, *Politique, religion et science de l'homme chez Philippe Buchez* (Paris: Cujas, 1967).

10. On Leroux see especially Robert Flint, *The Philosophy of History in Europe,* 2 vols. (Edinburgh and London: Blackwood, 1884), 1:252–58; David Owen Evans, *Social Romanticism in France, 1830–1848* (Oxford: Clarendon Press, 1951); Charlton, *Secular Religions in France,* 82–87; and Jack Bakunin, *Pierre Leroux and the Birth of Democratic Socialism* (New York: Revisionist Press, 1976).

11. [William B. Greene,] *Remarks on the Science of History: Followed by an A Priori Autobiography* (Boston: William Crosby and H. P. Nichols, 1849), 37; Peabody, *Channing,* 439–40; also see Greene, *The Incarnation,* 28–29.

12. [William B. Greene,] "First Principles," *Dial* 2 (January 1842), 281.

13. William B. Greene, *The Doctrine of Life and Some of Its Theological Applications* (Boston: B. H. Greene, 1843), 57–58, 74; Peabody, *Channing,* 364.

14. William B. Greene, *Transcendentalism* (West Brookfield, Mass.: O. S. Cooke and Company, 1849), 12–14.

15. Ibid., 6, 18.

16. Ibid., 21–22, 32, 41.

17. Greene, *The Incarnation,* 25–27.

18. Ibid., 41–43.

19. Ibid., 25–27.

20. William B. Greene, *Equality* (West Brookfield, Mass.: O. S. Cooke and Company, 1849), 32. Also see *Mutual Banking* (West Brookfield, Mass.: O. S. Cooke and Company, 1849).

21. Greene, *Equality,* 71–73.

22. William B. Greene, *The Blazing Star; with an Appendix Treating of the Jewish Kabbala* (Boston: Rand, Avery, & Frye, 1872), 80.

23. [George Wood], *Peter Schlemiel in America* (Philadelphia: Carey and Hart, 1848), 244.

24. Ibid., 255.

25. See *Boston Transcript*, February 29, 1881, p. 1, for her obituary.

26. Cooke, *Historical and Biographical Introduction*, 2:109.

27. Ibid., 2:101–103. Her verse appeared in *Dial* 2 (July 1841) and 3 (July 1842).

28. Charles A. Dana, review of *Studies in Religion, Harbinger* 1, no. 23 (November 15, 1845), 362.

29. Frederic Henry Hedge in Eliza Thayer Clapp, *Essays, Letters, and Poems* (Boston: privately printed, 1888), ix–x. On Clapp see Cooke, *Historical and Biographical Introduction*, 2:101–12; and Myerson, *New England Transcendentalists and the Dial*, 125–26.

30. Cooke, *Historical and Biographical Introduction*, 2:110–11.

31. Ibid., 2:111, and Dana, "review of *Studies in Religion*," 362.

32. [Eliza Thayer Clapp,] *Studies in Religion, by the Author of Words in a Sunday School* (New York: C. Shepard, 1845), 11–16.

33. Ibid., 75.

34. Ibid., 27–31, 34.

35. Ibid., 84, 86.

36. Ibid., 115, 123–24.

37. Ibid., 168, 218.

38. Cooke, *Historical and Biographical Introduction*, 2:111.

39. Ibid.

40. Judith Mattson Bean and Joel Myerson, eds., *Margaret Fuller, Critic: Writings from the New-York Tribune, 1844–1846* (New York: Columbia University Press, 2000), 335–36. The earlier notice is ibid., 210.

41. Cited in Philip Judd Brockway, *Sylvester Judd (1813–1853): Novelist of Transcendentalism* (Orono, Maine: University Press, 1941), 79. Also see Richard D. Hathaway, *Sylvester Judd's New England* (University Park: Pennsylvania State University Press, 1981).

42. Arethusa Hall, *Life and Character of the Rev. Sylvester Judd* (Boston: Crosby, Nichols, and Company, 1854), 74, 77–78.

43. Hall gives generous excerpts from Judd's "Cardiagraphy" in *Life and Character of Judd*, 80–103.

44. Ibid., 131.

45. Brockway, *Judd*, 24, 26.

46. Hall, *Life and Character of Judd*, 112.

47. Ibid., 353–54.

48. Ibid., 354.

49. Elizabeth Palmer Peabody, "A Glimpse of Christ's Idea of Society," *Dial* 2 (October 1841), 214–28.

50. Hall, *Life and Character of Judd*, 357.

51. Ibid., 356; review of *Margaret, Southern Quarterly Review* 9 (April 1846), 507–22.

52. Frederic Dan Huntington, review of Judd's *Margaret, Christian Examiner* 39 (November 1845), 418–20. It was also reviewed by W.B.O. Peabody in the *North American Review* 62 (January 1846), 102–40.

53. James Russell Lowell, review of *Kavanagh: A Tale*, in *North American Review* 69 (July 1849), 209.

54. Orestes Brownson, *The Works of Orestes A. Brownson, collected and arranged by Henry F. Brownson*, 20 vols. (Detroit: T. Nourse, 1882–1907) 6:113–15, and passim.

55. Hall, *Life and Character of Judd*, 364–69.

56. Andrew Preston Peabody, review of *Philo, North American Review* 70 (April 1850), 434, 440. It was also reviewed in William Henry Channing's *Spirit of the Age*; see 2, no. 5 (February 2, 1857), 76.

57. Hall, *Life and Character of Judd*, 456.

58. Henry David Thoreau, *Journal*, John C. Broderick, general editor, 7 vols. to date (Princeton: Princeton University Press, 1981–), 1:277–78.

59. Henry Thoreau to Mrs. John Thoreau, June 8, 1843, in Walter Harding and Carl Bode, eds., *The Correspondence of Henry David Thoreau* (New York: New York University Press, 1958), 141.

60. Ibid., 111, for Brisbane.

61. Ibid., 139.

62. Henry Thoreau, "Paradise (to Be) Regained," *United States Magazine and Democratic Review* 13 (November 1843), 451–63.

63. Henry Thoreau to Ralph Waldo Emerson, June 8, 1843, in *Correspondence of Thoreau*, 112.

64. For Etzler's thought see John Hydahl, "Introduction," *The Collected Works of John Adolphus Etzler* (Delmar, N.Y.: Scholars' Facsimiles & Reprints, 1977), vii–xxxi.

65. Henry David Thoreau, "Paradise (to Be) Regained" in *Reform Papers*, ed. Wendell Glick (Princeton: Princeton University Press, 1973), 20, 22, 39–40, 42, 45–46.

66. Ibid., 47.

67. Ralph Waldo Emerson, *Dial* 3 (July 1842), 19.

68. Henry Thoreau, "Natural History of Massachusetts," *Dial* 3 (July 1842), 19–40.

69. Ibid., 27, 37. Also see Henry David Thoreau, *Walden*, ed. J. Lyndon Shanley (Princeton: Princeton University Press, 1971), 234–36 and 304–09.

70. Thoreau, "Natural History of Massachusetts," 39–40.

71. Henry David Thoreau, "A Walk to Wachusett," in *Writings of Henry David Thoreau*, 20 vols. (Boston: Houghton, Mifflin, 1906), 5:142.

72. Ibid., 151.

73. Henry David Thoreau, "A Winter Walk," in *Writings*, 5:166, 167, 169.

74. Ibid., 171.

75. Thoreau, *Walden*, 19–20.

76. Ralph Waldo Emerson, *Journals and Miscellaneous Notebooks*, eds. William H.

Gilman et al., 16 vols. (Cambridge: Belknap Press of Harvard University Press, 1960–82), 8:96.

77. Caroline Healey Dall, *Transcendentalism in New England: A Lecture* (Boston: Sold by Roberts Brothers, 1897), 20–21.

8: SELF AND SOCIETY

1. Linck C. Johnson, "Reforming the Reformers: Emerson, Thoreau, and the Sunday Lectures at Amory Hall, Boston," *ESQ: A Journal of the American Renaissance* 37 (1991), 235–89.

2. "Priestcraft," *Congregational Journal*, February 29, 1844, p. 2.

3. Ralph Waldo Emerson, "New England Reformers," in *Collected Works of Ralph Waldo Emerson*, vol. 3, *Essays, Second Series; Historical Introduction and Notes by Joseph Slater; Text Established by Alfred R. Ferguson and Jean Ferguson Carr; Textual Introduction and Apparatus by Jean Ferguson Carr* (Cambridge: Harvard University Press, 1983), 149.

4. Ibid., 154.

5. Ibid., 155–57.

6. Ibid., 157.

7. Ibid., 167.

8. Elizabeth Palmer Peabody, *Reminiscences of the Rev. William Ellery Channing, D.D.* (Boston: Roberts Brothers, 1880), 371, 365.

9. Helen R. Deese, ed., *Selected Journals of Caroline Healey Dall*, in Massachusetts Historical Society, *Collections* 90 (2006), 81, 217.

10. Francis Bowen, "Locke and the Transcendentalists," *Christian Examiner* 23 (November 1837), 184, 193.

11. Simeon Doggett, *Sermon on Transcendentalism* (Taunton, Mass.: J.W.D. Hall, 1843), 6.

12. Ralph Waldo Emerson, *Collected Works of Ralph Waldo Emerson*, vol. 2, *Essays, First Series; Historical Introduction and Notes by Joseph Slater; Text Established by Alfred R. Ferguson and Jean Ferguson Carr* (Cambridge: Harvard University Press, 1979), 27–29.

13. Ibid., 30–31.

14. Ibid., 44, 50–51.

15. Ibid., 47, 36.

16. Ibid., 47, 49.

17. Theodore Parker, "Writings of Ralph Waldo Emerson," in *The Collected Works of Theodore Parker*, ed. Frances Power Cobbe, 12 vols. (London: Trüber, 1863–65), 10:203.

18. Peabody, *Channing*, 373.

19. Elizabeth Palmer Peabody, "Egotheism, the Atheism of Today" (1858), reprinted in Elizabeth Peabody, *Last Evening with Allston and Other Papers* (Boston: D. Lothrop, 1886), 245.

20. *New-York Daily Tribune*, March 19, 1842, p. 3.

21. Henry James, *Moralism and Christianity; or, Man's Experience and Destiny* (New York: J. S. Redfield, 1850), 84.

22. Bruce A. Ronda, ed., *Letters of Elizabeth Palmer Peabody: American Renaissance Woman* (Middletown, Conn.: Wesleyan University Press, 1984), 246–47, 253.

23. Helen R. Deese, ed., *Daughter of Boston: The Extraordinary Diary of a Nineteenth-Century Woman* (Boston: Beacon Press, 2005), 138.

24. Parker, *A Sermon of the Perishing Classes in Boston* (1846), in *Collected Works*, 7:58–59.

25. *A Sermon of the Moral Condition of Boston* (1849), ibid., 7:115–16.

26. Ibid., 7:144–45.

27. Ibid., 7:145.

28. *A Sermon of War* (1846), ibid., 4:5–6.

29. Ibid., 4:16.

30. Ibid., 4:25.

31. Ibid., 4:29.

32. *A Sermon of the Mexican War* (1848), ibid., 7:42–43.

33. Ibid., 7:59–60.

34. Ibid., 7:76.

35. Elizabeth Peabody, "Introduction," *Aesthetic Papers* 1 (1849), iii.

36. Henry David Thoreau, *Journal*, John C. Broderick, general editor, 7 vols. to date (Princeton: Princeton University Press, 1981–), 2:263–64.

37. Henry David Thoreau, "Resistance to Civil Government," in *Reform Papers*, ed. Wendell Glick (Princeton: Princeton University Press, 1973), 67, 74–75.

38. Ibid., 68–69.

39. Ibid., 72–73.

40. Ibid., 75.

41. Ibid., 89.

42. On the Fuller-Emerson relationship, see especially Christina Zwarg, *Feminist Conversations: Fuller, Emerson, and the Play of Reading* (Ithaca: Cornell University Press, 1995). See also Joel Myerson, "Margaret Fuller's 1842 Journal: At Concord with the Emersons," *Harvard Library Bulletin* 21 (July 1973), 320–40.

43. See Adam-Max Tuchinsky, "'Her Cause Against Herself': Margaret Fuller, Emersonian Democracy, and the Nineteenth-Century Public Intellectual," *American Nineteenth Century History* 5, no. 1 (Spring 2004), 66–99.

44. For a good description of the *Tribune*'s operations at this time, including descriptions of Fuller's coworkers, see Catherine C. Mitchell, ed., *Margaret Fuller's New York Journalism: A Biographical Essay and Key Writings* (Knoxville: University of Tennessee Press, 1995), 3–50.

45. Judith Mattson Bean and Joel Myerson, eds., *Margaret Fuller, Critic: Writings from the New-York Tribune, 1844–1846* (New York: Columbia University Press, 2000), 5.

46. Robert N. Hudspeth, ed., *The Letters of Margaret Fuller*, 6 vols. (Ithaca: Cornell University Press, 1983–94), 6:294, 296 n. 6.

47. Margaret Fuller, *Woman in the Nineteenth Century* (1845; reprint, New York: W. W. Norton, 1971), 38–39.

48. Ibid., 115–16.

49. Ibid.

50. Ibid., 171.

51. Ibid., 62, 38.

52. Ibid., 40.

53. See Jeffrey Steele, *Transfiguring America: Myth, Ideology, and Mourning in Margaret Fuller's Writings* (Columbia: University of Missouri Press, 2001), 240–50, for a discussion of Channing's influence on Fuller.

54. See Octavius Brooks Frothingham, *Memoir of William Henry Channing* (Boston: Houghton, Mifflin, 1886), 210.

55. Margaret Fuller to Elizabeth Hoar, October 20 (28?), 1844, in *Letters of Fuller*, 3:237.

56. Ibid., 3:238.

57. Bean and Myerson, eds., *Margaret Fuller, Critic*, 8–13.

58. Ibid., 134–37.

59. Ibid., 128–30.

60. These and subsequent quotations from this article are ibid., 98–104.

61. See Jerzy Jan Lerski, *A Polish Chapter in Jacksonian America: The United States and the Polish Exiles of 1831* (Madison: University of Wisconsin Press, 1958), esp. 3–13.

62. Charles Kraitsir, *The Significance of the Alphabet* (Boston: E. P. Peabody, 1846). The same year she also published his *First Book of English* (Boston: E. P. Peabody, 1846), a textbook for children.

63. See Philip F. Gura, *The Wisdom of Words: Language, Theology, and Literature in the New England Renaissance* (Middletown, Conn.: Wesleyan University Press, 1981) for a general discussion of the Transcendentalists' interest in language.

64. Margaret Fuller to Caroline Sturgis, November 16(?), 1846, in *Letters of Fuller*, 4:239–40.

65. Margaret Fuller to Ralph Waldo Emerson, March 15, 1847, ibid., 4:261.

66. Margaret Fuller, *"These Sad But Glorious Days": Dispatches from Europe, 1846–1850*, Larry J. Reynolds and Susan Belasco Smith, eds. (New Haven: Yale University Press, 1991), 119.

67. Margaret Fuller to William Henry Channing, May 7, 1847, in *Letters of Fuller*, 4:271.

68. Margaret Fuller to William Henry Channing, March 29, 1848, ibid., 5:58.

69. Margaret Fuller to Richard Fuller, February 23, 1849, ibid., 5:192.

70. Fuller, *Dispatches from Europe*, 165.

71. Ibid., 230.

72. Margaret Fuller to Marcus and Rebecca Spring, February 5, 1850, in *Letters of Fuller*, 6:55. Fuller's European years are illuminated by Charles Capper in *Margaret Fuller: An American Romantic Life: The Public Years* (New York: Oxford University Press, 2007).

73. See Donald S. Spencer, *Louis Kossuth and Young America: A Study of Sectionalism and Foreign Policy, 1848–1852* (Columbia: University of Missouri Press, 1977).

9: THE INWARD TURN

1. William C. Gannett, *Ezra Stiles Gannett: Unitarian Minister in Boston, 1824–1871* (Boston: Roberts Brothers, 1875), 407.

2. Caroline Healey Dall, *Transcendentalism in New England: A Lecture* (Boston: Sold by Roberts Brothers, 1897), 38.

3. Octavius Brooks Frothingham, *Transcendentalism in New England: A History* (New York: G. P. Putnam's Sons, 1876), 331.

4. On the Compromise of 1850 see Hamilton Holman, *Prologue to Conflict: The Crisis and Compromise of 1850* (Lexington: University of Kentucky Press, 2005).

5. See Len Gougeon, *Virtue's Hero: Emerson, Antislavery, and Reform* (Athens: University of Georgia Press, 1990).

6. Ralph Waldo Emerson, *Journals and Miscellaneous Notebooks* (hereafter JMN), eds. William H. Gilman et al., 16 vols. (Cambridge: Belknap Press of Harvard University Press, 1960–82), 8:360.

7. Ibid., 11:152.

8. Ibid., 11:345–46.

9. Ibid., 11:349.

10. On antislavery in Concord see Sandra Harbert Petrulionis, *To Set the World Right: The Antislavery Movement in Thoreau's Concord* (Ithaca: Cornell University Press, 2006).

11. This account follows Emerson's in his address; see Joel Myerson and Len Gougeon, eds., *Emerson's Antislavery Writings* (New Haven: Yale University Press, 1995), 14–15.

12. Ibid., 20.

13. Ibid., 24–25.

14. Ibid., 32.

15. Ralph Waldo Emerson, "Address to the Citizens of Concord on the Fugitive Slave Law," ibid., 53.

16. Ibid., 53–54.

17. Ibid., 56.

18. Ibid., 58.

19. Ibid., 60, 62, 66, 68, 70.

20. Ibid., 73, 76, 78, 82.

21. Ralph Waldo Emerson, "Historic Notes on Life and Letters in New England," *Lectures and Biographical Sketches* (1883), in *Complete Works of Ralph Waldo Emerson*, ed. Edward Waldo Emerson, 12 vols. (Boston and New York: Houghton, Mifflin, 1903–04), 10:324.

22. John White Chadwick, *Theodore Parker: Preacher and Reformer* (Boston: Houghton, Mifflin, 1900), 235.

23. Theodore Parker, *A Letter to the People of the United States . . . Touching the Matter of Slavery* (1848), in *The Collected Works of Theodore Parker*, ed. Frances Power Cobbe, 12 vols. (London: Trüber, 1863–65), 5:34, 79.

24. *Speech at the New England Anti-Slavery Convention* (1850), ibid., 6:115, 132.

25. *The Chief Sins of the People* (1851), ibid., 7:262, 267.

26. Ibid., 7:274–75.

27. Ibid., 7:292–93.

28. Ibid., 7:294.

29. *The Boston Kidnapping* (1852), ibid., 5:177.

30. Ibid., 5:209, 219.

31. See Albert J. Von Frank, *The Trials of Anthony Burns: Freedom and Slavery in Emerson's Boston* (Cambridge: Harvard University Press, 1998), for the definitive account of the Burns affair.

32. Parker, *The New Crime against Humanity* (1854), in *Collected Works*, 6:48–49, 59.

33. *The Rights of Man in America* (1854), ibid., 6:121, 125, 136, 155–56.

34. John Weiss, *Life and Correspondence of Theodore Parker*, 2 vols. (New York: D. Appleton and Company, 1864), 2:140.

35. Octavius Brooks Frothingham, *Theodore Parker: A Biography* (Boston: J. R. Osgood and Company, 1874), 429.

36. Parker, *The Great Battle between Slavery and Freedom* (1856), in *Collected Works*, 6:215 for Garrison.

37. *The Present Crisis in American Affairs* (1856), ibid., 6:242–43.

38. Ibid., 6:252.

39. Ibid., 6:268-69, 270–72, 285.

40. On Brown see David S. Reynolds, *John Brown, Abolitionist: The Man Who Killed Slavery, Sparked the Civil War, and Seeded Civil Rights* (New York: Alfred A. Knopf, 2005).

41. Weiss, *Life and Correspondence*, 2:162.

42. Ralph Waldo Emerson to William Emerson, October 23, 1859, *Letters of Ralph Waldo Emerson* (hereafter LRWE), eds. Ralph L. Rusk and Eleanor M. Tilton, 10 vols. (New York: Columbia University Press, 1939–95), 5:178.

43. Weiss, *Life and Correspondence*, 2:170–71, 178.

44. Ralph Waldo Emerson, "Affairs in Kansas," *Miscellanies*, in Emerson, *Complete Works*, 11:248.

45. Henry David Thoreau, *Reform Papers*, ed. Wendell Glick (Princeton: Princeton University Press, 1973), 139.
46. Henry David Thoreau, "Slavery in Massachusetts," ibid., 94.
47. Henry David Thoreau, "A Plea for Captain John Brown," ibid., 112–15.
48. Ibid., 122–23.
49. Ibid., 137.
50. Cited ibid., 364.
51. Ralph Waldo Emerson, "Thoreau" in *Lectures and Biographical Sketches*, in Emerson, *Complete Works*, 10:429–30.
52. James Redpath, *Echoes of Harper's Ferry* (Boston: Thayer and Eldridge, 1860).
53. Ralph Waldo Emerson to Moncure Daniel Conway, June 6, 1860, in LRWE, 5:221.
54. Emerson, JMN, 14:352–53.
55. See Gougeon, *Virtue's Hero*, 264–65, quoting a report in *The Liberator* of February 1, 1861.
56. Emerson, "American Civilization," *Miscellanies*, in Emerson, *Complete Works*, 11:277–79, 283.
57. Ibid., 286–87.
58. Ibid., 297.
59. See Charles R. Crowe, *George Ripley, Transcendentalist and Utopian Socialist* (Athens: University of Georgia Press, 1967), 234.
60. Patrick W. Carey, *Orestes A. Brownson, American Religious Weathervane* (Grand Rapids, Mich.: W. B. Eerdmann's Publ. Co., 2004), 268–81.

10: FREE RELIGION AND THE DREAM OF A COMMON HUMANITY

1. Thomas Wentworth Higginson, *Cheerful Yesterdays* (Boston: Houghton, Mifflin, 1898), 168–69.
2. On *The Atlantic*'s early years see Bliss Perry, *Park Street Papers* (Boston: Houghton, Mifflin, 1908), 205–77; and on the magazine's cultural influence, Ellery Sedgwick, *The Atlantic Monthly, 1857–1909: Yankee Humanism at High Tide and Ebb Tide* (Amherst: University of Massachusetts Press, 1994).
3. Ralph Waldo Emerson, *Collected Works of Ralph Waldo Emerson*, vol. 5, *English Traits; Historical Introduction by Philip Nicoloff; Notes by Robert E. Burkholder; Text Established and Textual Introduction and Apparatus by Douglas Emory Wilson* (Cambridge, Mass.: Harvard University Press, 1994), 18–19.
4. Ibid., 60–61.
5. Ibid., 131–32.
6. John B. Stallo, *General Principles of the Philosophy of Nature: With an Outline of Some of Its Recent Developments among the Germans, Embracing the Philo-*

sophical Systems of Schelling and Hegel, and Oken's System of Nature (Boston: Wm. Crosby and H. P. Nichols, 1848).

7. See Loyd D. Easton, *Hegel's First American Followers: The Ohio Hegelians: John B. Stallo, Peter Kaufmann, Moncure Conway, and August Willich, with Key Writings* (Athens: Ohio University Press, 1966).

8. Theodore Parker, review of J. B. Stallo, *General Principles, Massachusetts Quarterly Review* 1 (1847), 263–65.

9. Henry A. Pochmann, *German Culture in America: Philosophical and Literary Influences, 1600–1900* (Madison: University of Wisconsin Press, 1957), 199.

10. See Henry A. Pochmann, *New England Transcendentalism and St. Louis Hegelianism* (Philadelphia: Carl Schurz Memorial Foundation, 1948).

11. Octavius Brooks Frothingham, *Transcendentalism in New England: A History* (New York: G. P. Putnam's Sons, 1876), 341.

12. Cyrus Bartol, *Discourses on the Christian Spirit and Life* (Boston: Crosby & Nichols, 1850), 20.

13. Ibid., 40.

14. See Stow Persons, *Free Religion, An American Faith* (New Haven: Yale University Press, 1947), 45, and chapter 3 passim for a discussion of the organization's founding.

15. Ibid., 49.

16. Cyrus Bartol, *Radical Problems* (Boston: Roberts Brothers, 1872), 106.

17. Frederic Hedge, "The Destinies of Ecclesiastical Religion: A Concio ad Clerum," *Christian Examiner* 82 (January 1867), 5.

18. See Mrs. John T. Sargent, ed., *Sketches and Reminiscences of the Radical Club of Chestnut Street, Boston* (Boston: J. R. Osgood and Company, 1880), passim.

19. Bartol, *Radical Problems*, 110. See also David M. Robinson, "'The New Epoch of Belief': *The Radical* and Religious Transformation in Nineteenth-Century New England," *New England Quarterly* 79, no. 4 (December 2006), 557–77.

20. Bartol, *Radical Problems*, 112.

21. Ibid., 228. Bushnell presented these ideas most forcefully in the preface to his *God in Christ* (Hartford: Brown and Parsons, 1849).

22. Cyrus Bartol, *Principles and Portraits* (Boston: Roberts Brothers, 1880), 3, 6, 9–10.

23. Ibid., 73, 87, 94, 110.

24. Ibid., 411.

25. John Weiss, *American Religion* (Boston: Roberts Brothers, 1871), 2–3, 6.

26. Ibid., 42, 47, 56–59.

27. Ibid., 71.

28. Ibid., 86, 89, 107.

29. Ibid., 137.

30. Bartol, *Principles and Portraits*, 399, 402, 412.

31. Biographical information comes from Octavius B. Frothingham, "Biographical Sketch," in David A. Wasson, *Essays: Religious, Social, Political, with a Biographical Sketch by Octavius B. Frothingham* (Boston: Lee and Shepard, 1889); Charles H. Foster, *Beyond Concord: Selected Writings of David Atwood Wasson* (Bloomington: Indiana University Press, 1965), 3–60; and Frank Preston Stearns, *Sketches from Concord and Appledore* (New York: G. P. Putnam's Sons, 1895), 134–79.

32. Frothingham, "Sketch of Wasson," in Wasson, *Essays*, 43–44.

33. Frank Preston Stearns, *Cambridge Sketches* (Philadelphia: J. B. Lippincott, 1905), 148.

34. Frothingham, "Sketch of Wasson," in Wasson, *Essays*, 64–65, 60.

35. Ibid., 66.

36. David A. Wasson, *The Radical Creed* (Boston: Walker, Fuller, and Company, 1865), 3–4.

37. Ibid., 10.

38. Ibid., 13.

39. Ibid., 22.

40. Wasson, *Essays*, 182–83, 191–92.

41. Ibid., 195, 201, 203.

42. Ibid., 173.

43. Helen R. Deese, ed., *Daughter of Boston: The Extraordinary Diary of a Nineteenth-Century Woman* (Boston: Beacon Press, 2005). A longer version of her diary has recently been published; see Helen R. Deese, ed., *Selected Journals of Caroline Healey Dall*, in Massachusetts Historical Society, *Collections* 90 (2006). Also see Tiffany K. Wayne, *Woman Thinking: Feminism and Transcendentalism in Nineteenth-Century America* (Lanham, Md.: Lexington Books, 2005), chapters 3 and 4.

44. On *The Una* see Mari Boor Tonn, "The *Una*, 1853–1855: The Premiere of the Woman's Rights Press," in Martha M. Solomon, ed., *A Voice of Their Own: The Woman Suffrage Press, 1840–1910* (Tuscaloosa: University of Alabama Press, 1991), 48–70; and Phyllis Cole, "The Literary Landscape of a Woman's Rights Periodical: The *Una*, 1853–1855," in *ESQ: A Journal of the American Renaissance* 49, nos. 1–3 (2003), 81–94.

45. Deese, *Daughter of Boston*, 111.

46. Mrs. [Caroline Healey] Dall, *Historical Pictures Retouched* (Boston: Walker, Wise, and Company, 1860), 243, 227.

47. Caroline Wells Healey Dall, *The College, the Market, and the Court; or, Woman's Relation to Education, Labor, and Law* (Boston: Lee and Shepard, 1867), 116–17, 119.

48. Ibid., 440.

49. Caroline Wells Healey Dall, *Essays and Sketches* (Boston: Samuel G. Simpkins, 1849), 84.

50. Dall, *College, Market, Court,* 116, xvi, xvii.
51. Ibid., 358.
52. The lecture was published as a pamphlet in Boston in 1897.
53. Elizabeth Palmer Peabody to Caroline Healey Dall, February 21, 1859, in Bruce A. Ronda, ed., *Letters of Elizabeth Palmer Peabody: American Renaissance Woman* (Middletown, Conn.: Wesleyan University Press, 1984), 297.
54. Elizabeth Palmer Peabody to Caroline Healey Dall, January 4, 1860, ibid., 298. This was the New England Women's Rights Convention of 1859, held in Boston.
55. Ibid., 313–14.
56. Samuel Johnson, *Lectures, Essays, and Sermons, with a Memoir by Samuel Longfellow* (Boston: Houghton, Mifflin, 1883), quoting D. H. Jaques. The best account of Johnson is Roger C. Mueller, "Samuel Johnson, American Transcendentalist: A Short Biography," *Essex Institute Historical Collections* 115 (January 1979), 9–67, to which I am indebted throughout; but see also Arthur Versluis, *American Transcendentalism & Asian Religions* (New York: Oxford University Press, 1993), chapter 8.
57. Ralph Waldo Emerson to Elizabeth Hoar, September 12, 1840, *Letters of Ralph Waldo Emerson,* eds. Ralph L. Rusk and Eleanor M. Tilton, 10 vols. (New York: Columbia University Press, 1939–95), 2:331.
58. For James Walker, for example, he read Cousin's "Lectures on Psychology" (*Elements of Psychology* [1834]) in Caleb Sprague Henry's translation, and Jouffroy's "Ethics" (*Introduction to Ethics*) as William Henry Channing had rendered them for Ripley's *Specimens of Standard Foreign Literature.* Later Johnson recalled this as "the most delightful textbook" he had ever studied and as well lavished praise on Ripley's whole series. See Longfellow, "Memoir," in Johnson, *Lectures, Essays, and Sermons,* 4–5.
59. Ibid., 14–15.
60. Ibid., 27.
61. Ibid., 33–34, 39–40.
62. Ibid., 41–42; Persons, *Free Religion,* 79–80.
63. Samuel Johnson, *A Ministry in Free Religion* (Boston: Rand, Avery, & Frye, 1870), 24.
64. Longfellow, "Memoir," in Johnson, *Lectures, Essays, and Sermons,* 47; Samuel Johnson, *Oriental Religions and Their Relation to Universal Religion: India* (Boston: J. R. Osgood and Company, 1872), 1.
65. Longfellow, "Memoir," in Johnson, *Lectures, Essays, and Sermons,* 106–07, letter to Lucy Osgood; and 97.
66. Ibid., 97.
67. Johnson, *India,* 1.
68. Ibid., 3.
69. Ibid., 13–14.
70. Ibid., 2, 30.

71. Roberts Brothers to Samuel Johnson, September 19, 1870, cited in Mueller, "Samuel Johnson," 47.
72. James Freeman Clarke, "Comparative Theology of Heathen Religions," *Christian Examiner* 62 (March 1857), 183–99.
73. *Atlantic Monthly* 23 (May 1869), 548–62; 23 (June 1869), 713–28; and 24 (September 1869), 336–51.
74. Johnson, *Ministry in Free Religion*, 15.
75. *Atlantic Monthly* 51 (June 1883), 852.
76. Johnson, *Lectures, Essays, and Sermons*, 420, 423–24.
77. Ibid., 431.
78. Ibid., 447, 450.

11: TOWARD THE GENTEEL TRADITION

1. Stedman, Edmund C., *Octavius Brooks Frothingham and the New Faith* (New York: G. P. Putnam's Sons, 1876), 3–4.
2. Ibid., 7–8.
3. See Moncure Daniel Conway, ed., *The Sacred Anthology: A Book of Ethnical Scriptures* (New York: Henry Holt and Company, 1874).
4. Stedman, *Frothingham*, 10–18.
5. Ibid., 8–9, 15–16.
6. Ibid., 15–18.
7. Octavius Brooks Frothingham provided reminiscences of his father in *Boston Unitarianism, 1820–1850: A Study of the Life and Work of Nathaniel Langdon Frothingham* (New York: G. P. Putnam's Sons, 1890).
8. One of the few modern considerations of Frothingham is J. Wade Caruthers, *Octavius Brooks Frothingham, Gentle Radical* (Tuscaloosa: University of Alabama Press, 1977).
9. See ibid., chapter 3.
10. Free Religious Association, *Proceedings* (1892), 12. Also see Stow Persons, *Free Religion, An American Faith* (New Haven: Yale University Press, 1947), passim.
11. Octavius Brooks Frothingham, *Recollections and Impressions, 1822–1890* (New York: G. P. Putnam's Sons, 1891), 120–21.
12. Octavius Brooks Frothingham, *The Religion of Humanity* (New York: D. G. Francis, 1873), 12–15.
13. Ibid., 15–17.
14. See, for example, ibid., 59, where Frothingham quotes the famous "transparent eye-ball" passage from Emerson's *Nature*.
15. Ibid., 22–23.
16. Ibid., 32–34.
17. Ibid., 90, 108.
18. Ibid., 108–09.

19. Octavius Brooks Frothingham, *Transcendentalism in New England: A History* (New York: G. P. Putnam's Sons, 1876), vii–viii.

20. Ibid., 353, 355.

21. Samuel Osgood, "Transcendentalists in New England," *International Review* 3 (1876), 761. Hedge was more acerbic. In the early 1880s, when he told a correspondent that he had provided Frothingham with his own, corrective reminiscences of the movement when Frothingham talked of preparing a new edition (never completed), Hedge added tartly, "between ourselves [*Transcendentalism in New England*] is a very poor book & one which [Frothingham] had no vocation to write." Frederic Henry Hedge to James Elliot Cabot, November 20, 1883, in Mathew Fisher, "Emerson Remembered: Nine Letters of Frederic Henry Hedge," *Studies in the American Renaissance, 1989* (Charlottesville: University Press of Virginia, 1989), 325–26.

22. The best account of this venture is in F. B. Sanborn and William T. Harris, *Bronson Alcott: His Life and Philosophy*, 2 vols. (Boston: Roberts Brothers, 1893).

23. Caroline Healey Dall, *Transcendentalism in New England: A Lecture* (Boston: Sold by Roberts Brothers, 1897), 22.

24. Santayana, in Norman Henfrey, ed., *Selected Critical Writings of George Santayana*, 2 vols. (Cambridge: Cambridge University Press, 1968), 2:88–89.

25. Ibid., 2:90–91.

26. Ibid., 2:91–92.

27. Ibid., 2:93.

28. George Santayana, "Emerson" (1900) ibid., 1:119.

29. George Santayana, "The Genteel Tradition in American Philosophy," ibid., 2: 98–100.

ACKNOWLEDGMENTS

I have been reading and thinking about Transcendentalism for forty-odd years and can date the beginning of my interest. I was barely a teenager in a November that stands out from all other damp, drizzly New England Novembers by the horror of the gunshots in Dallas: 1963. One afternoon near a field of uncut hay I saw a chokecherry tree full of chattering yellow birds. Only as large as robins, in their aura they seemed immense and surreal, with black wings and oversize finch bills, working their way through fermenting fruit with such dispatch that I watched the ground chalk beneath. Twice as big and amazingly bright, these were not goldfinches, at this season also attired in duller garb. Against a crystalline late-autumn sky these birds were startlingly garish, so noisy as to be brash, and unforgettable when, five minutes later, as oblivious to me as I was entranced by them, they flew when the last cherry was gone.

This visitation transformed my life. What were they? When I discovered that Roger Tory Peterson's bird guide was checked out of our small public library and no other book pictured them, I convinced the librarian to help me locate the addresses of natural history museums whose scientists, I was convinced, would be excited about my discovery. I sent off several handwritten letters, addressed to the "Curator of Birds," at the Smithsonian Institution, the Museum of Comparative Zoology, and other such august institutions.

Months passed without any answer, but one day there appeared in the mailbox a handwritten envelope from the American Museum of Natural History in New York City, with a few lines hastily written on the stationery of the Curator of Ornithology. "Undoubtedly Evening Grosbeaks, a large cousin of the Goldfinch. [signed] Dean Amadon." My next trip to the library yielded Peterson's field guide, returned by whoever had checked it out prior to my first foray, and there were my birds, evening grosbeaks! Their visit was not so remarkable, as it turned out, for in severe winters they often wander from northern forests to regions like New England, where food is more readily available. Rather, as I subsequently learned, the extraordinary thing was that one of the world's foremost ornithologists, Dean Amadon, had taken the time to answer a schoolboy's scrawl! That note was the beginning of my serious interest in nature study. Through the enthusiasm of an eighth-grade teacher I soon found the works of Thoreau and, eventually, through him, the Transcendentalists and their world.

I date the genesis of this particular book to April 20, 1971, when, after spending two semesters with Warner Berthoff reading nineteenth-century American literature, he inscribed to me his copies of the first two volumes of George Ripley's *Specimens of Foreign Standard Literature*, "to commemorate a fine tutorial year." I have treasured these books and have eventually acquired and read Ripley's remarkable series in its totality. More than anything, these works pushed me to consider the transatlantic dimensions of the Transcendentalist movement.

I owe much to other teachers, too. The late Joel Porte, who directed my doctoral dissertation, early on offered guidance in studies of Emerson and Thoreau. Shortly before he died, I was able to tell him of this project as well as share our mutual love of Thoreau a last time. Two other scholars whom I miss, Alan Heimert and his colleague William Hutchison, alerted me to the significance of the religious dimensions of the Transcendentalist movement. The remarkable nonagenarian Daniel Aaron insisted that I consider the political activities of Theodore Parker, Orestes Brownson, and others. His *Men of Good Hope* remains an inspiration. Elsewhere I have indicated my indebtedness to Richard Rabinowitz, but I want to note here that, among other things, he encouraged my work on James Marsh by sharing his own unpublished essays on this fascinating thinker. I mention, too, one memorable erratum from my student years, my not having taken Richard Niebuhr's legendary course, "Kant, Coleridge, and Schleiermacher." Now I know what the topic meant and why it matters, and had I enrolled in it, this no doubt would have been a better book.

For a decade I was privileged to contribute the evaluative essay on "Emerson, Thoreau, and Transcendentalism" to the annual volume *American Literary Scholarship*, a task that kept me abreast of the scholars who make possible the study of Transcendentalism. Foremost among these are Lawrence Buell, Joel Myerson, Robert D. Richardson, Jr., and David M. Robinson, who comprise what we jokingly call our modern Transcendental Club, meeting together or in rump session at the Modern Language Association conventions and occasionally at other venues for good talk and much cheer. For years we toyed with the idea of writing a collaborative history of the movement, but other projects took us elsewhere. These individuals know how much I am indebted to their scholarship and support. I also wish to acknowledge David D. Hall and Daniel Walker Howe, whose work in cognate fields has much helped me to write about my subject. These two are models of professionalism.

I thank Ellen S. Dunlap, the president of the American Antiquarian Society, for appointing me Mellon Distinguished Scholar in Residence for 2006–07 and thus allowing me to reacquaint myself, after thirty years, with New England's four seasons. Those who have had the privilege of working at this national library of American history know its incomparable resources and its infallibly helpful and courteous staff. I single out Joanne Chaison, John B. Hench, and Caroline Sloat for years of support there.

Finally, I thank my loving children, David, Daniel, and Katherine, and my wife, Leslie, all of whom have been ever tolerant of my habits and eccentricities, and who survived an academic year when all five of us lived in different locations.

INDEX

Russell, Amelia, 167
Russell, William, 85–86, 88

Sacred Anthology (Conway), 296
St. Louis, Mo., 271, 272–73, 293,
    303
St. Louis Philosophical Society, 272
Saint-Simon, Claude-Henri de, 73, 78,
    137, 161, 187
Sanborn, Franklin, 8, 256, 257, 260,
    286, 303
Sand, George, 124, 131, 235
Sand, Karl, 30
Santayana, George, 271, 304–305
Sartor Resartus (Carlyle), 91, 93, 280
Saxton, J. A., xi, 12
Saxton and Pierce, 147
Schelling, Friedrich Wilhelm Joseph
    von, 12, 54–55, 67, 115, 195,
    217
Schlegel, A. W. von, 26
Schleiermacher, Friedrich, 28, 47,
    66–67, 78, 79, 91, 297; Norton's
    attack on, 107, 110–11, 112–13;
    Parker and, 118, 218; Ripley and,
    80–81, 83
Scott, Dred, 265–66
Scott, Walter, 86
Scriptural Interpreter, 117
Second Letter to Mr. Andrews Norton
    (Ripley), 113, 114
"Secret Six," 258–60, 281
Sedgwick, Catharine Maria, 195
Selections from German Literature
    (Edwards and Park), 113
"Self-Reliance" (Emerson), 207,
    213–14, 215
Seminole War, 182
Semler, J. S., 35, 40
Separatists, 153
Sermon of the Mexican War (Parker),
    220
Sermon of War (Parker), 220
Shackford, Charles, 145, 146
Shakers (United Society of Believers in
    Christ's Second Appearing), 153,
    177, 178
Shakespeare, William, 86
Shaw, Lemuel, 86
Shaw, Robert Gould, 160
Shelley, Percy Bysshe, 124

Significance of the Alphabet, The
    (Kraitsir), 234
Sims, Thomas, 245, 247, 250, 251–52
Sing Sing prison, 229, 230
Skaneateles Community, 165
"Skepticism of the Present Age"
    (Jouffroy), 58
Sketches of Modern Philosophy
    (Murdock), 10, 12–13
slavery, xiv, 18, 179, 208, 209, 210,
    218, 220, 222, 224–25, 227,
    232, 241–66, 297
"Slavery in Massachusetts" (Thoreau),
    261
Smith, Gerrit, 258, 260, 301
Smithsonian Institution, 264
*Social Destiny of Man; or, Association
    and Reorganization of Industry*
    (Brisbane), 153, 154, 161, 163,
    202–203
socialism, xv, 137, 140–41, 161, 178,
    181, 183–84, 186, 197, 216, 236
Society at Amory Hall, 209–10
Society for Philosophical Inquiry,
    286–87
Society for the Promotion of Christian
    Union and Progress, 76, 119–20
Society of the Friends of Progress,
    118
"Some Further Remarks on the
    Characteristics of the Modern
    German School of Infidelity"
    (Norton), 110–11
"Soul's Errand, The" (Raleigh), 260
*South-Boston Unitarian Ordination,
    The* (Saxton and Pierce), 147
*Specimens of Foreign Standard
    Literature* (Ripley), 46–48, 53,
    55, 56, 57, 58, 119, 136, 227
Spinoza, Baruch, 112, 113
spirit: Bartol's acknowledgment of,
    276; Emerson's view of, 94, 95
Spirit of the Age, 178
Spirit of the Age, The (Channing), 131
spiritualism, materialism's reconciliation
    with, 76–79, 298–99
Spring, Marcus, 234–37
Spring, Rebecca, 234–37
Springfield Republican, 193
Staël, Anne-Louise-Germaine de,
    Baronne de Staël-Holstein